THE ROWS OF CH

The Chester Rows Research F̲

THE ROWS OF CHESTER
The Chester Rows Research Project

Andrew Brown, Peter de Figueiredo, Jane Grenville,
Roland Harris, Jane Laughton, Alan Thacker, and Rick Turner

with contributions by
Cathy Groves, Jennifer Hillam, Malcolm Hughes,
and Pat Leggett

Editor: Andrew Brown

ENGLISH HERITAGE

1999
ARCHAEOLOGICAL REPORT 16

First published 1999 by
English Heritage, 23 Savile Row,
London, W1X 1AB

Printed and bound by Snoeck-Ducaju & Zoon, Gent

ISBN 1 85074 629 X
Product Code XC10852

A CIP data record for this book is available from the
British Library.

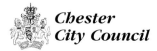 

English Heritage is greatly indebted to Chester City
Council and to Cheshire County Council for a generous
grant towards the cost of publication.

Editors: Josephine Turquet (Consultant), Margaret
Wood (English Heritage)
Project management, design: Andrew McLaren (English
Heritage)
Layout and cover design: Pauline Hull (Consultant)
Artwork adjustment: Chris Evans (English Heritage)
Assessment of Appendix B: Alix Bayliss (English Heritage),
Ian Tyers (University of Sheffield)

Contents

List of illustrations

Colour plates (between pages 94 and 95)

Figures

List of tables

Acknowledgements

To organisations

The Chester Rows Research Project acknowledges the support and generosity of the following, without whom little would have been achieved:

The British Academy
The British Archaeological Research Trust
Chester City Council
Chester Civic Trust
Cheshire County Council
English Heritage
The Royal Commission on the Historical Monuments of England
Colin Stannanought and Associates
The St John's House Trust, Chester
Samuel Smith Old Brewery (Tadcaster) Ltd

To individuals

The Chester Rows Research Project has drawn in individuals from many disciplines. Graham Holme's perspective drawings of some of the key buildings illustrated the work and thus helped the process of funding. The authors are equally grateful to Brian Howes, the field investigator for the pilot study, whose work in Italy made further involvement impossible, to Jill Collens and Adrian Tindall of Cheshire County Council for their administrative help and analytical support, and to Chris Bardsley and Jane Hore who provided much-needed voluntary assistance during the survey.

Our thanks go to the many people who have commented, criticised, and argued over our various theories, particularly Peter Howell, Derek Keene, John Maddison, Gwyn Meirion-Jones, Nick Molyneux, and the late David Black. Our especial thanks go to Oliver Bott, Frank Kelsall, Robin Thornes, and Simon Ward, who read through the draft, and were able to see the whole structure when we had got lost in the details of the timber framing.

Thanks go also to Margaret Deakin, who typed most of the archive and, despite this experience, was still willing to tackle various drafts and redrafts of the book, and to Roger Thomas and Bob Skingle of the Royal Commission on the Historical Monuments of England, who took most of the photographs.

Finally, we offer especial thanks to the owners and tenants of all the Row buildings, who suffered many interruptions and only occasionally asked if we could come back at a more convenient time.

For illustrations

The Chester Rows Research Project is grateful to the many organisations, particularly Chester Archives and the Chester Archaeological Society, who have kindly given permission for the reproduction of illustrations in this publication. (Acknowledgements to *CAS Library* in figure captions refer to the Library of the Chester Archaeological Society, held by Chester Archives.) Despite considerable efforts, The Research Project and English Heritage have been unable to trace the copyright holders of some of the illustrations used. Apologies are offered to those whom it has proved impossible to contact. In any future edition of this volume, English Heritage would be happy to make good any omissions: none has been intentional.

The watercolours by Louise Rayner (1829–1924) were probably painted when she lived in Chester between the years 1871 and 1886. Those by Edward Harrison Compton (born 1881) were signed and dated 1909: little is known of this artist, who spent much of his working life in Bavaria.

Preface

If every building in the four main streets could be examined and recorded rapidly as alterations take place, in the same way that cleared sites are excavated prior to rebuilding, the truth about the Rows and about that obscure period between 907 and *c* 1300 would become a good deal clearer. The thoroughness of modern reconstructions destroys the evidence of the past so completely that if the work is not begun soon it will be too late.

With these words, P H Lawson and J T Smith concluded their important paper on the Rows of Chester in 1958. However, it was not until 1984 that a day conference organised by the Chester Archaeological Society inspired us to start the Chester Rows Research Project, and thus to attempt the comprehensive survey that they had envisaged. We are very aware that in the 26 years that had elapsed, much had been destroyed by reconstruction and repair and that, for some buildings at least, it was too late.

Funds for a pilot survey were provided by Chester City Council, Cheshire County Council, and the Chester Civic Trust, and the results of this stimulated interest in the project, enabling a survey of all the Row buildings to be undertaken. During its latter stages, the project was primarily financed by English Heritage and the Royal Commission on the Historical Monuments of England: the two local councils continued to provide support, along with many other groups and individuals. The results of the fieldwork, together with some of the other information gathered, forms an archive which has been deposited with Chester Archives (formerly Chester City Record Office) and with the National Monuments Record.

This book is not a series of independent essays. Individual team members took responsibility for preparing the first draft of a chapter or part of a chapter, which was then circulated for comments or passed to another member of the team for rewriting. In some cases this was repeated several times before all the chapters were drawn together by the editor to form what we trust is a coherent volume. Despite this joint responsibility, it is possible to ascribe the prime work behind the chapters to individuals. Chapters One and Five were drafted by Andrew Brown and Rick Turner, although Five was then radically reworked as a result of comments from other team members, particularly Roland Harris. Chapter Two was the work of Roland Harris and Alan Thacker. Chapters Three and Four were mainly the responsibility of Roland Harris and Rick Turner. Jane Grenville and Jane Laughton provided the substance of Chapters Six and Seven, while Chapter Eight was largely the work of Jane Laughton and Rick Turner. Chapters Nine and Ten were almost entirely the responsibility of Peter de Figueiredo, who also put in a great deal of work on the Gazetteer. Appendix A is the result of work by Alan Thacker and Jane Laughton, while Appendix C was produced by Rick Turner and Jane Laughton. Pat Leggett, Malcolm Hughes, Jennifer Hillam, and Cathy Groves provided important dendrochronological information and were responsible for Appendix B.

The project was always intended to be an inter-disciplinary effort, as we believed that only by involving archaeological investigation and historical research, together with an appreciation of the architectural and social influences that inspired the creation of the buildings, could we begin to understand the origins and survival of the Rows. We have therefore been grateful for the way in which the project has grown, and for the involvement of our fellow authors, all of whom have given much time and effort to the development of the project. We are also conscious that the research is continuing, both through the work of Jane Laughton and Alan Thacker on the Chester documents and Roland Harris' study of medieval town houses. Also, as time goes on, we expect there to be other discoveries in the buildings. However, you have to draw a line somewhere and we believe that the project has uncovered sufficient new evidence to justify publication.

Andrew Brown and Rick Turner
Co-founders, Chester Rows Research Project

Note on authors

Andrew Brown was Conservation Officer for Chester City Council from 1983–88, and is now with Woodhall Planning and Conservation in Leeds. A co-founder of the Chester Rows Research Project, he was the chairman and editor during its later stages.

Peter de Figueiredo is the author of books on Cheshire country houses and the Victorian architecture of Manchester and Salford. He replaced Andrew Brown as the Conservation Officer for Chester City Council in 1988, and has recently joined English Heritage as an Inspector of Historic Buildings.

Jane Grenville was the field investigator for the Chester Rows Research Project from 1987–88 and is now a lecturer in the Department of Archaeology, University of York.

Roland Harris was the field investigator for the Chester Rows Research Project from 1988–90, completed a doctorate on English medieval town houses, and is now Director of the Historic Buildings Recording Unit in the Department of Archaeology, University of Reading.

Jane Laughton is working on a research project on medieval towns at the University of Birmingham, having completed a doctorate on late medieval Chester.

Alan Thacker was Editor of the Victoria County History of Cheshire until 1994, and of the Journal of the Chester Archaeological Society from 1987–1994, and is now Deputy Editor of the Victoria County History at the Institute of Historical Research, University of London.

Rick Turner was County Archaeologist of Cheshire from 1984–1989 and is now an Inspector of Ancient Monuments with CADW. He was a co-founder of the Chester Rows Research Project.

Summary

The Rows of Chester are a unique system of walkways that run through the frontages of the buildings on the four main streets of the city. These walkways pass above the shops at street level and provide access to a second level of shops at Row (first floor) level. The walkway is normally separated from the street frontage by Row stalls or stallboards. These are sloping sections that provide headroom for the steps that lead down from the street into the lower shops, that occupy the undercrofts of the buildings. The Row and its associated stallboard are now public spaces controlled by the City Council, despite the fact that they are within the structure of the buildings and the building owners are responsible for their maintenance.

The Rows have been the subject of speculation for centuries and, although it has been clear that they date from the medieval period, no entirely satisfactory theory about their origin or development has been established. The Chester Rows Research Project was set up in 1984 to survey all the Rows buildings using an interdisciplinary approach that combined archaeological investigation and historical research with an appreciation of the architectural and social influences that inspired the construction and modification of buildings. The ultimate aim was to understand the origins and the survival of the Rows.

The Rows and their special characteristics are described, and the differences from structures in other medieval towns noted. The differing views on the origins and development of the Rows are set out.

The topography and early history of the city, from Roman times to the early thirteenth century, is established and the development of buildings along the main streets in the period before 1350 is assessed. Using both the documentary evidence and detailed surveys of the surviving buildings the different elements of the buildings, undercrofts, Rows, stallboards, shops and domestic spaces, are analysed. The authors conclude that by 1350 a recognisable, but incomplete, Row system had emerged along the four main streets of Chester. However, some sections of the Rows existed well before this date and the system possibly evolved over a period of 100 years or more.

Detailed analysis of the early medieval building materials and techniques is presented; with walls, vaults, arches, corbels, doorways and windows in stone; and timberwork in the arcades, beams, corbel tables, floors and framing. The recognition and dating of a range of early timber structures within the Rows buildings has proved one of the most important findings of the Project, helping to correct the previous impression that timber structures of the thirteenth and fourteenth centuries were likely to occur in southern and eastern England.

On the origins of the Rows, the authors conclude that there is no simple explanation; all previous theories having given undue weight to single factors.

The detailed and interdisciplinary study of the evidence suggests that the origins of the Rows are complex and result from a range of factors, which together are peculiar to Chester. These factors may be summarised as: physical and topographical; the commercial advantages of a double-level trading system; and the prosperity and building expertise brought to the city by the Edwardian campaigns in North Wales. English and foreign parallels for the various elements of the Row buildings are cited but these are found to be evidence of the general development of early medieval town houses rather than directly linked to the origins of the Chester Rows. Experimentation with urban forms such as the bastides of south-west France may have influenced the development of the Rows but there is no evidence for an imposed planning scheme. It is likely that the Rows are the result of a general undertaking by the citizens of Chester, possibly with specific encouragement at a key period as a result of royal interest.

The equally remarkable story of how the Rows survived to the present day is traced. The trading advantages of the system meant that, although the buildings were modified and reconstructed to meet the needs and aspirations of successive generations, the Rows were not totally destroyed.

Chester's prosperity declined from the mid-fourteenth to the mid-sixteenth century. These years of depression were crucial to the survival of the Rows, since there was no extensive rebuilding that might have led to a loss of continuity and thus destroyed the incentive to maintain the system of walkways. Another factor was that the street level spaces were usually independent of the houses above and were often occupied or owned separately, so that total rebuilding was difficult. Those buildings that were constructed show new arrangements of internal planning, with an increasing number of rooms, and more sophisticated carpentry techniques.

In the later part of the sixteenth century and the first half of the seventeenth century Chester was party to the general rise in wealth in England. After centuries of neglect there was a need to rebuild and this, coupled with rising prosperity and a desire to follow new trends, led to a great period of reconstruction and adaptation of the town houses of Chester. A substantial number of timber frames survive from this period, together with decorative plasterwork, richly ornamented fireplaces and other rich furnishings. The desire to create spacious well-lit domestic accommodation more separate from commercial activities resulted in the loss of approximately one third of the Rows system. This process of rebuilding and enclosure provided a source of much needed revenue for the city authorities. However, the heart of the Rows remained protected by the Assembly, who presumably recognised the continuing commercial advantages of the system. From the 1770s to the present day almost no further losses occurred.

The years 1670–1830 saw significant changes to the appearance of the Rows as timber-framed frontages were replaced with brick. There were similar changes to the functions of the buildings; no longer used for small shops and stalls, warehouses, fairs and street markets, but for a more modern style of retailing with larger and larger shops that gradually took over complete buildings. By the mid-nineteenth century antiquarianism produced a revolt against the 'heavy Athenian architecture' of the city and a new era of timber-frame design began. This established the external character of the Rows as seen today but it also swept away many of the medieval structures that had survived up to that time.

During the second half of the twentieth century the Rows continued to adapt and change. New buildings incorporated galleries, and pedestrian bridges were constructed across some of the side streets so that the continuity of the system was reinforced. A major programme of repair and restoration was launched in 1968 and the emphasis is now on the conservation and reuse of what already exists. The Rows of Chester have survived for over 600 years but their evolution is a reflection of the ever-changing patterns of habitation and trade.

Summary text: *Josephine Turquet*

Résumé

Les 'Rows' de la ville de Chester constituent un système unique de galeries qui courent sur toute la longueur des façades des édifices dans quatre des principales artères de la ville. Ces galeries surmontent les magasins situés au niveau de la rue et permettent d'accéder à un second niveau de boutiques de plain pied avec le 'Row', c'est à dire au premier étage. La galerie est normalement séparée des devantures en bordure de rue par des planches ou des plateformes. Ce sont des sections inclinées qui permettent de descendre ou monter les marches qui conduisent de la rue aux boutiques situées en contrebas sans se taper la tête. Le 'Row' et les plateformes qui l'accompagnent sont maintenant des lieux publics administrés par le conseil municipal, malgré le fait qu'ils font partie intégrante de la structure des édifices et que les propriétaires des bâtiments sont chargés de leur entretien.

Les 'Rows' ont fait l'objet de maintes spéculations au cours des siècles et, bien qu'il ait été évident que leur construction remonte à la période médiévale, on n'a jusqu'à présent pas émis de théorie totalement satisfaisante sur leur origine et leur développement. Le projet de recherche sur les 'Rows' de Chester fondé en 1984 pour étudier tous les édifices des 'Rows' a adopté une approche pluridisciplinaire qui associait analyse archéologique et recherches historiques à une évaluation des influences architecturales et sociales qui ont inspiré la construction des bâtiments et les modifications qui ont suivi. Le projet avait comme but ultime de comprendre les origines des 'Rows' et d'expliquer les raisons pour lesquelles ils ont survécu.

On décrit les 'Rows' et leurs caractéristiques spécifiques et on note les différences par rapport aux constructions dans les autres villes médiévales. On met en évidence les divers points de vue sur les origines et l'évolution des 'Rows'.

On établit la topographie des lieux et retrace les débuts de l'histoire de la ville, de l'époque romaine jusqu'au treizième siècle, et on évalue le développement des bâtiments qui longent les rues principales dans la période qui précède 1350. A partir de témoignages provenant de documents, associés à une série d'études détaillées des bâtiments qui subsistent encore, on a analysé les différents éléments des édifices: les échoppes en contrebas, les 'Rows', les plateformes, les boutiques et les lieux consacrés à la vie domestique. Les auteurs en arrivent à la conclusion que dès 1530 un système de 'Rows', peut-être incomplet mais reconnaissable, était apparu le long des quatres artères principales de Chester. Toutefois, certaines sections des 'Rows' existaient bien avant cette date et il se peut que le système ait évolué sur une période de cent ans ou plus. On présente une analyse détaillée des matériaux et techniques de construction du début du Moyen-âge avec murs, voûtes, arches, consoles, embrasures de portes et fenêtres en pierre mais bois pour les arcades, poutres, encorbellements, planchers et charpentes. L'identification et la datation d'un échantillon des premières structures en bois à l'intérieur des bâtiments des 'Rows' se s'est avérée une des plus importantes trouvailles du projet, et nous a permis de rectifier l'impression jusqu'alors prédominante que les structures en bois des treizième et quatorzième siècles étaient plus susceptibles de se trouver dans le sud et l'est de l'Angleterre.

Quant à l'origine des 'Rows', les auteurs concluent qu'il n'existe pas d'explication facile, toutes les théories émises précédemment ont accordé trop de poids à un facteur particulier. L'étude détaillée et pluri-disciplinaire des témoignages donne à penser que l'origine des 'Rows' est complexe et résulte de divers facteurs dont l'association fait la particularité de Chester.

On peut résumer ainsi ces facteurs: aspects physique et topographique, avantages sur le plan commercial d'un système permettant de faire des affaires sur deux niveaux, prospérité et expertise en matière de bâtiment introduites dans la ville à la suite des campagnes du roi Edouard Premier dans le nord du Pays de Galles. On cite des exemples similaires, en Angleterre et à l'étranger, pour chacun des divers éléments des bâtiments des 'Rows' mais ceux-ci s'avèrent témoigner de l'évolution générale des maisons citadines au début du Moyen-âge plutôt que de démontrer l'existence de liens directs avec les origines des 'Rows' de Chester. Des expériences sur des structures urbaines telles que les bastides du sud-ouest de la France ont peut-être eu une influence sur le développement des 'Rows', mais rien ne prouve qu'un plan d'aménagement ait jamais été imposé. Il est probable que les 'Rows' résultent d'une action générale entreprise par les citoyens de Chester et peut-être spécifiquement encouragée à une époque clé à la suite de l'intérêt manifesté par la royauté.

On retrace l'histoire, tout aussi remarquable, de la survivance des 'Rows' jusqu'à nos jours. Les avantages du système pour le commerce eurent pour conséquence que, bien que les bâtiments aient été modifiés et reconstruits pour satisfaire aux besoins et aux aspirations de générations successives, les 'Rows' n'ont jamais été complètement détruits.

La prospérité de Chester déclina à partir du milieu du quatorzième siècle jusqu'au milieu du seizième siècle. Les années de dépression jouèrent un rôle crucial dans la survivance des 'Rows' car on n'entreprit pas de grands travaux de reconstruction qui auraient pu conduire à la disparition de la continuité et ainsi on n'aurait plus eu de raison de conserver le système de galeries. Un autre facteur fut le fait que les emplacements au niveau de la rue étaient en géneral indépendants des maisons au niveau supérieur et n'appartenaient, ni n'étaient occupés par les mêmes personnes, ça aurait donc été une tâche difficile de reconstruire l'ensemble. Ceux des bâtiments qui ont été reconstruits mettent en évidence de nouvelles normes dans l'agencement intérieur des édifices, en particulier une augmentation du nombre des pièces ainsi que des techniques de menuiserie plus sophistiquées.

Dans la seconde partie du seizième et la première moitié du dix-septième siècle Chester bénéficia de l'enrichissement général de l'Angleterre. Après des siècles de négligence, on éprouva le besoin de reconstruire, et ce fait, associé à une prospérité grandissante et un désir de suivre les nouveaux courants, conduisit à une grande période de reconstruction et d'aménagement des maisons de la ville de Chester. Un nombre important de colombages de cette époque survivent, ainsi que des ouvrages décoratifs en plâtre, des cheminées richement ornées et d'autres ornements de valeur. Le désir de faire vivre sa famille dans un endroit spacieux et bien éclairé, plus éloigné des activités commerciales, eut comme conséquence la disparition d'environ un tiers du système des 'Rows'. Ce processus de reconstruction et de cloisonnement fournit aux autorités de la ville une source de revenus dont elles avaient bien besoin. Cependant le coeur des 'Rows' continua à être protégé par l'assemblée probablement consciente de la pérennité des avantages commerciaux du système. On ne constata quasiment aucune disparition entre les années 1770 et nos jours.

Les années 1670 à 1830 furent témoin de changements importants dans l'aspect des 'Rows' car les façades en colombages laissèrent place à des briques. Des changements similaires affectèrent le rôle des bâtiments, ils n'abritaient plus de petites boutiques, étals, entrepôts, foires ou marchés mais s'étaient adaptés à un style de vente plus moderne avec des magasins de plus en plus grands qui, petit à petit, accaparèrent la totalité des bâtiments. Vers le milieu du dix-neuvième siècle le mouvement des antiquaires s'éleva contre la lourde architecture athénienne de la ville et une nouvelle ère de styles à colombages commença. Celle-ci établit l'aspect externe des 'Rows' tel que nous le connaissons aujourd'hui, mais elle balaya maints édifices médiévaux qui avaient survécu jusqu'à cette date.

Au cours de la seconde moitié du vingtième siècle, les 'Rows' continuèrent à s'adapter et à changer. De nouveaux bâtiments dotés de galeries et de ponts pour piétons furent construits en travers de certaines petites rues ce qui contribua à maintenir l'uniformité du système. Un important programme de réparations et de restauration fut lancé en 1968 et on met maintenant l'accent sur la sauvegarde et la réutilisation de ce qui existe déjà. Les 'Rows' de Chester ont survécu pendant plus de six cents ans mais leur évolution reflète les changements constants dans la manière de vivre et de faire du commerce.

Traduction: *Annie Pritchard*

Zusammenfassung

Die 'Rows' von Chester sind ein einzigartiges System von Fußgängerpromenaden, die in den vier Hauptstraßen der Stadt durch die Gebäude-Vorderseiten verlaufen. Diese Promenaden befinden sich oberhalb der Geschäfte auf Straßenniveau und ermöglichen Zugang zu einem zweiten Geschoß von Geschäften auf Row-Niveau. Die Promenade ist normalerweise durch Row-Stände oder begehbare Vordächer von der Straßenfront abgetrennt. Dabei handelt es sich um nach außen hin leicht ansteigende Bretterdächer, deren Neigung für Kopfraum in den darunterliegenden Treppenabgängen sorgt, die von der Straße in die unteren Geschäfte in den Kellergewölben der Gebäude führen. Die Row und die mit ihnen verbundenen Vordächer sind heute öffentlich zugänglich und werden von der Stadtverwaltung kontrolliert obwohl sie sich eigentlich innerhalb der Gebäude selbst befinden und die Hauseigentümer(innen) für ihre Instandhaltung verantwortlich sind.

Die Rows sind seit Jahrhunderten Gegenstand von Spekulationen gewesen. Es war zwar immer klar, daß sie in das Mittelalter datieren, aber über ihre Ursprünge und ihre Entwicklung haben sich keine gänzlich befriedigenden Theorien durchsetzen können. Das Chester-Rows-Forschungsprojekt wurde 1984 mit der Aufgabe ins Leben gerufen, alle Row-Gebäude mit einem interdisziplinären Ansatz zu untersuchen, der archäologische und historische Forschungen mit einer kritischen Würdigung der architektonischen und sozialen Einflüsse verbindet, die die Konstruktion und Modifizierung der Gebäude inspirierten. Das Endziel war es, die Ursprünge der Rows und die Gründe für ihren Fortbestand zu verstehen.

Die Rows und ihre speziellen Charakteristika werden beschrieben sowie Unterschiede zu Strukturen in anderen mittelalterlichen Städten angeführt. Dargestellt werden auch die unterschiedlichen Sichtweisen der Ursprünge und der Entwicklung der Rows.

Die Topographie und frühe Geschichte der Stadt (von römischer Zeit bis ins frühe dreizehnte Jahrhundert) wird dargelegt; ferner wird die Entwicklung der Gebäude entlang der Hauptstraßen in der Zeit vor 1350 begutachtet. Die unterschiedlichen Gebäudeelemente – Kellergewölbe, Rows, eingebaute Vordächer, Geschäfte und Wohnräume – werden unter Einbeziehung sowohl von Schriftquellen als auch von detaillierten Untersuchungen der erhaltenen Gebäude analysiert. Die Autorinnen und Autoren kommen zu dem Ergebnis, daß sich im Jahr 1350 ein erkennbares, aber noch unvollständiges Row-System entlang der vier Hauptstraßen von Chester entwickelt hatte. Einige Abschnitte der Rows gab es freilich schon erheblich früher; das System entwickelte sich möglicherweise über einen Zeitraum von mehr als 100 Jahren.

Es werden detaillierte Analysen der frühmittelalterlichen Baumaterialien und -techniken vorgestellt. Stein wurde verwendet für Mauern, Gewölbe, Bögen, Kragsteine, Eingänge und Fenster; Holz für Arkaden, Balken, auf Kragsteinen ruhende Vorbauten, Fußböden und Fachwerkgerippe. Das Erkennen und Datieren einer Reihe von frühen Holzstrukturen in Row-Gebäuden erwies sich als eines der wichtigsten Ergebnisse des Projektes; es trug dazu bei, den früheren Eindruck zu korrigieren, demzufolge Holzstrukturen des dreizehnten und vierzehnten Jahrhunderts am ehesten in Süd- und Ostengland zu finden seien.

In Hinsicht auf die Ursprünge der Rows kommen die Autorinnen und Autoren zu dem Schluß, daß es keine einfache Erklärung dafür gibt. Alle früheren Ansätze haben einzelnen Faktoren unangemessen viel Gewicht beigemessen. Das detaillierte und interdiszi-plinäre Studium der zur Verfügung stehenden Informationsquellen legt nahe, daß die Ursprünge der Rows komplex sind und auf eine Reihe unterschiedlicher Faktoren zurückgehen, die in ihrer Kombination Chester-eigentümlich sind. Diese Faktoren können zusammengefaßt werden wie folgt: physische und topographische Faktoren; kommerzielle Vorteile eines doppelgeschossigen Gewerbesystems; schließlich Wohlstand und baulicher Sachverstand, den die nordwalisischen Feldzüge König Edward I in die Stadt brachten. Es werden englische und ausländische Parallelen zu den verschiedenen Elementen der Row-Gebäude angeführt, aber diese stellen sich vor allem als Anhaltspunkte für die allgemeine Entwicklung frühmittelalterlicher Stadthäuser heraus und haben wenig mit den speziellen Ursprüngen der Rows von Chester zu tun. Das Experimentieren mit städtischen Formen, wie etwa den befestigten Städten (bastides) in Südwestfrankreich, mag die Entwicklung der Rows beeinflußt haben, aber nichts deutet darauf hin, daß ein Plan von außen aufgezwungen worden wäre. Es ist wahrscheinlich, daß die Rows das Ergebnis eines Gemeinschaftsprojektes der Bürger von Chester waren, möglicherweise mit besonderer königlicher Ermunterung in der entscheidenden Phase.

Verfolgt wird dann die gleichermaßen bemerkenswerte Geschichte wie die Rows bis in die Gegenwart fortbestanden. Die gewerblichen Vorteile des Systems führten dazu, daß die Gebäude zwar in Hinsicht auf die Bedürfnisse und Wünsche späterer Generationen modifiziert und umgebaut, doch die Rows nie völlig zerstört wurden.

Von der Mitte des vierzehnten bis zur Mitte des sechzehnten Jahrhunderts ging Chesters Wohlstand zurück. Diese Krisenjahre waren entscheidend für den Fortbestand der Rows, da es damals zu keinen umfangreichen Umbauten kam, die einen Verlust von Kontinuität mit sich gebracht haben könnten und damit den Anreiz, das System der Fußgängerpromenaden instand zu halten, zerstört hätten. Ein weiterer Faktor war der Umstand, daß die Räume auf Straßenniveau normalerweise unabhängig von den Häusern darüber waren; sie wurden oft separat genutzt oder hatten andere Eigentümer(innen), so daß ein völliger Umbau kompliziert war. Zu dieser Zeit errichtete Gebäude zeigen neue Raumanordnungen im Inneren, mit einer größeren Anzahl von Räumen, sowie weiter entwickelte Zimmerhandwerkstechniken.

Im späteren sechzehnten Jahrhundert und in der ersten Hälfte des siebzehnten Jahrhunderts hatte Chester teil an der allgemeinen Zunahme des Wohlstandes in England. Nach Jahrhunderten der Vernachlässigung waren Umbauten nötig, was, zusammen mit wachsendem Reichtum und einem Verlangen neuen Trends zu folgen, zu einer großen Periode des Neu- und Umbauens der Stadthäuser von Chester führte. Aus dieser Phase sind eine beträchtliche Anzahl von Fachwerkgerippen erhalten geblieben, ferner dekorative Putzarbeiten, reich geschmückte Kamine und andere prächtige

Einrichtungen. Das Verlangen, geräumige, gut beleuchtete Wohnräume zu schaffen, die von den kommerziellen Aktivitäten stärker abgetrennt waren, führte zum Verlust von etwa einem Drittel des gesamten Row-Systems. Dieser Prozeß des Umbauens und Abgrenzens bedeutete jedoch dringend benötigte Einnahmen für die städtischen Behörden. Die Stadtversammlung schützte allerdings das Herzstück der Rows, da sie vermutlich die anhaltenden kommerziellen Vorteile dieses Systems begriff. Von den siebziger Jahren des achtzehnten Jahrhunderts bis heute ist es zu praktisch keinen weiteren Verlusten gekommen.

Die Jahre 1670–1830 sahen bedeutsame Veränderungen im äußeren Erscheinungsbild der Rows, als die Fachwerk-Vorderseiten durch Backsteinfassaden ersetzt wurden. Zu ähnlich grundlegenden Veränderungen kam es, was die Funktionen der Gebäude betrifft: sie wurden nicht mehr für kleine Geschäfte und Stände, Lager, Jahr- und Straßenmärkte verwendet, sondern für ein moderneres Einzelhandelssystem mit größer und größer werdenden Geschäften, die nach und nach komplette Gebäude übernahmen. In der Mitte des neunzehnten Jahrhunderts hatte jedoch die Begeisterung für alles Alte zu einem Aufstand gegen die 'schwere athenische Architektur' der Stadt geführt, und eine neue Ära des Fachwerkdesigns begann. Dies führte zu dem heute sichtbaren äußeren Charakter der Rows, aber es machte auch viele der mittelalterlichen Strukturen zunichte, die bis dahin erhalten geblieben waren.

Während der zweiten Hälfte des zwanzigsten Jahrhunderts wurden die Rows weiterhin neuen Bedürfnissen angepaßt und veränderten sich kontinuierlich. Neue Gebäude nahmen Gallerien auf, und über einige der Seitenstraßen wurden Fußgängerbrücken gebaut, so daß die Kontinuität des Systems zusätzlich unterstrichen wurde. 1968 wurde ein großes Reparatur- und Restaurierungsprogramm begonnen; der Schwerpunkt ist heute auf Konservierung und Wiederverwendung von bereits existierenden Strukturen. Die Rows von Chester als solche sind über 600 Jahre hinweg erhalten geblieben, aber ihre Entwicklung spiegelt gleichzeitig sich ständig wandelnde Wohnweisen und Gewerbepraktiken wider.

Übersetzung: *Cornelius J Holtorf*

Editor's note

by Andrew Brown

Dendrochronological re-analysis
Recent work on timbers from the Blue Bell, 63–65 Northgate Street, has indicated that the structure may be significantly earlier than previously thought (see pp 139 and 145). Because production of this volume was already well advanced when the dendrochronological re-analysis became practicable, it was not possible to incorporate discussion of this new information into the relevant chapters, although brief adaptations to text have been made as space permitted (pp 23, 53, 54, 69, and 71).

Referencing
The Harvard style of referencing has generally been used for published sources, with the author's name and the date of publication in brackets within the text and a full reference in the bibliography.

Citation of sources
Unpublished sources are given in the endnotes: in those cases where there are both published and unpublished sources, it has been convenient to include the references together in an endnote.

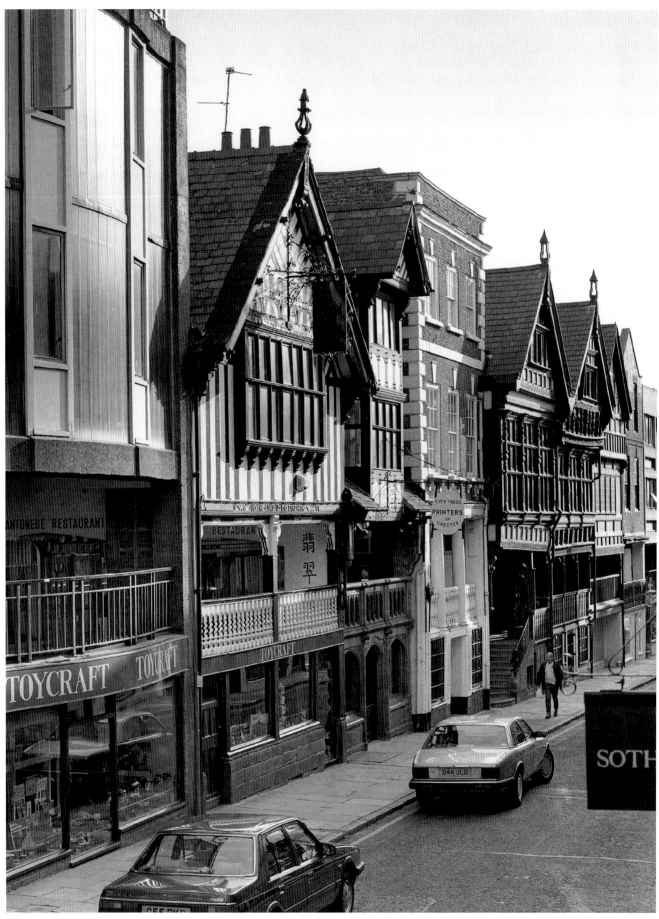

Fig 1   South side of Watergate Street showing the Row walkway running through buildings dating from different periods (RCHME © Crown Copyright)

1 Introduction

Here is a property of building peculiar to the City (of Chester) called the Rows, being Galleries, wherein Passengers go dry without coming into the streets, having shops on both sides and underneath. The fashion whereof is somewhat hard to conceive, it is therefore worth their pains, who have money and leasure to make their own Eyes the Expounders of the manner thereof. The like being said not to be seen in all England, no nor in all Europe again.

(Fuller 1662, 290)

The Rows of Chester are a unique system of walkways that run through the frontages of the buildings on the four main streets of the city[1]. These walkways are in the form of covered galleries that pass above the shops which are at street level, and provide access to a second level of shops at Row, or first floor, level. They are contained within buildings of various dates and architectural styles, all of which appear to have been designed to accommodate the Row walkway. The Rows are continuous within each block; access from the street is by way of steps at the ends of each section and between the street-level shops at every third or fourth property. Figures 1 and 2 show the continuous nature of the Row as it passes through different buildings, and Figure 3 shows the arrangement of a typical Row building. Beneath the Row there is an undercroft, which accommodates the street-level shop. The floor level of these undercroft spaces is usually below street level and in a few of the Row buildings there is also a true cellar underneath. The Row walkway is normally separated from the street frontage by a Row 'stall' or 'stallboard', which is a raised sloping area providing the necessary headroom for the steps down into the undercroft. The ground level to the rear of the Row buildings is usually at the level of the Row walkway, approximately a storey higher than the street level.

The Row and its associated stallboard are now public spaces despite the fact that they are within the structure of the buildings and might therefore be considered private property. This public right of access has been jealously guarded for centuries by the City Council who resist any effort to enclose the walkway or to encroach on to the Rows and stallboards. Nevertheless the building owners are responsible for the maintenance of the Rows, the Council being responsible only for the steps at the ends of each section. This division of responsibility is found in many of the documents in Chester Archives (formerly Chester City Record Office), and is now enshrined in the Cheshire County Council Act 1980.

In many of the Row buildings there is a horizontal division of ownership, with the premises at street level being owned separately from the building above. Thus the Rows are effectively independent streets and the Row-level properties have separate postal addresses from the street-level shops. This can cause confusion as the two numbering systems do not normally coincide; 57 Bridge Street Row, for example, being located above 49 Bridge Street. Therefore for the purposes of this book the Row-level numbering has been ignored and buildings are identified only by their street number (see Gazetteer for both numbering systems).

In other English medieval towns and cities the word 'Row' is commonly applied to groups of buildings along street frontages (see pp56–7). The 'Rows' of Chester are very different, both in their form and in the fact that they extend along all the main streets of the city. Nowhere else is there a system of raised galleries identical to the Chester Rows. Other English towns have stretches of covered pavement with the buildings above supported on columns, such as the Pentice, Winchester, the Butterwalks at Totnes[2] and the north end of Broad Street, Ludlow, but all these covered ways are at street level. Some of the buildings in Chester, in Northgate Street, Foregate Street, and formerly in Lower Bridge Street (Fig 4), are built out over the pavement in this fashion, but these are very different from the Rows which stand alongside and above the pavement. Similar street-level arcades exist in many European towns and cities, such as Berne, Switzerland. Walkways above undercrofts also exist elsewhere, as at Meersburg, Germany, but these generally pass through only a few buildings.

Throughout this book the word 'Row' will be used to indicate the peculiar Chester galleries, and what so impressed Thomas Fuller will be described and analysed.

The debate about the Rows

People have been speculating about the peculiar character of the Chester Rows for over 400 years (Harris 1984). The earliest antiquarian reference to the Rows was made rather obliquely by John Leland in his *Itineraries* of the 1540s. In describing a street in Bridgnorth, Shropshire, he stated '...that Men may passe drye by them yf it rayne, according to some strets in Chestar citie' (Smith 1908, 85). A much fuller description was made by William Smith, a Cheshire man, writing in the 1580s

The Buildings of the City are very ancient; and the Houses builded in such sort, that a man may go dry, from one place of the City to another, and never come in the street; but go as it were in Galleries, which they call, The Roes, which have Shops on both sides and underneath, with divers fair staires to go up or down into the street. Which manner of building I have not heard of in

Fig 2 Row walkway on the east side of Bridge Street (RCHME © Crown Copyright)

any place of Christendome. Some will say, that the like is at Padua in Italy, but that is not so. For the houses at Padua, are builded as the Suburbs of this City be, that is, on the ground, upon Posts, that a man may go dry underneath them; like as they are at Billingsgate in London, but nothing like to the Roes...

(King 1656, 40)

About 40 years later, another Cheshire historian, William Webb, made special mention of the Rows in a description of the city. He recorded that '...the principal dwelling houses and shops for the chiefest Trades, are mounted a Story higher; and before the Doors and Entries, a continued Rowe on either side the street, for people to pass to and fro...' (King 1656, 19–20). Webb then began to conjecture about the origin of the Rows. Drawing on the speculations of an earlier antiquary, he concluded that the Rows originated as a means of defence. He believed that the early inhabitants of Chester lived in the undercrofts, under the ground surface rather than above. New additions were then added on top of these earlier foundations for more comfort and convenience, however '...because their conflicts with Enemies continued long time, it was needful for them to leave a space before the doors of those their upper buildings, upon which they might stand in safety from the violence of their Enemies horses, and withall defend their houses from spoyl...' (King 1656, 19–20).

From this time onwards many visitors to Chester record their comments on the Rows, perhaps encouraged by the quotation from Thomas Fuller given at the opening of this chapter, which reads like an early example of a tourism promotion. However, not all visitors were as impressed by this strange form of building, particularly as architectural taste began to turn against timber-framed buildings. Celia Fiennes and Daniel Defoe, in particular, were strongly critical, the latter describing the Rows as 'both old and ugly' (see p111). Along with the visitors came many of the most famous antiquarians and it is through their speculations that the debate on the origins of the Rows developed.

Several of the descriptions at the turn of the eighteenth century described the Rows as 'piazzaed' (Trappes-Lomax 1930, 105; Cowan 1903, 167–9) implying a similarity in appearance to Italian cities.

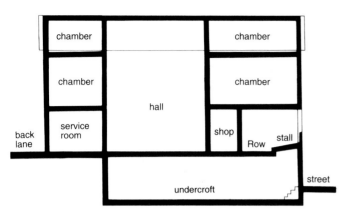

Fig 3 Section through a typical medieval Rows building (after J Grenville)

Later in the eighteenth century William Stukeley (1776, 59) proposed that they were connected with the Roman tradition of colonnaded streets. Thomas Pennant, who lived in Flintshire near Chester, subscribed to the same idea and in 1773 he described the Rows as follows

> The structure of the four principal streets is without parallel. They run direct from east to west, and north to south; and were excavated out of the earth, and sunk many feet beneath the surface. The carriages drive far below the level of the kitchens, on a line with ranges of shops; over which on each side of the streets, passengers walk from end to end, secure from wet and heat, in galleries (or rows, as they are called) purloined from the first floor of each house, open in front and balustraded. The back courts of all these houses are level with the rows: but to go into any of those four streets, it is necessary to descend a flight of several steps...
>
> (Pennant 1883, 142)

This passage highlights the disparity of levels between the front and back of the Row buildings and the oddity of having a public footway passing through private houses. The Roman connection was supported by Joseph Hemingway in his *History of the City of Chester*, published in 1831, and he attributed the excavation of the streets to the Roman legionaries, to ease the slope from the river to the centre of their fortress (Hemingway 1831, 389–97).

The first writer to consider the architecture of the individual buildings and the bearing this had on the development of the Rows was John Hewitt. In a paper published in 1887, he looked at parallels to the buildings surviving in Chester, particularly their 'crypts' or undercrofts. He concluded that the front walls of the medieval houses rose straight up from the street, with the principal floor reached by a flight of external steps. Subsequently, the upper floors were brought forward over these steps as much as nine or ten feet into the main streets. Within these encroachments, the Row

was created by demolishing the original front walls, and this was a 'general undertaking' made by the citizens of Chester (Hewitt 1887).

The Chester Archaeological Society held discussions on the origins of the Rows in 1893 and 1894. Hewitt restated his case, that the Row was created through adjacent buildings to make shopping at this first-floor level more convenient, and suggested that this change took place between about 1490 and 1520. Another member of the Society, Dr T N Brushfield, could not see how the self-interested citizenry would surrender 'to the public good, the best portion of the best room in his house', and concluded that the elevation of the Row came about by the accumulation of debris in front of the early houses on which the walkway was created, with the undercrofts then being excavated underneath (Brushfield 1895).

New light was thrown on these issues by the publication in 1894 of Canon R H Morris' book, *Chester in the Plantagenet and Tudor Reigns*. This was the first history of Chester to be based on extensive research into the city's records, and it set the documentary sources alongside the architectural and archaeological evidence, which had already been widely discussed. This book included the then earliest known reference to the Rows in a deed of grant by Richard Russel to his son, David, in 1330 (Morris mistakenly gives 1331). These consisted of the 'Iurnemongerrowe', 'Baxterrowe' and 'Cokesrowe' in Northgate and

Fig 4 Buildings formerly on the east side of Lower Bridge Street with a covered walkway at street level (RCHME © Crown Copyright)

Fig 5 South side of Watergate Street by G Pickering, 1829 (photograph RCHME © Crown Copyright, from print in CAS Library, Chester Archives)

Fig 6 Row walkway on the south side of Watergate Street by G Pickering, 1852 (photograph RCHME © Crown Copyright, from print in CAS Library, Chester Archives)

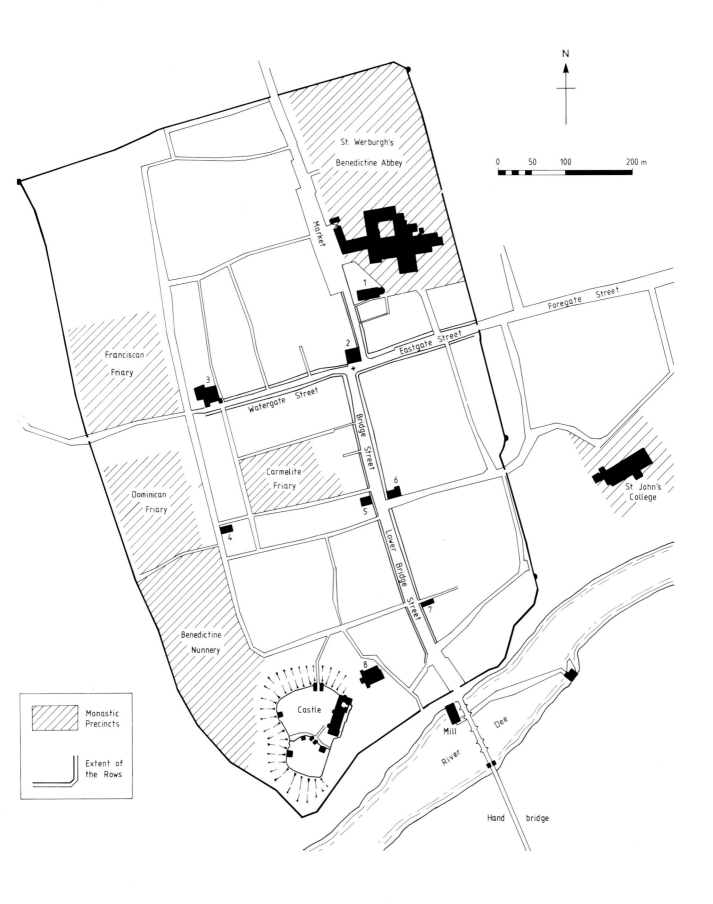

Fig 7 Plan of medieval Chester showing the parish churches: **1** *St Werburgh's;* **2** *St Peter's;* **3** *Holy Trinity;* **4** *St Martin's;* **5** *St Bridget's;* **6** *St Michael's;* **7** *St Olave's;* **8** *St Mary's*

Eastgate Streets (Morris 1894, 292). Like Hewitt, Morris favoured the theory that the origins of the Rows developed from the encroachment of the buildings into the street and he recognised the commercial aspect of the Rows. Seven years later, in another paper published in the Archaeological Society's journal, H D Harrod (1902) contradicted Morris and Hewitt by suggesting that the colonnaded Row was derived directly from Roman colonnaded streets and their presumed associated shops, a refinement of the arguments put forward by Pennant and Hemingway.

No further significant research into the history and architecture of the Rows was undertaken until 1957. During that year the Chester Archaeological Society was given two lectures, one by J T Smith and the other by P H Lawson, who later published a joint paper (Lawson and Smith 1958). Their work consisted of the first comprehensive study of the surviving buildings, together with a consideration of the associated documentation. This remains a very valuable source of information, for a number of the buildings which they discussed have since been demolished. In considering their evidence, however, they reached different conclusions. Smith based his ideas firmly on the architectural evidence of the stone undercrofts and the other stone structures. He believed that these were all of the period 1270–1330, and argued that this was supported by the record of a fire in 1278, said to have almost totally destroyed the area within the walls. Smith postulated that the Rows were devised immediately after that date as part of a plan for a fireproof town which would be able to survive the type of disasters which had ravaged the city since the Conquest.

Lawson's arguments were largely intended to contradict some of the major points made by Smith. He argued for the steady evolution of the system from a period before the fire, with evidence for substantial stone houses within the Rows dating from as early as 1208. Lawson and Smith ended their paper with a plea for a systematic record to be made of all the Row buildings, especially when they were being altered or rebuilt. This challenge was eventually taken up in 1984 with the establishment of the Chester Rows Research Project (see Preface) and the comprehensive study that lies behind the publication of this book.

The early development of Chester

Two major factors contributed to Chester's development. The first was its strategic importance. It stands at the lowest bridging point of the River Dee and at the limit of its tidal range. Over the river is Wales, which throughout much of the medieval period was a source of unrest and rebellion against the rulers of England. Across the sea is Ireland, a base for raiding parties in the Viking period and the scene of English conquests, often led from Chester. The second factor was trade, which underlay the activity and wealth of the city. No doubt the Romans used sea and river transport to service the army[3] and the importance of external trade and Chester's dependence upon imported food can be documented back into Saxon times (Thacker forthcoming).

The topography of Chester and its early history as a Roman fortress is of special significance for the layout of the later city and the development of its buildings. The city centre is contained by the medieval and earlier walls, and within these the four main streets, Bridge Street, Eastgate Street, Northgate Street, and Watergate Street, lead from the principal gates to the centre, forming a cross. Bridge Street and its continuation, Lower Bridge Street, run south to the river and the bridge, while Watergate Street was the main entry from the port. The point where the main streets meet is the focus of the city and is known as the Cross (Fig 8).

Chester is built on the end of a low, broad promontory of Old Red Sandstone, surrounded to the south and west by the River Dee. The centre of the city is about 30m above sea level and the land falls gently to low cliffs above the river (Mason 1976). A number of small stream valleys underlie the present city; the most significant of these, in terms of the development of the Rows, runs south along the line of Lower Bridge Street.

The sandstone provided a readily available building stone and several early quarry faces can be seen across the river in Handbridge. The rock is very close to the surface, so deep foundations are unnecessary and the floors of the medieval undercrofts are only slightly below street level. True cellars, below the undercrofts, had to be cut out of the rock.

The traditional bridging point across the River Dee is at the south end of Lower Bridge Street, where the former stream valley joined the river. There is evidence for the survival of the Roman bridge into the medieval period, possibly until the present bridge was constructed in 1347 (Strickland 1984, 25–7). Immediately upstream of the bridge is the great weir built diagonally across the river on a natural shelf of rock. This provided the site for the medieval and later mills, and also prevented ships progressing further upstream. Thus the port developed below the bridge, on the south and west sides of the city.

There is little indication of pre-Roman settlement at Chester. The legionary fortress established in the 70s by the governor, Agricola, was laid out over cultivated fields (Mason 1976, 19). It was of a typical rectangular form, covering 24ha, and was sited some distance back from the river. There were some stone buildings from the beginning but the fortress and its associated civilian settlement evolved during the next 300 years (Strickland 1984). The plan of the fortress established the framework of the later Saxon *burh*, and thus of the medieval and modern city; and the survival of the ruins of major Roman buildings must also have been a factor in later development[4]. As in other Roman fortresses and towns in England, many of the structures seemed to survive into the Middle Ages (Greenhalgh 1989). Ranulph Higden, a monk of St Werburgh's

Fig 8   The Cross looking west down Watergate Street (RCHME © Crown Copyright)

Abbey in Chester, wrote in his chronicle of the 1340s: 'when I behold the ground-work of buildings in the streets, laid with many strong high stones, it seemeth that it hath been founded by the painful labour of Romans or giants...' (Babington 1869, 76–84).

As shown in Figure 9 there is an obvious relationship between the developed plan of the Roman fortress and the modern street pattern. The two main Roman streets – the *via principalis* running east–west, and the *via praetoria* running north–south – are broad and straight. These correspond to the more irregular and narrower Eastgate, Watergate, and Bridge Streets. Of the four main streets only Northgate Street does not have an immediate relationship with the fortress plan. Although it used the Roman north gate[5], it wanders rather irregularly across the site of Roman buildings, widens to form a market place in the area of the Roman hospital courtyard and joins Eastgate Street over the corner of the *principia* or headquarters building. The lines of several of the minor Roman streets are also still in use. Weaver, Trinity, and Water Tower Streets follow the line of the *intervallum* road on the west and north side of the fortress, and Whitefriars rather less precisely on the south side. Commonhall, Crook, and Goss Streets are on the lines of minor throughfares.

The collapse of the Roman buildings has led to a peculiarity in Chester's topography that is significant in the development of the Rows. Look up any of the minor streets from Bridge Street or Watergate Street and the ground level will be seen to rise away from you (Fig 10). The present surface of the major streets has remained at, or at some stage was cleared back to, the Roman street level. Some of this difference in height can be attributed to a layer of Roman debris (Strickland 1984, 31) and excavation has also shown that soil and rubbish deposits continued to accumulate behind Row buildings during the medieval period (Ward 1984), so increasing the disparity in height. This means that, although the Row level may be as much as 2m above street level at the front of a property, at the rear it usually corresponds with the ground level. A similar arrangement exists on either side of Lower Bridge Street, but here the natural slopes on either side of the stream valley are largely responsible because this is outside the area of the Roman fortress. Away from the main streets the buildings of the fortress were less massive, being largely barrack and stable blocks probably of timber-framed construction on low stone walls. In these areas the 'debris slope' is less significant, and medieval stone cellars that are completely below ground survive, or have been excavated, in Whitefriars (Grenville and Turner 1986) and Northgate Street (Davey 1973).

The Roman buildings may have provided a useful source of building stone for later construction and the

Fig 9 Plan of the Roman fortress related to the later street pattern (reproduced by courtesy of Chester Archaeology)

Fig 10   View looking up Commonhall Street from Bridge Street showing rise in 'ground level' (RCHME © Crown Copyright)

Fig 11   Part of the north wall of the Roman fortress incorporated into later defences (RCHME © Crown Copyright)

archaeological evidence indicates that stone robbing was common (Ward 1984, 45). Yet almost no reused Roman masonry has been identified in Row buildings, with the exception of a fragmentary inscription taken from the undercroft of 64 Watergate Street (Webster 1951).

The evidence for the immediate post-Roman period is very scanty. Some imported Mediterranean pottery and a timber-framed building at Abbey Green suggest the short-term survival of a Romanised settlement. For later centuries there are a few references in the Welsh and Danish annals and in Bede's *Historia Ecclesiastica* (Thacker 1987, 237–8). As with most English towns, the archaeological evidence suggests that Chester was largely abandoned until the eighth or ninth centuries. In 893–4, when the area was firmly within the Mercian kingdom, a party of Danes reached and briefly occupied '...a deserted city in Wirral, which was called Chester' (Thacker 1987, 249). The Mercians regained much of their territory from the Danes in the early tenth century and Queen Aethelflaed refortified Chester as a *burh* in 907. It later acted as the centre for a line of smaller *burhs* stretching from Rhuddlan to Manchester, which protected Mercia's northern frontier (Thacker 1987, 250). This was the beginning of Chester's appearance as an English town.

The reuse of the line of the Roman fortifications to the north and east as part of the defences of the early tenth century *burh* (Fig 11), together with the river to the south and west, controlled the physical expansion of Chester. The walls retained their strategic importance into the fourteenth and fifteenth centuries

because of intermittent threats from the Welsh, and the growth of suburbs was limited to Foregate Street, and Handbridge, across the river; the latter was repeatedly burnt by the Welsh during the thirteenth century. Alldridge (1981) contends that some of Chester's present land divisions date from the pre-Norman period. By the late Saxon period there were three parish churches, St Werburgh's, St John's, and St Peter's, and the parish boundaries on Eastgate Street are significant. The parish of St Peter's was perhaps created out of St Werburgh's as the result of a grant of land by a lay patron; the parish of St Werburgh, however, retained two linear plots fronting on to each side of Eastgate Street, which isolated part of St Peter's parish (Fig 12). The shape of these boundaries may be evidence for the existence of long, narrow burgage plots at this early date.

In late Saxon times Chester was one of the largest and most important towns in northern England and was substantial even by national standards. It had a considerable population of perhaps 2–3000 inhabitants, probably concentrated in the southern two-thirds of the area enclosed by the walls (Sawyer and Thacker 1987; Thacker forthcoming). In the less densely populated areas north of Eastgate and Watergate Streets there are indications that there was discontinuity between the late Saxon and post-Conquest building patterns and that the long thin plots associated with the medieval city were introduced only after 1066 (Ward 1984). Further south, however, it seems likely that there were early plots which were increasingly densely occupied and subdivided in late Saxon times to form continuous built-up frontages along the principal streets. Unfortunately the archaeological evidence gives little indication of the type of houses present at this time, apart from a group of semi-basement buildings in the backland area west of Lower Bridge Street (Mason 1985) and a timber hall-type structure on Princess Street (Ward 1984, 41). The street frontages have been so extensively redeveloped that there is no evidence for the Saxon and early Norman use of these areas.

Following the Norman Conquest, Chester became the centre of an independent earldom, acting as a buffer against the unruly Welsh. The Domesday Book provides the first evidence for the number and ownership of houses within Chester (Sawyer and Thacker 1987, 325–7). On the eve of the Conquest a total of 508 houses was recorded, with 431 paying rent to the King and Earl and 56 to the Bishop. The Mercian rebellion and subsequent military campaigns in 1069–70 reduced the income from the city and 205 fewer houses are recorded in 1086. The construction of the castle in the south-west corner of the city may account for some of this loss[6], but the castle and its demesne lands were peripheral to the main settlement. The reduction in house numbers may have been the result of a disenfranchisement of Saxon burgesses and their replacement by a smaller number of Norman tenants, controlling larger blocks of land within existing boundaries. Such large blocks may have been subdivided as

the population grew in later centuries, resulting in the long, thin plots which were typical of medieval settlements. This certainly happened to some of the larger medieval houses.

In Chester there is little indication of the houses erected during the twelfth century, and although the majority would probably have been of timber, the earliest surviving English town houses are of stone construction and were probably the houses of very wealthy merchants (Wood 1965, 6). These have the domestic accommodation at first floor level above an undercroft and this is the basic building form that was later to be found in the Chester Rows. As in other towns the buildings of Chester were constantly threatened by fire and it would therefore have been logical for stone to be used for the houses of the wealthy. One of the local laws recorded in the Domesday Book sets penalties for anyone whose house was the source of fire (Sawyer and Thacker 1987, 326) and two fires are recorded in the twelfth century (Morris 1894, 277, 292), but the extent of the destruction is not known.

The Domesday Book lays emphasis on Chester's port and trading activities, detailing an elaborate system of tolls, and throughout the medieval period the city controlled various creek ports in the Dee and Mersey estuaries, including Liverpool (Wilson 1965; Woodward 1970). Chester has never had an important role in manufacturing, its wealth being almost entirely the result of trade. The most important links were with Ireland, where there are charters confirming the liberties of Chester merchants from the twelfth century (Hewitt 1967, 81). Imports to Chester were primarily grain and other foodstuffs. Exports consisted of salt, salted fish, cloth, and metals. There was also the regular movement of government officials and troops. Imports peaked during the military campaigns against the Welsh in the late thirteenth century, when food was needed for the army and to provision the new castles. Chester was also used to tranship provisions to Carlisle and Skinburness on the Solway Firth when Edward I's attention turned to Scotland.

Chester's ships travelled further afield, particularly to Gascony for wine, a trade which also peaked during the Welsh campaigns. There were also some connections with the wealthy Italian city states, for the production of wool at three of Cheshire's abbeys appears in *La practica della mercatura* (Hewitt 1967, 38), produced as a guide for Italian merchants. However, Chester was not an important woollen port and Cheshire's wool was shipped via Boston and Ipswich (Hewitt 1967, 70–89). Behind the international links was a thriving coastal and estuarine trade, and Chester also acted as the market place for its hinterland.

The earliest surviving reference to a market dates from *c* 1080 (Chibnall 1969–80, IV, 136). The first reference to a fair is 1121–9 and by the early thirteenth century there were fairs at both midsummer and Michaelmas (Barraclough 1988, 21–2). Trade with Ireland was particularly important from an early date

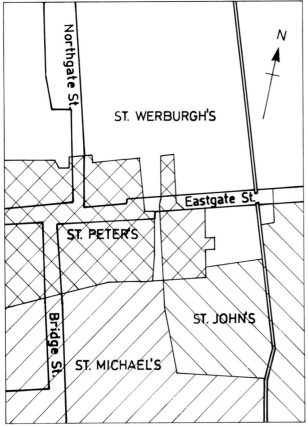

Fig 12 Plan of parish boundaries in Eastgate Street and Bridge Street (after Alldridge 1981)

and William of Malmesbury wrote in *c* 1125, 'Goods are exchanged between Chester and Ireland, so that what the nature of the soil lacks, is supplied by the toil of the merchants' (Hamilton 1870, 308).

The twelfth century appears to have been a period of steady expansion for Chester. The defences were extended to the south and west, linking the castle to the existing walls[7]. While there were obvious military requirements for this expensive work, it may also have been prompted by a hope for growth. In this the earls of Chester were to be disappointed, for the western extension appears to have remained undeveloped until the foundation of the Franciscan and Dominican friaries in 1237[8].

At the end of the twelfth century, Lucian, a monk of St Werburgh's Abbey, wrote a poem in praise of Chester; this is the second oldest description of an English town[9] and is of interest despite its elaborate allegorical style. He saw '...the two excellent straight streets in form of the blessed Cross, which through meeting and crossing themselves, then make four out of two, the heads ending in four gates... in the middle of the city... there to be a market for the sale of goods.' He also described '...beneath the city walls... a harbour for ships coming from Aquitaine, Spain, Ireland and Germany, which by Christ's guidance and by the labour and skill of the merchants, come and unload at the city bay, with many goods, so that comforted in many ways, by the grace of our God, we may drink wine more often and more plentifully...' (Palliser 1980, 6–7).

So, the picture of Chester at the beginning of the thirteenth century is of a prospering city with a well-established pattern of settlement and longstanding property divisions. Much of the area within the walls would still be open space devoted to gardens, orchards, and even vineyards (Morris 1894, 569), but the houses would have clustered along the main streets, probably providing almost continuous frontages. During the thirteenth century, three events occurred which may be of great significance for our understanding of the Rows: the fire of 1278, which reputedly destroyed a significant section of the town; Edward I's use of Chester as his base for the military campaigns against the Welsh; and his grant of the city's first charter in 1300, which gave the citizens greater control over the development of the city.

The *Annales Cestrienses,* written by a monk of St Werburgh's Abbey, records that on 15 May 1278 almost the whole of Chester within the walls of the city was burned down (Christie 1887, 104–5). J T Smith gives considerable emphasis to this event in his discussion of the origin of the Rows (Lawson and Smith 1958, 33). A major fire would undoubtedly have led to a need for extensive rebuilding, with many new houses being erected at the same time. Smith contends that this would have provided the incentive for a planned reconstruction, with all new buildings required to incorporate Row walkways. Despite the documentary record for an extensive fire in 1278, there is, however,

considerable doubt about the scale of the destruction caused. No evidence of the fire debris that could be equated with such an event has been uncovered in any of the extensive archaeological excavations in the city centre and this raises the possibility that the fire was not as widespread as the chronicler suggested (Ward 1984, 44–5).

Fires were undoubtedly frequent occurrences in medieval towns and the threat that they posed did result in early regulations. For example, fireproofing measures were introduced into London by its first mayor between 1192–3 and 1212 (Schofield 1984, 75). In Chester the occurrence of stone party walls to many undercrofts, often in conjunction with massive floor thicknesses at Row level, suggests that some form of medieval building regulation may have existed by the end of the thirteenth century. More puzzling is the very limited number of stone party walls at higher levels. It seems that the merchants of Chester were prepared to risk their houses being destroyed by fire, but not the valuable goods stored in the undercrofts. This theory is supported by evidence from the nearby royal borough of Flint which was deliberately burnt in 1294, in advance of an anticipated attack by the Welsh, so as to provide an unimpeded field of fire from the castle. Every burgess was compensated for the loss of his house, grain, and other goods. Nearly all the houses seem to have been timber-framed and of relatively low value compared to the goods that they contained (Taylor 1982). So domestic accommodation may have been cheap and relatively easy to replace, while wealth was in stored merchandise.

At the end of the thirteenth century, Chester's status changed from that of a provincial city, with a modest but steady trade and a small garrison, to a strategic military base of national importance (Grenville 1990, 449–51; Thacker forthcoming). Edward I mounted two massive campaigns against the Welsh, in 1277 and 1282–3, with Chester acting as the main mustering point on both occasions. From January to July 1277, the Earl of Warwick's force was billeted in the city at the huge cost of £1,094 in wages, before being joined by the main muster from Worcester. In February, an order was sent to Ireland for 600 quarters of wheat and 1000 quarters of oats to be shipped to Chester, and 26 ships of the fleet arrived from the Cinque ports. Strong forward bases were established at Flint and Rhuddlan, and, for the purposes of castle building, quantities of timber were brought from the Wirral via Chester, and picks, axes, and other equipment were purchased in the city.

The second campaign, sparked off by a Welsh rebellion, was a far greater undertaking aimed at the total submission of North Wales. Chester again served as a mustering point and as a major market for supplies. The organisation of the immense army (up to 8000 foot and 276 heavy cavalry) for over a year was effected from 'a great central victualling depot at Chester under William de Perton' (Prestwich 1988, 199).

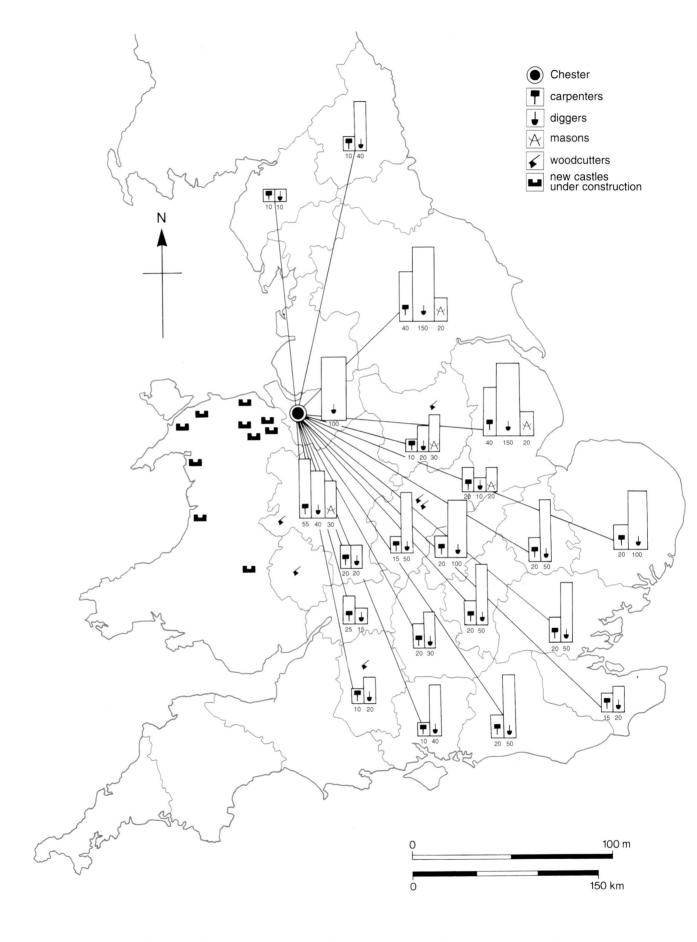

Fig 13 Movement of labour 1282–3 for Edward I's building works in North Wales (after J Grenville)

By the summer of 1283, the power of the princes of Gwynedd had been destroyed, but Edward was determined to maintain his advantage, and a massive programme of castle building was initiated.

Thus, after its years as a major military base, Chester found itself playing host to the army of skilled workmen employed in the impressive ring of castles designed by Edward I's military architects, James of St George and Richard the Engineer being chief amongst them. This workforce was drawn from across the country (Fig 13) and involved up to 6530 woodcutters, 1100 diggers, 410 carpenters, and 115 masons (Brown *et al* 1963, 182–3). Building campaigns were vigorous throughout the 1280s and further work took place after an unsuccessful rebellion in 1294. With construction work generally suspended over the winter, many of the craftsmen, for whom the journey home was impracticable, may have sought temporary lodgings and work in Chester. So, in the 1280s and 1290s, and to a lesser extent into the early fourteenth century, Chester experienced a considerable economic boom. Quantities of food and other supplies were channelled through the city; soldiers, craftsmen and labourers, paid in cash for their services, flooded in, boosting trade. Thus, the end of the thirteenth century and the first half of the fourteenth saw Chester at the height of its medieval prosperity.

By the early thirteenth century the citizens were beginning to emancipate themselves from government by the appointed officials of the earl, a process probably accelerated by the annexation of the earldom by the Crown in 1237. Throughout the thirteenth century power was passing from the sheriffs, who were originally the earl's nominees, to the mayor as the principal representative of the merchant class, a position that is first mentioned in the 1240s (Thacker forthcoming). This growing self confidence was strengthened by Edward I's charter of 1300 which granted or confirmed to the citizens a wide range of rights, including control over vacant plots within the city (Morris 1894, 490–3). Such privileges can only have enhanced the role of the merchant élite in the development of the city and hence in the construction of the buildings which contain the Rows.

Several merchant families came to dominate Chester's political life. Examples include the Hurel and Brickhill families, who dealt in prestige commodities such as wine and wool, and whose members held the mayoralty 15 times between 1278 and 1315 (Hewitt 1967, 72). But the most enterprising of this generation of merchants was William of Doncaster, king's merchant, citizen of Chester, and mayor in 1316 and 1319. He imported wine in great quantities; one of his ships, the *Mariote*, being engaged in stocking the Welsh castles with wine in 1295. He had agents in Gascony for wine and in Ireland for corn, and he shipped wool to Flanders via Ipswich. He farmed the lead mines of Englefield on the Welsh side of the Dee estuary and supplied the king with horseshoes. Although convicted of introducing bad money into Chester in 1300, he was made 'searcher for money' in the ports of Chester and North Wales. With his increasing wealth he began to buy land around Chester and in North Wales (Hewitt 1967, 73, 81). More significantly for the development of the Rows he and his family steadily purchased a large number of properties along the main trading streets of the town, Eastgate and Watergate Streets. This pattern of ownership was matched by another merchant family, the Russells, probably reflecting a desire to control much of the commercial frontages.

The merchants were the beneficiaries of the prosperity, built on the back of the king's Welsh campaigns, and it was the merchants who gained the power to govern their city following the charter of 1300. This substantial increase in wealth and power appears to have been expressed in an extensive rebuilding of the commercial core, and it is the evidence for these buildings that must now be considered. The antiquarians and architectural historians quoted at the beginning of this chapter were trying to seek a single factor or mechanism that was responsible for the Row system. The Rows Research Project, however, has attempted to consider the topographical, historical, documentary, and architectural evidence together. This has not thrown up any single factor which explains the Chester Rows. There is no easy answer to the questions of origin and early development, as different emphases can be given to the different strands of evidence. Following a discussion of the general documentary and structural evidence in the next chapter, and two more detailed chapters on the early medieval stonework and timberwork, our conclusions regarding the origins of the Rows are presented in chapter 5. The later chapters then explore how the Rows have been adapted through the centuries.

2 Early medieval buildings

This chapter considers the development of buildings along the main streets of Chester in the period before 1350, when the city was at the height of its medieval prosperity, and assesses the extent of the Rows at this time. In order to build up a picture of these town houses, use has been made of both the documentary evidence and the detailed surveys of the surviving buildings carried out by the Rows Research Project between 1984 and 1990.

One important prerequisite for the development of the Rows was a reasonably continuous run of buildings along the street frontages. This is likely to have existed in Chester, at least in the central area of the city, from an early date. The long narrow plots running back from the main streets, typical of medieval towns, were already in existence by the thirteenth century and may well date back to late Saxon times (see pp 9–10). The documentary record provides important evidence of numerous buildings along the principal thoroughfares, and it seems likely that the street frontages were largely occupied by buildings from the time that the records become available, and that a semi-continuous system of Row walkways was thus possible. The bulk of the evidence comprises local deeds which first occur in considerable numbers from the first decades of the thirteenth century and which relate to property

variously termed land (*terra*), plots (*placeae* or *placeae terrae*), messuages (*messuagia*), tenements (*tenementa*), and burgages (*burgagia*)[1]. Most of these terms are highly unspecific (see Appendix A), but in many instances it is clear that they were applied to sites with buildings[2].

In contemporary newly-planted towns, the use of such terminology might well imply plots of a uniform statutory size, an arrangement which if it had existed in Chester would have considerable significance for the development of the Rows (Reynolds 1977, 53–6, 192). In fact, however, the documentary evidence on this subject is very limited, and there is nothing in the twelfth- or thirteenth-century records to imply any uniformity in the size of contemporary holdings in the four main streets[3]. Equally the dimensions of the surviving medieval undercrofts vary considerably, from 3.7m to 8.8m in width and from 10m to 40.85m in length[4]. Thus there appears to be little evidence of urban planning in post-Conquest Chester. The only hint of uniformity lies in the frequency with which measurements involving an 11ft (3.35m) or half a chain unit occur in the frontage dimensions along the principal streets. From the 1875 edition of the 1:500 Ordnance Survey map it has been possible to identify some 45 frontages measuring 55ft (16.76m) and a further 14 frontages measuring about 66ft (20.12m) out of a total

Fig 14 Nineteenth-century view of Eastgate Street by W Batenham; the buildings on the left beyond St Peter's Church occupy the site of the Buttershops. (Photograph RCHME © Crown Copyright, from print in CAS Library, Chester Archives)

of approximately 150 properties. Several half-plots also derive from measurements that are a multiple of 11ft. That links up with documentary evidence of a large holding on the north side of Watergate Street with a street frontage of 55ft[5]. Such uniformity in the width of frontages, if it existed, would date from the establishment of the plots and thus probably predates the development of the Rows by a considerable period.

The elements of the buildings

By the thirteenth century domestic and commercial structures were very closely intertwined. In the 1250s, for example, the section of Northgate Street that was already – or was soon to become – known as Ironmongers' Row contained dwellings (*domus*) as well as shops and undercrofts. Deeds of that date refer to plots whose frontages included both shops and the door (*hostium*) to the house behind[6]. Similar arrangements were to be found in the Cornmarket, on the south side of Eastgate Street, where in 1275 the entrance to the house of the wealthy citizen, Robert le Barn, lay next to two shops, also owned by Robert[7]. On the opposite side of Eastgate Street (Fig 14), the Buttershops similarly contained dwellings; in 1293, for example, Hugh of Brickhill owned four *domus* on the site, all with porches (*porcheria*) in front of them[8].

Dwellings could of course vary greatly in size and status, ranging from the simplest accommodation (no more than one or two rooms) to substantial merchants' houses with spacious halls. The grander structures were often stone-built throughout, and hence more of their upper storeys remain (see Chapter 3). Moreover, because of their high status and the comparatively unusual and expensive fabric which expressed it, they also attracted more attention in the documentary record. As early as the late twelfth century, the stone house (*domus lapidea*) of Peter the Clerk, the earl's chancellor, was singled out for mention. It lay at the corner of Castle Street and Lower Bridge Street, and is probably to be identified with the mansion in Castle Street subsequently known as 'le Stonehall', which in the mid-fourteenth century belonged to Sir Peter of Thornton and incorporated an undercroft (*celarium*)[9]. Elsewhere in the city there were stone structures termed 'chambers' (*camerae* or *solaria*). In the mid-thirteenth century, for example, Ranulph of Oxford, a chamberlain of Chester, owned a *camera lapidea* in the lane of Alexander Hare (now Whitefriars)[10], while in the early fourteenth century the sheriff, Richard of Wheatley, had a stone *solarium*, which lay some 15 'royal' ells (13.72m) behind the frontage of the western side of Northgate Street[11]. Other important houses stood in Lower Bridge Street, including the house of the royal official, Richard the Engineer, later known as Pareas Hall after its sale in 1321 to Robert Pares or Praers. Originally stone-built and with a high tower, it stood next to St Olave's church, which probably originated as its chapel[12].

Although all these buildings have now disappeared, the late fourteenth-century deeds give occasional glimpses of the internal arrangements of similar substantial dwellings. The Bultinghouse, which stood next to the church of St Mary on the Hill in 1390, was the chief Chester residence of the wealthy local landowner, Hugh de Holes. Among its apartments were several 'lower rooms' (*bas chambres*) next to the kitchen, and a principal chamber, a grange and stables, which Hugh reserved to himself when letting the rest to a pelter called William de Kerdyne[13]. In 1369, the Black Hall (*le Blakehalle, aula nigra*) in Pepper Street was the subject of a similar agreement[14]. In this instance the grantor reserved to himself the stables, the principal apartments, and the stone and painted chambers (*camera lapidea et camera depicta*) in what seems to have been a grand house, originally the home of a mayoral family, the Daresburys[15]. Although neither of these houses was situated on the four main streets, similar large structures would probably have existed there, such as the property in Bridge Street which included a chapel, a dovecote and a garden[16].

Almost all these structures combined commercial and domestic use, with the domestic element behind and above the commercial frontage. They often included shops, usually small lock-ups with modest accommodation for the shopkeepers[17]. A well-documented example is the house in Northgate Street subdivided between members of the Doncaster family in 1342. The deed recording the division shows that the property included at least one undercroft, over which lay a shop or 'seld' (*seude*) with a chamber (*soler*) above that[18]. The more substantial houses might have as many as five Row-level shops above a number of undercrofts. Such dual use was normal in medieval urban buildings and in Chester the walkway or Row, with its associated shops and oversailing chamber, formed an integral part of the design of surviving thirteenth- and fourteenth-century buildings.

Undercrofts, Rows and shops

At street level the four main thoroughfares were dominated by semi-subterranean stone-walled undercrofts. Such structures were numerous in thirteenth- and fourteenth-century English towns, doubtless because of the security which they afforded for the storage and sale of valuable commodities. In addition they doubled the amount of street frontage available for commercial purposes by allowing space for smaller shops above. In Chester the *celaria* so frequently referred to in late thirteenth- and fourteenth-century deeds[19] are most impressively exemplified by the five surviving stone-vaulted undercrofts (see Chapter 3 and Fig 15). Many others also survive with stone party walls (there are 36 such undercrofts in Watergate Street alone) and some retain massive timber ceilings, often supported by timber posts (see Chapter 4). As in other towns these structures were often quite elaborate and impressive,

Fig 15   Vaulted undercroft at 28 Eastgate Street (RCHME © Crown Copyright)

some being divided into two aisles by an arcade, as at 11 Watergate Street. Several are singled out in the deeds by being expressly described as stone-built (*celaria lapidea*)[20] and, in one instance at least, an undercroft seems to have been considered sufficiently noteworthy to provide a citizen with his soubriquet, 'de la Celer' (Irvine 1904, 26).

In one respect, however, the undercrofts in Chester are unlike those in the majority of other English towns: they are set unusually high with floors scarcely lower than the street (Fig 3). One reason for this is the presence of bedrock immediately below street level which rendered it unnecessary and indeed undesirable to sink the undercroft walls to any great depth. Another is the peculiar topography across the main thoroughfares. The fact that the ground level at the rear was up to 2 or 3m higher than the street front made it advantageous for the ceilings of the under-crofts to be at the higher level. This not only allowed access from the rear at Row level[21], but had the added benefit of ensuring that the timber-framed structures above the undercrofts were not in contact with the soil. The only exceptions, at the east end of Eastgate Street (south side) and on the west side of Northgate Street, significantly coincide with a lower rear ground level and the limit of the extent of the Rows.

The undercroft frontages, which could be quite elaborate, are exemplified at the Falcon (6 Lower Bridge Street), 28 Eastgate Street (Fig 16), and the lost 25 Watergate Street (recorded *c* 1816). Each had a central doorway up to 1.5m wide with flanking windows. A similar arrangement was adopted for the timber-framed frontage to the undercroft at the Leche House, 17 Watergate Street and a central doorway without flanking windows survives at 22 Northgate Street.

Fig 16   Doorway and windows in the front wall of the undercroft at 28 Eastgate Street (RCHME © Crown Copyright)

Only one undercroft, at 12 Bridge Street (Fig 17), is known to have had a rear window, and it therefore appears that both access and illumination were usually from the front only. The subdivision of the undercrofts into discrete sections each requiring separate doors and windows rendered illumination and access from the front even more essential. At 32–34 Watergate Street, for example, the surviving timber arcade is grooved to take wattle and daub partitions, implying a division of the undercroft into three longitudinal sections, each only 2.6m wide internally.

In a number of the surviving and recorded undercrofts there is clear evidence for a staircase linking to the house above (Lawson and Smith 1958). This was usually at the rear, but at 12 Bridge Street there is a stair within the party wall. In these cases at least, the undercroft was clearly intended to be used by the occupier of the house at Row level for storage or as an impressive space for the sale and display of wares (Brown *et al* 1986, 122–3). By the early fourteenth century, however, it is clear that they were often held separately from the accommodation on the upper levels. A good example of the evolution of this pattern of tenure occurs in Eastgate Street in 1311–12, when a *celarium lapideum* (perhaps that at No 6), which had hitherto been in the same ownership as the premises above, was exchanged for another undercroft and thus passed into separate occupancy[22]. This raises interesting possibilities about the later use of these spaces. Once separated from the premises above, they may well have served as shops, like those in the *celaria* under Fleshmongers' Row in the early fifteenth century[23]. Some may have housed taverns; this perhaps was the function of the undercroft in Eastgate Street known in the mid-fourteenth century as 'Helle'[24]. Such changes in use may help to explain the subdivision which is such a characteristic feature of Chester's undercrofts by the fourteenth century.

Undercrofts and shops clearly existed together in the same structures from an early date. From its first appearance in the Chester records the word 'Row' was used to designate small assemblages of shops grouped by trade, and perhaps even owned by a single merchant. Such rows of shops were common in medieval times and were not necessarily elevated above undercrofts. In the main streets of Chester, however, the evidence of the surviving buildings and the sheer numbers of medieval undercrofts strongly suggest that these early groupings of shops were already at an upper level. This would naturally have encouraged the desire for a common walkway at that level to promote access to traders and to reduce the number of inconvenient

Fig 17   Undercroft at 12 Bridge Street showing window in rear wall (RCHME © Crown Copyright)

stairs from the street. At present such steps occur on average at every third plot, a distribution which appears to have been relatively consistent since medieval times. This arrangement may therefore reflect commercial groupings within thirteenth- and fourteenth-century Chester.

The early development of shops can be observed most clearly in the centre of the city around St Peter's church (Fig 18). It is here that commercial activity was most intense and the documentary sources record the first references to Rows. As early as the 1220s at least four shops abutted the church[25]. Although their exact location was not then recorded, they are perhaps to be identified with those four shops which in the 1250s occupied two plots immediately to the north of the church, on the west side of Northgate Street[26], and by 1293 known as Ironmongers' Row[27]. That the area's main trade was indeed hardware is suggested by a case which came before the justice of Chester in that year, involving the sale of a stolen bronze bowl at a shop within the Row[28]. Although the early deeds are unspecific about the nature of the buildings in Ironmongers' Row, it is fairly clear that by the early fourteenth century they were situated over undercrofts and hence formed a Row in the traditional Chester sense. A multi-storeyed house with an undercroft can be located within the Row by the 1340s, and in fact there are references to *celaria* in Northgate Street as early as the 1280s[29].

Equally interesting is the evidence from the east end of Watergate Street (north side). Here, abutting the other side of St Peter's Church, was Flesher's Row, in which the influential Doncaster family had owned property from at least the 1290s[30]. A deed of 1330 reveals that one of the Doncasters' holdings on this site had an undercroft, but the nature of the property becomes clear only in 1345–6. Deeds from those years show that the Doncasters' holding lay next to St Peter's and included two adjacent messuages comprising shops and rooms over undercrofts, clearly a Row-like arrangement[31]. By 1398, the Row, which still contained at least one butcher ('fleshewer'), ran westwards as far as Goss Lane[32].

Opposite St Peter's on the north side of Eastgate Street stood a building or group of buildings known by 1270 as the Buttershops. The first reference to a Row within these buildings occurs in 1369, when a tenement was said to front on to 'le Buttershoprow' and to extend northwards to land belonging to the Abbey of St Werburgh (*Cheshire Sheaf*, 3rd ser, xxxvi, 34). By then this Row was apparently located within substantial buildings more than one storey high; a deed of 1361 mentions a shop in the Buttershops with two *solaria* above and one adjacent[33]. The Buttershop Row was sometimes known as 'Baxter' or Bakers' Row, a name more properly applied to the contiguous stretch immediately to the east. That part of the Row, which derived its name from the proximity of the important bakehouse belonging to the leper hospital of St Giles, was certainly in existence by 1293, when it was said to contain

Fig 18 The earliest documentary references to Rows refer to properties around St Peter's Church (RCHME © Crown Copyright)

four 'vacant houses' (*domus vacuas*)[34]. Although none of these references mentions *celaria*, it seems likely that the Row ran over undercrofts from an early date; certainly it was associated with such structures by 1375.

All these examples (and they could be multiplied) show that by the late thirteenth and early fourteenth centuries at the very latest the central areas of the four main streets were lined with sections of Row of indeterminate length associated with a single trade and perhaps with a single important structure such as a bakehouse or cornmarket. In the instances cited above, the shops were in individual ownership, but there are examples of a number of adjacent premises all in the hands of a single owner. Corvisers' (or Shoemakers') Row, on the west side of Bridge Street, had its origins in a group of at least 11 such, the *shopae* or *seldae sutorum*, all in the hands of Robert le Barn in 1275[35]. These, however, may have been in a different type of structure or organised in a somewhat different way (see following section).

Selds

The structures referred to in the local sources as *seldae* (selds) have long been thought to have made an important contribution to the development of the Rows. In the past it has been suggested that they were

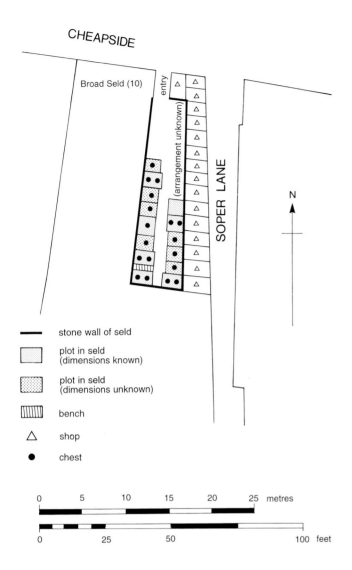

CHEAPSIDE

Broad Seld (10)

entry

(arrangement unknown)

SOPER LANE

N

— stone wall of seld

▢ plot in seld (dimensions known)

▢ plot in seld (dimensions unknown)

▥ bench

△ shop

● chest

0   5   10   15   20   25 metres

0   25   50   100 feet

Fig 19   Plan of a seld in Cheapside, London, as reconstructed by Keene

long strips of property running in front of the undercrofts, the construction of which enabled the Row walkways to be developed above them (Lawson and Smith 1958, 26–7). Modern research on London (Fig 19), Winchester, and elsewhere has shown that this theory is based upon a misconception of the nature of selds (Keene 1985, 137–8, 1091–2, 1098; Keene 1990, 12–13). Although the word has a variety of meanings (see Appendix A), its dominant, and for the purposes of this study most relevant, usage was to describe a substantial structure, which contained a number of stalls (*tabula* – see Appendix A) selling a particular form of merchandise, such as skins or woollen cloth, perhaps under specially privileged regulations. Selds were, in fact, 'private bazaars', in some ways resembling the souks or covered markets of Arab *medinas;* their heyday was the thirteenth and early fourteenth centuries, after which the term became virtually obsolete. In Cheshire, the best documented reference to such a structure comes not from Chester itself but from Middlewich, where two prominent townsmen

undertook to build a 'house' 100ft (30.48m) long and 22ft (6.71m) wide as 'selds' (*pro seldis*) for the use of foreign merchants[36]. That this building, later known as the 'great hall' (*aula*) of Middlewich, did contain stalls is clear from the records of the mid-fourteenth century [37].

In Chester the term 'seld' was undoubtedly applied to substantial structures. In the mid-thirteenth century, for example, the mayor John Arneway was granted half a seld with the dimensions 10 x 52ft (3.05 x 15.85m) (Tait 1920–3, vol 82, 464). Where the term relates to such large spaces the location (when it is given) is always Bridge Street, usually on the western side and near the lane (then known as Norman or Moothall Lane) which gave access to the Common Hall[38]. It looks very much as if the core of the selds lay in the area of Bridge Street in front of the Common Hall itself, though they probably also extended northwards towards the Cross. The northern limit of the area was the corner formed by the junction of Bridge Street and Watergate Street, where there was a structure, known by the late fourteenth century as the 'Stone' or 'Staven Seld', which is probably to be identified with the *selda lapidea* mentioned in deeds of the 1270s[39]. The whole quarter was sufficiently distinctive to be known in the thirteenth and fourteenth centuries simply as 'the selds'. The early fourteenth century 'roll' of the gild merchant, for example, recorded that the gild met *in celdis* until 1251, after which it seems to have moved to new premises, perhaps to the newly-built Commonhall[40].

This quarter of the city undoubtedly contained a Row by the mid-fourteenth century. In 1356 the mayor and *communitas* granted to William de Burgh, citizen of Chester, a small piece of land, 2 x 3 royal ells (1.83 x 2.74m), which was said to lie in Bridge Street 'next to the new steps *(novum gradum)* which lead towards 'le Covyserrowe' at the end of the fishboards, next to the pillory of Chester, in that corner *(cornerio)* towards the church of St Peter'[41]. Here the word 'Row' is used unambiguously to denote an elevated walkway reached by steps and running along the west side of Bridge Street southwards from the corner opposite St Peter's[42].

Although these steps were new in 1356, it seems likely that the Row was much older. In 1275, Robert le Barn leased to Alexander Hurel, a former sheriff and soon to be mayor, *inter alia* a group of 11 shops *(shopae)* for the substantial sum of 40 marks[43]. The lease, originally intended to be for 12 years, was apparently soon terminated, perhaps at the behest of the king, since soon afterwards (by 1278 at the latest), Robert granted the same properties in perpetuity to the king's new foundation of Vale Royal Abbey[44]. This later transaction refers to the 11 shops as selds and reveals that they were known collectively as the *seldae sutorum*, the 'Shoemakers' selds'. Significantly, they were said to lie in Bridge Street between the land of the hospital of St John and that of Ralph of the Pillory, perhaps a reference to the pillory which in the mid-fourteenth century was known to stand next to the steps leading to Corvisers' Row. By 1334, Vale Royal Abbey owned 15 shops and a burgage in Chester, all apparently on a single continuous site, and one of the shops was expressly said to be held by a corviser (Brownbill 1914, 113). The connection with Corvisers' Row is clear and it therefore seems possible that the Row was already in existence in the 1270s when the Shoemakers' selds enter the record.

Where known, their dimensions suggest that the selds were long narrow structures, like the hall at Middlewich. The half seld granted to Arneway, for example, perhaps indicates a building 104ft (31.5m) long[45]. Such a shape would accord quite well with the present undercrofts and tenement plots in Bridge Street to the east of the site of the Commonhall[46]. More difficult to determine are the internal arrangements of these structures, and hence the way they related to the Rows. That they resembled market halls or bazaars is suggested by the fact that there were disputes over rights of way through them (see Appendix A). Interestingly, the eleven shops known as the Shoemakers' selds were all adjacent to a building known as the Abbot of Vale Royal's Hall, which may well have been a seld like the great hall of Middlewich (Brownbill 1914, 113).

At least some of the selds in Chester stood above undercrofts. This is indicated by the fact that the Shoemakers' selds evolved into the elevated Corvisers' Row, and also by deeds of 1314 and 1425 which describe the 'selda lapidea' on the corner of Bridge Street and Watergate Street, as comprising a seld at Row level above two *celaria*[47]. Similar arrangements are also known from Cheapside in London, where in the 1230s there were selds fronted by shops above vaulted undercrofts (Keene 1990, 38). If that was the form taken by the group of selds in Bridge Street, the emergence of an elevated Row walkway to serve them is readily comprehensible.

In Chester, then, there is evidence of substantial structures, termed 'selds', which could be stone-built and which were concentrated on the west side of Bridge Street, in the area nearest the Commonhall. Clearly important and profitable forms of property, they were being increasingly intensively developed in the late thirteenth century. Although the exact nature of the selds cannot be fully determined, they were undoubtedly closely related to one of the earliest recorded Row walkways.

Stallboards and encroachment

The Row 'stallboards', sloping areas along the street side of the Row walkway, are a distinctive element of the Row system. They appear to have developed from the construction of porches *(porcheria)*, in front of the undercrofts to shelter their entrances from rain (see Fig 60). The term *porcheria* is indicative of light timber structures added to the stone-walled undercrofts.

None of the stone structures surviving from the thirteenth and fourteenth centuries originally extended further forward than the front of the Row walkway. Although stallboards supported by a stone-built encroachment do occur in substantial town houses such as 38–42 Watergate Street, they seem to belong to later phases of construction, and in many cases, such as 19 and 37 Watergate Street, 22 Northgate Street, and 28 Eastgate Street, the side walls below the stallboard are predominantly of eighteenth- and nineteenth-century brickwork.

Such extensions involved encroachment on to the highway, and in the commercially active streets of thirteenth- and fourteenth-century Chester this was bound to be contentious. It is therefore not surprising that as early as 1293 indictments were made before the eyre of the justice of Chester regarding the erection of various obstructions in the public highway, including both steps and *porcheria*[48]. A particularly significant instance is that of the *porcheria* erected by Hugh of Brickhill in front of four vacant houses *(domus vacuas)* in Bakers' Row *(Baxterrowe)* in Eastgate Street. Although in 1293 all these structures were condemned by the court as injurious to the highway, and some at least were certainly removed, it is significant that encroachment was taking place in front of Row buildings at this early date.

Encroachment also posed another problem. Who owned the land that had been encroached upon? In Chester, it seems that it was deemed to be still in

Fig 20 Wide stallboards fronting the Row walkway on the west side of Bridge Street (RCHME © Crown Copyright)

public ownership, like the highway from which it was annexed. That is certainly implied by the fact that in 1508 the Staven Selds, at the corner of Bridge Street and Watergate Street, were fronted by narrow strips of land which were in separate ownership from the selds themselves and belonged to the mayor, sheriffs and citizens of Chester[49]. In Bridge Street this strip was 2½ virgates (2.29m) wide and some 18⅝ virgates (17.03m) long, dimensions which correspond with the length of the street frontage of the seld and with the width of the pre-nineteenth-century stallboard on this site. In Watergate Street, where the corresponding dimensions were 2 virgates (1.83m) and 21½ virgates (19.66m), it

may be significant that the medieval frontage lay 2.4m back from the line of the present street (Brown *et al* 1986, 123–4).

The strips which fronted the Staven Selds had probably long been in civic hands. As early as 1356 the mayor and citizens owned a plot of land *(unam placeam terrae)*, two ells (1.83m) wide and three ells (2.74m) long, lying next to the steps leading to Corviser Row[50]. It looks then as if at some point between the 1290s and the mid-fourteenth century the local authorities abandoned their attempts to prohibit the encroachment of Row properties into the street, but that they retained ownership of the land in question. That this develop-

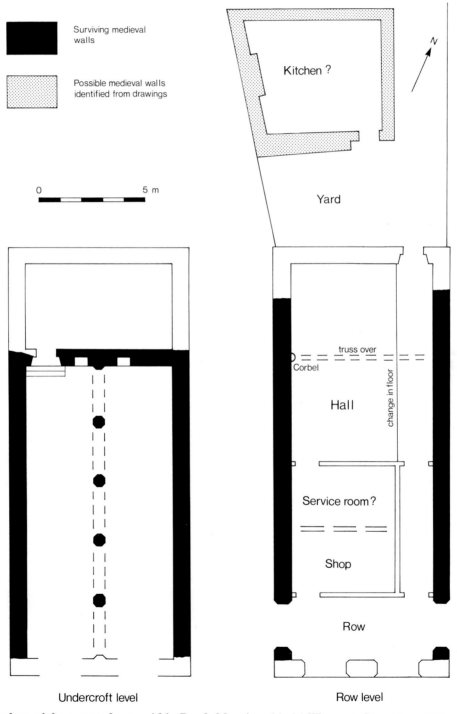

Fig 21 Reconstructed plans of the eastern house within Booth Mansion, 28–34 Watergate Street (see p23)

ment had powerful supporters in the late thirteenth century is indicated by the fact that among those indicted of encroachment in 1293 was Hugh of Brickhill, a leading citizen who was then mayor or was soon to become so. It may be that Edward I's charter of 1300, with its grant of jurisdiction over Crown Pleas to the mayor and bailiffs and the accompanying licence to the citizens to build on the vacant sites *(vacuas placeas)* of the city, removed any final constraint on this process (Morris 1894, 490–3).

Analysis of the term *tabula* in local usage throws further light on the early development of the building frontages. *Tabula* has a variety of meanings (see Appendix A). In Chester, as in London's Cheapside, it could be used to designate trestles within a seld or on the street. Nevertheless in a number of instances Cestrian *tabulae* are expressly said to have been in front of the seld or to have leasable property beneath them[51]. Given that the selds were generally at Row level, the most likely meaning is 'stallboard'. Such an interpretation of *tabula* would suggest that in the area of the selds (ie in Bridge Street) stallboards had already developed by the late thirteenth century, presumably to create as much space as possible for the display of merchandise. Many references connect both the selds and the *tabulae* with cloth or tailors, and in at least two instances the sale of cloth at *tabulae* was also linked with fairs. It is possible that the stallboards represented special trading facilities set up for the duration of the fairs,

when commercial space was at a premium, and these gradually became established as permanent features of the Rows.

The form of the buildings

During the medieval period the main streets of a city such as Chester were probably lined with substantial merchants' houses. The Rows Research Project has identified two main types of early medieval town house coincident with Pantin's typology (1963a). The dominant type, in which a single undercroft supports a structure orientated at right angles to the street, is poorly represented among the surviving thirteenth- and fourteenth-century buildings, probably because many of these buildings had timber superstructures, of which little has survived. Nevertheless, the greater proportion of the houses along the main streets were probably of this form, something of which is still preserved at the Leche House, 17 Watergate Street, although it is mostly later in date (see Chapter 6). The grandest structures occupied wide plots and this allowed the construction of halls parallel to the street above a number of undercrofts. Many of these houses occupied large corner sites, where a side street joined the main thoroughfare, since such locations allowed for easy access to the side and rear and provided greater wall-space for windows and hence better lighting. These houses were of the highest status, and like those mentioned in the documentary

Fig 22 Eastern undercroft at Booth Mansion, 28–34 Watergate Street, showing the stone arcade, wall cupboards, and part of the rear doorway (RCHME © Crown Copyright)

record, may have included richly decorated chambers, chapels, and a variety of service buildings such as stables, barns and dovecote. They almost certainly formed the residences of wealthy citizens, such as Richard the Engineer, Stephen Saracen, and William of Doncaster (see pp 15, 18, 27, and 33).

Right-angled halls

The arrangement of an early medieval Chester town house with its hall at right angles to the street can be reconstructed from the early elements of the eastern house within Booth Mansion, 28–34 Watergate Street (Fig 21 and Pl 12), which date from the late thirteenth century (see Appendix B). The double-aisled undercroft and stone party walls, up to eaves height, reveal this to have been a building of quality, but the basic form appears to have been common along the main streets of Chester. Significantly, it incorporated a Row walkway from the outset.

The double-aisled undercroft (Fig 22) with an internal span of about 6.8m is divided longitudinally by an arcade of four (originally five) two-centred arches with octagonal piers. A blocked doorway in the rear wall of the undercroft may have led to a stairway or, more probably, a separate rear chamber. Such secondary chambers behind undercrofts existed within other Row buildings, as at 39 Bridge Street and 63–65 Watergate Street. The stone party walls are carried over the Row walkway by two-centred chamfered arches (Fig 23), similar in profile to those in the undercroft. These arches demonstrate that the walkway was an integral part of the original layout and also that it was designed to link up with the adjacent buildings. The plan at Row level is similar to later and more intact examples such as the Leche House and 63 Northgate Street (see Chapter 6). A surviving internal doorway (Fig 58) marks the front entrance of the hall and, therefore, the position of the passage leading from the Row walkway. Alongside this enclosed passage, and in front of the hall, was a space 5.9m long x 4.9m wide. This has been considered too large to have been used purely for commercial purposes and it has been suggested that it incorporated a service room at the rear, connected with the hall (Brown *et al* 1986). It should be noted, however, that although the dimensions of shops in medieval Chester are rarely recorded, there is sufficient evidence to suggest that they could on occasion be substantially larger than the usual 2 x 3m lock-ups[52]. In the absence of any evidence that there was a buttery or pantry in front of the hall at Booth Mansion, or indeed elsewhere in Chester, it is perhaps more reasonable to interpret this room as given over solely to trade, forming one or more shops fronting the Row walkway.

The present rear wall of the undercroft coincides with the central truss of the Row-level hall, the position of which is marked by a surviving corbel (Fig 44). In other buildings there is some evidence that the super-

structure did not always coincide with the length of the undercroft[53]. However, it seems reasonable to postulate that normally the rear wall of both levels would have aligned. Thus, the reconstruction (Fig 21 and Pl 12) shows a rear chamber at undercroft level and a Row-level hall approximately 8.5 x 6.8m. The eastern wall survives to eaves level providing clear evidence for the height of the building. Comparisons with the Leche House and 63 Northgate Street suggest that there was originally a rear doorway directly opposite the front entrance into the hall. The route along the eastern wall between these front and rear doorways may have been screened from the hall to form a passage. Three mortices in the north face of the timber door frame which formed the hall entrance are consistent with a timber screen in this position and evidence from the stone paving suggests that this area may have been floored differently from the main body of the hall. Plans made of the building before recent development suggest that the rear doorway from the hall opened into a small yard beyond which lay a detached kitchen. The yards and gardens behind these houses presumably contained other outbuildings, but most of the evidence has been destroyed by later developments and demolition during slum clearance in the 1930s.

This basic layout of Row walkway, shop, and hall, all over an undercroft at right angles to the street, remained largely unchanged for many centuries in most of the Row buildings. Later examples can be seen at the Leche House and at 63 Northgate Street (but see p145).

Fig 23   Two arches over the Row walkway at Booth Mansion, 28–34 Watergate Street (RCHME © Crown Copyright)

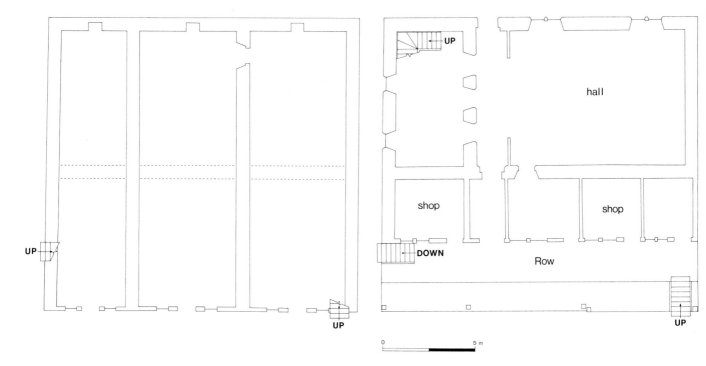

Fig 24 Reconstructed plans of 38–42 Watergate Street, street level (left), Row level (right)

Parallel halls

Despite the loss of its original facade, rear wall, and roof, 38–42 Watergate Street is the best preserved parallel hall town house in the Rows and its form can be easily reconstructed (Fig 24). Only slightly less complete is the town house at 48–52 Bridge Street, which, since it is largely of the same date and type, serves as a useful comparison. The Falcon, 6 Lower Bridge Street, with its reused passing-brace roof and substantial (though reconstructed) ground plan, also probably had a hall parallel to the Row.

At 38–42 Watergate Street, the chimney stack, floor and partition walls inserted in the seventeenth century are the only major alterations to the medieval plan, which remains readily discernible (Fig 24). Situated as it was between Crook Street to the west and an apparently vacant plot to the east[54], the substantial fourteenth-century town house built on this site must have carried an isolated length of Row walkway. The Row-level structure was designed over three undercrofts, which are at right angles to the street. Excluding the east wall of 38 Watergate Street, which survives from an earlier period, the medieval fabric is of one phase, although a short building break is detectable after the completion of the undercrofts. The ashlar stone blocks are of different dimensions in the two sub-phases and the junction can be seen over the arch in the undercroft of 38 Watergate Street. The central and eastern undercrofts form an identical pair, connected by a doorway at the rear; the less intact western under-croft is 1.3m narrower. This arrangement is directly linked with the plan at Row level, where there was a service bay to the west, overlooking Crook Street, and an open hall over the two undercrofts to the east. The

integration of the two levels is further demonstrated by the fact that the stone arches and rear walls at under-croft level correspond exactly with the front and rear walls of the hall above.

In the west wall of the hall there are three doorways, now blocked (Fig 47). They are identical in form and presumably provided access to the service rooms from a cross passage at the lower end of the hall. Further evidence for a cross passage is provided by the partly preserved segmental-headed doorways in the front and rear walls of the hall. The north (rear) doorhead and west jamb are well preserved, although somewhat obscured by modern stucco, and contain a seven-teenth-century door frame with a flat lintel. The remains of the south doorway suggest a form similar to the internally rebated hall entrance at 48–52 Bridge Street (see below), a house of the same type and date. In addition, there is a socket in the front wall, some 2.13m (7ft) from the west wall, which probably received a horizontal timber from the screen, which is no longer there, but formerly separated the cross passage from the hall. Three holes in the masonry of the cross passage probably indicate the location for a lamp or torch bracket. The location of the parallel hall above the rear of the undercrofts allowed space for the Row walkway and a run of small shops overlooking the street. Doorways in the front wall of the hall provided access to these shops, and perhaps to chambers over the shops and Row. One such doorway remains; a low fourteenth-century opening, rebated on the Row side, and hence opening out from (rather than into) the hall. Above it there is a line of corbels clearly intended to carry the joists of a floor at Row + 1 level.

Two late nineteenth-century paintings by Louise Rayner (Plates 2 and 3) show a stone frontage to

42 Watergate Street directly alongside the Row walk-way. The Row-level frontage to Watergate Street is pierced by two round-headed arches and the steps down into the side street and a window alongside have similar surrounds. This may represent, or be the form of, the fourteenth-century frontage.

The medieval building at 48–52 Bridge Street, on the corner with Whitefriars, formed the largest early structure yet discovered in the Rows (Fig 26). Much survives, and a late nineteenth-century record of some of the lost fabric assists with an understanding of the earliest phases. The most obvious feature is the frontage of No 48, known as the 'Three Old Arches', a line of three round-headed stone arches at Row level (Fig 40). Semicircular arches can be taken to be typical of Romanesque buildings and thus predate *c* 1200. However, they are found in later medieval buildings and there is some evidence that the same form was used in the fourteenth-century frontage of 42 Watergate Street (see above). Nevertheless, the 'Three Old Arches' do not align with the masonry behind, nor do they correspond with the two-centred arches used elsewhere in the building (see p39). The undercroft of No 48 is wider than the structure of the frontage and this, together with the fact that the spacing of the 'Three Old Arches' cannot be applied to the frontage widths of Nos 50 and 52 may make it reasonable to assume that an earlier frontage was retained when the substantial early or mid-fourteenth-century parallel-hall town house was created behind.

The east wall at Row level provides most interest, as it contains four doorways (Fig 25). That at the south is the widest and was presumably the entrance doorway, indicating that, as at 38–42 Watergate Street, the cross-passage and service bay access was at the end towards the side street. This doorway has a pointed arch with moulded exterior and rebated interior. On the Row side of the wall there is a vertical groove north of the doorway to receive a wattle and daub partition. An identical groove exists on the other side of the wall to receive the screen. North of the screens passage is a pair of doorways. The southern is smaller and has a two-centred arch on the hall face, with a segmental arch on the off-Row shop face, while the other simply has a segmental head. Their close juxtaposition would suggest that one led to a shop off the Row, while the other gave access to a stair up to the chambers over the Row. At the north end of the east wall of the hall, a fourth doorway survives. This should most logically lead to an off-Row shop, but its position at the upper end is unexpected as it would have conflicted with the usual arrangement of a hall. The sixteenth-century fireplace in the north wall is located centrally to the hall and could incorporate earlier fabric; this, together with the fourth doorway, suggests that there was no dais at the upper end. The west and south walls of the hall do not survive, but the former must have contained substantial fenestration and a doorway to the cross-passage, while the latter would have provided

access to the service rooms and probably also to the chamber over the service bay.

In both 38–42 Watergate Street and 48–52 Bridge Street there is a close relationship between the layout of the undercrofts and the superstructure above. It is particularly noticeable that the halls in both buildings are precisely rectangular in plan, indicating that they were the dominant element in the design. The same phenomenon is even more evident at the Falcon, where the hall was almost rectangular, despite being sited on an irregular corner plot. The main irregularities were absorbed in the Row walkway, shops, and service wing. The surviving late medieval and early post-medieval structure of the Falcon consists of the undercroft and two separate timber-framed constructions above, with a narrow gap between the two internal walls. The stone walls and doorway of the undercroft, together with the stone piers fronting the Row walkway above, are contemporary with the octagonal pier and its associated arcade plate, that support the undercroft ceiling. Dendrochronological tests on this plate have produced an estimated felling date of 1253–84 (see Appendix B). The other undercroft arcade is constructed of reused timbers from a passing-brace, crown-post roof that spanned 6.38m (Figs 27, 59), a dimension that is the same as the width of the present rear structure. The reused timbers have produced an estimated felling date of 1200–30, some 50 years earlier than those in the remainder of the undercroft, an indication that there was a radical rebuilding in the mid-thirteenth century. It looks as if the earlier structure was demolished and its roof timbers reused in the new undercroft, but that the dimensions of the building were retained. That probably means that the general arrangement of two blocks was also repeated. From the evidence of other buildings it seems reasonable to assume that this arrangement consisted of a block fronting Lower Bridge Street containing the commercial element, while the rear block was domestic, presumably incorporating an

Fig 25 Doorways in the front wall of the medieval hall at 48–52 Bridge Street (RCHME © Crown Copyright)

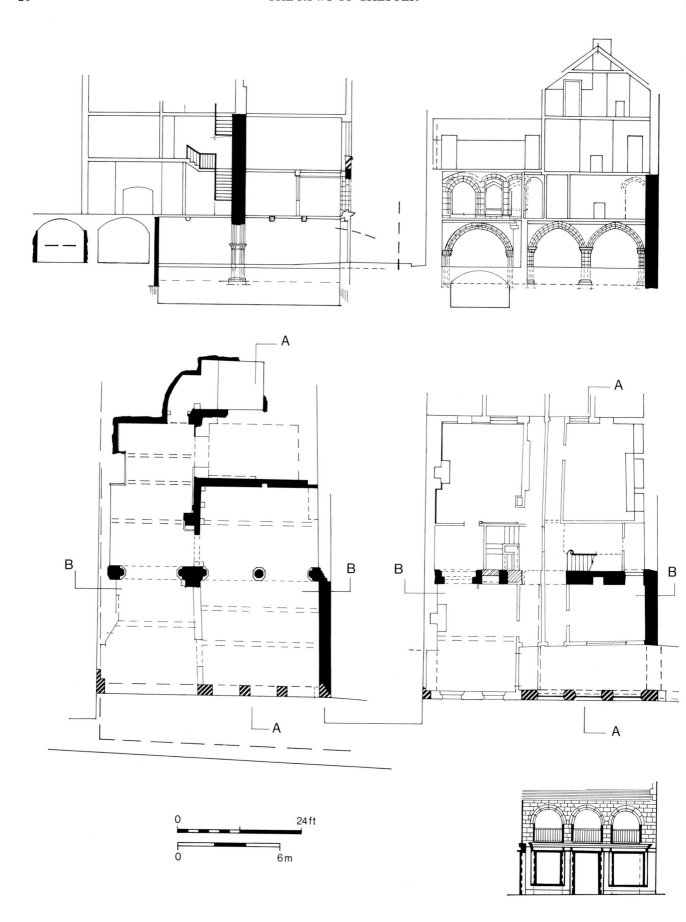

Fig 26 Plans and sections of 48–52 Bridge Street (after Lawson and Smith 1958, with acknowledgement to the Chester Archaeological Society)

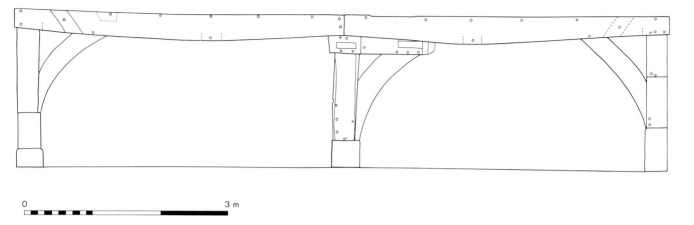

0   3 m

Fig 27   Timber arcade in the undercroft at the Falcon, 6 Lower Bridge Street, showing the reuse of the earlier tie beams (see also Fig 59)

open hall. It is therefore suggested that the reused tie beams originally formed part of the truss over the open hall in the rear structure. The centrally-placed arcade column on the surviving part of the front elevation suggests that this part of the front block had twin gables facing the street. As the medieval building extended further south, incorporating Nos 8–10, it is likely the Falcon originally presented a four-gable frontage to the street. Given that the width of the front block appears to have remained unchanged from the earliest phase of this building, and that the later phase certainly contained a Row walkway, it is possible that the early phase of the Falcon also incorporated a gallery from the early thirteenth century. Alternatively, the motive for the rebuilding after only two generations might have been in order to incorporate such a walkway.

There is one recorded building on the main streets of Chester that bears a superficial resemblance to medieval courtyard houses such as Scaplen's Court, Poole, or Marshall's Inn, Oxford (Pantin 1963a, 213, 223), although it is in fact more closely related to the parallel halls discussed above. The property, which lay on the site of 14–16 Northgate Street at the southern corner of Leen Lane, was recorded before partial demolition in the 1890s and 1950s (Lawson and Smith 1958, 14–15) and evidence was found of a pair of interconnecting undercrofts at right angles to the street. The length of these undercrofts would have allowed a superstructure consisting of a parallel hall, fronted by shops and a Row walkway (Fig 28). Behind a courtyard entered from Leen Lane, there was a second building over a single undercroft, parallel to the street. Briefly recorded before its demolition in the 1890s, it was largely timber-framed and was linked to the front structure by a two-storey wing, which partially survived along the south side of the courtyard. An unusual feature of the rear building was that it consisted of two large spaces one above the other. This two-tier arrangement may have been carried across the courtyard by the connecting wing and reproduced in the front building. It is unclear whether this property was

in normal domestic use or whether it served some other function, such as lodgings or apartments. The additional accommodation may indicate that this property acted as a hostel or that it housed a dignitary or court official. It is the only recorded example of a structure with principal spaces behind a courtyard, instead of the more usual arrangement of kitchen, stables, and outbuildings loosely grouped behind a hall. The stone *solarium* recorded in the early fourteenth century on the other side of Northgate Street may have been part of a similar arrangement, as it evidently lay behind the buildings on the street frontage[55].

None of these parallel hall houses can be linked to the written record with any certainty. It is however likely that the house at 48–52 Bridge Street was Roger Derby's 'Stone Place', which in the early fifteenth century lay in Bridge Street near St Bridget's and Whitefriars Lane (Lawson and Smith 1958, 30). A similar building which can be documented, although no trace of it now remains, is the residence (*placea*) known as the 'Shelter Yard' (*Erbereyert*). Inhabited in 1289–90 by Stephen Saracen, a prominent citizen of Chester, it almost certainly lay on the corner of Watergate Street and Goss Lane[56]. The wide frontage (55ft = 16.8m) seems to have run eastward from Goss Lane, terminating at a point, later (if not then) marked by steps and an entry, so it probably occupied the site of 16–20 Watergate Street. Like 38–42 Watergate Street, which it may have resembled in other ways, the house encompassed three undercrofts.

The effect of the Row

The combination of commercial and domestic elements found in the early Row buildings was normal for medieval urban buildings, as was the arrangement of an undercroft, with shop and house above (see p57 and Fig 60). The incorporation of the Row is, however, unusual and provided the opportunity for very large chambers at Row + 1 level, extending over the Row-level shop and walkway, and later the stallboard. Such

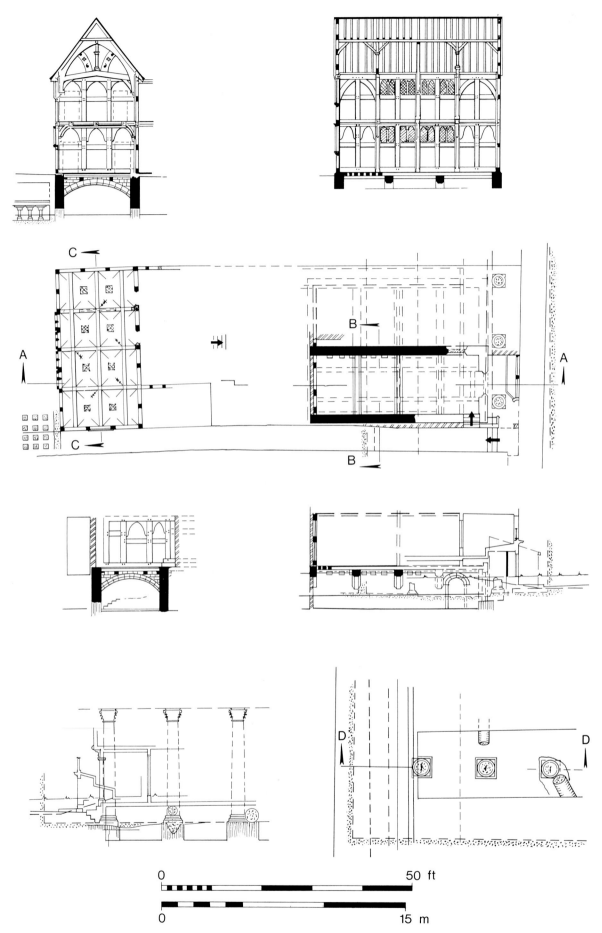

Fig 28   Reconstruction of 16 Northgate Street (after Lawson and Smith 1958, with acknowledgement to the Chester Archaeological Society)

oversailing appears to have been an integral part of the design of the thirteenth- and fourteenth-century frontages, but little medieval timber-framing survives at this level and it is therefore difficult to assess the arrangements that were produced. Most probably the extra space was used to create an extended solar, considerably larger than the comparable space in other medieval town houses. At 63 Northgate Street, a later building outside the Rows, the first-floor encroachment was utilised in this way to construct an impressive two-bay solar (3.9 x 3.7m) over the walkway and stallboard, leaving a separate, rather ill-lit chamber over the shop (Fig 73). The written record, however, indicates that these spaces did not necessarily form part of the main house; it seems that they were often associated with the lock-up shops below, providing either storage or accommodation for the tenant.

The other way in which the commercial frontage affected the domestic quarters was in the provision of access between the two. Access from the Row walkway to the house was by means of a passage alongside or between the shops. What is more unusual is the additional doorways in the front walls of the parallel halls, not all of which necessarily gave on to shops. At 38–42 Watergate Street, for example, a doorway next to the entrance to the cross passage could have provided access to a staircase leading to the spaces above Row level. At 48–52 Bridge Street, however, the proliferation of doorways is firm evidence of intercommunication between the small Row-level shops and the hall beyond.

The existence of the Row walkway also raises the question of access from the street. The present arrangement provides steps at approximately every third undercroft and at the ends of each section, where the Row was interrupted by a side street. The location of these steps may have remained almost unaltered since the creation of the Rows. Surprisingly, there is no evidence for steps opposite the main entrances to the larger houses. It is clear that access to the parallel hall houses was by way of steps from the side street into the Row. At the Falcon, for example, the present doorway on the Lower Bridge Street elevation is a much later insertion into the previously uninterrupted facade of *c* 1260. At 48–52 Bridge Street the only steps were those at the south end providing access from Whitefriars; at the north end the gallery simply connected with the Row in the adjacent house. A similar arrangement obtained at many of the smaller right-angled hall houses. At Booth Mansion, for example, the Row walkway was clearly designed to connect with the adjacent houses and there is no indication of any steps up from the street.

The present steps between the Row walkways and the streets are accommodated within the plan area of the stallboards, except at the ends of each section. Originally, however, they would have projected into the street. Clearly, flights of steps, 2–3m high, to each property would have been a major inconvenience, obstructing the street and difficult to incorporate into

the frontages of the undercrofts without restricting possible door and window positions. It is possible that intermediate steps, between the ends of the Row sections, were not originally provided. The present distribution of steps may have evolved only to serve a recognised need, alongside the general process of encroachment that resulted in the stallboards.

Conclusions

From the surviving documentary and structural evidence it seems relatively certain that by the mid-fourteenth century the following frontages along the four main streets incorporated Row walkways, albeit not yet necessarily continuous and interlinked (Fig 29).

Bridge Street – East

Medieval undercrofts at Nos 15 and 35–39 suggest Rows extending south to Pepper Street (Lawson and Smith 1958, 10–12). Mercers' Row was located in this area by the late fifteenth century.

Bridge Street – West

Corvisers' or Shoemakers' Row ran south from the High Cross through the selds by the mid-fourteenth century at the latest, and probably by the 1270s. Structural evidence in the form of undercrofts at Nos 12, 32, 36, and 48–52 suggest a Row along the full length of the street (Lawson and Smith 1958, 2–6).

Lower Bridge Street – East

Medieval masonry has been noted at Nos 27 and 29–31. The Row may have run southwards to Duke Street, incorporating Richard the Engineer's house, although some sections were probably of a different form, with no oversailing buildings. The terrace which still survives in front of the church of St Olave may be part of this Row system.

Lower Bridge Street – West

The Falcon (No 6) contains a substantial medieval undercroft and early evidence of a Row walkway. Nineteenth-century etchings show that Nos 2–4 (Lamb Row) also incorporated a Row. Further south there may have been a raised open walkway, such as that which still exists at Gamul House (Nos 52–68), perhaps extending as far as Shipgate Street.

Eastgate Street – North

The stretches of Row in this area were known variously as Dark Row, Buttershop Row, Bakers' Row, and Cooks' Row. There is clear evidence that Buttershop Row ran into Bakers' Row by the early fourteenth century, and that a Row extended as far east as

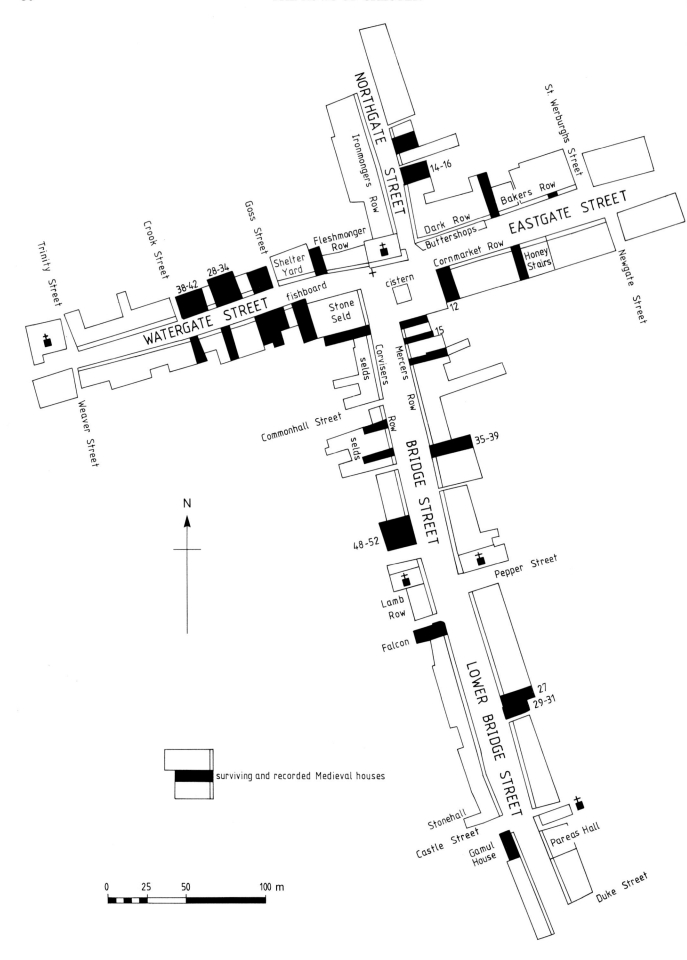

Fig 29 Plan of high medieval Chester city centre showing the likely extent of the Rows (mapping data © Crown Copyright)

St Werburgh's Street by the fifteenth century (Montgomery 1918, 131). Hardly any medieval structures survive, although a stone arch spanning the walkway was recorded at 31 Eastgate Street (just west of St Werburgh's Street) about 1840 (Lawson and Smith 1958, 15) and the eastern party wall of the undercroft below the Boot, 17 Eastgate Street, appears to be of medieval date.

Eastgate Street – South

A Row, known as Cornmarket Row, is first mentioned in 1342 (Dodgson 1981, 22), and presumably ran through the complex of cornmarket, shops, kilns and houses, known to have existed in this area from the 1270s[57]. Evidence of the medieval Row survives in the form of the fine stone undercroft at 28 Eastgate Street and of the two-centred chamfered arches shown in a nineteenth-century print spanning the walkway at No 32. Another stone-vaulted undercroft was recorded at 12 Eastgate Street in 1855, but has since been demolished (Lawson and Smith 1958, 12). The Honey Stairs, a substantial house with a stone arcaded front, also stood on this side of the street (see p40). Rows probably extended to Newgate Street; beyond that the walkway was presumably at street level, as at present, although a deed of 1383 proves that buildings with shops and undercrofts extended as far as the walls[58].

Northgate Street – East

Medieval undercrofts, surviving at No 22 and recorded at Nos 8 and 14–16, indicate that the Row probably extended northwards to the market square from an early period (Lawson and Smith 1958, 15).

Northgate Street – West

Ironmongers' Row probably ran northwards to the market square from the late thirteenth century, if not before.

Watergate Street – North

Fleshers' or Fleshmongers' Row ran westwards to Goss Lane; beyond that the sequence of undercrofts and walkways at Booth Mansion and Nos 38–42 show that it continued at least to Crook Street, if not to Trinity Lane. Medieval arches spanning the walkway at Booth Mansion provide the earliest structural evidence of a gallery connecting adjacent holdings.

Watergate Street – South

The survival of a large number of medieval undercrofts, including three substantial stone structures, suggests that the Rows extended at least to Weaver Street (Lawson and Smith 1958, 19–23).

It is therefore clear that a recognisable Row system had emerged by *c* 1350 in the four main streets of the city. The crowded frontages had undercrofts at street level, while the shops and domestic areas above were linked by a common walkway which, in some sections at least, ran through several properties. It is also clear, however, that some sections of the Rows existed well before this date. In fact there is little reason to doubt that by the time the term 'Row' is encountered in the written records (*c* 1293), the Rows were already beginning to be well-established in the central area. It is therefore possible that the system evolved over a period of approximately 100 years.

It is of course difficult to establish what the Rows looked like in this early period. Generally, it seems likely that the walkway itself would have been open at the front. In the earliest phases, it probably looked out directly on to the street, an arrangement that still exists at the 'Three Old Arches' (Figs 30, 40) and can be seen enclosed within The Falcon, 6 Lower Bridge Street, but by the late thirteenth century it was often separated from the street by a stallboard or *tabula* (see Appendix A). The streets in front of the buildings were in civic ownership and therefore any encroachment for the erection of these stallboards or for the use of the area below them required the payment of a rent or fine. By the early fourteenth century, however, in major buildings such as 38–42 Watergate Street, the stallboards may well have been envisaged as an integral part of the structure. In only one instance – the Dark Row – does the walkway seem to have been screened from the street by solid building, in the configuration still preserved on the corner of Eastgate Street[59].

Fig 30 Row walkway without stallboard at the 'Three Old Arches' 48–52 Bridge Street (RCHME © Crown Copyright)

This was probably the result of the location of the Buttershops as an independent structure in front of the main building line. That this was unusual and made the Row notably ill-lit is indicated by the name.

It would appear that it was normal for there to be an upper chamber above the Row walkway. In this regard, certain stretches of Lower Bridge Street, where there was no oversailing structure, an arrangement that can be seen in old prints and still survives at Gamul House, were probably unusual (Fig 164). The evidence from the 'Three Old Arches' and a number of other buildings suggests that chambers over the Row were original features.

The walkways seem, as later, to have belonged in some sense to the owners of the properties in which they were embedded. Richard the Clerk's possession of a right of way through a seld, in which he and three other merchant families had an interest, provides an obvious analogy (see Appendix A). The Rows were, however, obviously intended to be used by the general public, and by the early seventeenth century there is documentary evidence to show that the civic authorities were exercising powers over the walkways (Kennett 1984, 51). It is possible that some form of control over what were to become accepted as public rights of way was being exercised at a much earlier date.

3 Early medieval stonework

The most immediately obvious, and therefore the most discussed, medieval structures in the Chester Rows are the series of stone-vaulted undercrofts (Lawson and Smith 1958; Wood 1965, 81). However, they form only a small part of the surviving stonework; the majority of this is at undercroft level, although in a few properties the sandstone walls of the medieval Row-level halls and shops have been preserved.

The specific use of stone is documented in town houses in Chester as early as the late twelfth century, at Peter the Clerk's residence in Castle Street (see p15), and, in the mid-thirteenth century, at Ranulph of Oxford's house in Whitefriars[1]. With both these men holding high office locally[2], it is not surprising that their houses should be of stone rather than of timber. Pareas Hall, the house of Richard the Engineer, a royal castle-builder, was also built of stone (see p15) and the stone *solarium* at 1 Northgate Street (modern street number) belonged to the sheriff, Richard de Wheatley, in 1310 (Taylor 1897, 55–6). Given the ready supply of stone in Chester, it is to be expected that many of the more wealthy or powerful residents of the city would wish to live in imposing stone-built town houses. However, houses with all their external walls of stone would probably have been in the minority; the evidence suggests that the majority of the early medieval town houses on the principal streets would have been of mixed construction, partly stone and partly timber-framed.

Stone does appear to have been extensively used, however, for the construction of the outer walls of the undercrofts, albeit in varying degrees of sophistication. This is hardly surprising as the semi-subterranean nature of these spaces meant that they had to resist a great mass of earth at the rear, and the stonework provided some isolation between the ground dampness and any timber framing above. The use of stone at this level may also have related to the need to keep the undercrofts secure against theft and fire. It is not possible to state that all the early medieval undercrofts were stone-walled, as it is unlikely that any timber structures at this level would have survived. However it is noteworthy that in Watergate Street all the properties that still contain any historic fabric have stone party walls at street level, with the exception of the wall between Nos 22 and 24 (see p47). It is possible that this represents the physical evidence of some form of bye-law controlling the construction of party walls[3].

Very little of the stonework found in the Row buildings has any details that make it possible to ascribe a close date to the buildings. Fortunately many of the structures incorporate timber elements, which are described in Chapter 4, and dendrochronological analysis has consistently supported a predominantly thirteenth- and fourteenth-century dating for these buildings (see Appendix B).

Walls

The sandstone masonry within the medieval Row buildings has a general uniformity. It usually consists of large, well-coursed blocks of the local red sandstone and any variations appear to be the result of insertions or later alterations to the original fabric. This form of masonry was in common usage from the thirteenth to the sixteenth centuries. Stonework in Chester from earlier periods is identifiably different. Stone sizes in Roman walling tend to be very erratic, as exemplified in the exposed amphitheatre walls, and the small squarer blocks used by the Romanesque masons at the Abbey of St Werburgh (now the Cathedral) are equally distinct.

It is the stonework above Row level that has suffered most losses from rebuilding and development. Nevertheless, walls from two of the grander open halls are preserved to their full height. At 38–42 Watergate Street the west and south walls largely remain, and at 48–52 Bridge Street the east and north walls survive. Both are parallel-hall structures, over several undercrofts, and the intact walls provide vital information for the dimensions, location, and dating of the open halls. Unfortunately, in neither of these structures has the rear wall survived. Survival of the walls of other stone-built halls is fragmentary, although the eastern part of Booth Mansion, 28–34 Watergate Street, preserves its eastern party wall largely intact up to an eaves cornice, which shows that this building stood higher than its neighbour. Largely devoid of architectural detail, it appears to be part of the thirteenth-century building.

There is evidence that the internal faces of some of the stone walls were decorated. On the front wall of the undercroft at 11 Watergate Street there are the fragmentary remains of arcading. Also, during the demolition of 12 Eastgate Street in 1861 it was recorded that a number of round marble shafts resembling Purbeck were found, possibly suggesting that the walls of the undercroft had been decorated with an applied arcade (Lawson and Smith 1958, 12).

Vaults

The majority of the undercrofts in the Row buildings are spanned either by some form of timber structure or by brick vaults, which were probably inserted in the seventeenth century or later. Five undercrofts do have stone vaulting (12 Bridge Street, 28 Eastgate Street, and 11, 21, and 37 Watergate Street), although in some cases the vault was clearly not intended to be the ceiling of the whole of the undercroft, and there are vaults over two small spaces at the rear of a sixth undercroft. Two more vaulted undercrofts were recorded before demolition (Lawson and Smith 1958, 12, 23)

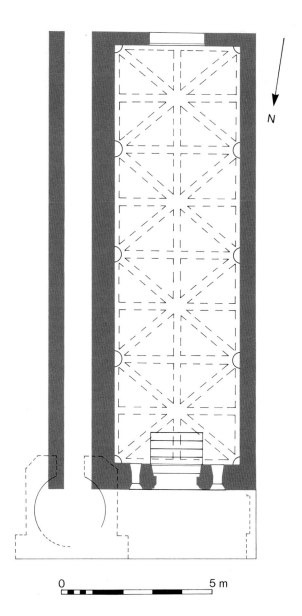

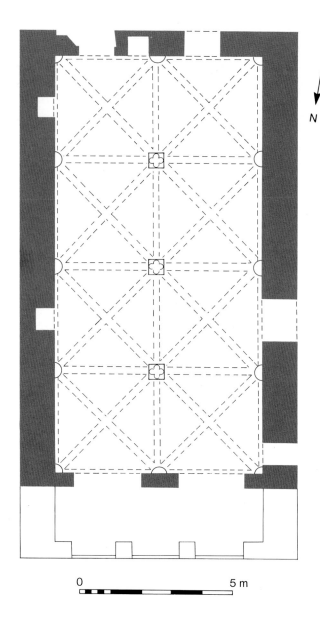

Fig 31 Plan of undercroft at 28 Eastgate Street

Fig 32 Plan of undercroft at 11 Watergate Street

and there is evidence for one other. Although these nine examples are only a small proportion of the total number of medieval undercrofts in Chester, they provide evidence for the construction of some very high quality town houses fronting the main streets of the city. No doubt the fireproof qualities of a vaulted undercroft were realised by the builders, but the motivation for their construction was more probably an indication of wealth or a reflection of the quality of the merchandise stocked.

Three different types of stone vault are found in the Row buildings; quadripartite rib vaults, segmental barrel vaults, and one example of a ribbed segmental vault. Six of the known stone vaults are of a quadripartite form with chamfered ribs. In four of these examples, the vaulting springs from the side walls of the under-croft, and the bays are rectangular (Fig 31). In the other two undercrofts there are central lines of piers dividing the space into two aisles, and here the bays are

almost square (Figs 32 and 34). The detailing of these vaults provides some dating evidence, although quadri-partite rib vaulting is not in itself a chronologically or regionally confined construction technique.

Of more use in dating are the various mouldings used on the associated responds and pier capitals. At 37 Watergate Street, the crudest of the surviving rib vaults, there is little such detail, with the central octagonal pier of the two-aisled structure having no imposts. This is itself indicative of a thirteenth-century date, confirmed by the moulded corbels in the side walls. Also the irreg-ularity of the vaulted bays suggests that they were inserted into a pre-existing late twelfth- or early thirteenth-century undercroft (Fig 33). A similar two-aisled vault, probably three or four bays in length, at the rear of a plain walled undercroft was demolished in 1861, at 12 Eastgate Street[4]. As at 37 Watergate Street, the chamfered ribs sprang from octagonal columns without imposts, and so a similar dating is suggested.

Fig 33 Undercroft at 37 Watergate Street (RCHME © Crown Copyright)

The two-aisled vault of 11 Watergate Street has a central row of three octagonal piers with typical fifteenth-century mouldings (Fig 34), but the semicircular shafted responds are evidently earlier, the undercut abacus and heavily projecting bell indicating a date *c* 1250–90 (Fig 35). This suggests that the vault was rebuilt during the fifteenth century, of necessity utilising the rib profiles of the mid-thirteenth-century springers (J M Maddison, pers comm). In the somewhat simpler vaulted undercroft of 21 Watergate Street, the ribs spring from corbels, which, despite being somewhat mutilated, appear to date from the mid- to late thirteenth century.

An analysis of the five-sided rib profiles of these vaults establishes a consistency of dimensions at 11, 21, and 37 Watergate Street (Fig 36). This implies a relationship between these vaults and, together with the evidence from the mouldings discussed above, suggests that they were originally constructed during the second half of the thirteenth century. The quadripartite vault ribs at 12 Bridge Street are more steeply chamfered than those elsewhere in Chester and the trefoil heads to the associated doorway and windows are indicative of a late thirteenth-century date (see p42). At 28 Eastgate Street, the four-bay vaulted undercroft

is the most precisely executed in the Rows, with a ridge rib and carefully cut stones in the vault web (Fig 15). The mouldings of the doorway into this undercroft suggest an early fourteenth-century date (see pp41–2). The undercroft at 28 Eastgate Street is 12.95m (42ft 6in) long internally. This dimension may be of significance, as the vaulted section of the undercroft at 12 Bridge Street is also 12.95m long and appears to be an extension behind a presumably earlier and unvaulted undercroft, of identical length. Interestingly, the Marlipins, Shoreham, Sussex (Packham 1924) is the same length (see p47 and Fig 53).

Within the western undercroft of Booth Mansion there is a pair of parallel two-centred barrel vaults, each spanning *c* 3.3m. These lie behind the thirteenth-century undercroft, approximately 16m from the street frontage. The end walls to the north are original, but the southern ends have been truncated. Such vaults are common throughout Britain and Europe in medieval and later buildings. There is a short section of barrel vault at the rear of the undercroft below the Boot, 17 Eastgate Street. At 27 Northgate Street an angled string course, similar to the springing technique found in the shallow barrel vaults of Southampton, survives

Fig 34 Undercroft at 11 Watergate Street showing doorway and wall cupboard in rear wall (RCHME © Crown Copyright)

Fig 35 Respond of vaulting in undercroft at 11 Watergate Street (RCHME © Crown Copyright)

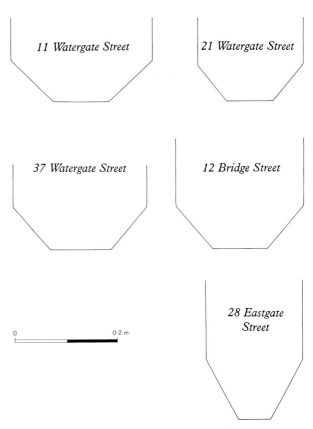

Fig 36 Rib profiles of quadripartite rib vaulting in Chester

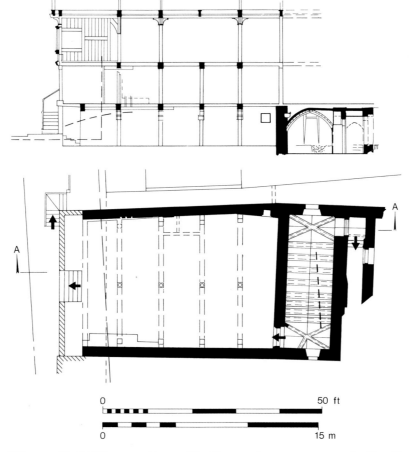

Fig 37 Former building at 63–65 Watergate Street. The Row and street are on north side of building, left. (After Lawson and Smith 1958, with acknowledgement to the Chester Archaeological Society)

along part of the south wall. A shallow barrel vault may
have been adopted over this wide undercroft, because
the Row walkway in this part of Northgate Street
is extremely low and it would have been difficult to
introduce a higher vault. This plot appears, from post-
medieval map evidence (eg 1:500 OS map, 1875), to
have been a northwards encroachment into the market
place; a late medieval date is therefore proposed. The
use of a shallow vault is obviously an advantage when
the available height is restricted, either by the existence
of a building above, as in Southampton, or by the
general level of the Row walkway, as in Chester. In this
regard it is noticeable that the seventeenth-century and
later brick vaults inserted into so many of the medieval
undercrofts of Chester are all of a segmental profile.

At the rear of 63–65 Watergate Street, a demolished
medieval undercroft is recorded (Lawson and Smith
1958, 22–3) as having contained a ribbed vault of
segmental pointed profile, with single bays of quadripartite vaulting at each end (Fig 37). This was located
in a chamber, 3.28 x 9.1m, parallel to the street and
directly behind an undercroft with a timber arcade.
The eight chamfered ribs were irregularly spaced, the
four to the west being more closely spaced than those
to the east. The rib profiles and the associated doorways were similar to the early to mid-fourteenth-century
fabric elsewhere in the Rows. The presence of corbel
sockets and the traces of plaster above the springers
provide evidence that this vault was inserted into a
chamber which had previously had a timber floor above.

Quadripartite rib vaults are predominant amongst
the few vaulted undercrofts in Chester and there is little
evidence for the widespread construction of barrel
vaults in the thirteenth and fourteenth centuries. It
is therefore likely that the Row walkway level and
the near street level floors of the undercrofts were
established prior to the period of vault construction.
This would have restricted the vertical space that was
available, making the use of rib vaults necessary to
span the wide undercrofts.

Arches

Three types of stone arches are found within the Row
buildings; a single shallow arch spanning the width of
an undercroft, a single arch spanning the Row walkway, and arcades.

At 15 and 36 Bridge Street, and formerly in the
recorded town house at 16 Northgate Street (Lawson
and Smith 1958, 14–15), a number of chamfered
arches span the width of the undercrofts (Figs 38, 39).
These are associated with the support of a timber
superstructure, and at 36 Bridge Street (Fig 161)
dendrochronological analysis of the *in-situ* medieval
joists indicates a mid-fourteenth-century date (see
Appendix B). This type of stone arch was more applicable
to those undercrofts below stone-walled halls parallel
to the street. At 38–42 Watergate Street, chamfered
arches support the front wall of the hall (Fig 54), and

Fig 38 Arch across undercroft at 36 Bridge Street

*Fig 39   Arches across undercroft at 15 Bridge Street
(RCHME © Crown Copyright)*

dendrochronological analysis of the associated joists
corroborates an early to mid-fourteenth-century date
(see Appendix B). Likewise, a segmental two-ordered
arch, springing from responds with imposts, survives at
50 Bridge Street. This supported the front wall of the
parallel hall, which also spanned the undercroft to
the north (48 Bridge Street – see below). This wall is
largely intact, with various moulded doorways which
indicate an early to mid-fourteenth-century date
(see pp41–3). The best dated parallels for chamfered
arches of this type are those inserted into the Great
Hall of Conwy Castle in 1346 to carry the new roof
(Brown *et al* 1963, 337–53). This confirms that the
technique was favoured in the mid-fourteenth century
and therefore postdates the quadripartite rib vaults.

Only two examples now exist of stone arches spanning the Row walkway, but there is print evidence for
others. Two-centred chamfered arches carry the stone
party walls of the eastern part of Booth Mansion,
28-34 Watergate Street, over the Row (Fig 23). There
is no reason to doubt that these were an integral part
of the house that has been dated dendrochronologically
to *c* 1267–80 (see Appendix B). Early nineteenth-century
prints record an identical pair of chamfered arches over
the Row at 32 Eastgate Street.

Two examples of the use of stone arcades exist in
Row buildings and a third is known from a published
drawing; however, all three examples occur in differing
situations. The most notable example is the arcade
which fronts the Row at 48 Bridge Street, giving the
building its name, the 'Three Old Arches' (Fig 40).
This comprises three round-headed arches at Row level
with simple chamfers. Whilst such arches are most
commonly associated with Romanesque buildings,
these and the other two known examples of the form in
the Rows – in the undercroft of 37 Watergate Street
and the lost frontage at 42 Watergate Street – do not

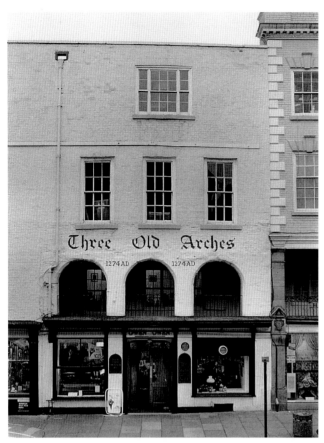

Fig 40 Facade of the 'Three Old Arches', 48 Bridge Street (RCHME © Crown Copyright)

Fig 41   Former building at St Michael's Passage, Southampton (after Minns 1913)

have typical Romanesque decoration. Round-headed arches occur in the Edwardian castles of North Wales, for example in the gatehouse at Harlech, the Queen's Gate, Caernarfon, and in the entrance from the west barbican to the outer ward at Conwy. Taylor (1989, 3) has shown that this type of arch was one of the features of contemporary architecture in Savoy, brought to Wales by Master James of St George and his associates. A large round-headed arch spans the passageway from the kitchen to the great hall at the Bishop's Palace, St Davids, dating to the 1340s (Evans, 1991, 32). Above the Row the structure must have been timber-framed as the thinned spandrels of the arches make the support of further stonework impossible. The stone piers continue down to street level, but the insertion of large shop windows during the nineteenth century, probably replacing similarly sized post-medieval fenestration, means that the nature of the inter-pier spaces is not certain. It seems likely that there would have been a central doorway flanked by windows, similar to the arrangement that survives at 28 Eastgate Street. A similar frontage existed at St Michael's Passage, Southampton (Faulkner 1966, 130–1; Minns 1913, 1–2), and whilst the internal arrangement of this building is unclear, the lower two levels of the facade were of stone and appear to have carried a timber-framed structure. A low central arch provided an entrance to the space below street level, this being flanked by tall arches of a similar size to those at Chester (Fig 41). All three arches in

the Southampton building were round-headed and chamfered.

Also in 48 Bridge Street, a two-bay arcade with two-centred arches parallel to the street was recorded (Baker 1895). These arches had two chamfered orders and were supported by semi-octagonal responds and a central octagonal pier. The arcade was in line with the single stone arch over the undercroft at 50 Bridge Street, the whole arrangement being designed to carry the stone wall of the hall above (see above). The use of both a single arch and an arcade to support this wall above adjacent undercrofts in the one structure was presumably because of the different spans involved. A stone arcade at right angles to the street survives in the eastern undercroft of Booth Mansion. This arcade originally had five bays, with chamfered two-centred arches springing from octagonal columns, and resulted in a ground plan similar to that achieved in the two-aisled stone-vaulted structures, although costing substantially less. Booth Mansion has been dated to the late thirteenth century (see Appendix B).

In the undercroft of the Falcon, 6 Lower Bridge Street, two octagonal stone piers of differing girth carry a timber bridging beam. This structure is aligned at right angles to the street and therefore serves the same function as the stone arcade in Booth Mansion and the comparable thirteenth-century timber arcades (see Chapter 4). At Row level in the same building there are two square-plan stone piers which originally

Fig 42 Corbel table and part of the rear doorway in eastern undercroft at Booth Mansion, 28–34 Watergate Street (RCHME © Crown Copyright)

formed part of the Row frontage. Both arches and piers are reported from a lost building on the south side of Eastgate Street known as the 'Honey Stairs', '...the great stone building which in the front to the streetward is supported with five arches and strong pillars on the steps, at honey time, the country people bring their honey in ye combes in vessels of wood to be sold....'[5]

The sockets in the soffits of the arcade arches at Booth Mansion imply that the undercrofts were sub-divided along the line of these structural supports. Such arcades must however have restricted the use of the space and it seems that efforts were made to devise alternative techniques for supporting the floors above broad undercrofts. Early in the fourteenth century this led to the use of stone arches parallel to the street, simultaneously with an identical process in the development of the equivalent timber structures (see Chapter 4).

Corbels

Stone corbels were regularly used to support the timber floors above the undercrofts in Chester and the most common form is a plain stone with a near quarter-circle profile. These either directly support the common joists or carry a timber corbel plate which, in turn, supports common joists (see Chapter 4). The most impressive instances of closely set corbels, supporting a corbel plate, have been dated by dendrochronology of the associated timbers to the late thirteenth century (see Appendix B; at the Falcon and the eastern undercroft of Booth Mansion, the latter having the original corbel plate and joists in situ). In the Falcon the corbels are 280mm wide and are set at *c* 450mm centres, while at Booth Mansion they are 300mm wide at *c* 600mm centres (Fig 42). The technique continued into the fourteenth century, being used above the stone arches in 38–42 Watergate Street. In this building it also occurs above Row level, where a line of irregularly spaced corbels carried the floor over the shops and Row walkway.

At 39 Bridge Street, a more elaborate arrangement of corbels survives, with successively projecting stones forming a four-part corbel (Fig 43). Elsewhere in the Rows such a sequence of projecting corbels appears to be associated with a function other than ceiling support. At 51 Watergate Street, for example, an extensive area of burning between two double corbels could imply an early smoke hood. A comparable arrangement at 9 Watergate Street may also have been an early attempt at heating the undercroft. The fully developed hooded fireplace in The Undercroft, Simnel Street, Southampton (Faulkner 1966, 131) demonstrates that this did occur in mercantile undercrofts.

Some evidence for sculpted corbels survives. The description of the demolished undercroft at 63–65 Watergate Street (Lawson and Smith 1958, 22–3)

Fig 43 Corbels in undercroft at 39 Bridge Street (RCHME © Crown Copyright)

Fig 44 Sculptured corbel at Row level in the eastern part of Booth Mansion, 28–34 Watergate Street (RCHME © Crown Copyright)

records that the six remaining corbels which supported the ends of the bridging beams were carved with heads. Several of these are preserved at the Grosvenor Museum, Chester. In a different context, a single carved corbel in the form of a squatting human figure remains at Row level in the west wall of the eastern part of Booth Mansion (Fig 44). This corbel probably coincides with the central truss of the former open hall and therefore may have supported the foot of a post or brace (see Chapter 2).

Doorways and windows

With the loss of virtually all the early medieval street frontages in the Rows, and also of many of the rear undercroft walls, few doorways and fewer windows survive. However, it is possible to demonstrate that a wide range of stone doorways was used and the same may also be true of the windows. In many of the buildings the evidence suggests that only simple stone mouldings were used. At 22 Northgate Street the doorway in the centre of the front wall of the undercroft is preserved up to a height of 1.4m and is completely devoid of architectural detail, without even a rebate.

Other undercrofts offer evidence of an elaborate treatment of doors and windows. At the Falcon the front wall of the undercroft is relatively intact and contains a two-centred arched doorway, 1.48m wide (Fig 45), flanked by the remains of two windows. These windows had sills below ground level and would have required light wells. The shouldered arch at Row level in the southern party wall is a later insertion; the flat arch head is in two pieces and the doorway does not tie in with the thirteenth-century phase of the stonework. Similarly the Row-level arch on the Lower Bridge Street elevation appears to be of late medieval date.

Despite a severe, though accurate, nineteenth-century restoration, the front wall of the undercroft at 28 Eastgate Street preserves an identical arrangement to that at the Falcon, but displaying the use of more refined mouldings (Fig 16). The sunk chamfers on the

Fig 45 Doorway in front wall of undercroft at the Falcon, 6 Lower Bridge Street, 1966 (RCHME © Crown Copyright)

*Fig 46 Doorway in undercroft at 12 Bridge Street
(RCHME © Crown copyright)*

central doorway, clearly of the same phase of construction as the undercroft beyond, preclude a date much before *c* 1300. This moulding appears at the Queen's Gate, Caernarfon Castle, possibly between 1283 and 1292 (Maddison 1983, 41). Elsewhere in Chester, the sunk chamfer occurs both at the Abbey Gatehouse (*c* 1300) and, more surprisingly, in the piers of the western two bays of the Abbey choir which date from the early fourteenth century. The robust qualities of this moulding, which seemingly played a role in its military origins, were equally applicable in other contexts.

Chamfers are found on a number of doorways through the rear walls of undercrofts of varying date. They include the late twelfth- to early thirteenth-century round-headed doorway of 37 Watergate Street, the late thirteenth-century two-centred arched doorway of 11 Watergate Street (Fig 34), and the four-centred arched doorway, formerly providing access up to the hall at the Falcon.

One doorway connecting adjacent undercrofts survives and another is recorded. A doorway in 38–42 Watergate Street has a flat lintel with a supporting double-cusped corbel, similar to a Caernarfon arch. This presumably dates from the early to mid-fourteenth-century phase of the building. In the 1950s a three- or four-centred chamfered arch was recorded

connecting 14 and 16 Northgate Street (Lawson and Smith 1958, 14–15). At 12 Bridge Street a more elaborate, but narrow, trefoil-headed doorway in the southern party wall provides access to a stair within the thickness of the wall (Fig 46). The form of this doorway and the tightly-radiused shoulders of the trefoil-headed windows to the rear light well (Fig 17), discernible in spite of the harsh nineteenth-century restoration, are indicative of a late thirteenth-century date.

Several of the doorways to the Row-level halls and service rooms are preserved. The three doorways to the former service wing in 38–42 Watergate Street are identical. They take the form of two-centred arches, with single stones forming each side of the arch, backed by wider, pointed, segmental-headed arches on the rebated side, in this case facing the service bay (Fig 47). The same type occurs on a smaller scale in the wall between the off-Row shops and the hall. The two-stone two-centred arch is a common type[6], and its conjunction with a segmental head on the rebated side is found occasionally. In a similar fourteenth-century context, the same form is used at 48–52 Bridge Street for one of the doorways in the front wall of the hall (Fig 25). Here the segmental head is unpointed and there is no rebate. The adjacent door, to the north, is similarly unrebated, and is without the inner arch. The main entrance to the cross passage in this building is on a grander scale, having a typically early fourteenth-century roll- and hollow-moulded pointed arch with a segmental arch on the inner face. The fragmentary remains of an identical arrangement can be seen at 38–42 Watergate Street. In Chester, the earliest instance of this juxtaposition of pointed and segmental head occurs in the blocked rear doorway of the eastern undercroft at Booth Mansion (Fig 42), datable to *c* 1267–80 (see Appendix B).

Cupboards

Cupboards occur frequently in the Chester undercrofts (Figs 22, 34). While lacking distinctive datable features such as the ogee-headed cupboard in the merchant's town house at 3–4 West Street, New Romney (Parkin 1973, 124–7), the plain, square, rebated examples in the Rows are contemporary with the walls and thus range across the thirteenth and fourteenth centuries. The rebate for a door and their most frequent occurrence in the rear walls of the undercrofts, as at 11 Watergate Street and 12 Bridge Street, or in the small rear chambers, as at 57 Bridge Street, indicate that they may have functioned as repositories for precious objects, accounts or money.

Conclusions

The early medieval stonework within the Row buildings demonstrates that substantial structures were built along the main streets of Chester during the thirteenth and fourteenth centuries. However, it is the two surviving, and one recorded, instances of early medieval stonework

Fig 47 Service doorways to the medieval hall at Row level, 38–42 Watergate Street (RCHME © Crown copyright)

directly associated with a Row walkway that provide the most remarkable evidence.

At 48 Bridge Street the 'Three Old Arches' are the only surviving remains of an arcaded stone frontage directly alongside the Row walkway, with no later stallboard intervening. Although there has been some suggestion that this frontage could date from *c* 1200, round-headed arches are found elsewhere in the region in buildings dating to the 1280s. The insubstantial thickness of the upper part of this facade indicates that an oversailing timber structure above the Row walkway was an integral part of the design from the outset. The surviving stonework of the parallel hall behind and modifications to the undercroft indicate that substantial remodelling of No 48 and the adjacent properties took place in the early or mid-fourteenth century.

The pair of arches over the walkway at Booth Mansion and the similar arches recorded at 32 Eastgate Street are indicative of a partially established Row system. The former can be dated to *c* 1267–80 from associated timber elements (see Appendix B), and demonstrate the existence of adjacent galleried buildings at the time of construction. They also suggest that the building originally had a substantial stone arcade frontage as at 48 Bridge Street.

The evidence of these structures points to the construction of galleried buildings during the early thirteenth century, but it also suggests that initially this development may have been very fragmentary and it was probably not until the mid-fourteenth century that a continuous system began to emerge.

4 Early medieval timberwork

The detailed examination of every Row building has revealed a surprisingly high density of thirteenth- and early fourteenth-century timber structures, particularly within the undercrofts. The survival of any such structures in the West Midlands and north-west England was hardly known before this project began (Turner 1988), and their identification helps to redress the balance, which has previously been heavily weighted to the south and east. Unfortunately there is little evidence of the carpentry of the thirteenth and fourteenth centuries at Row level and above. Similarly, few timber structures have been identified from the mid-fourteenth century to the end of the fifteenth century, probably reflecting the depressed state of the city's economy at that time (see Chapter 6). Datable carpentry elements begin to reappear in the early decades of the sixteenth century and survive in profusion from the later Elizabethan period onwards.

Thus it is the timber structures surviving within the undercroft or street level of the Row buildings which provide the main interest. They should not, however, be viewed in isolation from the stone structures described in the previous chapter, for they occur within stone undercrofts and have their structural equivalents in stone. Originally there were probably many more undercrofts incorporating timber structures than those with stone vaulting. Many of the undercrofts which now contain eighteenth-century and later brick barrel vaults, as a result of decay or fire, are likely to have been constructed with timber elements.

Arcades

The most common, datable, and sophisticated of the early timber structures is the arcade, consisting of a line of posts, often raised on pad stones, carrying a plate. This results in an aisled plan and presumably provided an inexpensive method of supporting a floor above wide undercrofts. Although frequently found elsewhere in major stone structures[1], its usage in Chester is in the smaller houses. These did not exert the massive mid-undercroft thrusts of the stone-walled parallel halls, which demanded more substantial support. The continued existence of the Row system has resulted in the survival of a homogeneous group of undercrofts with timber arcades dating from the mid-thirteenth to the late sixteenth centuries. To these can be added two further examples that were recorded before demolition.

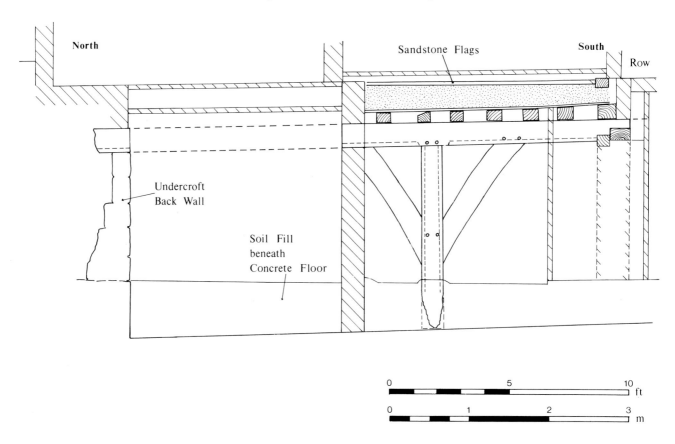

Fig 48 Longitudinal section through rear part of undercroft at 12 Watergate Street before demolition (reproduced by courtesy of Chester Archaeology)

Fig 49 Part of the timber arcade in the western undercroft at Booth Mansion, 28–34 Watergate Street; the post in front belongs to later alterations when the ceiling was raised (RCHME © Crown Copyright)

This group provides sufficient evidence to suggest a development from a simple form through a transitional type to a complex design. Dendrochronological sampling, carpentry detail, and comparable dated

structures suggest that this classification indicates a chronological evolution. The first two forms will be described in this chapter, but the final, complex form does not occur in Chester until the later medieval period and is therefore included in Chapter 6.

The undercrofts of 11 Bridge Street, the Falcon (6 Lower Bridge Street), Booth Mansion (28–34 Watergate Street), and 12 Watergate Street, demolished in 1985 (Ward 1988), all have timber arcades in their simplest form. These consist of vertical posts, usually chamfered, and either tenoned directly into the soffit of a plate or into a bolster which in turn supports the plate. The arcade runs the length of the undercroft and carries lodged joists. The arcade in 12 Watergate Street had a single central post (350 x 270mm) tenoned into a plate of the same scantling (Fig 48). Curved upward braces extended from near the base of the post to the plate. The one surviving post at 11 Bridge Street (Fig 151) is similarly massive (370mm square) and appears to have been one of a pair, the rear section of the arcade having been removed when an eighteenth-century wall was inserted. The comparable arcade in the western undercroft of Booth Mansion is of more slender and decorative design (Figs 49, 50) and was probably one of a pair that originally divided the undercroft into three aisles. It is constructed of posts (185mm square) that are chamfered so that they are almost octagonal. The bolsters between the post and the plate are 1.32m long and have moulded ends. The arcade now forms part of a brick wall, but a groove is visible on one of the posts revealing the former existence of a partition.

In the undercroft of the Falcon, 6 Lower Bridge Street, there are two arcades (Figs 27, 51), one with massive timber posts supporting a plate consisting of two inverted tie beams from an earlier phase of the building (see p27). The adjacent near-central arcade comprises a substantial timber plate carrying lodged joists, but resting on two octagonal sandstone piers (Fig 51). The use of stone in this situation may simply

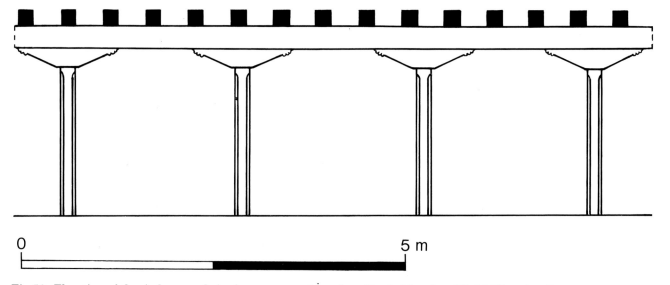

0   5 m

Fig 50 Elevation of the timber arcade in the western undercroft at Booth Mansion, 28–34 Watergate Street

Fig 51 Undercroft at the Falcon, 6 Lower Bridge Street (RCHME © Crown Copyright)

reflect the greater compression stresses involved, as the beam also carries the flying sill beams of the two separate parts of a timber-framed structure above.

Dendrochronology has provided dates for several of the arcades (see Appendix B). Cores from the arcade at 12 Watergate Street proved undatable, but the contemporary timber structure above provided an estimated felling date in the range *c* 1226–57. The arcade posts and associated timbers in the western undercroft at Booth Mansion provided a range *c* 1250–63. The arcade plates in the undercroft of the Falcon provided differing dates because of the reuse of timbers (see p25) but it is likely that the central arcade dates from the mid-thirteenth century. No significant dendrochronological matches were obtained from 11 Bridge Street. This evidence indicates that simple arcades were being constructed in Chester during the mid- to late thirteenth century.

The relationship of these early carpentry structures to the Row walkway is of interest. Despite the independence of the timber structures at undercroft and Row levels, which includes dissimilar bay widths, it can be seen that three of the simple arcades carried Row walkways, almost certainly from the outset. The arcade at 12 Watergate Street, which was inserted into an earlier undercroft (Ward 1988), extended forward to a masonry wall, level with the front of the Row walkway. At Booth Mansion the surviving arcade plate is sawn off at the front, but still extends 0.85m under the present Row walkway. This walkway must have existed by the time of the construction of the eastern part of the mansion, which has arches spanning the Row, demonstrating the existence of a gallery connecting with the neighbouring properties. Since the timbers in the eastern undercroft of the mansion have provided an estimated felling date range of *c* 1267–80 (see Appendix B), it would appear probable that the arcade in the western undercroft supported a walkway from its construction, perhaps a decade or two earlier. The arcade plate at the Falcon runs under the full width of the former Row and terminates above the southern jamb of the thirteenth-century doorway. This timber is part of a phase of construction which included the stone piers at the front of the building, which can only relate to the Row. At 11 Bridge Street the section of arcade plate in front of the post now stops well short of the walkway and it is therefore impossible to be certain that the arcade carried the Row in this building.

It is significant that none of these thirteenth- and fourteenth-century timber structures extend under the stallboards that now separate the Row walkway from the street. This confirms what has already become clear from the stone frontages, that the stallboards represent later encroachment into the street (see p20). Thus, in at least some buildings erected during the mid-thirteenth century, the Row walkway appears to have been designed as an integral part of the structure, with the stallboard being a later addition.

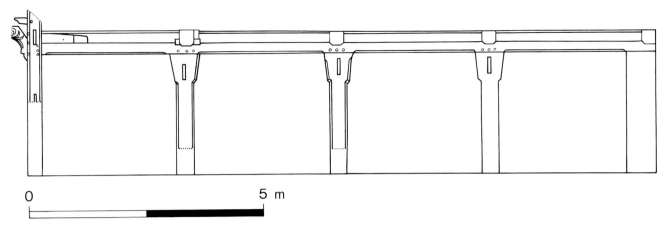

Fig 52 Elevation of western party wall in undercroft, 22 Watergate Street

A subsequent development of the simple arcade is found at 22 Watergate Street, where the remains of an arcade can be seen incorporated into the western party wall (Figs 52 and 181). This may originally have been an open arcade in a larger building. The chamfered posts are *c* 350mm wide but thicken with gunstock heads up to 600mm. In these heads there are blocked mortices *c* 350 x 630mm for diagonal braces which have been removed. The braces joined the posts to the soffits of transverse beams trenched on to the arcade plate. There is no evidence for bracing in the arcade itself. As the transverse beams span *c* 6m on either side of the arcade it is clear that this arrangement was adopted to reduce the span of the common joists and thus remove the need for further arcades to support the floor. The thickening of the post heads is part of the evolution from the carpentry techniques used for the simple arcades to the universal acceptance of the jowl, and would seem to date the structure to the very end of the thirteenth century. This makes the mortice and tenon joints in the common joists the earliest such occurrence in Chester.

The arcade at 22 Watergate Street extends under the present Row walkway and, in view of the dating proposed above, it is not surprising that this appears to be an original arrangement. Most significantly, an arcade post stands directly below the transverse beam that runs along the rear of the walkway.

It is possible to trace a number of parallels to Chester's timber arcades. Hewett (1980, 293) produced a list, which includes Great Chesterford Manor, Essex; St Etheldreda's Church, Ely Place, London; 39–43 The Causeway, Steventon, Berkshire; St Mary's Church tower, Wethersfield, Essex; The Old Palace, Croydon; and King John's Hunting Lodge, Romsey, Hants. More examples are likely to survive but there is sufficient evidence to test the typological and chronological sequence just presented.

The jointing technique used in the simple arcades is one in which no more than two members are jointed together, regardless of the number converging, and is universal in carpentry structures up to the late thirteenth century, when thickened heads, or prototype jowls appear. The earliest example of a simple arcade in Hewett's list is from Great Chesterford Manor, Essex, but the Royal Commission's inventory dates the associated screens passage doorways to the early thirteenth century (RCHME 1916, I, 174). This has braces like those at 12 Watergate Street, but they rise to a bolster underneath the arcade plate. A more exact parallel survives in the Marlipins, Shoreham, Sussex, (Packham 1924) where a central beam, 12.95m long, was originally supported by three posts (Fig 53 see also p35). The posts at the front and centre had braces, and all were tenoned directly into the soffit of the beam. The date of this structure is not certain but its association with the chequerwork stone facade and datable moulded doorways and windows suggests that it cannot be earlier than *c* 1300[2]. An analogous structure, but without any freestanding posts, survives in the undercroft of the solar of Stokesay Castle, Shropshire, dated to *c* 1291 (Pevsner 1958, 295).

The more elegant treatment of the arcade in Booth Mansion has a close parallel with the structure in the undercroft of the Guard Room of the Old Palace, Croydon, Surrey, which formed part of one of the many medieval palaces of the Archbishops of Canterbury[3]. It is on a more massive scale than the Chester example, with the bolster 3m long and the lodged joists 300 x 220mm in size. The stepped chamfered stops on the post are very similar to those at Booth Mansion, but no accurate date is known for this part of the palace[4].

Within the palace of another medieval bishop there is an arcade of a transitional form, but different from that at 22 Watergate Street. This survives in the undercroft of St Etheldreda's Church, Ely Place, London, the former domestic chapel of the palace of the Bishops of Ely. The chapel is thought to have been constructed by Bishop William de Luda between 1290 and 1299 (Hewett 1980, 123–4). Here a central arcade of seven irregular bays carries the usual massive lodged joists. Between each post and the arcade plate is a long shaped bolster. There are stout braces rising from the posts to the arcade plate while more slender braces rise to the common joists. At the east end, under the altar area, the posts are more closely spaced and only the common joist is braced.

The use of timber arcades in the undercrofts of merchants' town houses was probably widespread. In medieval Southampton, Platt (1973, 41–2) describes the roofing of the undercrofts of the thirteenth- and fourteenth-century town as being 'with a simple structure of pillars and beams'. Recent investigations at 55 Sheinton Street (Bastard Hall), Much Wenlock, Shropshire, have revealed a ground-floor timber arcade with an ornate octagonal post (estimated felling date 1255–89) with an equally elaborate bolster (estimated felling date 1246–80). The bolster supports an arcade plate, with the floor above being made of flat, lodged planks laid transversely and carrying a solid floor at least 150mm thick (Moran 1994, 34). This structure is very similar to the arcade in the western undercroft of Booth Mansion and the floor structure in the eastern section of the same building. One isolated example survives from the far north in the undercroft of the Guildhall, Carlisle. It was built as the house of the merchant, Robert de Redness, between 1396 and 1407, on a key corner site on the market square, and the form of the arcade is analogous to that in 22 Watergate Street. The comparative rarity of timber arcades surviving in England is not a fair reflection of the extent of their original use. After identifying the form, it becomes possible to reconstruct the arcades which existed elsewhere from the evidence of the sockets and ledges remaining in many stone structures. Also, the pad stones for the posts sometimes survive.

From this evidence it appears that timber arcades were widely used within stone undercrofts, beneath first-floor halls. Presumably they would also have been used in timber structures where the span of the joists required a central support.

It is clear that this form of construction was widely used in high status buildings, despite the fact that it is less ornate than stone vaulting. In Chester, there are two undercrofts with stone equivalents to the timber arcade: the Falcon, 6 Lower Bridge Street (described above) and the eastern undercroft of Booth Mansion, where the span is broken by an arcade of two-centred stone arches (see p39). The solution to carrying the Row level floors seems to have varied, but this may not necessarily reflect the status of the building as a whole. The uses of the different undercrofts may also have varied, ranging from the storage of household goods to the sale of wine and other high value products. It is possible that the choice of stone vaulting, rather than a cheaper timber arcade, may have resulted from a wish for obvious display within the undercroft and a desire to impress prospective customers.

Arch-braced beams

An alternative way of reducing the span of the floor above undercrofts in Chester is the use of a braced beam. This consists of the elaboration of a normal transverse beam by the introduction of massive upward

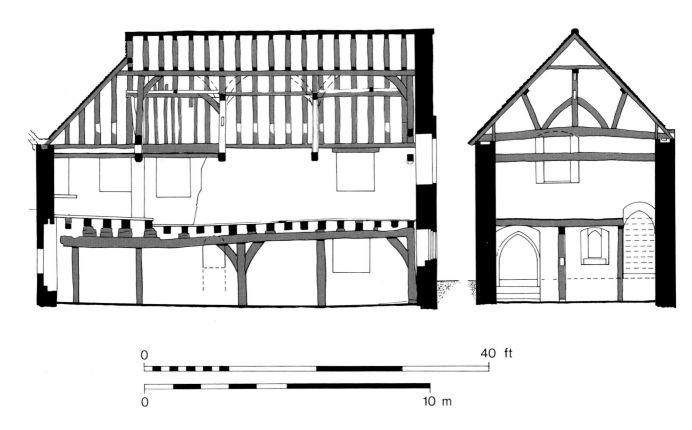

Fig 53 Cross section of the Marlipins, Shoreham, showing the timber arcade (after Packham 1924)

Fig 54 Depressed arch and arch-braced beam in undercroft at 38–42 Watergate Street (RCHME © Crown Copyright)

braces, similar to those found in the timber arcades. However, in these cases the ends of the beams are set into the stone walls and the curving braces rise from stone springers or corbels. Only two examples survive, and no evidence has been found for the use of this construction in other Row buildings.

At 38–42 Watergate Street, one of the undercrofts (5.1m wide) is spanned by braced transverse beams, one on either side of a segmental stone arch (Fig 54). The arch carries the weight of the stone wall of the hall above, whilst the beams carried the lesser weight of the hall floor and timber-framed shop frontages. The beams are of massive scantling (c 440mm square) and made of dressed, whole trunks of fast-grown timber (see Appendix B). These are supported by short curving braces of a similar size, rising from stone springers (Figs 55 and 183). The common joists (230mm square) were originally lodged on the beam but were subsequently raised. An identical braced transverse beam survives in the adjacent undercroft and this, together with a section of a segmental stone arch, shows that the space was originally spanned in exactly the same way. There is no evidence to show how the floor over the third undercroft within the building was constructed. The original joists were reused for the modified floor and they have provided a felling date of the early to mid-fourteenth century (see Appendix B). This date is confirmed by the fact that one of the curving braces has a scribed shoulder to a central tenon, over the chamfer of the beam. The joint is akin to scribing over waney edges and is in response to the erroneous running through of the chamfer. Such scribing is indicative of the early fourteenth century[5].

The second example comes from the undercroft of the Leche House, 17 Watergate Street, where the dimensions of the arched braces are smaller and they rise from stone corbels. The common joists (c 200mm square) are flush with the top of the beams, to which they are jointed by barefaced soffit tenons. This type of joint[6] and the slighter timbers suggest an evolution of the form and may date from the mid- to late fourteenth century. Unfortunately, dendrochronological analysis failed to produce a conclusive result (see Appendix B).

Given the relatively late date of this type of timber structure, it is not surprising to find that in both these examples the joists extend under the Row walkway.

The arch-braced beams are analogous to, and are perhaps contemporary with, the segmental stone arches found in other undercrofts (see p38). At 38–42 Watergate Street they occur together, and the line of the transverse beams in 17–19 Watergate Street is paralleled by the stone arches in 15 and 36 Bridge Street and the demolished 16 Watergate Street. The only surviving parallel to Chester's arch-braced beams is within the late thirteenth-century south range of the Blackfriars, Gloucester. Only one of the original six arch-braced beams in that building remains. The main beam (0.33 x 0.31m) spans 6.71m supported by arch braces and wall posts rising from stone corbels. The large square joists are closely spaced and planted on top of the beam (Rackham *et al* 1978). A similar structure with straight braces and no wall posts is recorded from the Dominican Priory, Bristol (Taylor 1878–9).

Corbel tables

One of the problems associated with timber floor construction within a stone building is how the ends of the joists are to be supported. In the thirteenth- and fourteenth-century Row buildings this problem was often solved by the use of a corbel table, on either the side or end walls (see p40). This comprises a line of closely set plain stone corbels carrying a plate, 100–150mm deep (Fig 42). The ends of the common joists are placed on top of the plate. The spacing of the joists and corbels is not necessarily the same, and in many instances the joists occur directly over the space between the corbels. The plate serves to spread the load on to the corbels. This construction involves less sophisticated masonry than where each corbel carries the end of an individual joist or beam, a form which occurs elsewhere in the thirteenth and four-teenth centuries[7], and in Chester later in the medieval period, for example in the now demolished undercroft at 63–65 Watergate Street (Lawson and Smith 1958, 22–3).

Corbel tabling is a feature of the early undercrofts in Chester, although the technique continued through-out the thirteenth and fourteenth centuries. At 12 Watergate Street, the corbels belong to the first phase of construction, predating the timber arcade, and therefore date from before the middle of the thirteenth century (Ward 1988, 49). The stone superstructure of the first phase of this building was replaced by a timber-framed structure, which could not counterbalance the weight of the joists on the projecting corbels. This necessitated the lowering of the joists so that they could be set on to the top of the remaining stone walls. The corbels were left in position although they no longer served any function.

Complete corbel tables survive in a number of Chester undercrofts (see p40) and these together with many partially intact examples and the record of others from Row buildings that have been demolished shows that the technique was used extensively. Those

in the eastern undercroft of Booth Mansion can be dated to 1267–80 from the associated joists (see Appendix B), while those recorded at 48 Bridge Street (Baker 1895) and 16 Northgate Street (Lawson and Smith 1958, 14–15) are of the early to mid-fourteenth century. However, it is reasonable to suppose that the other examples all fall within the period from the early thirteenth to the mid-fourteenth century.

The use of corbel tables is a refinement of earlier methods of carrying the common joists. At Scollands Hall at Richmond Castle, and in the Great Tower at Chepstow Castle, both dating from the late eleventh century, the joists were set into regular-spaced sockets within the stone walls of the undercrofts. This method continued as late as the third quarter of the thirteenth century when it was used in the western hall of the Bishop's Palace, Lamphey (Turner 1991) and in the Great Hall of Ludlow Castle. In other cases, the joists rested on a continuous ledge formed in the stonework. Corbel tables were an improvement on such arrange-ments; by setting the ends of the joists out of the wall the life of the floor was increased, as it was less prone to rot.

There are several comparative examples of corbel tables from the Chester area, all of late thirteenth-century date and all with the same technique of lodging the joists over the plates. The timber and stonework survives in the undercrofts of Adam's Tower, Chirk Castle (Dean 1983, 33–4) and the former west cloister range of Vale Royal Abbey, near Winsford (McNeil and Turner 1987–8, 62). The corbelling alone can be seen in the monastic lodgings of Ince Manor, near Ellesmere Port (Thompson 1981).

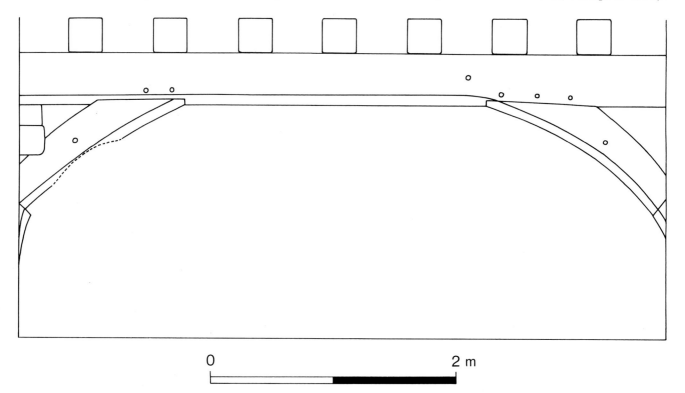

0   2 m

Fig 55 Arch-braced beam in the undercroft of 38–42 Watergate Street

Floors

All the above techniques were designed to carry floors over the undercroft spaces, and it is noticeable that where the original thirteenth-century floor still exists the construction is peculiarly massive. For example, the joists above the eastern undercroft at Booth Mansion are 200mm square and are set at *c* 400mm centres. The reason for such substantial construction becomes clear when it is realised that the joists had to carry oak boarding, a layer of sand and rubble, and the stone flags of the floor above. Thus at Booth Mansion the total floor construction is 600mm deep. A similar form of floor was found at 12 Watergate Street(Fig 48) and partly survives at 36 Bridge Street.

This technique continued into the fourteenth century, as it is possible to deduce that the same construction also existed at 38–42 Watergate Street. Here the floor joists have clearly been raised by *c* 300mm, but the floor level still coincides with the level of the Row walkway, which is unlikely to have been altered significantly because of the need to maintain continuity with the Row through the adjacent properties. It would therefore appear that a layer of sand, rubble, and flags *c* 300mm deep was removed and the joists raised in order to maintain the same floor level. The weight of this construction presumably accounts for the substantial size of both the transverse beams and the joists. Conversely the absence of a rubble layer would seem to account for the smaller section timbers in the Leche House (see p49).

It is possible that this massive form of construction represents an attempt to fireproof the undercroft without going to the expense of using a stone vault. However, it may also be connected to the existence of open fires in the centre of the halls above the undercrofts. Obviously such an arrangement would only be possible if at least part of the floor were fireproof.

Timber framing

There is very little evidence of the timber-framing of the thirteenth- and fourteenth-century Row buildings. However, the fragments that do exist provide an indication of the types of structure that existed at undercroft and higher levels. Unfortunately, there is not enough information to reveal the precise dating and structural details of the frontages as successive encroachment in later centuries has left little evidence of any timber elements that may have existed.

The only evidence for a timber frontage is at the Leche House, where a fourteenth-century beam remains below the rear of the stallboard. This provides evidence that the stone-walled undercroft had a timber frontage. The beam contains soffit mortices for the lost facade studwork, indicating that there was a central doorway. It is level with the transverse beams and common joists, and therefore there was no jetty projection. This accords with the print evidence for medieval Row

Fig 56   West side of Bridge Street, W Batenham 1839 (photograph RCHME © Crown Copyright, from print in CAS Library, Chester Archives)

buildings (Fig 56) and the surviving seventeenth-century timber-framed buildings where substantial jetties occur only at levels above the Row walkway.

While there is an absence of demonstrably medieval posts carrying timber-framed chambers over the Row walkway and stallboard, there is structural confirmation that such oversailing was typical from the earliest Row buildings. As noted on p39, at 48 Bridge Street the spandrels of the stone arches are only half the thickness of the piers, indicating that there was timber framing at Row + 1 level.

Only small sections of the framing of the party walls are visible and these are not often of a diagnostic character. The study of 12 Watergate Street (Ward 1988) identified the remains of the western party wall (Fig 57). It rested on a wall plate set on the outer edge of the stone wall of the undercroft. The rather irregular framing formed bays 1.7–1.8m wide with the rails tenoned into three of the four uprights and in one case the post tenoned into the rail. There was a substantial mortice for a bracket and rail continuing the framing across the Row, and two other posts and the top rail from the original Row frontage also survived. Dendrochronology suggested an estimated felling date soon after 1237. Unfortunately the only feature of the framing was the existence of proto-jowls on two of the corner posts and therefore there is no other evidence to support this surprisingly early date.

There is only one survival of internal timberwork from the early Row buildings; a doorway in the eastern part of Booth Mansion. This has a rectangular wooden frame within which two curved braces form an

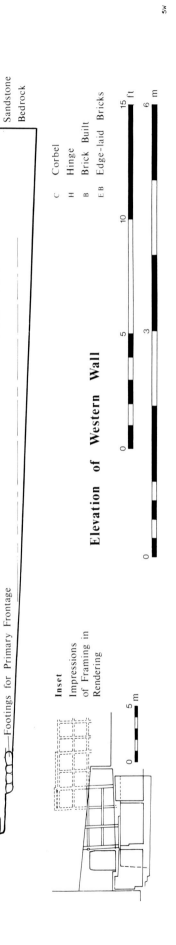

Fig 57 Elevation of the western party wall of 12 Watergate Street, recorded during demolition (reproduced by courtesy of Chester Archaeology)

Fig 58 Top section of thirteenth-century doorway to the open hall at Row level in the eastern part of Booth Mansion, 28–34 Watergate Street (RCHME © Crown Copyright)

approximately two-centred arched opening (Fig 58). The inner face is chamfered. Empty mortices suggest that it was part of the timber-framed partition wall at the Row end of the open hall. The door seems to have opened from a short passage leading to the Row walkway. It can be dated to *c* 1260–80 by its association with the undercroft timbers beneath. An almost identical doorway exists in the solar undercroft of Stokesay Castle, Shropshire, dated to *c* 1291 (Pevsner 1958, 295).

Roofs

The paucity of extant medieval timber structures above undercroft level includes roof structures; there are no *in-situ* roofs in the Rows earlier than the late fifteenth or early sixteenth century, with the possible exception of the roof over the hall at Gamul House, 52–58 Lower Bridge Street, and the Blue Bell, 63–65 Northgate Street (see pp 145 and 176). This dearth of material can be attributed to the constant pressure to enlarge the buildings. One of the few ways of gaining additional accommodation was to build upwards and most of the Row buildings were regularly enlarged by the addition of extra storeys, leading to the loss of the earlier roof. This process can be seen most graphically at 24 Watergate Street where the tie beams of the sixteenth- and seventeenth-century roofs can be seen integrated into the timber framing of the present stairwell.

Lack of information does not however preclude all discussion of the medieval roof structures. Details of construction are revealed by roofing timbers that have been reused, and from the records of demolished buildings. Furthermore, the necessary interrelationship between the roofs and the structures below means that the overall layout of the former can frequently be deduced from the latter.

The buildings on narrow plots, arranged at right angles to the street, were easily roofed with a gabled frontage. This needed only additional length to cover

the Row and stallboard, as in the later medieval houses (see Chapter 6). More sophisticated roofs were required for the larger parallel-hall houses. These needed multiple roofs, but the core of the building is always an exactly rectangular hall, despite any irregularity in the shape of the plot. At 48–52 Bridge Street, the remaining stone walls and the repositioning of the northern undercroft party wall indicate that the fourteenth-century rebuilding was dictated by the shape of the new hall rather than by the inherited plot widths. The screen of this hall, the position of which is indicated by a groove in the east wall, was aligned with the apex of the central facade gable, implying both the existence of a spere truss and a correlation in the design of the hall and street-facing gabled roofs. This would have resulted in the tie beams in the hall corresponding with the locations of the valleys and ridges in the front roof structures. Such precise integration of roofs at right angles to each other emerged in the early thirteenth century, both in early H-plan houses such as Priory Place, Little Dunmow (Hewett 1980, 129–30) and in

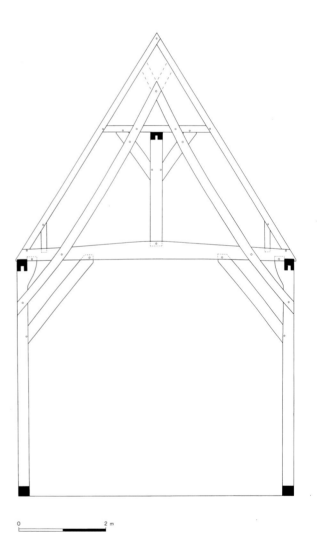

Fig 59 Reconstruction of passing-brace roof truss formerly at the Falcon, 6 Lower Bridge Street

ecclesiastical architecture at the junctions of nave and transept. At 48–52 Bridge Street, the same technique was adopted, despite the resultant irregularity of the gable widths, which was doubtless seen as subservient to the structural superiority of this method.

A more balanced version of this arrangement occurs at 38–42 Watergate Street, where the western valley was aligned with the upper face of the service bay end of the hall truss. In the absence of any evidence for a spere truss, the two symmetrical undercrofts beneath the hall point to two – or less plausibly four – gables to the street. The seventeenth-century roof now on this building probably repeats the earlier form, and comprises two gable roofs with jack rafters and valleys connecting to the hall roof and a separate roof over the service bay.

Although the only surviving example of crown post construction in medieval Chester is at 63 Northgate Street, a mid-fifteenth-century building (Fig 174), there is evidence for the earlier use of this roof type (but see pp 145 and 176). During demolition of the rear of 16 Northgate Street in 1892, a detailed description was made of a two-storey, timber-framed hall above a stone undercroft and Lawson subsequently produced a reconstruction (Lawson and Smith 1958, 14–15). This would appear to have been the rear wing of a courtyard building, and the description clearly implies crown-post roof trusses with braces to the tie beams and crown plate (Fig 28). It can be assumed that the trusses were contemporary with the early fourteenth-century undercroft.

At the Falcon, 6 Lower Bridge Street, there is surprising evidence of an earlier roof. Within the undercroft there is a pair of reused tie beams and what is assumed to be a related crown post from a passing-brace roof (p25, Figs 27, 59)[8]. These now function as the plate and one post of an arcade. One end and the centre of each tie beam survive, giving a reconstructed span of 6.38m, with mortices showing that the original wall posts were inset by 40mm. This span is exactly equal to the width of the rear section of the present seventeenth-century superstructure, which occupies the expected site of a parallel hall. The tie beams have central mortices on their top faces, indicating the use of a crown-post. Final tree-ring dates of 1180 and 1181 from the tie beams suggest a date in the early thirteenth century for the construction of the roof (see Appendix B). This is in accord with similar roof trusses elsewhere[9].

Conclusions

The recognition and dating of a range of early timber structures within the Rows of Chester has proved one of the most important of the project's findings. The work of Hewett and others had created the impression that timber structures of the thirteenth and fourteenth centuries are likely to occur only in southern and eastern England, but this is being corrected by recent research.

It is the peculiarities of the Row system which have ensured the survival of these early timber structures in Chester. The need to retain the Row walkway, and the early subletting or separate ownership of the undercrofts from the house above, have made wholesale redevelopment almost impossible. Most of Chester's undercrofts will have contained timber structures of the types described in this chapter. Many must have decayed over the past 600 years to be replaced by brick barrel vaults, but a precious few have survived. These show that timber structures extended under and over the Row from the early thirteenth century, indicating that the walkway was planned as an integral part of the buildings and was not a later insertion.

These timber structures required a good supply of timber and the drain on the woodlands of Chester's hinterland must have been enormous during the period 1250–1330. For example, the volume of wood required for the undercroft at 6 Lower Bridge Street can be estimated at 15.5 cubic metres, the product of seven or eight mature oak trees. Quantities of timber would also be required for any timber-framing, upper floors, and roofs. During this period timber was also required for purposes other than new buildings in the town. Chester acted as the campaign base for Edward I's advance into North Wales and, as late as 1295, the two leading military engineers, James of St George and Richard the Engineer, had ordered the felling of 2300 trees on the lands of St Werburgh's Abbey around Chester to help construct and prefabricate a pontoon bridge over the Menai Straits (Brown *et al* 1963, 396). Modern estimates for lowland Cheshire give an average of 135 oak trees per square kilometre in order to produce suitable structural timber (Forestry Commission 1984). The effect on the landscape of this medieval demand for timber can therefore be gauged.

The growing scarcity of timber towards the end of the thirteenth century across England may have provided a stimulus for the development of new framing and jointing techniques. By the mid-fourteenth century, grants of trees from the Earl of Chester's forests were marks of special favour[10]. The use of square-section lodged joists creates structures that are substantially over-designed in structural terms. Later techniques allowed the use of shorter members of smaller scantling, many of which could have been drawn from coppiced or underwood trees.

Despite the very limited survival of thirteenth- and fourteenth-century timber structures from levels above the undercroft, the Rows of Chester preserve enough, frequently scientifically datable, evidence of carpentry techniques to advance both an understanding of the Rows and, more broadly, the evolution of methods of construction.

5 Origins of the Rows

In the preceding chapters we have studied the early history of the Chester Rows, presenting at some length the architectural and documentary evidence for the buildings of the thirteenth and early fourteenth centuries. This chapter will attempt to answer the two questions which have puzzled antiquarians, historians, and archaeologists for over four hundred years. What were the origins of the Rows and why do they appear to be unique to Chester?

The physical evidence and the documentary record make it clear that the Row system was largely in existence by 1350 (see pp 18–20). It is also clear that Row walkways were an integral part of many of the buildings that were erected before this date, with some of the dendrochronological data indicating that Row walkways may have been constructed as early as *c* 1250. Whilst the system may not have been continuous at the beginning, it must have developed reasonably rapidly as its advantages became apparent. The development of public thoroughfares within private properties distinguishes the Rows from other medieval arcaded streets. The system brought mutual benefits, but it also resulted in constant tensions, as will be seen in our investigation of its development in later centuries.

There is no simple explanation for the origins of the Rows. All previous theories have given undue weight to single factors, such as defence, or the accumulation of Roman debris, or the effects of the fire recorded in 1278 (see Chapter 1). Our detailed study of the evidence suggests that the origins of the Rows are more complex and result from a range of factors, which together are peculiar to Chester. We therefore have to analyse what is known about Chester in the thirteenth and fourteenth centuries in order to suggest what may have occurred.

Physical and topographical factors

Inevitably, physical and topographical factors have played a significant part in shaping the city of Chester and determining the form of its medieval buildings. In themselves, they are not directly responsible for the Rows, but it is useful to reconsider them first.

The undercrofts of the medieval buildings in Chester are only slightly below ground level, probably because there is rock very close to the surface. This is in contrast to the similar undercrofts in many other English towns, which tend to be sunk 2–3m below street level (Wood 1965, 81). In a number of Row buildings an additional cellar, below the undercroft, has been cut out of the rock but this generally appears to have occurred in post-medieval or modern periods.

The accumulation of debris from collapsed Roman buildings and rubbish deposits behind the main street frontages – and the existence of a former stream valley along the line of Lower Bridge Street – allowed the main domestic elements of the Row buildings, which were located above the undercrofts, to have ground level access to the rear. It is of note that where this change of level between the front and rear of buildings does not exist, as at the east end of Eastgate Street, true Rows did not develop.

Following the Norman Conquest, the layout of the area within the walls changed radically. The castle was laid out in the south-west corner of the city and this quarter was developed with houses for the officers of the Palatinate. The north-east quarter of the town was almost entirely occupied by the precinct of the refounded Benedictine Abbey of St Werburgh. The land on the western side remained largely undeveloped until it was granted to three religious houses in the early thirteenth century. The continuing threat of Welsh incursions restricted development outside the walls. All this limited the area available for commercial building. The development of a two-tier system effectively doubled the frontages available for trading and hence increased the value of individual buildings.

Early evolution of the Rows

The physical and topographical factors provided the essential preconditions for the development of the Rows but two other historical factors also seem significant: wide (though increasingly subdivided) plots and a growing commercial prosperity, enhanced by the city's expanding strategic and military role in the late thirteenth century.

Chester's street frontages appear to have been originally divided into wide plots, possibly laid out as part of the Anglo-Saxon *burh*. These wide plots allowed the development of several small shops across the width of each plot above the undercroft, making a first-floor gallery desirable. As population and commercial pressures increased, these plots were subdivided into different ownerships and tenancies, all of whom would have had an interest in the continuity of the gallery system. As in most medieval towns, traders and craftsmen with similar wares located close to each other and this would have further encouraged the development or extension of galleries. It may be significant that the earliest recorded Rows are named after buttersellers, ironmongers, bakers, butchers, and the like.

Chester's economic activity reached a peak during the late thirteenth century when it became the base for Edward I's military campaigns in North Wales and then the mustering point and winter quarters for the thousands of craftsmen employed on the subsequent building programme. The impact of Chester's growing prosperity on the buildings of the city in general, and those of the four main streets in particular, is clear.

From the mid-thirteenth century, there is evidence of the subdivision of undercrofts and selds and an increasingly intensive use of the street frontages, with the appearance of numerous small shops at Row level, alongside the entrance to the house or seld behind. The city's prosperity continued into the second quarter of the fourteenth century when the two largest stone houses still surviving in the Rows were built.

Edward I and his followers were responsible for founding many new towns in England, Wales, and Gascony, experimenting with new plan forms. It is, therefore, tempting to see the Rows as one of these experiments, assisted by the apparent loss of many of the city centre buildings in the fire of 1278 (Lawson and Smith 1958). There is, however, evidence for Row buildings before 1277 and no clear evidence of extensive fire debris dating to 1278 (Ward 1984, 44). Also there is no indication of replanning or rapid rebuilding during the immediately post-1278 period. In addition there is no evidence for any royal or comital decree enforcing such an arrangement on the landholders in the four main streets.

The combination of evidence argues for the gradual development of the Rows, albeit achieved for the majority of the frontages over a relatively short period as the dates of the early Row buildings are largely restricted to the period 1250–1350. It is, however, difficult to believe that the Row system could have been established through private properties entirely as a result of haphazard factors. The documentary evidence links the earliest sections of the Rows with the selds on the west side of Bridge Street and the properties adjacent to St Peter's Church at the Cross, both areas in which the civic authorities are likely to have been influential. It is possible that the idea for the Row system came from the royal interest in the city and was sustained by the civic authorities until there was a common recognition of the mutual advantages of such a system.

Whatever the process by which the Rows evolved, it is inevitable that the initial idea and its subsequent development would have been influenced by other buildings of the time, and particularly by other systems of walkways or arcades. The Rows could hardly have evolved in isolation and we therefore need to consider parallel developments.

English parallels

In seeking to explain the Rows, some people have sought comparisons with other towns and cities in England. Many English towns have streets or groups of buildings called Row. The word is not specific to the raised walkways found in Chester, having presumably originated simply as the description of a row of buildings. The term was often used to describe adjacent buildings that were linked to particular trades or the sale of certain goods, with each building containing both domestic accommodation and a shop or workshop (Schofield 1984, 88). Less frequently, the word was applied to a group of small tenements, such as Our

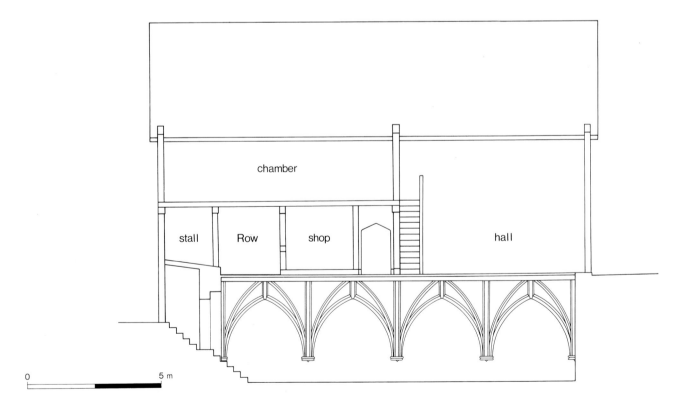

Fig 60 Speculative section of medieval building at 28 Eastgate Street with Row, shop and hall over surviving undercroft. Also shows encroachment into the street with a stall over the steps down into the undercroft. Compare with section through 58 French Street, Southampton (Fig 61).

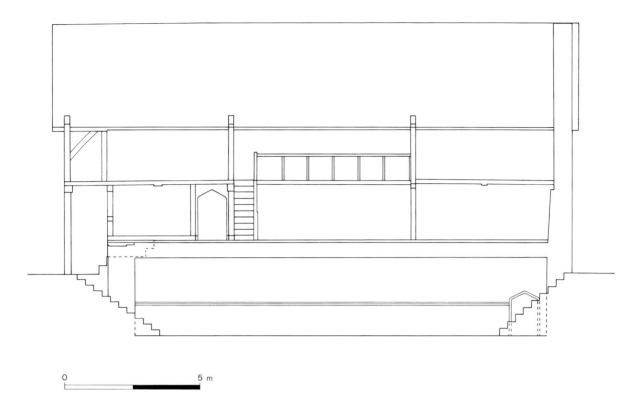

0   5 m

Fig 61   Section, 58 French Street, Southampton

Lady's Row in York, that were just workers' cottages (RCHME 1981, 143–5).

The study of medieval town houses in England is in its early stages and the evidence is scattered, and it is therefore difficult to generalise. It is possible that the twelfth century saw the appearance of a dedicated urban form of architecture, as exemplified by the Jew's House, Lincoln, but the larger town houses of the thirteenth century appear to be adaptations of the almost universal tripartite plan. In urban situations the arrangement of open hall, service rooms, and solar was constrained by limitations of space and the wish to maximise use of the commercial frontage. The buildings described in Chapter 2 show how this was achieved in Chester, and houses with similar plans can be found in many English towns. In fact the basic split-level arrangement of the early medieval town houses in Chester follows the normal pattern for English buildings of that period. The Red Lion in the High Street, Southampton has a shop 'with a chamber above' in front of an open hall with further chambers behind the hall. There is an undercroft below with access only from the hall, suggesting that it was used for storage (Platt 1976, 61). An even more direct comparison can be made between the Chester buildings and 58 French Street, Southampton (Figs 61 and 62) where the undercroft is not completely subterranean and there was access from the street. The floor level of the shop and hall is raised above the street, requiring an access stair[1]. Both these examples are of the right-angled hall type, but the same comparisons can be made for

Fig 62   58 French Street, Southampton

parallel hall buildings. Although it does not include an undercroft, 28–32 Coppergate, York has the same general layout as 38–42 Watergate Street, but with shops at street level there is no need for a gallery (RCHME 1981, 128). Tackley's Inn at Oxford (Fig 63) has also been shown to have had a similar form (Pantin 1963a, 217–19 and Faulkner 1966, 128–30). Five shops above an undercroft fronted the street and there was an open hall behind. Faulkner suggests that there was a gallery along the frontage to provide access to the shops, but the evidence for this is uncertain (Harris forthcoming). Some form of access would have been required, however, and if each shop was provided with its own flight of steps from the street the disadvantages are obvious.

The consistent use of undercrofts is one of the elements that distinguishes the Row buildings of Chester. Approximately 180 undercrofts survive in whole or in part, and originally there may have been over 250. Stone-built undercrofts do not occur in every English medieval town, although they seem to be ubiquitous in the surviving town houses of the twelfth and early thirteenth centuries. From the mid-thirteenth century, however, as plan forms evolve and timber houses survive, differences begin to appear. Later undercrofts can be found in significant numbers in some towns, such as Southampton, Winchelsea, Norwich, and Oxford, but in others, such as York, Salisbury and Stamford, they are almost entirely absent[2]. The evidence for Chester can be compared to Norwich, where 54 undercrofts survive and there are records of another 34. These occur on steeply sloping ground, but are not necessarily adjacent to the street. Many of these undercrofts survived the fire of 1507, which destroyed the timber-framed structures above (Smith and Carter 1983).

Medieval builders would undoubtedly have experimented with alternative variations of the basic town house forms, adapting it to particular circumstances and needs. In a number of other towns the undercrofts were adapted to the local topography. In Haverfordwest, Dyfed, three medieval houses, 2–6 St Mary's Street, exploit a change in the natural levels that is the reverse of the debris slope in Chester. All three properties have stone barrel-vaulted undercrofts that are below ground on St Mary's Street yet open at ground level to the rear. At 2 St Mary's Street the original layout of the upper floor can be identified, consisting of a shop on the street frontage, a double-height hall behind, and a chamber to the rear[3]. This situation is repeated on the north-west side of Pride Hill, Shrewsbury, where a combination of archaeological, architectural, and documentary evidence has shown the existence of a number of late thirteenth- and fourteenth-century halls opening on to courtyards, set behind lines of shops, with chambers above, facing the street. Underneath the halls are stone undercrofts with access from the lower level at the rear, as the ground falls away to the river (Baker et al 1993).

Undercrofts appear to occur in significant numbers where the topography requires the creation of a solid, level platform for the house above. They often appear to have been designed to provide secure, fireproof accommodation, which implies the storage of high-value goods, the relative value of which is perhaps indicated by the variety of embellishment to the interiors. However, no other town or city in England seems to have an undercroft in every building on the main street frontages. It is possible that the key factor in the consistent use of the one type of town house along Chester's main streets is the peculiar topography of the city, which lends itself to a two-level system.

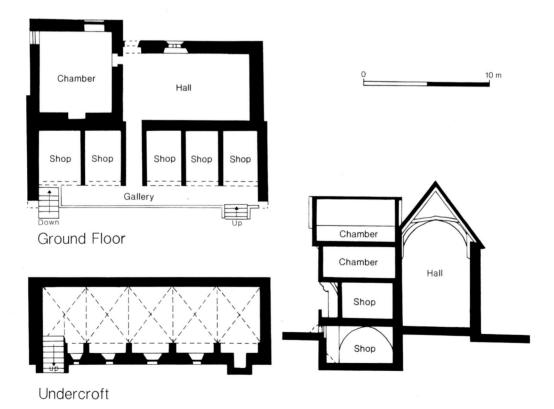

Fig 63 Tackley's Inn, Oxford (after Faulkner)

The Row walkway essentially consists of an arcade above an undercroft, and whilst this arrangement is unique to Chester, evidence for arcades linking series of buildings can be found elsewhere – notably at the Pentice in Winchester. The early fourteenth-century date of this development, together with its High Street location next to the Buttercross in Winchester and its occupation by a single group of traders, make it interestingly comparable with the early lengths of the Chester Rows. Recent research demonstrates that the development of this arcade was sporadic and gradual (Harris forthcoming).

William Stukeley made reference to Kendal as a parallel to Chester, but later authors have dismissed this idea because Kendal now consists almost exclusively of eighteenth- and nineteenth-century buildings. However there is evidence in the records of the Lonsdale family that the appearance of the main streets of Kendal was very different in Stukeley's time (Fig 64). One typical entry reads

These houses, one of which is now possessed by Mr. Redman and a shop thereto by Eden Howard and the other house by Thos. Kendal were about 20 years since rebuilt by Mr. Redman before which they had galleries hanging over the Street, supported by pillars from the Ground and in the building he took in the open part within those Pillars as far as the Galleries hung over, which might be a Yard deep and the Houses may be about 15 yards in Front[4].

Other entries would seem to imply that these galleries were at street level, although their owners appear to have been able to enclose the space that they oversailed without reference to the town authorities. Another description refers to a building that appears to have a plan very similar to that of a Row building, 'At the North end of the said Newbiggin and adjoining thereunto is a Shop with a Gallery and Warehouse over it and a Cellar under it....[5]'

Despite these intriguing references from Kendal and other examples, the evidence does not suggest the general existence of Row systems elsewhere in England during the medieval period. What is, however, becoming clear is that in the intensely commercial parts of large towns and cities the distributive trades commonly operated from two levels within town houses. Thus, the basic form of the Chester Rows buildings is not dissimilar to many other town houses being constructed at the same period and the Rows appear to have resulted from a specialised adaptation of an established building type. The peculiarity of Chester lies in its concentration of examples of this one type and their development into a coherent system.

Fig 64 A late nineteenth-century view of Stricklandgate, Kendal, showing raised galleries as described by Stukeley (reproduced by kind permission of Kendal Library, Cumbria County Council)

Foreign parallels

From the beginning, antiquarians and others have sought parallels for the Rows, not only in England, but in Europe and further afield. Comparisons have been made with Thun and Berne in Switzerland, with Padua and Bologna in Italy, the bastide towns of Gascony (Fig 65), and even Leptis Magna in Libya. Searching for such links is not unreasonable. The English kings had territory in, or connections by marriage with, much of western Europe. The gentry, their troops, monks, and other clerics commonly travelled on crusade or pilgrimage. Craftsmen for great royal and monastic building projects were sometimes drawn from the continent. The exchange of ideas and architectural styles in the medieval period is well documented[6].

However, whilst architectural style and decoration vary across medieval Europe, the houses of the merchant classes remain similar in form. Girouard (1985, 127) remarks

> A combination of forces all over Europe produced that most typical feature of medieval towns, the row of high merchants' houses usually from four to six storeys high, with the lower portion for business, a middle for residence and sometimes further space for storage in the attics.... There are contrasts in size, and in opulence of carved or moulded detail depending on the prosperity of the town and the richness of the individual merchant. But the basic pattern remains remarkably the same.

Given this similarity of form it would be surprising not to find, in one or two places at least, the evolution of a covered way at ground or first floor level. Girouard goes on to show how Italian merchants in particular would congregate in their own city states and abroad to exchange information and strike bargains. Eventually special loggias were built, the forerunners of the bourse and the exchange. In London, rather to their disgust, the Italians met in Lombard Street, '...walking in the rain when it raineth, more like pedlars than merchants' (Selfridge 1918, 216).

The earliest examples of arcaded and tiered market places are Greek and Roman in date. Trajan's Market, in the Forum at Rome, is perhaps the most spectacular example, where one of the huge hemicycles was surmounted by a high-rise structure with rows of shops on every floor, opening on to passages lit by semicircular arched arcades (Krautheimer 1982). Arcaded streets were a feature of Roman towns and cities, providing shade rather than shelter from the rain. It may have reached its most extensive and opulent form in the new capital of the empire at Constantinople. A long stretch of the main street, the *Mese*, was flanked by colonnades as it approached the Forum, as was its older continuation, the *Regia*, which led from the Forum to the palace gate. The Forum itself was a huge oval or circle enclosed by

Fig 65   The arcades of Castelnau de Montmiral, France (reproduced by kind permission of Peter Humphries)

double-tier colonnades. The original construction of these colonnades is credited to Emperor Constantine I (306–37), following the transfer of power from Rome to Byzantium in 330. Manuel Chrysoloras, a Greek scholar who taught in Florence during the fourteenth century, provides the comment, which is so reminiscent of sixteenth-century descriptions of Chester, 'that one might traverse the entire city completely under shelter' (Grenville 1990, 457). By that time, Constantinople had suffered many vicissitudes, including its sacking in 1204 during the Fourth Crusade. Yet this eyewitness account of the fourteenth century shows that the colonnades existed at that date. This form of building had a strong influence on some medieval squares and market places. In the twelfth century, St Mark's Square, Venice, was surrounded by two-tier arcades, fronting shops and commercial premises. This arrangement survived until the fifteenth century when redevelopment began. A similar form with an arcaded first floor was used at a later date on the exterior of the Doge's Palace, begun in 1343, and in the courtyard of the Fondaco dei Tedeschi of 1505, with its four tiers of arcades (Girouard 1985, 100–12).

Although there is no direct parallel with the Chester Rows in any of these examples, it is possible that the idea of arcaded commercial frontages was imported, particularly in view of Edward I's links with Europe and the Near East. The king had been involved in the crusades in 1270–73 and after an inconclusive campaign at Acre, he returned home via Savoy where he met his future military engineer, James of St George (Prestwich 1988). There were other links; the embassy headed by Geoffrey de Langley to the Il-Khan of Persia visited Constantinople in 1292. Harvey (1971) notes that the expedition included *Robertus sculptor*, 'who may well have been another artist equipped with a sketch book'.

The most convincing Byzantine parallel in a building project of the period occurs in one of the great architectural achievements of the reign of Edward I, Caernarfon Castle, begun in 1283 immediately after the subjugation of the Welsh. James of St George designed the castle with polygonal towers and dark bands of stone, reminiscent of the fifth-century Theodosian walls of the imperial city. Caernarfon was the capital of North Wales and the centre of Welsh resistance; also it was the legendary foundation of Magnus Maximus, father of Constantine I, who was adopted by the Welsh as a folk hero. In 1283, Edward I appropriated the legend for his own purposes, exhuming and reburying a body believed to be that of Magnus Maximus, and building a stronghold that was designed as a symbol of his own imperial intentions. Taylor (in Brown *et al* 1963, 370–1) argues that this similarity in style could only be achieved from a description by someone who knew the defences of the imperial capital and could instruct the master mason in the characteristics to be reproduced. A possible source of this description is suggested as Sir William de Cicon, constable at Flint and Conway, a protégé of Otto de Grandson, the justiciar of North Wales, whose seat of power was intended to be at Caernarfon.

We therefore have the intriguing possibility that the Rows of Chester may have been influenced in some way by the arcades of Constantinople, in the same way as the appearance of Caernarfon Castle was influenced by that city's walls. Or is it just that these two very

different cities realised the advantages that a two-tier commercial system could bring? The carefully designed classical arcades of Constantinople are certainly a far cry from the erratic widths, heights, styles, and materials of the Chester Rows and there is no evidence that the Rows were ever intended to form part of a coherently designed whole. It is therefore more likely that the inspiration, if any, came from nearer parallels.

Medieval arcades occur along street frontages throughout Europe. For example, the remains of what appears to have been a continuous street-level arcade passing through different medieval buildings can be seen at Dol in Brittany[7]. Berne in Switzerland exhibits a system of walkways not unlike the Chester Rows. The oversailed walkway is now virtually at ground level and the deep undercrofts have steps that are accessed via cumbersome trapdoor constructions in the street. This latter difficulty of access has possibly prevented the survival of a two-level commercial arrangement, except where there are shops under the Hochtrottoirs at the eastern end of the Gerechtigskeitgasse; the one part of the system where the walkway is raised as high as the Chester Rows.

Another European parallel is at Thun, also in Switzerland, where there are the same constituent parts of semi-subterranean undercrofts, raised walkways with

Fig 66 Raised walkways in the Obertor, Meersburg, Baden-Württemberg, Germany (reproduced by kind permission of Stadt Meersburg)

stallboards, occasional steps between the walkway and the street, and shops at the upper level. However, the walkway, which extends along both sides of the main street, is oversailed by only one building. It is therefore similar to the surviving stretch of raised walkway in front of Gamul House, 52–58 Lower Bridge Street (Fig 164).

In the small town of Meersburg, in Baden-Württemberg, Germany, there is a line of timber-framed houses in the Obertor, which are raised on street-level brick and stone undercrofts, with a galleried walkway at first-floor level (Fig 66). The earliest surviving buildings in this group are believed to date from 1620, significantly later than the Chester Rows.

Given the volume of building in Chester around the time of Edward I, Smith and others have sought comparisons with the bastide towns of south-west France. Many had a quadrilateral plan divided into quarters and were laid out around a market place, often with an arcade or cornière around it. However, this arcading is limited to the ground floor and the market place frontages, unlike the Chester Rows. Prestwich (1988, 308–11) believes that the bastides are as much a feature of urban centres in France, as the product of an imposed English policy. However, they do demonstrate the desire to create new towns in great numbers and to experiment with new forms of urban planning; over 50 being founded during Edward I's reign, mostly on new sites. Whilst the Crown was involved in the foundation of about three-quarters of these towns, many were partnerships with local lords or carried out by the king's officials or trusted allies[8]. The gridded and walled plan of New Winchelsea, laid out on a greenfield site after 1292, demonstrates that such ideas were transferable to England. Some of Edward I's courtiers also created towns in newly conquered Wales, such as Ruthin and Denbigh, and his court officials, and even some prominent merchants had a role to play in these new initiatives. It is therefore possible that the idea of experimenting with new urban forms is at least partly behind the development of the Chester Rows.

Conclusions

Reviewing the information and ideas presented in this and earlier chapters, the complexity of the factors and issues in considering the origin and evolution of the Rows is immediately apparent. Alternative conclusions can be argued. The antiquarians and early commentators seem to have had a desire to select one factor as the key to the origin of the Rows. All their hypotheses are unsatisfactory because it appears more likely that this raised gallery system is the result of the combination of a number of different factors, peculiar to Chester.

The major driving force must have been commercial. Towns were created for and prospered on trade. The livelihood of the merchants who built and occupied the houses that contain the Rows was trade. Such merchants lived and worked in a relatively small area in the centre of the walled city and when wealth and opportunity came there was little room to expand. The creation of the Rows effectively doubles the commercial potential of each property, making it possible to trade at both street and Row level. This two-level form of commercial building existed in other English and European towns and the idea was therefore available for transfer to Chester. The key difference is that Chester adopted this form of town house along all its main streets, thus allowing a continuous system to develop.

In the absence of any evidence for an imposed planning scheme, it is likely that the Rows are the result of a general undertaking by the citizens of Chester, perhaps reflecting their growing independence. There is, however, the possibility of specific encouragement at a key period, as a result of the royal interest in the city or from the civic authorities. The advantages of the Rows system are obvious. Both the undercrofts and the shops above had a street frontage, and the Row not only provided a raised walkway giving access to shops and the domestic accommodation, but provided shelter from the rain; this struck the sixteenth- and seventeenth-century commentators as being a very civilised idea. Also the change in ground level between the front and the back of the buildings meant that although the domestic accommodation was at Row level it was also level with the yard or garden behind the house. All this could be achieved through a simple adaptation of the two-level town house type to the peculiarities of the Chester topography.

The paradox remains; that the Rows are public thoroughfares incorporated into private property[9]; an arrangement which probably evolved at an early date. Despite its inherent tensions, this duality was maintained and is part of the story of how the Rows developed and changed in later centuries until they became the system we know today.

6 Late medieval buildings

In the preceding chapters we have described the evidence for the early existence of the Rows of Chester, have discussed how they were constructed and considered their possible origins. Just as remarkable is the story of how the system has survived to the present day, and how the buildings were modified and reconstructed to meet the needs of successive generations of Chester traders[1].

The prosperity enjoyed by Chester in the late thirteenth and early fourteenth centuries suffered a decline in the two centuries that followed. The effects of the outbreaks of plague in the mid-fourteenth century are unknown, but the physical fabric of the city did not go unscathed, with the castle, bridge, and mills all in need of restoration[2]. In the 1350s shops were reported empty and in danger of collapse, and ruined buildings were to be found throughout the city[3]. Among the untenanted properties were the important tenement north of the Stonehall in Bridge Street, the one next to St Bridget's Church (possibly the 'Three Old Arches'), and part of one of the selds[4].

A period of slow revival followed, perhaps accelerating in the closing years of the century when Chester benefited from the patronage of Richard II; for a brief period the city apparently enjoyed an influx of wealth and courtly patronage. This economic recovery was halted by the change in regime, by Chester's involvement in rebellions in 1400 and 1403, and by the revolt of Owen Glendower. The ensuing decades were marked by continuing decline and impoverishment. In 1445, 1484, and 1486 the citizens petitioned the king for a reduction in their fee farm, claiming that the silting of their harbour, the disruption of trade with Wales, and a consequent fall in population had rendered them unable to pay in full[5]. Similar petitions, phrased in what became a conventional format, were made by numerous towns during the fifteenth century and these pleas of urban poverty should not be accepted without question (Dobson 1977, 3–4, 10–3). Nevertheless, the fact that concessions were made by the royal authorities suggests that some of the cries of woe were genuine[6].

In the case of Chester, the records of the annual fee farm payments made to the Crown provide telling evidence of the realities of the economic situation. The fee farm had been set at £100 by Edward I in 1300, when Chester enjoyed considerable prosperity. Detailed accounts survive from 1387–8 until 1476–7[7]. These show that full payment was rarely made during the reign of Richard II, although lower arrears were recorded in the late 1390s. The farm was paid in full throughout the first decade of the fifteenth century, possibly as a result of strict control over a city of suspect loyalty, but from 1411–12 until the farm was reduced by half in 1445–6 full payment was achieved only three times. In other years the amount paid fell as

low as £20, while the cumulative arrears occasionally exceeded £100. John Rothley, the man unfortunate enough to serve as sheriff in 1443–4 and 1444–5, spent 36 weeks in prison for non-payment of the arrears and had all his possessions confiscated. The fact that his outstanding debt was excused and the farm significantly reduced is a clear indication that the authorities recognised the reality of Chester's malaise, which had been dramatically emphasised, but apparently not exaggerated, in the petition of 1445.

Even at the reduced level the fee farm proved impossible to collect and the sheriffs who served between 1449 and 1455 also received royal pardons for their arrears. Full payments were made, however, from the late 1460s until the accounts end in 1476–7. The end of the series at this juncture prevents an assessment of the economic realities underlying the petitions of 1484 and 1486, in which the citizens alleged that the city walls had fallen into decay and that a quarter of the city was 'vastata, desolata, ruinosa et minime inha[b]itata'. Other documentary evidence (see below) does suggest that there was some justification for their claims. Moreover, the archaeological survey of the Rows buildings has revealed a hiatus in building activity in the years 1350–1550. Material from the earlier medieval period (1250–1350) survives in relative abundance, as does fabric from the mid-sixteenth century onwards, but very few buildings or elements of buildings survive from the late fourteenth to the early sixteenth centuries.

The scarcity of references in the documents to building reinforces these archaeological findings. The late fourteenth- and early fifteenth-century records occasionally mention repairs to existing buildings. In 1354–5, for example, almost £1 was spent by the city on a house in Northgate Street; timber, boards, slates, and 'spikyng' were purchased, as too were lime and clay. The same year saw work on a property in Bridge Street; lead was obtained to make a gutter, and boards and nails were also purchased. Two years later both houses needed further repairs; a post was bought to support a wall at the Northgate Street property and a tiler and his servant spent several days working at the house in Bridge Street[8]. In 1404–5 similar repairs were carried out on a house belonging to the Fraternity of St Anne[9].

No building activity is attested in the next three or four decades, but during the 1440s and 1450s there is evidence of one or two citizens applying to rent sections of common land fronting properties in Bridge Street. In 1445 a prominent citizen was granted a piece of waste land extending from the house frontages towards the street (see *Tabulae* in Appendix A) and in 1456 a similar grant was made to another resident of Bridge Street. This waste ground measured 6ft in breadth and 18ft in length (approximately 2 x 6m) and stretched westwards from his entrance as far as Cuppings Lane. He was given permission to enclose and build upon this land and was to pay an annual rent of 6d (sixpence)[10]. In later years he is recorded as paying 6d a year for the encroachment of the stairs next to his home ('gradus iuxta mansum suum')[11]. It is possible that residents of other streets received similar grants, although Bridge Street perhaps witnessed most of this type of activity. Treasurer's rentals of the 1460s refer to shops (some of them newly built) in front of existing houses in Northgate Street and Foregate Street[12]. A few parlours were also built in the 1460s: two in Bridge Street and a third in Eastgate Street[13]. One of the Bridge Street parlours may have been added to a house near St Michael's Church, possibly extending over the Row or street as rent was due to the city for the posts

which supported it[14]. In October 1469 John Botiler was found guilty of causing an obstruction with the parlour built at his home outside the Northgate[15]. The sources therefore suggest that during the 1460s some encroachment was taking place along the main streets, perhaps with the intention of creating additional commercial space or extra domestic accommodation.

Even this modest activity appears to have come to an end in the following decade as the city's fortunes declined still further. A number of shops (perhaps in Foregate Street) were destroyed by fire in 1473–4 and six years later they had still not been rebuilt[16]. In 1476–7 the only evidence for building was the erection of a mud wall on the common soil[17]. Throughout the 1470s the fulling mills were in need of repair and often stood empty for months at a time; in 1479–80 their poor condition caused the adjacent fishery to be blocked[18]. Treasurer's rentals of the early 1480s list many rents in decay, including those due from shops in Eastgate Street, in Bridge Street, and also under the pillory, usually a prime site. Two shops in Watergate Street had fallen down and the building at the corner of Watergate Street and Bridge Street was described as 'ruinosa et prostrata'[19]. It was against this background that the citizens petitioned the king for relief and their claims that a great part of the city lay in ruins therefore had some justification. Some signs of economic recovery can be detected in the 1490s and in the early sixteenth century, but an outbreak of plague in 1517 again disrupted trade. Grass grew a foot high at the market cross and in other city streets (Ormerod 1882, 234).

It can therefore be seen that Chester was not prosperous during the late medieval period. Paradoxically these years of depression may have been crucial to the survival of the Rows, as extensive rebuilding might have led to a loss of continuity and thus destroyed the incentive to maintain the system of galleries. The few new buildings that were constructed during this period are of considerable interest, since they represent the end of one tradition of internal planning and employ more sophisticated carpentry techniques than hitherto.

Plan form

Although the national trend towards the replacement of the open hall by a series of smaller spaces had started in London in the early fourteenth century (Schofield 1984, 18), open halls continue to be at the heart of many houses well into the sixteenth and seventeenth centuries (see Chapter 7). A substantial open hall was the centrepiece of the fifteenth-century rebuilding of the Leche House, 17 Watergate Street (Figs 67 and Pl 7)[20]. In this building, the braced-beam construction of the undercroft ceiling echoes the early fourteenth-century undercrofts at 38–42 Watergate Street (see p24). Dendrochronological sampling of these timbers proved inconclusive (see Appendix B), but the evidence for a fourteenth-century date is supported by the fact that the upper storeys consist of

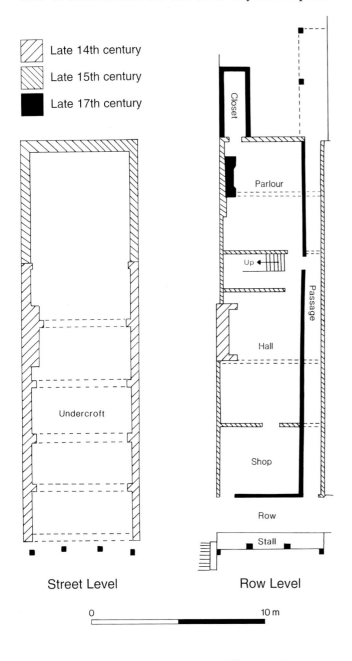

Fig 67 Plans of the Leche House, 17 Watergate Street

a box frame, dated on stylistic evidence to the late fifteenth century, which does not carry through the regular bay spacing of the undercroft. It therefore appears that the upper levels of the building were reconstructed at the later date and this is further supported by the fact that the undercroft required a rear extension to carry the full depth of the new building above.

The plan form of this second phase is a development of the early medieval right-angled hall plan (see Chapter 2). At Row level there is a shop in front of the open hall, which is accessed independently by means of a side passage running through from the Row to the yard at the rear. The position of the fireplace on the east lateral wall of the hall appears to be contemporary with the earlier medieval undercroft, for the stone jambs bond into the ashlar below. Behind the hall is a narrow bay which may have acted as a screens passage, and then there are two bays which probably provided service rooms at Row level with a chamber above. Presumably there was also a chamber above the Row walkway, stall, and shop, with access from a gallery along one side of the hall as at present, but this part of the building was reconstructed in the seventeenth century. This developing plan form must have created a problem with lighting the hall, as in the earlier period the hall appears to have had a window in its rear wall. The demand for more rooms to the rear meant that some form of top-lighting had to be created for the hall, and therefore the present dormer windows in the hall at the Leche House are presumably similar to the original arrangement.

The open hall at the Leche House survived the major seventeenth-century remodelling of the building (see Chapter 7), although it seems to have been sub-divided later (Lawson and Smith 1958, 38–9), only to have its open form subsequently restored. Some smaller houses also seem to have retained their open halls through seventeenth-century remodelling, probably indicating that their plan form and structure dates from an earlier period. These include St Michael's Rectory, 43 Bridge Street (Fig 154), and 8–10 Bridge Street. Both buildings display early seventeenth-century decorative elements, but contain halls that are open in the centre, with substantial galleries on three sides, and stairs on the fourth, although the hall at St Michael's Rectory is at Row + 1 level (Fig 68). Despite its seventeenth-century rebuilding 10 Bridge Street also retains the appearance of earlier buildings as there is no chamber at Row + 2 level (Figs 69,157). Another example of this plan type is 11 Bridge Street, although here a complete refit in the early twentieth century has obliterated all evidence of its origins and only the plan form survives.

At the Old King's Head, 48–50 Lower Bridge Street, a different plan form was adopted. Unfortunately the timbers here proved unsuitable for reliable dendrochronological dating (see Appendix B), but the stylistic evidence suggests a date in the mid-sixteenth century, indicating that this building probably marks the beginning of the great rebuilding discussed in the

Fig 68 Interior of Row + 1 level at St Michael's Rectory, 43 Bridge Street (RCHME © Crown Copyright)

next chapter. Its construction, however, appears to relate more to the late medieval period and therefore it is considered here. At Row level (the Row is now enclosed), the disposition of empty mortices and ceiling joists suggests that a series of small shops was backed by a hall-like space running parallel to the street, recalling the parallel-hall layouts found at 38–42 Watergate Street and 48–52 Bridge Street, which also occupy corner sites (see Chapter 2). However, it is clear that the space in the Old King's Head never formed an open hall, as enough structural evidence remains to show that it has always been ceiled. Nevertheless, the absence of similar mortice evidence for internal subdivision suggests that it was a large room, perhaps echoing the communal functions of the medieval open hall. It is quite unlike later parlours, in that it lies behind, rather than above, the Row, and therefore has no windows on to the main street. The original fenestration of the room is unclear and without clear information about the disposition of buildings to the north and west, or access to the framing behind modern plastering, it is difficult to reconstruct the means of lighting. This is the only building of its type surviving in Chester and it is possible that this is not simply the result of chance destruction of others. It could well be that the Row-level room was unsatisfactorily dark or that its windows prevented extension to the rear, and thus the plan form proved unsatisfactory until the Row was enclosed and adequate lighting could be admitted from the Lower Bridge Street facade (Fig 80).

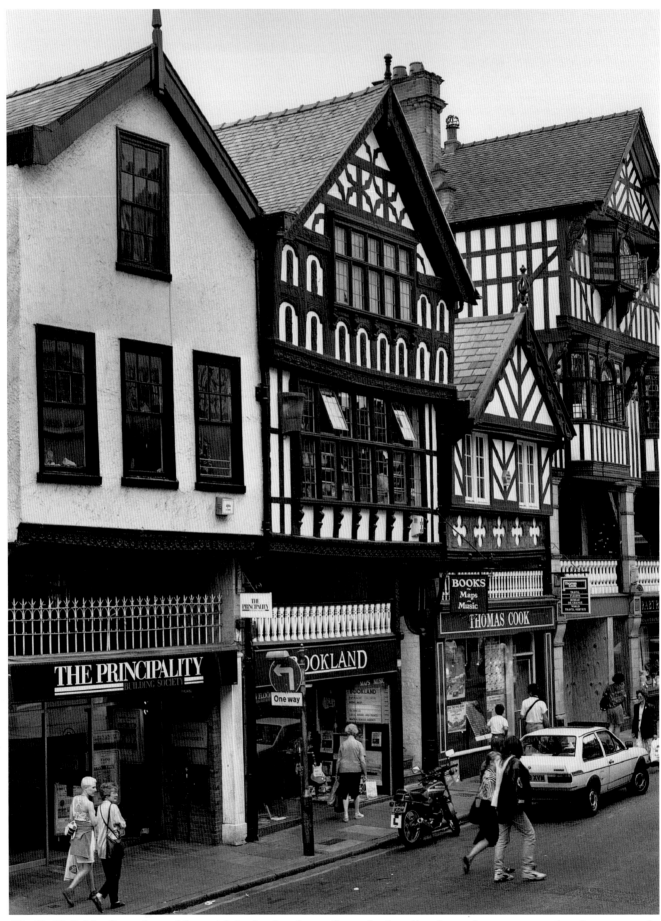

Fig 69 10 Bridge Street (second from right), showing the smaller scale of medieval town houses compared to the seventeenth- and nineteenth-century buildings on either side (RCHME © Crown Copyright)

All these buildings contained a Row walkway as an integral part of the structure, and there is no evidence that the difficult economic situation during this period led to an abandonment of the Row system.

Unfortunately no documentary material has been found relating to any of the specific buildings discussed above. The sources do, however, provide a little evidence of the layout of domestic structures. Tenements occupied by wealthy citizens typically comprised a complex of structures. In the 1380s the house of the Palatinate master mason contained *'cameras, subcameras, duas cameras iuxta coquinam, unam domum vocat, yatehouse et aulam'*[21]. In October 1419 the home of the mayor-elect, John Hope, was attacked by a group of armed men. They broke into his *'domos, aulam, cameram et coquinam'*, stole some of his possessions and caused his wife to miscarry[22]. Hope's property perhaps lay on the west side of Lower Bridge Street, near Castle Lane, and appears also to have had a garden in which a malt kiln had been built[23].

These, and other occasional, references to *'aula'* confirm that the hall was a feature of Chester's late medieval houses. One is attested in Foregate Street in 1385, and in 1445, when William Lely was granted leave to enclose and build upon a small piece of ground in Bridge Street, it was described as lying *'ex opposito ostium aule'*[24]. There is also considerable evidence for smaller rooms: chambers used as living and sleeping accommodation; solars leased out, often in association with shops; and cellars, which are presumably to be equated with the undercrofts, sometimes in separate occupation from the house above[25].

Building: construction

Although there are few buildings or building elements surviving in Chester from the late medieval period it is possible to comment on some of the apparent developments in building construction.

Timber framing

Little evidence for late medieval timber framing survives. Perhaps the most interesting complete facade is the Castle Street elevation of the rear wing of the Old King's Head (Fig 70). The precise date of this part of the building is uncertain, but it seems to have a raking strut roof with trenched purlins, which would place it in the late medieval period. However, it is demonstrably earlier than the main range, for which we have suggested a date in the mid-sixteenth century (see p65). This rear wing is thus one of the few buildings we can place securely in the later medieval period, before the great rebuilding of 1550–1640.

At street level the range is in stone and may be the remains of the *'domus lapidea'* of Peter the Clerk (see Chapter 2). Above is timber framing with square panels. The sill beam is of two pieces, jointed with a simple

through-splayed scarf. One stud has been removed for the insertion of a later window. The pattern of framing suggests that the midrail extends across two panels and is then interrupted by a post. Only one section of midrail survives intact; to the left it has been removed for the window, whilst to the right it has apparently been sawn off to frame into the post of the later range. The absence of peg holes for a stud over the left-hand window suggests that this is the position of an original opening. The storey above was originally jettied to the west as well as to the south, as evidenced by the survival of a dragon beam. To the south the jetty survives and is held on bull-nosed joists, very roughly cut, some laid upright, while others are laid flat. The pattern of wall framing is the same as the floor below, with an inserted three-light casement to the left and a three-light casement, possibly in an original opening, to the right.

A small undated corner building at 53 Lower Bridge Street is also of some interest (Fig 101). The long St Olave Street facade reveals a technique of framing not unlike that of the early range of the Old King's Head, although the scantling of the timber is slight and it may well be later in date. What is unusual here is the disposition of carpenters' marks. Rather than beginning at one end of the building and proceeding to the other, the post at the back of the shop on the Row level is number I and the other posts are numbered outwards from this in both directions. Thus both the Row and the house to the rear contain posts numbered II and III. The implications of this are interesting, as it suggests that, in this case at least, the demarcation

Fig 70 Castle Street elevation of rear wing at the Old King's Head, 48–50 Lower Bridge Street (RCHME © Crown Copyright)

between the Row walkway with its shop and the private house was implicit from the date of construction. Whether this suggests a split ownership from the outset, with one client for the Row and shop and another for the house, is uncertain.

Some vestigial timber framing of the late fifteenth century may also survive at the Falcon, 6 Lower Bridge Street. Here the survival of a jetty on bull-nosed joists, together with a substantial dragon beam and carrying joists laid on their backs, may represent work of this period, although the decorative exterior is clearly of sixteenth- or seventeenth-century date. Inside, at Row level, there is an element of heavily restored timber framing in the position of the rear wall of the former Row. This includes a window of diagonally-set wooden mullions, probably dating from the fifteenth century[26]. The dragon beam and large arch-braced corner post associated with the jetty at 86–88 Lower Bridge Street, which lies just outside the Row system, may also belong to this period.

Timber arcades

Two Row buildings of the later medieval period contain timber arcades that are a development of the arcades described in Chapter 4. At 10 Watergate Street the masonry side walls of the undercroft define a space 8.7m (28ft 6in) in width, originally divided by a central four-post arcade (Fig 71). The three posts to the rear survive and have provided an estimated felling date range of *c* 1528–59 (see Appendix B). The arcade is constructed of fully jowled posts, resting on pad stones, and measuring 280 x 350mm at the base. Curved braces support an arcade plate, one element of which survives, displaying single-pegged, splayed, bridled joints at each end to take extensions. It may be significant that this is the first known instance in Chester of an arcade plate constructed of more than one timber, possibly reflecting the fact that this technique is superior to the earlier arcades, described in Chapter 4, and therefore larger spaces could be spanned, rendering single timbers too short for the job. An alternative explanation is that by this date, the supply of trees was dwindling and carpenters were forced to use shorter elements. The cross beams are also massive, supported by upward bracing from the posts, resting on the arcade plate and contained within the jowled heads of the posts. Few original joists survive although the evidence of the cross beams suggests that they were approximately 150mm square, housed at their northern ends and tenoned to the south. This final development of the timber arcade in Chester created a rigid, gridded system of beams capable of flooring over wider areas than either of the earlier types.

The framed construction above the undercroft at 10 Watergate Street is clearly later in date, the upper structure being markedly narrower than the undercroft. Evidence observed in the east wall of the undercroft shows that there is no relationship between the framing

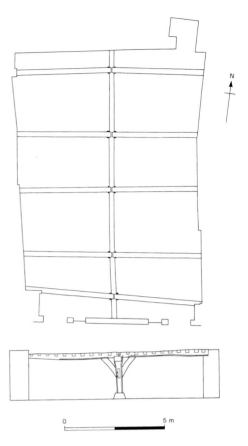

Fig 71 Plan and section of the undercroft at 10 Watergate Street

of the undercroft and that of the structure above, the latter simply resting upon the former in a rather precarious manner. There is no evidence in the building above of a subdivided open hall, and the survival of elements of an early seventeenth-century decorative scheme suggest that the upper levels were reconstructed *c* 1600–20. It is perhaps interesting to note that while the open hall of the Leche House survived the seventeenth century intact, albeit with the introduction of a new decorative scheme, 10 Watergate Street suffered far more radical treatment. Despite the fact that the building had been totally rebuilt in the mid-sixteenth century, the structure above the Row level was apparently entirely reconstructed only 50–70 years later, presumably to conform with the new fashion for a greater number of smaller rooms with ceilings.

The undercroft within the Old King's Head also contains a seven-post arcade of this later-medieval type (Fig 72). Notwithstanding the absence of dendrochronological dates (see Appendix B) it is strikingly similar to the arcade in 10 Watergate Street, possibly suggesting that it is the work of the same craftsman or workshop. In this building, and in the five-bay, late fifteenth-century undercroft of the demolished 63–65 Watergate Street (Lawson and Smith 1958, 22–23), the arcade posts of the undercrofts correspond with the bay divisions above, indicating a continuity of structure.

This type of construction follows closely that of the Merchant Adventurers' Hall, York, a building which contains a number of unusual features and is dated on documentary and dendrochronological evidence to 1357–61 (RCHME 1981, 82–8). In that building there is a slightly irregular arcade within the undercroft, which ranges between 11.1m and 12.6m wide. The heads of the posts thicken and clasp the arcade plate, and there is four-way bracing to both this plate and the transverse beams. There is a corresponding arcade directly above, the posts of which support the valley plate between two parallel roofs. The arcade at 10 Watergate Street dates from nearly two centuries later, yet the similarities are striking, suggesting that this technique was in use over a long period of time. Alternatively, the technique may represent a late export from the eastern to the western side of the Pennines.

A structure that formerly stood at the corner of Bridge Street and Watergate Street may also have contained an arcade of this form. Known as the 'Stone Seld' by 1425 and as the 'Staven Selds' by 1508, this massive building, 17.03 x 19.66m, may well have derived its conflicting names from having a stone-walled undercroft containing a timber arcade[27]. These dimensions are a little smaller than the space between the medieval undercrofts at 12 Bridge Street and 11 Watergate Street and the present building form may therefore represent encroachment into what was formerly public space, possibly a market.

Roofs

As was mentioned in Chapter 4, few medieval roof structures survive in Chester. During the substantial restoration in the 1970s of Gamul House, 52–58 Lower Bridge Street, the roof over the hall was recorded by RCHME[28]. This is now hidden by a barrel-vaulted plaster ceiling from which hang seventeenth-century carved wooden pendants (Fig 165), but the records show the survival of a number of common rafter trusses linked by a collar purlin. The span fits the presumably thirteenth- or fourteenth-century walls of the hall, so it is possible that, despite an irregularity in the spacing of the trusses which indicates some loss or reworking of the structure, this may be the earliest roof in Chester.

The other early roofs that survive *in situ* are over the hall at the Leche House, dating from the late fifteenth century, and that at 63 Northgate Street, a mid-fifteenth-century building outside the Row system (but see p145 and Tables 7 and 7a). Both these buildings have roofs at right angles to the street with a gabled frontage. This arrangement is obviously suited to buildings on narrow plots and must have been the dominant form in Chester. It needed only extra length to cover the Row and stall-board, as can be seen at 63 Northgate Street (Figs 73 and 76). In this building, which has a pavement level walkway rather than an elevated gallery, there is a direct correspondence between the bay divisions at roof level and the plan of the walkway, shop and open hall beneath. The two-bay chamber over the shop and walk-

Fig 72   Timber arcade at the Old King's Head, 48–50 Lower Bridge Street (RCHME © Crown Copyright)

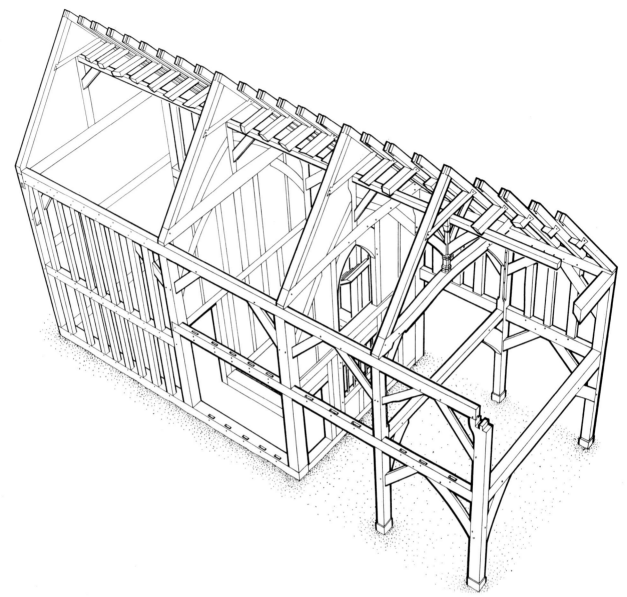

Fig 73 Axonometric projection of 63 Northgate Street, part of the Blue Bell

way provided the opportunity for an open, mid-chamber truss, which in this case is a crown post (Fig 174). The open hall at the Leche House is spanned by an arch-braced collar truss. At either end of the hall are king-post trusses: this form of truss is also found in the chamber at Row + 1 level behind the hall. Here the truss has a canted tie beam with broad curving braces to the bay posts (Fig 74). The Row chamber was remodelled and enlarged in the seventeenth century, and its central truss is a false hammer beam[29]. One of the purlins is a reused moulded bressumer which may have come from the fifteenth-century frontage (Fig 75).

With five medieval roofs known in Chester (including the evidence from the Falcon and 16 Northgate Street described in Chapter 4) it is just possible to suggest the variety of trusses used. The three crown-post roofs span the period from the early thirteenth century to the mid-fifteenth century. This confirms recent discoveries which indicate that crown-post roofs were used more commonly in north-west England than had been

previously thought[30]. It can therefore be demonstrated that the crown-post roof was one of a number of options used by medieval carpenters for both rural and urban buildings in the north-west over a long period. Its comparative scarcity must be not only a reflection of the survival of few buildings from this period in the region, but also of the fact that where these buildings have survived, as in Chester, they have been subject to considerable alteration.

The same problem exists when considering the common rafter roof over the hall at Gamul House. With the exception of the south aisle of St Andrew's Church, Tarvin (Harris and Lever 1966, 106), there is no other known medieval unpurlined roof surviving in Cheshire. Is the Gamul House roof an exception or is it the one remaining example of a type formerly common in Chester? In contrast, the arch-braced collar and king-post trusses of the Leche House fit much more easily into the known distributions of these forms of truss. The former was particularly favoured

Fig 74 Chamber behind the hall at Row + 1 level at the Leche House, 17 Watergate Street (RCHME © Crown Copyright)

above the open halls of manor houses of the late fifteenth and early sixteenth century, which survive in some numbers in Cheshire and adjacent counties[31].

The standard form of roof valley is for the common rafters to converge onto a plate or an obliquely set jack rafter. In Chester, however, several buildings exhibit a different form of valley construction in which there is no solid member at the bottom of the valley; in effect it 'flies'. In these cases the timber frames beneath each roof do not abut below the valley but are set between 300 and 600mm apart. Proof that such an arrangement was planned rather than accidental comes from the Falcon, where the early thirteenth-century passing-brace roof was carried by a timber-framed wall, spanning a single undercroft that extends below the void. The doubling up of sill beams and inner walls provided a necessary way of spreading the roofing thrusts. The benefits of a valley over a void, particularly in the reduction of problems with rot in the valley plate, may also have influenced the adoption of such a method of construction. Similar arrangements are preserved at 63–65 Northgate Street and 69–71 Watergate Street. In view of its excessive use of timber and despite later utilisation of the resultant void, which was particularly suitable for the insertion of chimney stacks and fireplaces, it is surprising to find the technique employed as late as the mid-fifteenth century at 63–65 Northgate Street (but see p145), although in this case it may have related to separate ownership of the two structures, albeit over a single cellar.

Fig 75 False hammer beam truss over the Row chamber at the Leche House, 17 Watergate Street: also showing the moulded bressumer reused as a purlin (RCHME © Crown Copyright)

Building: craftsmen and materials

The depressed state of Chester's economy in the late medieval period did not encourage ambitious building projects, but some new work was undertaken and there was an ongoing need for repair and maintenance which provided employment for building workers. The borough court rolls, which name those men who were involved in litigation, allow at least a percentage of these craftsmen to be identified. In the years 1350–1506 150 carpenters are attested, as well as 47 masons, 34 slaters, 18 painters, 17 glaziers, and 10 plumbers. As the fourteenth- and fifteenth-century houses of the city were predominantly timber-framed the numerical superiority of the carpenters is readily explained. The numbers of other building workers perhaps convey an impression of the relative quantity of work available for each craft.

Stone houses were unusual in late medieval Chester and therefore served as significant landmarks. Thus in June 1424 the men who took part in the Corpus Christi Day riot were said to have attacked the king's ministers at Castle Lane End '*iuxta le stouneplace que quondam fuit Petri de Thornton chivaler*'[32]. Surviving stone undercrofts were highly valued and specifically referred to as such in property deeds[33]. The masons were perhaps employed primarily on royal and ecclesiastical buildings or on public building projects. In 1464 the Pentice was rebuilt and, although most of the expenses involved the purchase of timber and the wages of carpenters and sawyers, 13 corbels were purchased and a mason and a carver were employed for two weeks[34]. The city wall also required regular repair, a task not helped by citizens appropriating stones from it for their own use[35]. Muragers' accounts reveal that in 1440 John Asser, master mason of the Palatinate, received £10 for building the upper section of the city wall extending from the tower on 'le Walshegate' to the old wall next to the bridge[36]. Accounts also survive of the weekly payments made by the muragers to John Southworth and his small team of quarrymen in 1477–8; the city mason received 3s (shillings) a week and the others half that amount[37]. The master masons of the Palatinate are mentioned occasionally in the sources and appear to have been prosperous individuals, as could be expected. In 1357, John de Tudenham was granted a messuage and cellar in Bridge Street, and in the early fifteenth century John Asser had a house with a cellar[38]. During the late fourteenth and early fifteenth centuries, however, masons were not a large occupational group and there was apparently little demand for their skills.

The carpenters were the most numerous of the building craftsmen; by the early fifteenth century, if not before, they had assumed a corporate identity and maintained a light in the church of the Carmelite friars[39]. Direct evidence for a gild comes in 1437 and thereafter occasional entries show their stewards demanding payment of customary dues and of contributions to the gild pageant[40]. Despite the existence of the gild, it is clear that throughout the period a percentage of carpenters were non-citizens who paid an annual fine to the authorities for permission to engage in their trade[41]. Apparently unable to earn a living from carpentry alone they are occasionally attested supplementing their income by brewing ale or brothel-keeping[42]. Others worked in the city on a more casual basis, paying for board and lodging for a few weeks, possibly during the summer months[43].

Other carpenters were more prosperous, employing servants and selling building materials[44]. The most successful became freemen. John Richardson, wright, entered the freedom in October 1455, and was followed by his son Richard in 1474[45]. Both men earned their living as carpenters, but a second son opted to become a draper, possibly viewing this as a more promising career[46]. Only one carpenter is known to have held high civic office in the fifteenth century; Roger Burgess who served as sheriff in 1482–3[47]. He was perhaps the leading city carpenter of his day and may well have been involved in the building programme underway at St Werburgh's Abbey in the closing years of the fifteenth century[48]. Evidently no prejudice existed which prevented carpenters joining the ruling élite; the fact that Burgess was the only representative perhaps indicates that there was little opportunity in late medieval Chester for these craftsmen to accumulate the necessary wealth. The master carpenters of the Palatinate stood slightly apart, as befitted men of their status and substance, but they occasionally became involved in the social life of the city. Robert Scot, for example, lived in Bridge Street and in his will asked to be buried in St Oswald's Church. He left his 'chyppynax' to the carpenters' light in the Carmelite church[49].

The predominance of timber-framed buildings resulted in an ever-present fear of fire, demonstrated by the regular presentments of people before the city's courts for '*affraia ignis*'[50]. Bakehouses, kilns and kitchens were often built as separate structures in order to minimise fire risk, while the hearths of the city cooks appear to have been sited in the street, on the common soil[51]. The occasional reference to '*caminus ferri*' and one mention of a chimney made by a smith, implies that attempts were made to contain fire and flame in non-combustible materials[52]. Such precautions were not always successful and the history of medieval Chester is punctuated by outbreaks of fire.

Somewhat surprisingly no building regulations or other controls over the use of combustible materials have yet emerged from Chester's medieval records, although they certainly existed by the seventeenth century[53]. London had regulated against the use of thatch as a roofing material as early as the twelfth century (Keene 1985, I, 172–3 and n1). It is possible that in Chester private restrictions were in force, at least within the walls. A lease of 1500 for a house in Watergate Street specified that it should not be roofed with thatch, shingles, or boards, but only with Welsh

Fig 76 Fifteenth-century roof at 63 Northgate Street, part of the Blue Bell (RCHME © Crown Copyright)

slate or tiles[54]. Moreover, few thatchers appear to have been at work in the city during the late medieval period, and of these only one, John Wright of Foregate Street, enjoyed a working life of any duration. He seems to have worked primarily outside the walls where the risk posed by thatched roofs was less serious[55].

There were, on the other hand, considerable numbers of slaters, so many in fact that the city sought to control their pay. In 1407 four slaters were accused of taking excessive wages and it was perhaps the prospect of regular and well-paid employment which encouraged a slater from the Kendal area to migrate to Chester a few years later[56]. He may have made the journey by ship, as did at least some of the slates. In July 1399 a cart laden with 'sclatstones' and pulled by seven horses was making its laborious way up from the Watergate when its left wheel slipped and ran over a man, killing him instantly[57]. A century later, a Beaumaris trader owed money for the carriage of 'sclatestones' from Wales to the Portpool[58].

None of Chester's slaters grew wealthy. There is no record of any slater becoming a freeman and many were known by an occupational by-name. Their wages were always slightly lower than those paid to carpenters: 4d (fourpence) a day compared to 5d or 6d[59]. They had no gild of their own, but were linked to that of the carpenters[60]. Like the poorer members of that craft, some may have come to the city on an occasional basis and their employment was no doubt uncertain in the winter months. One or two tilers occur in the records, and although it is impossible to be sure that there was always a clear differentiation between the terms, it does seem that clay tiles were occasionally used. Repairs to a house in St John's Lane in 1404–5 necessitated the employment of both a slater and a 'tegulator', each receiving the same daily wage[61]. Fragments of medieval roofing tiles were found on the Northgate Brewery site, including one with an olive green glaze and moulded decoration (Davey 1973). In the seventeenth century a property in this area was known as the Green Hall[62]. A building called 'le Tile howses' stood near Cow Lane in the 1490s and it is possible that tiles were manufactured in the city from clay obtained around Gorse Stacks[63]. Debts for tiles have been traced; 4000 cost 33s 4d (thirty-three shillings and fourpence) in 1489, and when Richard Slater broke 100 tiles in the custody of Patrick Slater, the latter demanded 6s 8d (six shillings and eightpence) in damages[64]. 'Shyngyls' and 'shyngil nayls' were purchased for repairs to a house in Northgate Street in the mid-fourteenth century, but only two shinglers have emerged from the documentary sources, Thomas Waltham who entered the freedom in 1495 and David Shingler who married a slater's widow[65].

Throughout the period there are occasional references to plumbers, but they seem never to have been a large occupational group in late medieval Chester. A major part of a plumber's work was undoubtedly the manufacture and maintenance of gutters. In c 1461 a gutter on the Pentice was repaired at a cost of eleven shillings and fourpence-halfpenny[66].Such work was vital. After 24lb of lead had been stolen from the gutters of his house in Bridge Street in 1501, Richard Wirrall complained that the walls had become 'putrid and corrupt'[67]. Lead was also used in windows and plumbers are not infrequently associated with glaziers, acting as pledge in court or as surety for a debt[68].

Chester was an important centre for window glass during the fourteenth century and glaziers are attested throughout the late medieval period (Blair and Ramsey 1991, 275, 277). Since they are often named together with stainers and painters their work was probably in ecclesiastical rather than domestic contexts. Thus John Glasier of St John's Lane, who sued three chaplains for trespass in 1428, may have been carrying out some work in the nearby Collegiate church[69]. Later in the century the glazier William Martin was in trouble with St Werburgh's Abbey for non-payment of a debt of 6s (six shillings) for two panes of glass[70]. There is no evidence for domestic window glazing in late medieval Chester, although such comfort had been known in London from the mid-thirteenth century onwards (Schofield 1984, 93). Painted chambers ('camera depicta') existed in the Black Hall, Pepper Street in 1369[71] and some of the painters recorded in the sources may have been employed by private individuals to decorate their homes, but there is no record of this. Only the abbot of St Werburgh's is known to have sought the services of a painter. In March 1485 he made an agreement with John Deyne who was to serve as a painter for a year, receiving a fee of 49s 10d (forty-nine shillings and tenpence) plus a robe. Three years later Deyne claimed that 16s 6d (sixteen shillings and sixpence) was still outstanding and took the abbot to court[72]. It seems likely that during the late medieval period the churches and religious houses were the best customers of the city's specialist craftsmen, such as the glaziers and painters. The vast majority of building work did not require the skills of such men, but were the product of the carpenters, the wrights, and the unskilled labourers who carried the raw materials and prepared the daub.

Conclusions

The limited survival of late medieval fabric in the Row buildings confirms the documentary evidence that this period was one of economic decline and limited building activity. There is no record of any major projects being undertaken by the civic authorities and virtually no church building work in progress until the late fifteenth century, with the exception of the Troutbeck Chapel at St Mary's, which was the result of a benefaction by one wealthy individual. The larger town houses were, however, developing during this period with an increasing number of rooms. Given the relatively few new houses being constructed, this must have been achieved largely by additions and alterations to existing structures.

The late fourteenth- and fifteenth-century sources contain few references to the Rows, possibly because they were an accepted feature of the city's landscape. Fleshmongers' Row remained the focus of the butchers' retail trade and butchers are attested occupying tenements at Row level and in the cellars below[73]. Retail outlets for prepared food continued to cluster in Cooks' Row and Baxter Row at the corner of Northgate and Eastgate Street. One prominent family of cooks is known to have rented a cellar and shop in this area from 1453–4 until at least the 1480s (Brownbill 1913, no 01028). There is mention of a Glovers' Row in Eastgate Street in 1426[74]. The earliest reference to the Mercers' Row on the east side of Bridge Street dates from 1493; its appearance may perhaps be interpreted as a sign of Chester's reviving economic fortunes at this time (Dodgson 1981, 21).

Shops were to be found throughout the late medieval city and commonly formed part of the property holdings of prominent citizens and local gentlemen[75]. The dimensions of shops are not recorded but it seems likely that they were small, as they had been in the preceding period. The few shops known to have been built in the fifteenth century as a result of encroachment, and sometimes described as 'iuxta portam', would also have been small[76].

Cellars were often mentioned in property deeds and were sometimes in separate ownership/occupancy from the dwelling above[77]. These were presumably the undercroft spaces. Some were doubtless valued for the secure storage space they provided, while others evidently served as retail outlets for ale. These ale-cellars were sometimes found beneath the homes of prominent citizens and could be named after these wealthy men, in whose households the ale was perhaps brewed[78]. The city's tapsters also rented cellars in which they plied their trade and the more elaborate undercrofts were possibly used as taverns[79]. Butchers traded from cellars in Watergate Street and there is a little evidence for the use of these spaces for the storage of fish[80].

It seems likely that the shops and undercrofts along the four main streets functioned as they had done in earlier years, although trading conditions were depressed and some rents were reduced. At times premises stood empty and in need of repair[81]. The selds, which had been highly valued in the thirteenth and early fourteenth centuries, had apparently lost their commercial significance. The fifteenth-century sources mention them only as a means of locating other property[82]. The Rows presumably continued to provide access to the upper-level shops, although there are few specific references to their function, with the possible exception of a testamentary bequest of 1396. In that year John le Armerer left 40s (forty shillings) to be distributed to 'pauperibus iacentibus in skopis'[83]. This enigmatic phrase could perhaps be interpreted to indicate that the city's poor slept on the Row stallboards.

The decline in commercial activity must have reduced the significance of the Rows and if there had been extensive rebuilding it is possible that they would have been lost. The evidence from the few remaining buildings of the period, however, indicates that Row walkways were being incorporated. There must therefore have been sufficient commercial advantage or sufficient pressure from the owners of adjacent properties for the system to be maintained, at least when individual properties were being rebuilt.

Fig 77 The Tudor House, 29–31 Lower Bridge Street (RCHME © Crown Copyright)

7 The great rebuilding

During the latter half of the sixteenth century and the first half of the seventeenth century, Chester was party to the general rise in wealth in England. Nowhere is this more apparent than in the rebuilding of the townhouses and shops of the merchant class, particularly those in the Rows, the commercial heart of the city[1]. The poor condition of many of the city's buildings was a matter for regular comment in documents during the late sixteenth century. Contemporary Mayors' Books and Quarter Sessions' files were filled with references to overflowing watercourses which render house walls rotten and concave, and to broken gutters which rot the timbers and posts of adjacent dwellings[2]. In 1588, a petitioner to the Assembly claimed that his house, which belonged to the city and lay just outside the Eastgate,

> '...partly by reason of the feeble and weake byldinge thereof and partly by the inhabylite of suche as of late yeres have inhabited and dwelt in the same ys now became soe ruinouse as of necessite yr. suppleant must be forced to plucke the same cleane doun and to buyld yt uppe againe from the verie fundacioun'[3].

This problem with the condition of the city's buildings was the consequence of the limited repairs and reconstruction undertaken in previous centuries, with the majority of the building stock being of considerable age; the house of Thomas Ince being described as dating from 'before the memory of man'[4]. Thus a combination of necessity, increasing prosperity, and a desire to follow new building trends explains the rebuilding of Chester, which peaked in the early seventeenth century. By the 1620s William Webb was able to record that 'the streets, for the most part, are very fair and beautiful, the Buildings on either side, especially towards the streets, of seemly proportion, and very neatly composed; whether of Timber, whereof the most are builded; or of stone, or brick.' (King 1656, pt 2, 19–20)

That this rebuilding in the Rows was more than a cosmetic refacing or renovation of predominantly medieval town houses is evidenced by the number of mid-sixteenth to mid-seventeenth-century timber frames which survive. Of the recorded Row buildings, 34 per cent have, or had, such a superstructure, usually above earlier stone undercrofts (Fig 78), while another 5 per cent exhibit major internal alterations and refacing from the same period. In view of the extensive rebuilding incurred in the nineteenth and early twentieth century this is a remarkably high proportion and demonstrates the scale of the building activity at that time.

Equally surprising is the fact that the Row walkways survived this major phase of new building. It appears likely that the continuing commercial success of the Rows ensured the retention of the system. Indeed, where there was less commercial activity, as in Lower Bridge Street, the Row system did fall victim to architectural fashion from the late seventeenth century onwards (see Chapter 8). Another factor, peculiar to Chester, which may also have ensured the retention of the Row system, is that the street-level spaces were almost always independent of the house above, usually had a different function and were often occupied separately. Where undercrofts were in separate ownership from the Row level and above, total rebuilding became difficult. It must often have been easier to reconstruct only the upper part of a property, in which case the Row would still have been required for access. The loss of a section of Row walkway would also have been unpopular with adjacent owners, who relied upon it for access and trade.

Inevitably the scale of building activity would have varied considerably, with many projects being no more than the remodelling or extension of a pre-existing structure; but other owners were more ambitious. Among them was Alderman John Aldersey, whose 'great new house' was built on the north side of Watergate Street early in 1604. It occupied a corner site, probably that adjoining Trinity Lane (68 Watergate Street), and evidently replaced an earlier house on the site which had been subject to a gable rent in 1523–3[5]. If Aldersey's house has been correctly located, then it made use of the medieval stone undercroft which survives to this day. However, the impressive house built outside the Row system in 1611 for the sheriff Thomas Whitby, on the corner of Northgate Street and Parsons Lane (the present Princess Street) seems to have involved a more radical rebuilding (Laughton 1988). The earlier structure on the site appears to have been completely demolished, for several hundred ashlars were purchased for new foundations and a new cellar was excavated. On this was set a timber-framed superstructure, probably with twin gables facing the street, for Whitby and subsequently his heirs paid an annual rent to the treasurers for five posts on the city ground[6]. The house took some eight or nine months to complete and cost in the region of £300, a figure which included some of the furnishings. Whitby died soon afterwards, heavily in debt.

Overspending on building projects remained habitual among prominent Cestrians throughout the century. Thomas Whitby's brother Edward, Recorder of Chester 1613–39, lamented the fact that the outlay on his house left him incapable of leaving such remembrances to his kindred and friends as he had proposed and desired[7]. In 1688, the skinner Robert Fletcher cited the £400 charges he had incurred building and repairing his dwelling in Bridge Street as the main reason for his indebtedness[8].

*Fig 78 Surviving Row buildings with evidence for sixteenth- and seventeenth-century timber framing (base mapping data ©
Crown Copyright)*

As well as the threat of financial difficulties, rebuilding also carried with it the risk of offending the neighbours. In November 1604, John Aldersey's neighbour to the east, the gentleman Thomas Rivington, complained that the height of Aldersey's new house was such that it completely shaded the light and that rainwater fell from it onto his walls, undermining them and rendering them putrid and hollow. Moreover, the new building was so close to Rivington's that he himself was prevented from building his own property any higher[9]. A few years later, in 1613, a new house in Goss Lane caused similar consternation, with the shoemaker Thomas Ince alleging that it stopped the light coming to his windows. A delegation appointed to view the property agreed and recommended that it be taken down[10]. The following year the authorities learned of the problems created by a new structure in the court behind Henry Crosby's house in Eastgate Street (probably in the vicinity of the Boot). This 'annoyed' the parlour and house of William Aldersey, darkening the light, and Crosby was accordingly ordered to 'cutt and sett the same building shorter by one foot and nine ynches'. He was also forbidden to have 'any syde light in the said buildinge towards the house of the said William Aldersey nor any made standinge stayres on that syde but onlie a loose or removinge ladder without any coverings over the same...'[11]. In order to avoid the inconvenience and expense of such injunctions it clearly made sense to obtain permission in advance. That this was sometimes done is attested by a postscript to a property transaction of the preceding century, involving a house in Watergate Street. The mayor and sheriffs witnessed that the neighbour had freely licensed the new owner to 'joyne and reare a bay of a house of ys unto myne'[12].

This process of renewal can be traced both through the surviving buildings (Figs 79, 80) and from the increasing documentation that exists from the beginning of the seventeenth century, particularly the probate records, which corroborate the physical evidence and attest considerable building activity in all parts of the city[13]. Indeed, in the early decades of the century, scarcely an inventory exists which does not mention a new room of some kind, be it hall, parlour, chamber, buttery, loft, or cellar.

Trading in the Rows

The seventeenth-century records show that there was a complex interplay between public and private interests in the Rows, in some ways analogous to that in operation in the common field system. Despite an acceptance that the Rows were in some sense public property, the owners of Row buildings appear to have had some responsibilities for, and rights over, their section of the Row walkway. For example, in November 1605 John Aldersey's widow was presented before the Assembly, '...for that she doeth not make a pere of stayers at the end of the Roe, at her now dwellinge house in the Wattergate strete and for want of them stayers and

Rayles w[hi]ch should bee ffor the same Roe, may indanger manie p[er]sons liffes'[14]. The dangers to life and limb were not exaggerated, and the Coroners' Inquests record several deaths due to people falling from the Row or from stairs with insufficient railings. Both young and old were vulnerable; the toddler, Grace Meire, fell to her death in Watergate Street in 1668, and an 85-year-old widow tumbled down stairs in Eastgate Street in December 1709 '...whereby she was sadly bruised and languishingly lived ab[ou]t an hour and then dyed'[15].

Seventeenth-century deeds often include the Row in the list of appurtenances enjoyed by the property, suggesting that there were private rights over the space[16].

Fig 79   The Falcon, 6 Lower Bridge Street (RCHME © Crown Copyright)

Fig 80   The Old King's Head, 48–50 Lower Bridge Street (RCHME © Crown Copyright)

The fact that the Row in front of a property in some way 'belonged' to it seems to have added to its value. In 1599 a hosier was granted part of a property in Eastgate Street including

> ...the third part of a board situate against the said shop... viz. the third part westward of that shop and the third part estward of that board which [he] held by lease as parcels of those buildings belonging to that messuage... together with the third part of the Rowe belonging to the said shop and board, with all lights and commodities beloging to the said third part of the said shop and board....[17]

Thomas Bolland, joiner, states in a petition of 1657 that he had lately purchased a house '...with a row thereunto belonging scituate in the Bridgate Streete...', and he was '...the rather induced to purchase the same house because the said row was then free...', and he set up a bench in it for himself and his servants[18].

Thus the Rows were not only important as public thoroughfares and as a means of access to adjacent properties, but were also used for trading. Methods of trading were, however, changing, with areas hitherto used for the erection of stalls being enclosed as permanent shops[19]. In 1597–8 the ironmonger, Robert Ambry, enclosed his stall in the corner shop of Mr Houghton, and two years later William Greene, a cobbler,

enclosed a stall situated under the house of John Hallwood, tailor. On the east side of Bridge Street four posts were enclosed and made into two candlemakers' shops. Other entries are less specific but appear to record the same activity, although there were sometimes advantages in being able to reverse the process. By 1628, for example, William Hincks had enclosed a great part of the Row in front of his house for a shop, but he was careful to remove this enclosure at fair-time for his own profit[20]. He could be certain of financial gain during the fairs because it was only during these midsummer and Michaelmas periods that non-freemen were permitted to buy and sell merchandise in the city without payment of a fine[21].

These fines, paid by traders from outside the city, were an important source of revenue and by the end of the century there are signs that some tightening up of the regulations was necessary since 'of late years' strangers and foreigners had presumed to keep open shop all year round and the Treasurers were ordered to take action against all such offenders[22]. The profits to be made from non-free merchants and traders at fair-time were evidently worth having, and both private individuals and the corporation jealously guarded their ancient rights[23].

The fairs occurred for only a short period each year; the midsummer fair, for example, lasted for four weeks but there appears to have been a core period around 24th June. Markets, on the other hand, were

Fig 81   Market in Eastgate Street in 1829 (photograph RCHME © Crown Copyright, from print reproduced by kind permission of Chester Archaeological Society)

twice-weekly events, held every Wednesday and Saturday, and there is plenty of seventeenth-century evidence that markets were held in the Rows. The flax and linen market is a particularly well-documented example and the petitions of its traders refer to the Row as their 'market place'[24]. Changing perceptions of retailing and an increasing desire for individual privacy resulted in a series of Assembly orders removing the linen market from one Row to another. The process appears to have begun in August 1654, with a petition from Sara Bennett, who kept a tavern at the 'higher end' of Watergate Street, on its south side. She complained that '...by reason of the throng of people at ffairs and on market dayes resorting thither to sell cloath' she had been much prejudiced in her way of trade[25]. The fact that she was a widow with six small children and had no other means of support may have influenced the Assembly, who ordered the market to be moved to the other side of Watergate Street. This did not suit the traders, who petitioned to be allowed to return to their former location, but the Assembly confirmed the previous decision[26]. Three years later the linen traders were still petitioning to return, since they found the Row on the north side of Watergate Street inconvenient, prejudicial to their trade, and '...destitute of places convenient to make stalls in for their wares'[27]. Moreover, Alderman Jonathan Ridge had built a shop in that part of the Row, further constraining the available space; strife and contention were the result. The Assembly therefore instructed that the market be moved to Eastgate Street, but in 1663 several Eastgate Street residents successfully petitioned for its return to Watergate Street Row near Jonathan Ridge's shop[28]. By February 1665 it was on the move again, to the Row on the south side of Watergate Street; then in June 1668 the flax, yarn, and linen cloth markets were removed to the Row in Watergate Street from Mrs Johnson's house downwards[29]. March 1677 saw a fleeting appearance in Bridge Street Row, but in April 1677 the Assembly ordered the market to the Row in Watergate Street where it had formerly been held[30].

These relocations of the linen market graphically illustrate the profitable use made of the Rows on market days and also the conflicting interests which were beginning to emerge. There had been permanent retail shops fronting the Row walkways since the medieval period, but the demand for more and larger permanent shop space was increasing in Chester, as elsewhere (Keene 1990, 42–3).

Encroachment

Throughout the history of the Rows there seems to have been a tendency for individual owners to extend their buildings into the streets and Row walkways, and it is possible to study this encroachment in some detail during the late sixteenth and early seventeenth centuries because of the documentary material that is available. Along the main streets, the Rows and the

Fig 82 Houses in Watergate Street with posts into the street (CAS Library, Chester Archives)

areas at street level in front of the houses were considered part of the 'common soil' of the city[31]. The seventeenth-century Assembly Books and Files amply attest both the Corporation's complete confidence in its powers over these areas, and the citizens' acknowledgement of the same. The street frontages and the Rows were considered to be public property (separate from the King's highway) and numerous petitions to advance streetward are recorded, as well as the subsequent granting or refusal of the request[32].

The treasurers' account rolls give some indication of building activity, particularly as it affected public land. The accounts of 1554–5 reveal that considerable encroachment upon all four main streets had already taken place. A string of entries record small annual payments for parlours, shops, cellars, and stairs built on the common soil, as well as for posts in the street upholding various tenements (Fig 82) and for house 'forefronts' built further than an individual's own land extended[33]. Bridge Street may have been in the vanguard of these developments. It was on the west side near the Cross that the tailor, Roger Siddall, was granted permission in 1601 to build a front to his shop to match that of Lewis Roberts next door[34]. By 1617, when William Fletcher applied to enlarge his shop, he could claim that all other shops on the same side of the street northwards to the Cross had been so extended[35]. His extension would therefore create a 'uniformity' of building, serving to beautify and adorn the city. His tenant, the ironmonger William Edwards, had more personal reasons for the extension. He feared for his livelihood as at present his shop was '...soe farre out of sight and soe distant from the strete...' as to be of no use whatsoever[36].

The construction of new town houses also resulted in encroachment. In 1590–1, for example, a new rent fell due from Alderman William Cotgrave for the five posts and two fronts over them lately erected in Foregate Street, just beyond the Eastgate[37]. In the following year 3 shillings was demanded from Sir Hugh Cholmondeley

Fig 83 Stanley Palace before the removal of the wing fronting Watergate Street (RCHME © Crown Copyright)

for the seven posts and three fronts recently built at his home nearby[38]. Cotgrave's house evidently had twin gables, while that of Cholmondeley seems to have been a grander structure, with a triple-gabled facade, but in form both resembled Stanley Palace in Watergate Street, their almost exact contemporary (Fig 83).

Similar activity, although on a smaller scale, is apparent within the Rows, mainly as a result of the pressures for permanent shop space. The Account Roll for 1589–90 includes rent from a shop in the Dark Row and from two more in Northgate Street Row[39]. The 1603–4 rental includes new entries for a shop or parlour in the Row before Alderman Philip's house and another similar enclosure made by Rowland Barnes[40]. These seem to relate to the creation of small shops on the street side of the Row walkways. This was not always popular. William Hincks applied for permission to build a shop in the Row before his house in Eastgate Street[41] and went ahead with the construction despite having his petition refused. Two of his neighbours asked for the removal of this shop on several occasions, stating that '...the said shoppe doth cleane take awaye the lighte of yor peticoner's shoppe and divers other neighbours shoppes neere thereunto and very much annoys them and furthermore it is a great shelter for lewde persons in the nighte time...'[42]. They also added some reasons for public concern, stating that if this

shop were not removed they '...doubteth not butt in shorte time a great part of all the Rowes within this Cittie wilbee in like manner taken in'. This they saw as '...an evill president unto all others to attempt the like...'[43]. Despite an order being given for the removal of this shop, Hincks appears to have taken it down only at fair-times and then only for his own profit. Such occasional refusals did not stem the increasing number of shops in the Rows and by 1662 most of the Rows had shops on either side (see Fuller's description, p1).

Periodically the Assembly ordered a 'view' of what was going on, as in December 1649 when nine surveyors were appointed to make a rental of city lands and of all encroachments[44]. By the late seventeenth century the impression is that these periodic surveys were less to prevent encroachment than to ensure that the city received its dues. These surveys may well be linked to the Assembly's wish to raise money for new building projects (see p113).

Plan form

The sixteenth and seventeenth centuries brought major changes to the character of the English town house. The new fashion was towards a multiplicity of rooms, seen quite clearly in the lists produced by seventeenth-century appraisers. The division of a Row house between two new owners in 1614 affords an indication of the variety of rooms that might be found in a house of the period. In that year David Evans and Robert Ince purchased a property on the south side of Eastgate Street for £130[45]. The latter apparently took over the rear portion of the structure, namely

> ...the back parlour, the chamber over the same, the gatehouse chamber, the cole-house under the same, the kitchen, a chamber over the kitchen, a little chamber adjoining to the kitchen, a cellar under the same kitchen, one garden next the same parlour, one stable and one house of office adjoining thereunto...

David Evans acquired the front section of the house, which consisted of

> ...two sellars streetward, two shops and two bords or stalls before the same..., a street chamber over the cellar and shops, ...a hall with a chamber in the north part of the hall, a closet at the entrance into the hall and the rooms over the same hall, a parlour or chamber over the south part of the hall with a buttery and closet adjoining to the same, together with a sellar descending out of and from the said buttery and the chamber over the parlour which lyeth southward of the same.

This assortment of rooms appears to have been typical of the large town house in Chester in the first half of the seventeenth century and it recurs time and again in

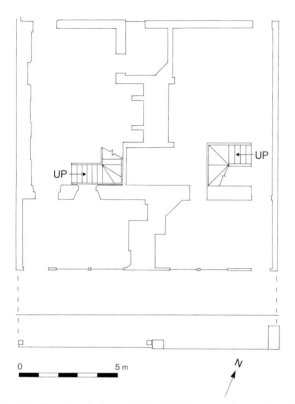

Fig 84 Row-level plan of 38–42 Watergate Street showing chimney stack and staircases inserted into the medieval hall

aldermanic inventories. An increased number of rooms was achieved in a number of different ways; by slightly modernising, extending, or adding a storey to an existing house, by subdividing the open halls of earlier houses through the insertion of floors and chimney stacks, or by building anew. It should be noted, however, that not all dwellings in the Row area were large, and great variations in wealth and status occurred, with the rich and the less well-to-do living in close proximity[46].

At the Leche House, 17 Watergate Street, this period is marked by alterations and additions which included the new great chamber over the Row and the early seventeenth-century decoration of the hall fireplace. In some new-built structures of the period variants of this plan form survive. Both 11 and 51–53 Bridge Street have galleries along one side of a two-storey Row-level room in the manner of the Leche House, although detailed reconstructions have not been possible. At 26 Eastgate Street, a modern gallery appears to perpetuate the arrangement of an early seventeenth-century rebuild.

Subdivision of an earlier open hall is most graphically illustrated at 38–42 Watergate Street, where the hall was divided into four, with a central stack heating two rooms on each floor (Fig 84). A staircase was inserted alongside the stack, but only the upper flight remains *in situ*. The front portion of the building and the roof were also rebuilt at this time.

The Tudor House, 29–31 Lower Bridge Street (Figs 77, 85), is probably the best surviving example of a new Row building of the early seventeenth century. It is a timber-framed town house of *c* 1610–36 (see

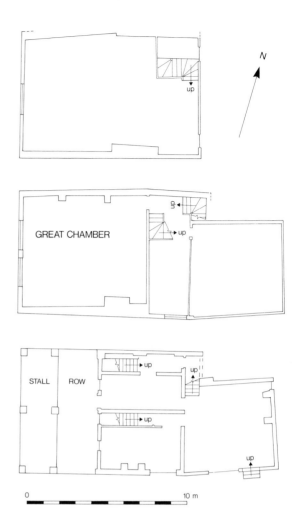

Fig 85 Reconstructed plans of the Tudor House, 29–31 Lower Bridge Street

Appendix B), and originally had a Row walkway, which has now been enclosed (Fig 86). A large street chamber occupies the whole space above the former stallboard and Row, plus half the depth of the former

Fig 86 Enclosed Row at the Tudor House, 29–31 Lower Bridge Street (RCHME © Crown Copyright)

off-Row shops. The Row-level parlour was smaller and ill-lit, a far cry from the grandeur of the open hall which would have occupied this location in earlier houses. The importance of the street chamber is also evident at Bishop Lloyd's Palace, 41 Watergate Street, where the size and decoration of the rooms over the Row clearly indicate they were the principal spaces.

Some of the more impressive timber-framed town houses of this period, such as the Tudor House and 36 Bridge Street, also made good use of the Row + 2 level, and it is not unusual to find chambers with plaster ceilings and decorative fireplaces at this level rather than simple attic rooms. As a result of all these changes the floor area of the domestic element of the typical Row building more than doubled, compared with its medieval counterpart. Unfortunately, as with the medieval town houses, little evidence of the other structures that existed beyond the main house remains from this period; outbuildings and gardens were swept away in later centuries. More happily, detailed documentation – chiefly in the form of inventories – proliferates, elucidating both the form and function of the domestic spaces.

Halls

Despite the reduction in the importance of the hall as the architectural and social centrepiece of the house, it continued to feature prominently in the sixteenth and seventeenth centuries, although often in a different form. In smaller homes it continued to function as the main living room, in larger ones as an important reception room. The majority of the inventories which name rooms mention a hall, and indeed often list it first, implying that it was a natural place to begin.

Halls invariably contained a hearth (Fig 96) and were usually panelled with wainscot, which cost between 14 pence and 2 shillings a yard in the early seventeenth century. The appraisers duly listed the amount they found, thus allowing some approximate estimate of room size. The amounts varied considerably, ranging from some 30 to upwards of 70 yards[47]. The glass in the windows was also occasionally noted. In 1606, the shoemaker Richard Lingley lived on the east side of Bridge Street close to St Michael's Church and his hall contained 15 feet of glass[48]. Ten years later the hall of his near neighbour, William Leycester, boasted over five times that amount, some 80 feet in all[49].

The quantity and quality of the tables, chairs, stools, and cupboards in a hall naturally reflected the wealth and status of the occupant. In 1662, the scrivener Daniel Butler lived next to the Eastgate and the goods in his hall – a table, a wainscot form, a wainscot chair, and four turned chairs, a court cupboard, six old pictures, and a collection of fire-irons were valued at under £2[50]. The halls of Chester's aldermen provided a striking contrast, for they normally boasted several tables as well as stools and chairs by the dozen. These were decked with a variety of cushions, made of silk, taffeta and satin, and were often gilt, fringed with silk, or worked with expensive embroidery. A court cupboard was standard, complete with cupboard cloths 'bordered with needlework', and there were normally other cupboards, plus desks and shelves for books. Playing tables and virginals were often found in the hall, as too were 'seeing glasses', pieces of armour, and hanging candlesticks. Glass globes and maps attested the mercantile interests of these wealthy Cestrians, while an array of scutcheons and coats of arms advertised their social status. A fortunate few could display the ultimate status symbol, the table for the sword and the iron for the mace, indicating that they had served their city as its mayor[51]. The adjoining butteries contained shelves and cupboards and here the pewter, dishes, napery, and knives were stored.

Street chambers

The new room that emerged in this period, at the front of the house above the Row, was usually described as the street chamber. In modest establishments these chambers apparently served as the principal bedroom, and indeed even in the more prestigious dwellings they commonly contained beds. It was in the wainscot bedstead in his street chamber that Robert Amery lay while writing his will in 1602 and the bed was still *in situ* 11 years later when his son bequeathed it in turn to his heir[52]. The street chamber of William Leycester also contained a 'fair standing bed' and that of Thomas Thropp a walnut tree bedstead with a covered tester and a valance fringed with tawny silk[53]. However, the street chambers of these wealthy aldermen contained many other items, suggesting that these rooms had come to function as the major prestige space which, if not entirely supplanting the hall, at least reduced its importance and relegated it to a subsidiary role. Indeed some inventories begin with the street chamber, indicative perhaps of its primary status[54]. There may have been a hierarchy among the guests, with an élite group entertained upstairs while the less favoured visitors were received below in the hall. Such an arrangement would have suited the city's mayors, whose homes were open to many visitors of varying degree.

The most impressive street chambers in Chester are at Bishop Lloyd's Palace, with their highly decorative plasterwork (Figs 90 and 91). Similarly large chambers can be found elsewhere; the three-bay chamber at 17 Eastgate Street, for example, extends 7.65m back from the frontage. The size of other street chambers can be judged from the amount of wainscot and glass they contained. The value of these two commodities in William Leycester's home exceeded £18, while the glass in Thomas Thropp's street chamber was contained in four casements[55].

The furnishings of these larger street chambers replicated those of the hall but were often even more costly[56]. The goods in Thomas Thropp's street chamber, for example, were valued in excess of £40, four times the value of the goods in his hall. A picture of the Three Kings of Cologne, the pageant put on each year by the Mercers' Company, hung on the wall of his street chamber, possibly suggesting that the gild met there on occasion. William Leycester kept the table for the city's sword and the iron for the mace in his street chamber. Given their role as dining and entertaining rooms, it is not surprising to find that street chambers often had an adjoining buttery, and occasionally an adjoining closet.

Row parlours, chambers and shops

Few inventories specifically mention the rooms which adjoined the Row itself, even when referring to houses known to have been in the Rows such as those of Leycester, Thropp, and Mainwaring. The reason may well be that these rooms were often in separate occupation from the house, possibly serving as shops, and their contents were therefore irrelevant as far as the appraisers were concerned. With windows opening directly on to the public thoroughfare, such rooms were ill-lit and undesirable at the start of the seventeenth century when the Rows were insalubrious areas, habitually used as 'places of easement' for the people living in the cellars below and described as being 'of very odious sight and savour'[57]. The Rows were also traditionally used as viewing galleries for various public spectacles, such as the Watch and the Midsummer Show, and were often thronged with people[58]. Given the choice, owners would eat and sleep elsewhere, using the rooms fronting the Row as a screen to protect their privacy[59].

In those inventories in which a Row chamber or parlour is mentioned (and only 15 examples have been found), it appears to have been of low status, containing little of value. Typically, the furniture of a Row parlour would include a table, forms, benches, chests, and cupboards; that of a chamber, bedsteads and bedding. Often these furnishings were described as coarse and old, and the impression is that such rooms were occupied by servants. Indeed, the parlour next to the Row in William Hunt's house contained a coarse bed specified as being for the maiden[60].

The Rows themselves, although not in private ownership (see pp79–80), were occasionally used by the householders for various purposes. Two benches of planks stood in the Row outside the White Bull Inn next to the Northgate in 1666[61], and the Rows were habitually used for storing various items including old timber and slates, much to the annoyance of the authorities[62]. The pipes and stone troughs for the water supply were also occasionally located in the Row walkway[63].

Rear parlours

In the larger houses there was usually a parlour at the rear, which apparently functioned as a private retreat for the family, whereas the hall and street chamber were used as the more public spaces in which visitors were received and entertained. This was certainly the case in contemporary London (Schofield 1984, 160). Most of these parlours have disappeared as a result of later alterations, but a good example survives at the Leche House looking out on to a rear courtyard. This house also retains an unusual first-floor gallery carried on wooden Renaissance columns along one side of the same courtyard (Fig 89).

The rear parlour was often next to the garden and occasionally enjoyed a vista of flowers and foliage. In 1602, for example, John Aldersey complained of the smoke coming from his neighbour's chimney, which was causing the fruit on his apple, pear and plum trees to wither and was preventing his family from enjoying the scent and sight of the herbs and flowers[64]. Among the herbs was rosemary, carried away in quantities by a thief some years later[65]. Other parlours must have looked out on less pleasing prospects – alleyways and courts containing an untidy assortment of outbuildings and utilitarian artefacts.

Kitchens, outbuildings and gardens

It seems that the kitchen normally lay to the rear of the hall, in the larger houses being separated from it by a buttery and closet. In some cases, as at the Leche House, the kitchen was a separate building, but this was probably unusual by this date.

The lead cistern containing the household water supply was commonly located at the rear of the house, adjacent to the kitchen, together with the brass cock and necessary water pipes[66]. Timber, slates, turf, gorse, barrels, and ladders are among the commodities most frequently stored at the back of the house and there were, in addition, various separate outbuildings. Most common was the brewhouse and kiln, but malthouses, storehouses, milk houses, boulting houses, houses of office (privies), turf lofts, and stables were familiar features of the larger dwellings. Privies often caused problems, for they habitually overflowed, resulting in excrement being washed into adjoining properties[67].

Sixteenth- and seventeenth-century maps of Chester indicate many open spaces and gardens behind the densely-packed street frontages (Fig 87), and contemporary deeds often refer to gardens and orchards adjoining the houses along the four main streets[68]. The size of these plots is rarely given, but that belonging to the house in Eastgate Street purchased by Evans and Ince extended to about half an acre[69]. Building on these open spaces continued throughout the period and probably intensified. The garden behind John Rock's house was subdivided and must have been largely overbuilt, with each tenant having a stable, coal house, privy, and 'midding' place[70]. Access to the spaces behind the houses clearly presented problems for properties which did not occupy a corner site and rights of way were carefully recorded and, if need be, vigorously defended. An inquest in 1596 detailed the common and lawful way which 'had always been and

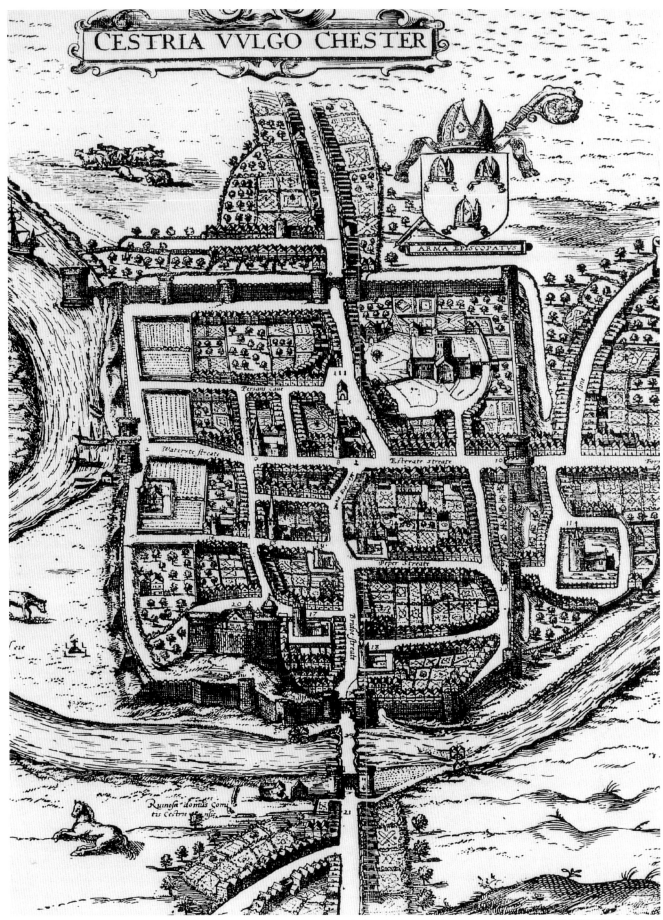

Fig 87 Part of Braun's plan of Chester, c 1580, showing gardens behind the main frontages (photograph RCHME © Crown Copyright, from original in Chester Archives)

ought always to be' between two houses in Bridge Street for the passage of the occupier, servants, and tenants, together with their animals, carts, and necessaries, to the back of the house[71].

Undercrofts and cellars

As in the medieval period, the street-level undercrofts or cellars were often in separate occupation from the building above and when listing goods, testators and appraisers alike took care to specify exactly where they lay. Thomas Fletcher's goods were to be found in the cellar under his hall; William Aldersey, on the other hand, had property in various cellars, one under his own house and others in Bridge Street and Watergate Street[72]. The probate records are full of similar examples.

Cellars were most obviously used for storage and throughout the city they functioned as repositories for an assortment of old 'trumpery' and other surplus household items[73]. The larger undercrofts on the four main streets, however, could be put to more commercial use and many inventories record the storage of quantities of expensive merchandise. At the start of the century Robert Brerewood kept a great store of leather in the cellar under the Row and a few years later John Aldersey's cellar contained 347 dozen calf skins and 20 tuns of Bordeaux wine, while the value of the goods in John Leche's cellar (lead, timber and cases of Irish tallow) amounted to approximately £250[74]. The nature of the goods stored could lead to complaint. In 1585, for example, fish stored in a cellar in Trinity Lane caused such a 'very stinking smell' that it put Mr Sheriff and his guests off their food[75].

Inventories attest the use of cellars as workshops and occasionally as brewhouses[76], and the use of some undercrofts as taverns, documented for the medieval period, persisted in the following centuries. In July 1610, the Assembly ordered that the windows and door of the cellar in which one of the councillors kept a tavern were to be shut so that he be prevented from doing any further trade[77]. Aldermen were also involved in this trade, and the inventory of Thomas Thropp actually begins with the goods in his cellar and tavern, which lay near the two churches in Bridge Street. The value of these goods was almost £90 and they included Gascon wine and claret as well as old wine and vinegar. The barrels, butts and tubs were kept in a storage area at the rear, divided from the tavern itself by a partition with glass windows. This was evidently an upmarket establishment, boasting a collection of valuable cups and bowls as well as linen for the tables and seats[78].

Other cellars were used as dwellings. During the plague at the start of the seventeenth century, the authorities were concerned about this, fearing that the 'narrow and close' restraint of such places, coupled with the lack of all amenities, could lead to the spread of disease[79], but the practice continued. In 1671, all the householders in the city, including those who lived in cellars, were ordered to share the responsibility of sweeping the streets before their doors[80]. Sometimes the servants lived in the cellars[81]; other cellars were rented out to poor townspeople who had nowhere else to live. The witness in a court case of 1605 revealed that she had lived in a cellar on the east side of Bridge Street for almost 20 years[82].

External appearance

The majority of the new buildings of the late sixteenth and seventeenth centuries in Chester were timber-framed, and double-, triple-, or even quadruple-gabled frontages were favoured. This form is well represented in the Rows by the Falcon, 6 Lower Bridge Street (Fig 79), and the Old King's Head, 48–50 Lower Bridge Street (Fig 80: see also Chapter 6). Where the less affluent owners could not afford such grand structures the existing medieval timber-framed structures were simply rebuilt with a single or double gable.

Fig 88 Detail of the façade of Bishop Lloyd's Palace, 41 Watergate Street (RCHME © Crown Copyright)

The Tudor House has a single gabled frontage, square-panelled, with wavy studs at Row + 1 and Row + 2 levels and diamond motifs to the gable end (Fig 77). More impressive is Bishop Lloyd's Palace, its front facade a riot of carved panels (Fig 88). The frieze above the Row includes representations of the Garden of Eden, Cain and Abel, Abraham and Isaac, and the Annunciation, along with the Royal Garter flanked by the initials IR for James VI and I and the arms of George Lloyd, Bishop of Sodor and Man (1599–1605) and of Chester (1605–15). The gable panels include heraldic emblems and fabulous beasts, such as lions, bears, mermaids, pairs of monkeys and serpents, green men, sea monsters and the elephant and castle, separated by crude caryatids (Morris 1899). Although the ensemble at the Leche House is less complete and the facade more Victorianised, elements of a decorative scheme on similar lines survive (Fig 176). At the rear of this building the influence is more Classical, with the gallery over the yard carried on Ionic columns (Fig 89).

Other houses were also elaborately decorated. A wooden turret with windows on all sides embellished Thomas Whitby's house, and it was surmounted by a weather vane emblazoned with the family coat of arms. There were two lesser vanes as well, plus a number of brightly coloured 'cartooses' (Laughton 1988, 104). A turret also featured on the house of his brother-in-law, William Aldersey[83], and it is likely that other aldermen embraced such opportunities for display with enthusiasm. Their efforts did not go unnoticed and contributed to the favourable impression of the city recorded by contemporary observers (see Webb quotation p77 above). At the Mainwaring House, 60–66 Watergate Street, the problem of creating an impressive entrance, while maintaining the Row walkway, was solved by building a typically Jacobean porch with side steps out into the street (Fig 102). This was a significant break from the treatment of even the major medieval parallel halls, where the entrance steps appear always to have been located at the end of the Row and did not coincide with the main door.

Stone does not appear to have been used for domestic architecture in seventeenth-century Chester and brick does not appear to have been widely utilised before 1600, despite its earlier use in the surrounding countryside. References to brick manufacture in various locations in and around the city become increasingly frequent as the decades progress. At the start of the century, however, its use was apparently restricted to chimneys and ovens, which were the province of specialist craftsmen. Whitby purchased some 25,000 bricks for the six chimneys of his house. However, William Webb's description of the city in the 1620s, quoted at the opening of this chapter, indicates that some brick houses had been built and in 1625 a brick house is recorded as having been 'lately' built by Randle Holme in Castle Lane; it was called the Red Nun Hall in 1688 and the Brick House four years later[84].

Fig 89   Timber post with classical details supporting the gallery at the rear of the Leche House, 17 Watergate Street (RCHME © Crown Copyright)

In 1671, the Assembly ordered that, before the following All Saints' Day, all houses in the main streets of the city were to be roofed with slate or tile and not thatch [85]. Previously the authorities seem to have relied upon owners to restrict the use of thatch. The number of slaters working in Chester makes it clear that many of the houses were roofed with slate before this date. Whitby's house was roofed with slate, as was the less prestigious building he erected in 1617[86].

Internal decoration

The late sixteenth- and early seventeenth-century changes in plan form were accompanied in Chester, as elsewhere, by an explosion in surface decoration. The loss of the symbolic vocabulary of the open hall, with its imposing size and hierarchical use of space (Harris 1989), left a vacuum which the plasterer and wood carver were able to fill. Unadorned, the single-storey parlours and chambers lacked the architectural power of the open hall. The art of decorative plasterwork was

Fig 90 Eastern room over the Row at Bishop Lloyd's Palace, 41 Watergate Street (RCHME © Crown Copyright)

Fig 91 Western room over the Row at Bishop Lloyd's Palace, 41 Watergate Street (RCHME © Crown Copyright)

revived in Renaissance Italy and introduced to this country under royal patronage in the mid-sixteenth century. This eyecatching form of decoration, a symbol of wealth and social status, flourished as a solution to the problem of how to delineate the principal formal rooms.

Ceilings and friezes

Two of the early plaster ceilings in Chester are very similar in style. The front section of the Tudor House is dated by dendrochronology to *c* 1610–36, and it contains a plastered ceiling, which is divided into three

Fig 93 Ceiling over the staircase at Bishop Lloyd's Palace, 41 Watergate Street (RCHME © Crown Copyright)

Fig 92 Fireplace at Row + 1 level at 10 Watergate Street (RCHME © Crown Copyright)

panels, between moulded cross beams. Each panel contains three large sub-circular, radial motifs with four small rectangular motifs at the corners. An almost identical ceiling exists in the western street chamber of Bishop Lloyd's Palace (Fig 91). The dating of both these buildings is fairly secure, and there is no reason to believe that the ceilings are not integral to the original design. At 12 Bridge Street an isolated pendant boss is embellished with strapwork of basically cruciform design. Although rather different from the sub-circular motifs of the Tudor House and Bishop Lloyd's Palace, it clearly belongs to this group of relatively plain ceilings.

At Bishop Lloyd's Palace, the western room is further enlivened by a vigorous frieze, depicting pairs of sea monsters, open-mouthed with lolling tongues, flanking abstract strapwork motifs. It is a delightful piece of work and it is therefore pleasing to see it appear identically, and without doubt from the same mould, at the top of the massive fireplace at Row + 1 level in 10 Watergate Street (Fig 92).

Two ceilings in the eastern half of Bishop Lloyd's Palace are perhaps more characteristic of the art of the plasterer, and also a little later in date. Neither appears to be *in situ*, since designs which are clearly intended to cover an entire ceiling are cut down in order to fit the space[87]. The ceiling above the staircase is a design of squares and kite shapes, defined by interlocking flat strapwork ribs with enriched soffits (Fig 93). In the eastern street chamber there is a ceiling with a highly complex design based on concentric ovals, with angel heads in the interstices (Fig 90). Though a common eighteenth-century motif, the angel's head is rare in seventeenth-century plasterwork[88]. A ceiling using the same moulds, though in a slightly different configuration, existed in the library of the Old Bishop's Palace and a

Fig 94 Hall fireplace at Gamul House, 52–58 Lower Bridge Street (RCHME © Crown Copyright)

Fig 95 Timber fire surround at Row level, 10 Watergate Street (RCHME © Crown Copyright)

similar ceiling still exists over the chancel of St Anselm's Chapel, which was formerly the private chapel of the Old Bishop's Palace. The palace was severely slighted during the Civil War, and seems likely to have been the original home of the ceiling in Bishop Lloyd's Palace.

These, plus the ornate ceiling in the Dutch Houses, 22–26 Bridge Street (Fig 159), form the corpus of major plasterwork ceilings within the Rows. To these should be added the simpler ceilings at the Boot, 17 Eastgate Street; 10 Watergate Street, where there are plaster mouldings to the cornices and beams; 9 Bridge Street, with its relief fleurs-de-lys and moulded beams; 15 Bridge Street, with its well-defined panels between moulded beams (Fig 152); and the fine ceiling at Row level in St Michael's Rectory, 43 Bridge Street. Also the rear chamber at Row + 1 level in the Leche House has a series of frieze motifs in the plasterwork.

Fireplaces

The introduction of the chimney flue heralded an opportunity for stone masons, woodcarvers, and plasterers alike to display their virtuoso skills. The hearth in Thomas Whitby's dining chamber was probably flanked by wooden pilasters, while over the mantel there may have been a decorative panel of plaster, painted in glowing colours by Randle Holme, herald painter. Similar embellishments adorned the hearths in Whitby's hall and parlour, while the three remaining chimney breasts were picked out in black (Laughton 1988, 105–6).

Of the stone fireplaces, perhaps the most adventurous is to be found at Gamul House, 52–58 Lower Bridge Street (Fig 94). Here, as at the Leche House, the open hall survived a major decorative reordering, which

included the installation of carved wooden pendants and inexplicable shelf-like structures held on carved consoles (Fig 165). The massive fireplace, of local red sandstone, is lavishly carved with primitive caryatids and stylised vegetation, and has no overmantel. By the middle of the seventeenth century, stone fireplaces had become far more restrained. A dated example of 1661 from 12 Bridge Street is very plain, the surround consisting of a moulded four-centred arch with a plain frieze and mantelpiece above. Three comparable fireplaces survive at the Dutch Houses, 22–26 Bridge Street.

A single timber fireplace of the period survives at 10 Watergate Street (Fig 95). It consists only of a fire surround, with complex mouldings to a series of arrises, and no overmantel. The width of the fireplace is so great that the chimney bressumer has developed a distinct sag. There is a stone fireplace with timber overmantel in the rear parlour of the Leche House (Fig 177).

Perhaps the most visually impressive fireplaces are those with decorative plaster overmantels. Five occur within Rows buildings: at the Leche House, at 10 and 38–42 Watergate Street, and two at Bishop Lloyd's Palace. The first of these is the most remarkable, with its massive plaster chimneypiece containing the coat of arms of the Leche family within a strapwork cartouche, supported by an Ionic colonnade. This chimneypiece extends virtually the whole height of the open hall (Fig 96).

Within the western street chamber of Bishop Lloyd's Palace there is a particularly engaging artisan plaster overmantel depicting Cupid mounted upon a lion (Fig 91). The whole composition demonstrates the very hazy understanding of classicism typical of provincial English work of the late sixteenth and early seventeenth centuries; columns flanking the fireplace

Fig 96 Hall fireplace at the Leche House, 17 Watergate Street (RCHME © Crown Copyright)

display pronounced entasis and are topped by ill-fitting capitals, whilst the overmantel itself is framed by an order of uncertain pedigree. The chimneypiece is clearly contemporary with the plaster ceiling of the room (see above), unlike its counterpart in the eastern street chamber. Here the very large chimneypiece has evidently been imported from another building, since the overmantel is higher than the ceiling and a small dome has been constructed in order to accommodate it (Fig 90). Plain Doric columns flank the fireplace and the overmantel consists of a central oval panel with four sub-rectangular panels surrounding it. The whole is surmounted by a representation of a phoenix. As with the plaster ceiling in this room, the most likely provenance seems to be the Old Bishop's Palace.

The fireplace at Row + 1 in 10 Watergate Street is flanked by stone columns, carrying a Doric frieze (Fig 92). The painted plaster overmantel depicts the Royal arms and those of the Corbett family (Dyke 1946, 29). The frieze above is identical to the sea monster frieze around the western street chamber at Bishop Lloyd's Palace, implying a late sixteenth- or early seventeenth-century date. The plaster chimneypiece in an upper rear chamber at 38–42 Watergate Street is much smaller than the other four within this group, but it shows that fine decoration was not confined to the principal spaces.

Staircases

The period of the great rebuilding saw a radical change in staircase construction nationally, with wood replacing stone as the principal material used, and open-well and dog-leg stairs with landings superseding spirals. In grander houses, the staircase became an architectural spectacle in its own right, and a vehicle for the skills of the woodcarver. In the Rows, restricted space precluded the possibility of major staircases, but nevertheless, a number of modest yet well-crafted examples survive.

A new departure in staircase design, perhaps influenced by the Renaissance revival of the classical balustrade, was the baluster and handrail. Earlier seventeenth-century examples of 'splat' balusters, with flat profiles but carefully carved to give the illusion of being turned, occur in a number of Row buildings, including the Tudor House and Booth Mansion, 28–34 Watergate Street (Fig 97). These vary in complexity, some being pierced while others are solid. The staircase at Booth Mansion is notable for the survival of cuboid finials to the newel posts, whilst at 10 Watergate Street the closed string is embellished with carved strapwork.

Later in the century turned and twisted balusters became more common and are to be found at 9 and 22 Bridge Street. These persisted into the next century, to be replaced by the more sophisticated column-on-vase balusters found in town houses from the mid-eighteenth century onwards.

Fig 97   Staircase in eastern part of Booth Mansion, 28–34 Watergate Street (RCHME © Crown Copyright)

Panelling

Inventories make it clear that the major rooms of the wealthy and also the not-so-wealthy were panelled with wainscot and provided with wainscot doors. In the first quarter of the seventeenth century the price of this 'sylyng' ranged between 14 pence and 2 shillings a yard. Thomas Whitby, who always chose the best quality, paid this latter sum for the wainscot in his new house, and he purchased it from a joiner in Nantwich, a town some 32km distant (Laughton 1988, 112). Robert Hood prefabricated this panelling in his home town and brought it to Chester by cart, accompanied by two of his men. The three spent two weeks in the city, putting it in position. A more expensive type of panelling was occasionally used. This was described as 'cut-work sylyng' and could cost twice as much as the plain variety. William Leycester accordingly contented himself with 9 yards of it[89].

Little panelling of this period survives in the Rows buildings. The parlour at the Tudor House is panelled, but this does not appear to be original, and there is one panelled room at 24 Watergate Street. There is panelling across one end of the hall at the Leche House, and some loose sections in 38–42 Watergate Street; but most seems to have succumbed to later fashions in interior decoration.

Conclusions

During the late sixteenth and early seventeenth centuries there was increasing self-confidence amongst the merchants of Chester as a result of the more buoyant economy. Within the Rows, many houses were rebuilt and others were extensively remodelled, replacing the many derelict properties that had survived from earlier centuries. In some cases, the expense of these houses, with their multiplicity of rooms, decorative plasterwork and rich furnishings, overstretched the financial resources of their owners.

All this new building must, in turn, have assisted with the growth of the city's economy. The Rows were retained, presumably because of the commercial advantage they provided. Existing Row-level shops were enlarged and new shops were added, so that the use of these elevated walkways could be maximised. Until the beginning of the Civil War, the Rows were once again operating as the commercial heart of the city, a role for which they had been designed by their medieval builders.

Plate 1 Cutaway reconstruction of medieval form of 38–42 Watergate Street (Graham Holme)

Plate 2 *Watergate Street* (watercolour by Louise Rayner, reproduced by kind permission of the Grosvenor Museum, Chester)

Plate 3 42 Watergate Street: round-headed arches in side elevation (left: detail of Pl 2) and front elevation (right: detail of water-colour by Louise Rayner): both paintings reproduced by kind permission of the Grosvenor Museum, Chester

Plate 4 Watergate Street (watercolour by E Harrison Compton, 1909)

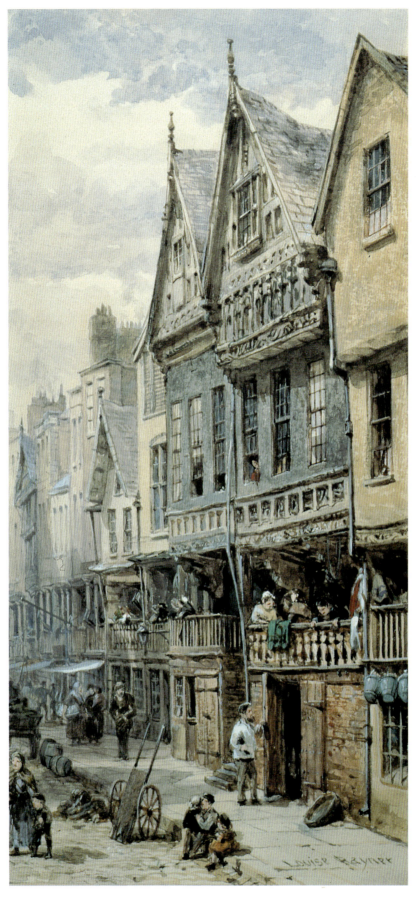

Plate 5 Bishop Lloyd's Palace, 41 Watergate Street (watercolour by Louise Rayner, reproduced by kind permission of the Grosvenor Museum, Chester)

Plate 6 Watergate Row (watercolour by E Harrison Compton, 1909)

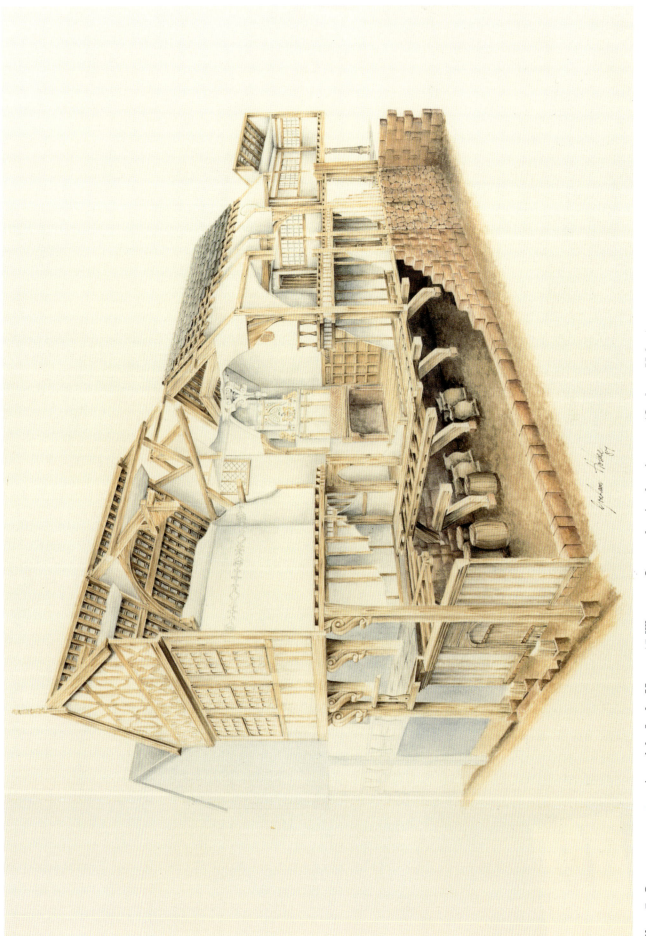

Plate 7 Cutaway reconstruction of the Leche House, 17 Watergate Street, showing key features (Graham Holme)

Plate 8 Lower Bridge Street, Gamul House at left: compare with Fig 164 (watercolour by Louise Rayner, reproduced by kind permission of the Grosvenor Museum, Chester)

Plate 9 Eastgate Street (watercolour by Louise Rayner, reproduced by kind permission of the Grosvenor Museum, Chester)

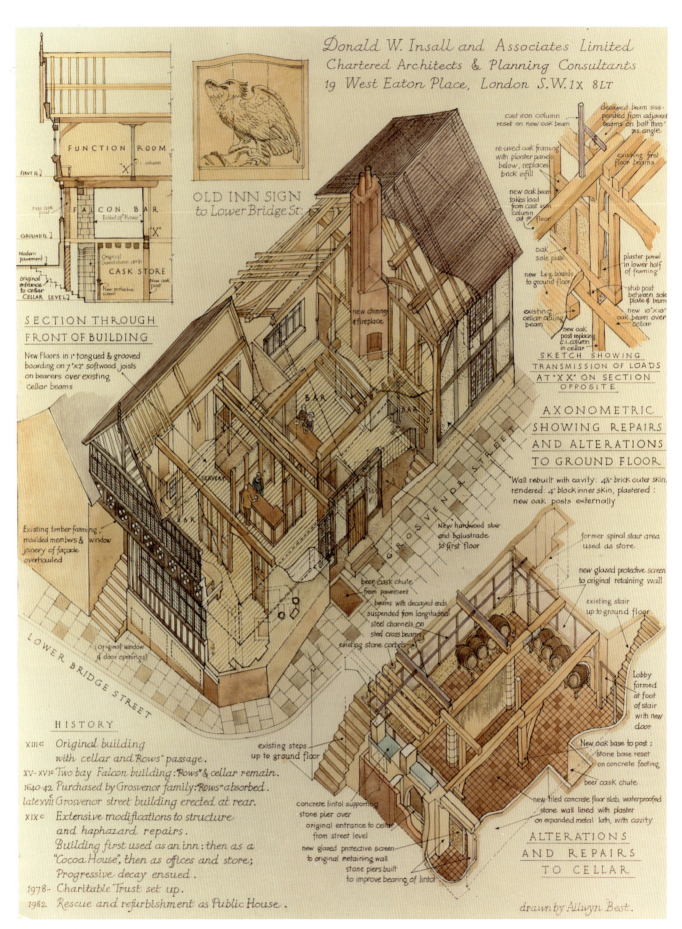

Donald W. Insall and Associates Limited
Chartered Architects & Planning Consultants
19 West Eaton Place, London S.W.1X 8LT

OLD INN SIGN
to Lower Bridge St.

FUNCTION ROOM

FIRST FL.

FALCON BAR
Extent of "Rows"

GROUND FL.

CASK STORE

CELLAR LEVEL

SECTION THROUGH
FRONT OF BUILDING

New floors in 1" tongued & grooved
boarding on 7"x2" softwood joists
on bearers over existing
cellar beams

Existing timber framing,
moulded members & window
joinery of façade
overhauled

(original window
& door openings)

LOWER BRIDGE STREET

GROSVENOR STREET

BAR

BAR

SERVERY

BAR

new chimney
& fireplace

cast iron column
reset on new oak beam

decayed beam sus-
pended from adjacent
beams on bolt thro'
as angle

re-used oak framing
with plaster panels
below, replaces
brick infill

existing first
floor beams

new oak beam
takes load
from cast iron
column at 1st floor

oak
sole plate

plaster panel
in lower half
of framing

new t & g. boards
to ground floor

stub post
between sole
plate & beam

existing
cellar ceiling
beam

new 10"x10"
oak beam over
cellar

new oak
post replacing
c.i. column
in cellar

SKETCH SHOWING
TRANSMISSION OF LOADS
AT "XX" ON SECTION
OPPOSITE

AXONOMETRIC
SHOWING REPAIRS
AND ALTERATIONS
TO GROUND FLOOR

Wall rebuilt with cavity: 4½" brick outer skin,
rendered: 4" block inner skin, plastered:
new oak posts externally

New hardwood stair
and balustrade
to first floor

beer cask chute
from pavement

beams with decayed ends
suspended from longitudinal
steel channels on
steel cross beams

existing stone corbels

former spiral stair area
used as store

new glazed protective screen
to original retaining wall

existing stair
up to ground floor

Lobby
formed
at foot
of stair
with new
door

New oak base to post:
stone base reset
on concrete footing

beer cask chute

new tiled concrete floor slab, waterproofed
stone wall lined with plaster
on expanded metal lath, with cavity

ALTERATIONS
AND REPAIRS
TO CELLAR

existing steps
up to ground floor

concrete lintol supporting
stone pier over
original entrance to cellar
from street level

new glazed protective screen
to original retaining wall

stone piers built
to improve bearing of lintol

HISTORY

XIII c   *Original building*
with cellar and "Rows" passage.
XV-XVI c *Two bay Falcon building: "Rows" & cellar remain.*
1640-42 *Purchased by Grosvenor family: "Rows" absorbed.*
late XVII *Grosvenor street building erected at rear.*
XIX c   *Extensive modifications to structure*
and haphazard repairs.
Building first used as an inn: then as a
"Cocoa House", then as offices and store;
Progressive decay ensued.
1978- *Charitable Trust set up.*
1982 *Rescue and refurbishment as Public House.*

drawn by Ailwyn Best.

Plate 10 The Falcon, 6 Lower Bridge Street: illustration of the repair work carried out during the early 1980s (drawing by Ailwyn Best for Donald W Insall and Associates Ltd)

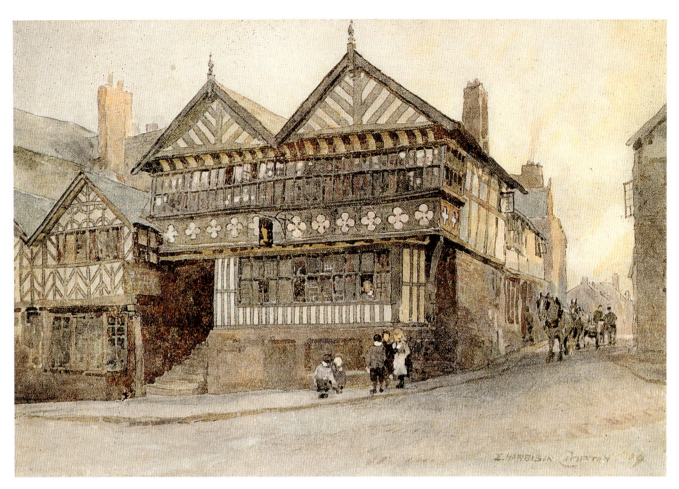

Plate 11a The Falcon, 6 Lower Bridge Street (watercolour by E Harrison Compton, 1909)

Plate 11b The Bear and Billet, 94 Lower Bridge Street
(watercolour by E Harrison Compton, 1909)

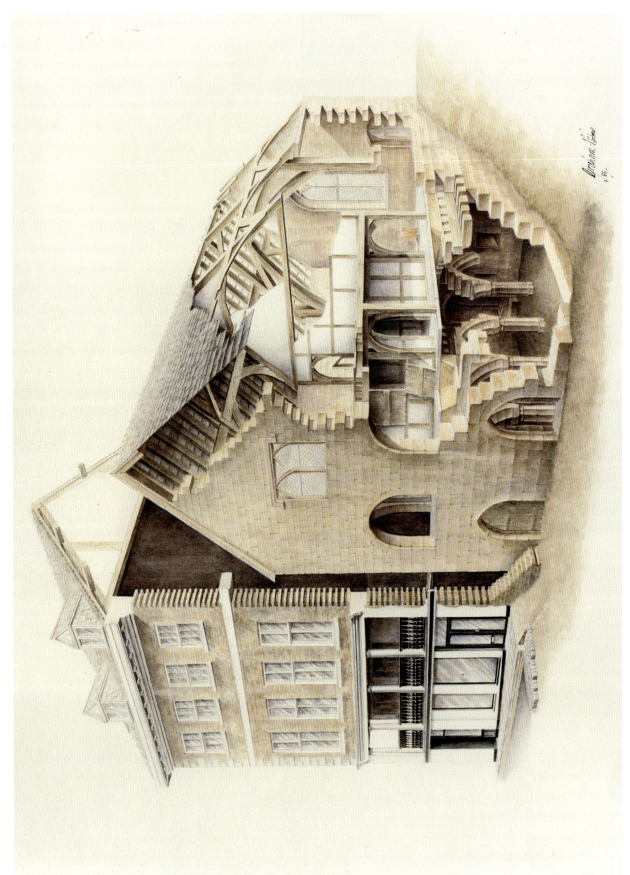

Plate 12 Cutaway drawing showing reconstruction of the medieval form of the eastern house within Booth Mansion, 28–34 Watergate Street, and the eighteenth-century facade (Graham Holme)

8 An ornament to the city

See Appendix C for all the documentary references to Row enclosures in this chapter.

> '...to take down the ffore part of her house in the Bridge Street by her lately purchased... and to rebuild the same roe as may bee a grace and ornament to the citty'.

Thus, Lady Mary Calveley petitioned the Assembly in 1676. This new house was the Baroque mansion, now called Bridge House, 18–24 Lower Bridge Street (see p101–2). Although it was built with its entrance and main rooms at first floor level there was no walkway passing through the front of the building and this loss of 19 yards of Row was allowed by the Assembly, although a hefty fine of £20 was imposed. Two years later a second petition was submitted for a pair of stairs out in the street, for which an additional fine of 40 shillings and an annual rent of 5 shillings was required.

These must be the curving imperial stairs shown on Batenham's view of 1816 (Fig 98).

The erection of Bridge House marked the beginning of a new era for the Rows. By the mid-seventeenth century pressure for retail space had led to the construction of permanent or semi-permanent shops on many of the stallboards along the street side of the Row walkways. The problems of light and access inherent in the Row system from its inception became acute, and the tensions between public and private interests increased. The obvious solution to these problems was, in the eyes of the wealthy, to seek to appropriate that section of the Row which fronted their properties. This permitted a radical break with the traditional form of Chester town house and allow the creation of spacious well-lit accommodation with a more dignified approach. No longer were owners prepared to alter and remodel the buildings that they had inherited, accepting the problems that this created. Now there was a wish by

Fig 98 Bridge House, 18–24 Lower Bridge Street, from print by G Batenham, 1816 (photograph RCHME © Crown Copyright, from print in CAS Library, Chester Archives)

Fig 99   Former Row within the Falcon, 6 Lower Bridge Street (RCHME © Crown Copyright)

Lady Mary Calveley and others to rebuild totally in the latest fashion. These aspirations meant dispensing with the Row.

Petitioners took care to stress the public benefit of their proposals, indicating that the new buildings would be an ornament to the city. Although to some extent these claims were the common form for such petitions, they may have had some significance, as increasingly critical comments were levelled at the Rows towards the end of the seventeenth century. In some cases, consent was granted for the enclosure of the Row, but the Assembly was not always amenable and some owners had to be content with redesigning their houses around the Row.

This chapter begins by examining the final stage in the evolution of the Rows, when improvements to individual properties resulted in the loss of approximately one third of the system of raised walkways during the hundred years, *c* 1640–1740. The method by which properties were improved naturally varied according to the means, energy, and ambition of the various owners. A few, like Lady Mary Calveley, embarked on entirely new buildings, but many others had less grandiose plans, often involving only a refronting or the absorption of the Row into their existing houses.

Enclosure of the Rows

The earliest recorded enclosure of a Row was granted to Sir Richard Grosvenor in 1643. His petition gave the following reasons: firstly the Row was an annoyance to his neighbours '...by reason of the moistinesse thereof...'; and secondly because his employment in the garrison of Chester '...tyeth him to inhabit in his said house which is far to little to receive his familie'. As a member of the local gentry, an MP, a member of the Assembly, and a leading Royalist responsible for the protection of Chester, he was a petitioner who could hardly be refused. His request was granted for a fine of 16s 6d (16 shillings and 6 pence) and an annual rent of 2s 6d. The enclosed Row can still be seen in the Falcon, 6 Lower Bridge Street, where the timber-framed wall fronting the walkway, with its former front door and window, and the stone piers of the Row arcade now form part of the bar (Fig 99). However, measurements given in the petition show it also included what is now the adjoining property (Nos 8–10).

Although the next petition to enclose a Row was not submitted for a further 25 years, the grant to Richard Grosvenor was crucial. Not only did it set a

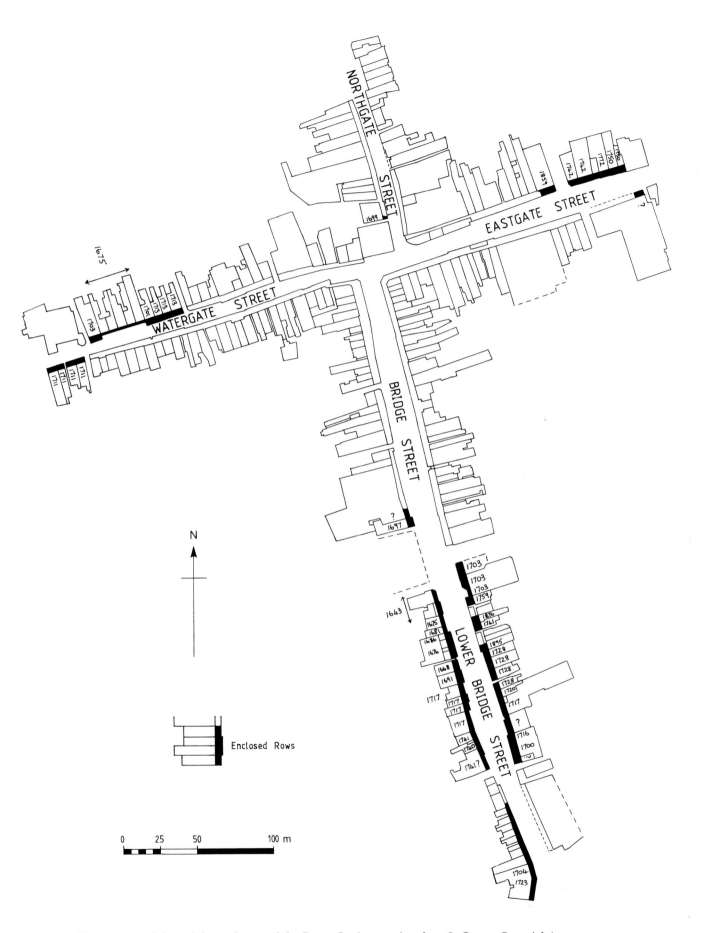

Fig 100 The extent and date of the enclosure of the Rows (basic mapping data © Crown Copyright)

Fig 101 51 and 53 Lower Bridge Street (RCHME © Crown Copyright)

precedent, but it also broke the continuity of this section of the Rows, thus making it easier for owners further down the street to show that the Row before their houses had become useless. By 1687, the remaining Rows between The Falcon and Lady Mary Calveley's house had been enclosed.

The enclosure of the Rows can be traced on all the four main streets (Fig 100) and it is possible to link many of the petitions to surviving buildings. The loss has been greatest in the present Lower Bridge Street, where, with two exceptions, all the former Rows have been enclosed. The early petitions relate to the west side of the street. Then in 1699 John Mather, gentleman, petitioned to build a major new house on the east side. He had recently purchased an old house and a small 'showing', or street level stall, and desired to build a new house which he hoped '...will be some ornament to that part of the street'. Permission was granted in 1700 to build the house, 51 Lower Bridge Street (Fig 101); and this reinforced the increasing trend for the newer properties in Lower Bridge Street

to be purely domestic rather than the mixed commercial-cum-domestic properties of earlier centuries. This could cause problems for the neighbouring owners.

The property to the south of 51 Lower Bridge Street was the Crown and Angel Inn (now No 53), owned by Richard Lawrence. He was required to pay an annual rent of 3s 4d (3 shillings and 4 pence) to the City for an encroachment of this building into the street. In a petition of 1708, he complained that he had '...lost forty shillings per annum in the rent of his said house for the tyme this City granted liberty to Mr Mather to inclose the Row which stopped the passage to this petitioner's said house, and whereas your petitioner having suffered so much by Mr Mather's taking up the Row.' He gave this as the reason for not having paid his rent to the City for the previous four years until he had been distrained by the sword bearer.

This illustrates how the new houses built by the gentry or members of the City Assembly effectively cut off the flow of people along the Row, rendering it 'useless'. Once these major new houses had been constructed the owners of adjacent properties with less influence could make their petitions for enclosure with every hope of success, as in 1716 when Peter Bristow's petition to build a new house, only a single bay wide, next to John Mather was granted. In some cases the City Assembly appeared to balance the loss of the Row against the improvement gained from a new building. In 1717 Madam Elizabeth Booth built Park House, 37–41 Lower Bridge Street, following the grant of the Row for a fine of £8. A previous petition to enclose in 1703, when she did not seem to have any intention of rebuilding, had been rejected.

Sometimes petitions were submitted in concert. One typical group of petitions was put forward in 1717 for 32–42 Lower Bridge Street. Thomas Leigh, Thomas Hunt, William Hunt, and Ambrose Wheawell all described their buildings in relation to that of the late Michael Croughton, whose house William Hunt had recently bought. The first three wished to bring their houses level with Croughton's frontage and to enclose the Row at the same time; the last only wished to add a shop or 'showing' at street level.

On the opposite side of the street three adjacent owners, Mary Whitfield, Roger Ormes, and William Bulkeley, all requested enclosure in 1725. A counter-petition was presented from John Dewsbury, a member of the Assembly, whose public house adjoined this group to the north. He stated that there was no convenient way to his pub other than along the Row, so an enclosure would be of great loss and damage. He estimated that if the Row were enclosed, the premises could only be let at half the current rate. The petitions were rejected. However, in 1727, the same three owners submitted identical petitions together with an agreement between Ormes, Bulkeley, and Dewsbury for the speedy erection of stone steps from the street to Dewsbury's property. These applications were successful and in the following year Dewsbury himself applied to enclose his section of the Row.

On a number of occasions, successful applicants did not carry out the enclosure and it is not therefore possible to rely on the date of a grant by the Assembly as the date of the alteration or construction. Two adjacent properties, 11 and 13 Lower Bridge Street, were both the subject of a number of successful petitions in the first half of the eighteenth century, but the Row at No 11 is one that has remained unenclosed and the Row at No 13 does not seem to have been completely taken into the house until 1876 (Lawson and Smith 1958, 9).

All the examples quoted above relate to Lower Bridge Street, but the same activity can be traced in all the streets with Rows. However, enclosure has generally only taken place at the ends of streets that are at a distance from the Cross. This is possibly the result of Assembly policy, or may reflect the lower value of the Rows away from the commercial centre.

Apart from Alderman Francis Skellern who was granted permission in 1697 to enclose the Row in the building on the north side of Whitefriars (52 Bridge Street) there appears to have been only one other attempt to enclose the Rows in Bridge Street, and this may have been rather more an attempt to influence the Assembly against another petition than a serious intention to enclose. In 1733, George Taylor applied to build his house out on pillars over the Row '...in the manner of Mr Soreton's house'. This prompted his neighbours, Joseph Soreton and Laurence Corless, to state that this action would block off windows to their houses, and to argue that if Taylor was granted this permission then they should be allowed to enclose their Rows in compensation. Not to be left out, Soreton's other neighbour, Robert Jones, requested the same. The Assembly were apparently unimpressed by their argument and granted Taylor's request rent-free, while firmly rejecting the other three.

Rows have been enclosed on both sides of Watergate Street. On the north side all the Rows west

Fig 102 'Alderman Mainwaring's house', 60–66 Watergate Street, from print by G Batenham, 1816 (photograph RCHME © Crown Copyright, from print in CAS Library, Chester Archives)

of Crook Street have gone, while on the south the
Rows have been enclosed west of Weaver Street. Both
these series of enclosures are distant from the commercial heart of Chester and form complete blocks of
buildings cut off from the surviving Rows by minor
streets. The process was begun by Sir Peter Pindar of
Iddenshall Hall. His petition of 1675 asked permission
to regularise an earlier grant; '...your pets. long since
by licence from the Treasurers did enclose the passage
or Row which fronted his house now in his holding in
the Watergate Street containing in about thirteen
yards, – in width and four stoopes or posts there and
for one pair of stairs adjoyning to the said house on the
street side...'.

This petition must refer to the building known as
Alderman Mainwaring's House, which occupied the
site of 60–66 Watergate Street until its demolition in
1852. The Batenham print of the building (Fig 102)
shows a timber-framed house with part of the Row
enclosed, but with the central section remaining open
for the stairs as described in the petition. The measurements given in the petition would correspond with
the enclosure shown by Batenham.

The majority of other enclosures in Watergate
Street were the result of joint action by the owners of
neighbouring properties. On the south side, enclosure
of all the Rows to the west of Weaver Street was
allowed in 1711, although in the case of No 69, confirmation had to be received by a new owner three
years later. In 1713, Sir Thomas Cotton re-started the
process of enclosure on the north side of the street by
asking to enclose the Row at 48–50 Watergate Street.
This prompted his neighbours Robert Bavand (Nos
44–46) and John Martin (No 52) to make similar
requests to the Assembly meeting at which Sir Thomas
Cotton's petition was being considered. During the
course of the meeting the Justices of the Peace were
sent from the Pentice to view the Rows in front of
Bavand's and Martin's houses. They reported
favourably and all three petitions were granted.
However the present frontage of 48–50 Watergate
Street is early nineteenth century (Fig 184) and behind
the window shutter of the front room at Row level can
be seen a Tuscan column which must previously have
supported the upper floors above an open Row (Fig
103). This suggests that the enclosure of this Row did
not occur until many years later[1].

It has proved more difficult to follow the pattern of
Row enclosures in Northgate Street and Eastgate
Street. In Northgate Street, there were some very early
petitions but although some petitioners appear to have
been successful, the evidence from mid-nineteenth-
century prints suggests that the enclosures were never
implemented on the west side at least. In Eastgate
Street the process of enclosure seems to have begun
later than in the other streets and was more actively
resisted by the Assembly. The Eastgate was the main
entry into Chester from early times, and always recorded
the highest collection of tolls taken by the four gates.

*Fig 103 Tuscan column within the shutterbox at 48–50
Watergate Street (RCHME © Crown Copyright)*

Fig 104 The enclosure of Rows destroyed the continuity which provided the commercial benefit of the system, as seen here at 11 Lower Bridge Street (RCHME © Crown Copyright)

As Row enclosure led to the loss of commercial potential both in those buildings where it happened and in the neighbourhood, there may have been a greater incentive to retain the Row walkway here. The nature of the commercial activity is clear in a letter of 1728 from William Hulton to the Governor of the Isle of Man giving details of the rents received from family properties in Eastgate Street[2]. As well as income from various houses, shops, and stables, there was money from the shops in the Row at the midsummer and Michaelmas fairs. During the 1740s, Eastgate Street Row was known as the Manchester Row since it was 'where Manchester tradesmen usually take shops for exposing their wares and merchandise to sale at the time of the Fairs'[3].

On the north side of Eastgate no Row survives in the block between St Werburgh's Street and the Eastgate. Rows also appear to have been lost on the south side from Newgate Street (now the entrance to the Grosvenor Precinct) to the Eastgate. It is not certain that any of these were true Row buildings, with a walkway raised above a line of properties at street level. On the north side, the remaining eighteenth-century buildings (Nos 39, 41, and 45) are not reached by a flight of steps up to the former Row level, as elsewhere in Chester. On the south side, the Row immediately to the west of Newgate Street is only a few feet above

street level, and the shops below are almost in true cellars. This situation can be confirmed by a remarkable sketch elevation of both sides of Eastgate Street (Fig 116). There the treatment of properties east of Newgate Street is different from those to the west, in which an extra storey is shown. Perhaps the properties in this area were like a number of those surviving beyond the Eastgate, in Foregate Street, where the houses are carried out on pillars or posts over the pavement.

New houses

The wish to enclose the Rows was a reflection of the desire for more elaborate accommodation. Three of the new houses built in Lower Bridge Street were substantial and departed from the plan form imposed by the Row walkway. The earliest of these was Bridge House, mentioned at the beginning of this chapter. Lady Mary Calveley had been recently widowed and seems to have expressed her new-found wealth and freedom in building new houses. Bridge House had a five-bay symmetrical frontage, articulated by Ionic columns, with a hipped roof over an elaborate cornice. The interior has a double-pile plan and retains many of its original fittings at Row level. The staircase has bulbous turned balusters, but may not be original[4], and the two

Fig 105 Panelling and carved chimney breast in Bridge House, 18–24 Lower Bridge Street (RCHME © Crown Copyright)

rooms at the rear retain bolection-moulded panelling and a profusely carved wooden chimney breast (Fig 105). Bridge House was altered in the eighteenth century and later; the eared window surrounds now contain sash windows, and the former central doorway and curving imperial staircase have gone. Also the building has acquired an additional bay to the right and a single-storey projection at street level along the whole elevation. A Venetian window has been inserted into the south wall to light the staircase and the rooms on the top floor have been remodelled in a Rococo style. The garden elevation however remains largely unaltered (Fig 106).

The second new house in Lower Bridge Street was that built by John Mather, gentleman, in 1700 (No 51). The interior is much altered and the original plan form is uncertain, but the entrance is very elaborate. The third of these houses was Park House (Nos 37–41), built in 1717 for Madam Elizabeth Booth. These houses appear to be major additions to the very small group of entirely new buildings erected along the main streets since the fourteenth century; not even in the undercrofts does any fabric from earlier buildings survive and the Row walkway also disappears in the process.

Fig 106 Rear of Bridge House, 18–24 Lower Bridge Street (RCHME © Crown Copyright)

Fig 107 Booth Mansion, 28–34 Watergate Street (RCHME © Crown Copyright)

Fig 108   11 Watergate Street (RCHME © Crown Copyright)

The early eighteenth century saw one large house created within the surviving Rows system. This was Booth Mansion, 28–34 Watergate Street, erected by George Booth, later Earl of Warrington. However, it was different from the Lower Bridge Street houses in that it incorporated major elements of the two medieval houses on the site, radically altering the plan, increasing them in height and encasing the whole in a new brick elevation. The resulting house had an eight-bay facade, with rusticated quoins and a heavily projecting wooden cornice below the hipped roof (Fig 107). The street level seems to have retained its shops, and six Tuscan columns were introduced at Row level to carry the building above. The plan of the building has changed, but two large panelled saloons survive at Row + 1 level overlooking the street. This is an early example of what Girouard (1992, 259) has called the double drawing-room, which appears on the first floor of Georgian town houses apparently for card parties

and later for dances. The creation of this new house brought George Booth into conflict with the Assembly. In order to make the house more prominent from The Cross, he angled the facade so that the western end encroaches into the street. This resulted in a fine of £10 and an annual rent of 5s (5 shillings)[5].

The enclosures in Lower Bridge Street produced a number of other new houses on narrow plots; the most elaborate of these is Shipgate House (No 84), built by Sir John Werden (Fig 166). Similarly, the enclosures at the western end of Watergate Street resulted in the substantial house built by Alderman Henry Bennett in 1729 on the corner of Trinity Street. This building (No 68), has a long and complex side elevation. In a lease of 1765 the property is described as a messuage with warehouses, vaults, cellars, a coach house, and three stables[6]. The interior was improved in the later eighteenth century when the large Venetian window was inserted into the Trinity Street elevation to light a fine open-string staircase.

There are a number of good smaller houses in the Rows that date from the first half of the eighteenth century. They are generally of three bays and are symmetrical above Row level. The largest, after Booth Mansion, is 26 Watergate Street, where the quoins and surrounds are of gauged and rubbed brickwork. The interior has a true double-pile plan, with a good turned-baluster staircase at its centre and panelled domestic rooms overlooking the Row walkway. Alderman and former mayor, Peter Ellames, bought the dilapidated timber-framed houses and shops above the vaulted, medieval undercroft of 11 Watergate Street, and was given permission in 1744 to rebuild these and take in the King's Board, the site of the weekly fish market, which had been recently moved to the Fish Shambles[7]. He built a four-storey brick house with rusticated quoins (Fig 108) and the window heads are almost identical with those at 39 Watergate Street, a house which retains most of its eighteenth-century fittings.

Refacing and other alterations

The erection of completely new houses in the Rows was rare; but in those areas where the City Assembly was able to resist enclosure or where the commercial benefits of the two-tier Row system were more apparent, there was still dissatisfaction with the unfashionable timber-framed facades. As a result, many Row buildings were refaced or otherwise altered during the late eighteenth and early nineteenth centuries. These were probably the properties of tradesmen, rather than of the gentry or members of the Assembly.

A typical petition was made by Philip Prestbury, cabinetmaker, in 1767. He had bought an old and decayed building on the east side of Bridge Street Row and was desirous of taking down and rebuilding the front so that it would correspond with the houses on either side[8]. Often in such houses, the earlier timber-framed structure still exists behind the brick facade. At 22 Watergate Street there is clear evidence of the jettied section of the timber-framed building having been sawn off, so that the new facade could be erected on the line of the undercroft frontage (Fig 109). At 21 Watergate Street, the early eighteenth-century brick front to the building contains only the rooms overlooking the street and the staircase behind. A lower range at the rear, dating from the mid-seventeenth century, was retained.

Sometimes only minor modifications were made to existing timber-framed buildings. Sash windows were inserted into the Row chamber of the Leche House, 17 Watergate Street, predating the graffito of 1736 scratched on one of the panes. On this building and elsewhere, the facades were plastered over so that Batenham's elevations of the early nineteenth century show little exposed timber-framing (Fig 110). Subsequently much of this plaster was removed during nineteenth- and twentieth-century restorations. One remarkable example of how existing buildings could be modernised survives in the Old King's Head, 48–50 Lower Bridge Street, where an arcade post of this timber-framed building has been laboriously carved into a Tuscan column, and an abacus inserted (Fig 111).

Refronting could cause problems in buildings with multiple ownerships and tenancies, and must have often prevented improvement. When Thomas Griffith came to rebuild the property on the corner of Watergate Street and Bridge Street, he petitioned the Assembly saying that, '...if he ever purchased Tim. Leftwiche's right to the stalls in the Row and the shops underneath, intermixed with the old houses and the intended new buildings, then he would alter the steps at the end of Watergate Row... and the slope of the corner... to make the turning less sharp and dangerous...'[9]; an arrangement that persists today in the late nineteenth-century building on the site.

The main design problem was how to incorporate the Row walkway into an eighteenth-century facade.

Fig 109 *Jetty bracket in undercroft at 22 Watergate Street (RCHME © Crown Copyright)*

Fig 110 *West side of Bridge Street, from print by G Batenham, 1816 (photograph RCHME © Crown Copyright from print in CAS Library, Chester Archives)*

Fig 112 4 Northgate Street from print by G Batenham, 1816 (photograph RCHME © Crown Copyright, from print in CAS Library, Chester Archives)

haphazard private enterprise, rather than an elegant terrace. The irregularity in the height of the Row storey, dictated by earlier surviving structures, prevented a unified classical treatment of the facades. Cast iron columns were introduced in the late eighteenth century, and these were often used, either singly or in pairs, to support the beam over the Row walkway opening. This was often combined with a less solid approach to the undercroft facade compared with that seen in earlier buildings. At 4 Northgate Street, for example, the late eighteenth-century refronting included a street level shopfront with large display windows, recorded by Batenham *c* 1816 (Fig 112). This is in marked contrast to the rusticated treatment and substantial columns and piers of 22, 24, and 26 Watergate Street (Fig 113), and may reflect the greater commercialism of this central area of the Rows. By the early nineteenth century the Row walkway was seen as an attractive feature in its own right, and was frequently heightened, given narrow cast iron columns, thinner brick piers, and simple iron balustrades; factors which combined to create a lighter, less claustrophobic Row system, more suited to the commercial requirements of the day.

Use of the Rows

The second half of the eighteenth century saw no new town houses in the Rows of the size and quality of those erected during the previous 50 years. The better housing had moved to other parts of the city as attitudes about living in the commercial centre changed. This period also saw significant changes in marketing and retailing which affected the character and use of the Rows. Special market halls were built to deal in specific commodities or to house specific traders; the earliest being the Manchester Hall, built behind Eastgate Street *c* 1751, to provide for the manufacturers of that city. A linen hall for the Irish trade was erected behind Northgate Street in 1755 and moved to

Fig 111 Tuscan column carved from a timber post at the Old King's Head, 48–50 Lower Bridge Street (RCHME © Crown Copyright)

With the predominantly narrow buildings having rather unimpressive levels above the Row, the undercroft and walkway frontages occupy almost half the area of the facade, clearly unsuited to the proportions of a Georgian building. Consequently, an uneasy solution was adopted, in which the undercroft level is treated as a rather squat podium with the Row as a colonnaded, intermediary storey, on which stands the implied order of Row + 1 and Row + 2 levels. There is no attempt to treat the walkway as a continuous colonnade, the party wall of each property usually being marked by brick piers. Like their medieval predecessors the effect is of

Fig 113 From right, 22, 24, and 26 Watergate Street (RCHME © Crown Copyright)

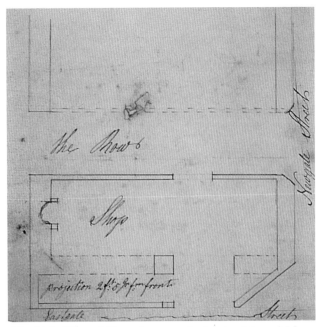

Fig 114 Plan of Row shop attached to petition of Mary Hand, 1771–2 (photograph RCHME © Crown Copyright from original in Chester Archives)

more commodious premises in 1778. The Union Hall of 1809 and the Commercial Hall of 1815 were both built around courtyards off Foregate Street, and each contained 76 stalls on tiered galleries (Kennett 1987, 16). The beast market was moved from Northgate Street as late as 1818, and weekly markets for farm produce and other goods continued in the main streets well into the nineteenth century.

A remarkable 'snapshot' of Eastgate Street and its occupants comes from a sketch elevation of both sides of the street (Fig 116), prepared by Alderman and Mrs Broster, and dated 1750–4, which identifies the occupier of each house and shop[10]. The south side of the street had, and still has, the more up-market shops, particularly at Row level. Interspersed with a number of linen and woollen drapers was a coffee room, a confectioner, two apothecaries, two goldsmiths, a milliner, a toyshop, and a silkmercer. At street level the shops are much more utilitarian, with ten butchers, two grocers, a bakehouse, two barbers, and a tobacconist. On the north side there was a much greater mixture of trades and goods, between a number of inns. A variety of hardware and metalworking shops operated at street level, together with two hatters, a cheesefactor, a tea warehouse, a wine merchant, and an apothecary; while at Row level there were a number of professionals, including a surgeon. Four people are given no trades, implying that their addresses are dwelling houses.

The document shows that Chester was maintaining its position as a sophisticated shopping centre. Mitchell (1980), in a study of retailing in three Cheshire towns during the eighteenth and early nineteenth centuries, showed that the city was stable in most of its trades, and had a higher percentage of luxury shops, such as wine merchants, furniture

dealers, printers, and booksellers, than Stockport or Macclesfield. Chester's shopkeepers not only became wealthy, but were important in the government of the city. Of the 176 sheriffs between 1730 and 1815, 109 were retailers, with mercers, grocers, druggists, wine merchants, and hatters being the most prominent trades.

Apart from the rebuilding and refronting of buildings, these sociological changes cannot be easily detected in the surviving buildings. Small shops continued to be built and modified on the stallboards of the Rows[11]. They were tiny premises, as shown by the plan appended to a petition of 1771–2 by Mary Hand for a street-level stall in Eastgate Street (Fig 114)[12]. However the style of some shops was changing and the displays of goods were more prominent, although the Assembly tried to limit such new developments. In 1762, Holme Burrows petitioned to extend his shop in order to lighten it and better display his toys and goods (Mitchell 1980, 46). In 1768, Mrs Edwards, a milliner in Watergate Street, and Mr Brown, a shoemaker in Bridge Street, were ordered to take down their show glasses, which obstructed the view and passage in the Rows[13], and in 1779, a more general order was made to remove any projections by bow windows or otherwise[14].

Two neo-classical buildings appeared in the Rows in the early nineteenth century. The first, designed by Thomas Harrison and built by subscription in 1807–8, was the Commercial Coffee Room and News Room, 1 Northgate Street (Fig 115). Its pedimented facade makes use of Grecian motifs and includes Harrison's favoured Ionic order (Ockrim 1988). The building does

Fig 115 Former Commercial Newsroom, 1 Northgate Street (RCHME © Crown Copyright)

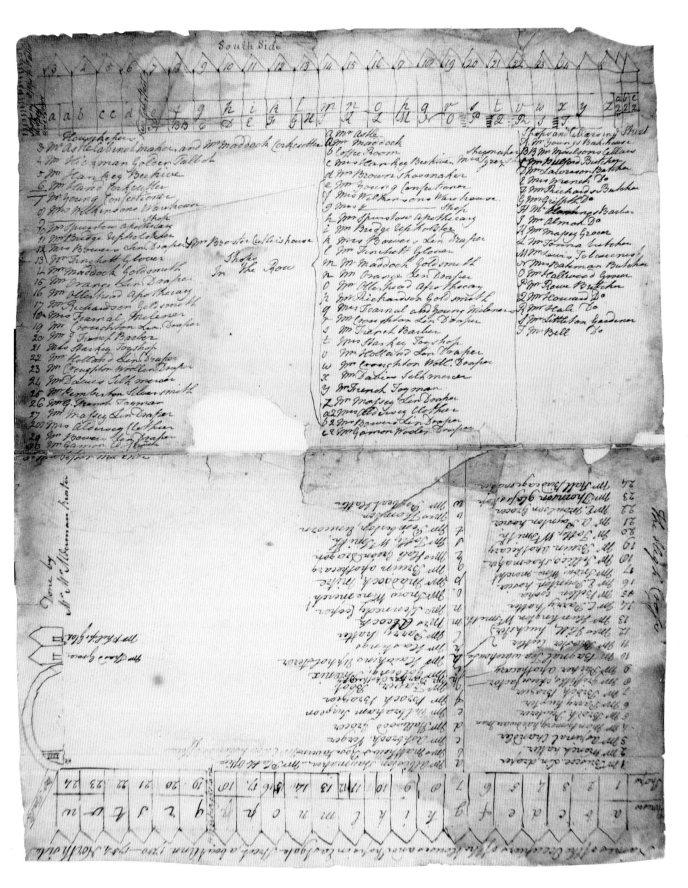

Fig 116 Sketch elevation and record of occupants of both sides of Eastgate Street, 1750–4, by Alderman and Mrs Broster (photograph RCHME © Crown Copyright, from original in Chester Archives)

EASTGATE STREET CHESTER.

Fig 117 Eastgate Street in 1831 from Hemingway's guide

not contain a Row and the street level walkway with its rusticated piers is a later addition. More significant was the erection of a new store by William Brown in Eastgate Street. He was a druggist, married to Susannah Towsey, an ambitious milliner, and they began to import the latest fashions from London. The plans for their new shop, the first purpose-built store in the city, were laid before the Assembly in 1828. It was in the fashionable Greek Revival style and incorporated a Row walkway (Fig 168). By the time it was built in 1831, Joseph Hemingway (1831) could write of the extensive improvements which had taken place in the city, and that the Rows were the best situation for retail shopkeepers.

During the early part of the nineteenth century the character of the Rows was changing rapidly. Writing in 1831, Hemingway described how 40 years earlier, '...there was hardly a shop in any of the rows which could boast a glass window. The fronts were all open to the row, in two or three compartments according to their size; and at night were closed by huge hanging shutters, fixed on hinges, and fastened in the daytime by hooks to the ceiling of the row.'

Most of the small shops and cabins, dating from the seventeenth and early eighteenth centuries, that occupied the Row stalls were removed during the early nineteenth century, to admit light and air to the Row walkways. Only three Row buildings still have the walkway separated from the street frontage by such cabins: 22 and 24 Eastgate Street, and 17–19 Lower Bridge Street.

Another remained at 18–20 Watergate Street, on the corner with Goss Street, until the property was redeveloped in 1970 (Fig 147).

These improvements were the result of an increasing concern for respectability, and were accompanied by constant attempts to combat rowdiness and disorder. The Assembly appointed additional constables in 1815 and gas lighting was introduced in 1818. By 1821, it was reported '...there is once more a chance for a quiet man to pass through the Rows in the evenings without being knocked down the steps, and for a woman to proceed through them without the usual risk of insult' (Mass Observation 1947). In 1823 the mayor urged the heads of households to prevent their children and servants from walking in the Rows in the evenings, and in 1828 a system of voluntary policing by the tradesmen who occupied the Row buildings was established. A view of Eastgate Street included in Hemingway's guide (1831), shows Brown's new store, the streets paved, and the gaslights in position (Fig 117), presenting quite a contrast to the hubbub of the market scene of two years earlier (Fig 81).

Pressures for change

Having considered some of the evidence for Row enclosure (see Appendix C for full details) it is appropriate to consider the motives of those who sought to enclose and those of the Assembly in granting the necessary permission.

The presence of a Row had been an important factor in retaining much of the fabric of the medieval buildings along the principal streets. It also appears to have encouraged separate tenure within single buildings, so that often the street level was in a different ownership from the Row level and above. This is reflected in similar ownership divisions today. Comprehensive rebuilding in such circumstances was obviously difficult. This, coupled with the relatively weak economy of the city in the late Middle Ages and early Tudor periods, ensured that the basic structure of many Row buildings often remained intact over the centuries, although rooms were subdivided and floors and fireplaces inserted as fashions changed. However, the existence of the Row created problems of lighting and privacy that could not be easily overcome. Enclosure of the Row allowed a fundamental change to take place, both to the appearance of the buildings and to their internal planning. It permitted 'modern' buildings in the architectural fashions of the day.

The end of the seventeenth and the beginning of the eighteenth centuries was a time of change in English towns and cities. Commercial activity became more centralised, there was an increasing tendency for the gentry and professional classes to move out to new suburbs, and towns began to develop a more active social life. The activities of Beau Nash in organising

Fig 118 The Exchange, built in 1698, became the centre for polite society (photograph RCHME © Crown Copyright from print in CAS Library, Chester Archives)

the entertainment of the polite society who visited Bath to take the waters is well known. In Chester, the Assembly built the new Exchange, completed in 1698 (Fig 118), to be the centre of their activities, but they also included an Assembly Room, a coffee house and, later, a subscription library. This became the setting of major public entertainments. A resolution of the Assembly of 1722 required that the Exchange could not be let for any ball or public dancing without their express order. During this period a well-established winter social season developed '...with a continual round of assemblies, card evenings and theatrical performances to amuse the landed families who migrated from their country estates to town houses in Chester' (Kennett 1987, 36).

The demand for such entertainments led to the conversion of Booth Mansion, Watergate Street, into another Assembly Room in the 1740s and a further move to the Talbot Inn in 1777. Its successor, the Royal, built in 1785, contained sumptuous premises for public entertainment. Although the first purpose-built theatre was not erected until 1773, Roger Comberbach records watching a number of plays in 1692 (Kennett 1987, 37). But the climax of the social season was the spring race meeting held on the Roodee in May. During this meeting, large numbers flocked in to the inns and privately rented houses.

Further evidence for the expansion in Chester's social life can be seen in the planting of the Groves, the riverside walk in 1732, close to the city's cockpit and a public bowling green. A map of 1789 shows that a two acre private park and garden had been developed behind the house built by Elizabeth Booth in Lower Bridge Street (Hunter 1789). A flavour of this life can be found on almost every page of Henry Prescott's diary for the years 1704–11 (Addy 1987). Deputy Registrar to the Chester diocese, he spent nearly every evening with a circle of professional and gentry friends, deep in drink, in many of Chester's 140 inns. The following morning was often spent circuiting the Roodee or the city walls to walk off his hangover, before he resorted to the coffee house.

For a family to enjoy this new social life, it had to have an appropriate town house. Not only did the period of enclosure coincide with social change, but also with a major change in architectural fashion, first to the Baroque and later to the neo-Classical styles. Chester's collection of timber-framed buildings were much criticised by contemporaries. Celia Fiennes, on a visit in 1697, commented on the main streets: 'There is one thing takes much from their appearing so and from their beauty, for on each side in most places they have made penthouses so broad set on pillars which persons walks under cover and is made up and down steps under which are warehouses.' (Morris 1982, 157)

A generation later Daniel Defoe (1726, 69–70) was blunter, saying, 'nor do the Rows... add any thing, in my opinion, to the beauty of the city; but just the contrary, they serve to make the city look both old and ugly.'

Enclosure had the greatest impact on Lower Bridge Street. This part of Chester had always had major houses (see p15), at least partly because the commercial aspect of the individual properties was less important than in those areas closer to the Cross. Therefore the loss of the Rows here had less commercial significance than elsewhere. New building following Row enclosure was less common elsewhere in Chester.

It seems that Sir Thomas Cotton had plans to build a substantial new house on the sites of 44 and 46 Watergate Street. However, on his death, his widow, Dame Philadelphia Cotton, rebuilt just one of the two properties with little architectural pretension and sold the other. The substantial house built by Alderman Henry Bennett on the same side of the street has already been described (p104). On the east side of Northgate Street, between Lees Lane and Music Hall Passage, Batenham's view shows a good mid-eighteenth-century house between very modest timber-framed Row buildings (Fig 119). Charles, Duke of Shrewsbury (see p154), built a new house on the site of the present Grosvenor Hotel, Eastgate Street in 1714, but nothing of its character is known. Indeed it was not until 1773 that Thomas Moulson erected 'handsome houses' to replace the dangerous Rows in that street.

Something of the impact of these social forces can be seen on the minor streets. There are a number of late seventeenth- and early eighteenth-century town houses in Castle Street, although at least one was just a reworking of a sixteenth-century timber-framed structure (Grenville and Turner, 1986). Whitefriars and King Street were also developed with seventeenth- and eighteenth-century town houses. However, from the middle of the eighteenth century onwards, fashionable houses were being built further from the commercial centre. They were either in terraces or squares, such as Abbey Square (1750s), Nicholas Street (1781) and Stanley Place (1780s), or in suburban locations like the new Bishop's Palace (1754–7) on The Groves and Forest House (1759) on Foregate Street (Fig 120).

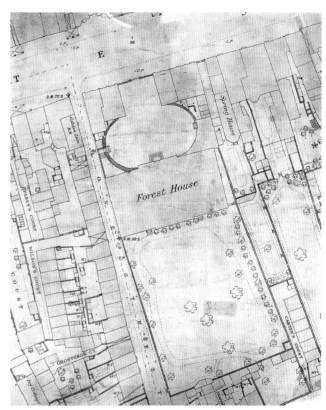

Fig 120   Extract from 1875 map, showing Forest House, Foregate Street, with an impressive oval forecourt and large garden (photograph RCHME © Crown Copyright, map Ordnance Survey © Crown Copyright)

If the prime motive of the gentry and merchant families in enclosing the Row, and later in building new houses away from the centre, was to take part in the social revolution, the Assembly's reasons for granting permission for the loss of the Rows are less clear. In previous and later centuries, the city's authorities resisted efforts to block or encroach upon the Row system. Nevertheless the Assembly cannot be divorced from the merchant and to a lesser extent the gentry classes; it also felt the pressures of architectural fashion

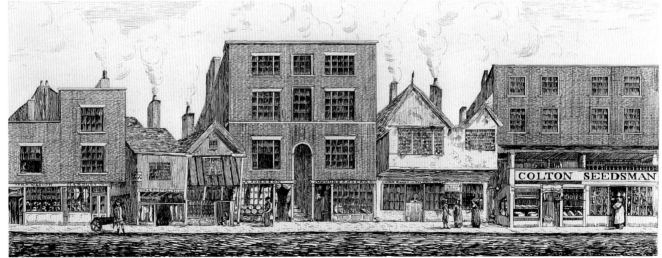

Fig 119   East side of Northgate Street, from print by G Batenham, 1816 (photograph RCHME © Crown Copyright, from print in CAS Library, Chester Archives)

and social pretension, and embarked on a programme of new building. This began with the Exchange, completed in 1698, and continued when the Pentice was encased in brick in 1704. In addition to these new buildings, £1000 was spent on the repair and maintenance of the city walls during the reign of Queen Anne, and the Assembly also faced considerable problems and expense in maintaining the Dee Navigation (Kennett 1987, 21). Some of this expenditure was covered by private subscription and donation. In 1702, the Assembly recorded its thanks to Sir Henry Bunbury MP for his gift of £100 towards the cost of the Exchange[15]. Much of the remainder of the money had to be found from tolls, taxes, fines and the rents from city property. Row enclosure, through its fines and rents, was a source of much needed revenue. Although this was never directly stated, an entry in the Assembly Book for 1700 betrays the need. It states that 'Mr Booth's fine for his encroachment (at Booth Mansion) and the fines for Mr Kenna's and Mr Simpson's freedom should be applied towards paying the debts contracted for building the new hall'[16].

The Assembly imposed a small fine and a substantial annual rent for the early enclosures to compensate for the loss of city property. However by the end of the seventeenth century this policy seems to have changed towards the imposition of a single cash payment. It is clear from the treasurer's accounts that small annual rents were difficult to collect, and this, together with the need to finance the building programme, was almost certainly the reason for the change. Fig 121 shows the frequency of petitions for Row enclosure and their success by each decade of the period studied. It also tries to show how much revenue was generated by granting petitions. There is a noticeable peak in the early eighteenth century, which coincides with the Assembly's own building works. The decade 1740–50 saw few approvals despite a very large number of petitions, possibly because there was less need to raise finance during this period.

The pressures for social and architectural change appear to have been too great to resist, and the Assembly themselves were caught up by the desire to erect new buildings. However, despite the loss of almost a third of the medieval raised walkways, the core of the system remained, protected by the Assembly, who presumably recognised the continuing commercial advantages of the Rows. From the 1770s to the present day, almost no further losses have occurred.

The years 1670 to 1830 also saw very significant changes to the appearance of the Rows. At the beginning of the period, the facades would have been almost exclusively timber-framed, but the construction of substantial brick houses and the refronting of many others led to a radically different appearance by the early nineteenth century. Just as important a change occurred in the use of the Rows. The essentially medieval pattern of trading, with small shops, stalls, warehouses, fairs, and street markets, was replaced by the modern style of retailing, with larger and larger shops that eventually took over the whole of the building. Also the Rows were no longer considered the smart place to live, and the wealthy began to move out of the commercial centre. The city centre, as we know it today, was beginning to be formed.

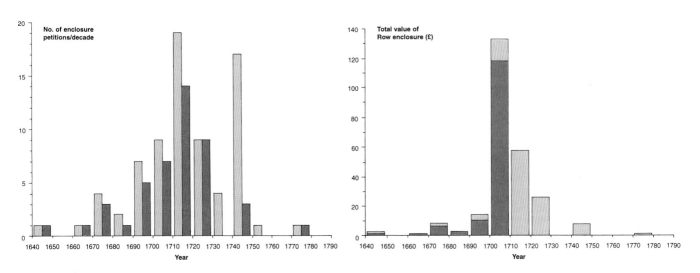

Fig 121 Tables showing the frequency of petitions to enclose the Row, their success and relative values. Rents have been multiplied by ten to give an approximate capital value. (In table left, petitions are denoted by dark tone, approvals by light tone. In table right, fines are denoted by dark tone, rents by light tone.)

9 The Vernacular Revival

For the mid-nineteenth-century visitor to Chester, the Rows had become an attraction of some appeal. Those following the guidebooks were informed that the Rows were 'as interesting to the antiquarian as they are convenient for a quiet lounge to ladies and others engaged in shopping' (Evans and Gresty 1857, 64). The preoccupation with shopping was nothing new; the Rows had their origins in commerce, and their later evolution has been no less dependent on economic forces. But antiquarianism was a new ingredient, for if there is a factor peculiar to the late nineteenth- and twentieth-century development of the Rows, it is a desire to capture the spirit of former times.

At a meeting on 31 December 1849, the Chester and North Wales Architectural, Archaeological and Historic Society was formed. The Society's objectives encompassed those of a modern civic society, and included: 'The Improvement of Architectural Taste, Science and Construction', and 'The recommending of Plans for the restoration, construction and improvement of buildings and other works' (*JCAS* 1857, 1–14). When the meeting came to be written up in the first issue of the Society's *Journal* it was accompanied by an article entitled 'Street Architecture in Chester'. The anonymous author of this piece regretted the replacement of timber-framed houses with their 'curiously carved fantastical gables' by 'miserable brick, and incongruous piles of heavy Athenian architecture' (*JCAS* 1857, 463). In an argument redolent of our own times, he warned

> ...that if Chester is to maintain its far-famed celebrity as one of the 'wonder cities' of England, if the great European and Transatlantic continents are still to contribute their shoals of annual visitors to fill our hotels, and the not too plenteous coffers of our tradesmen, one course only is open to us. We must maintain our ancient landmarks, we must preserve inviolate our city's rare attractions, ...our quaint old Rows, unique and picturesque as they certainly are, must not be idly sacrificed at Mammon's reckless shrine.

It was a call for conservation and respect for the buildings of the past. But the article also set out a stylistic programme for the future, for the author concluded 'every old house preserved or judiciously restored, or every new one erected after the same distinguishing type, will tend to raise the importance and perpetuate the fair fame of our venerable city.' This was the first public plea for the revival of half-timbering.

To reinforce this plea, the *Journal* also reported a lecture given in September 1850 by the architect Thomas Mainwaring Penson on the history of timber framing (*JCAS* 1857, 184). Penson's research was put to good effect, for in 1852, in Eastgate Street, he created the first half-timbered revival building in Chester (Fig 122). Although it followed the eighteenth-century trend of refacing an earlier structure, the house and chemist's shop for Mr Platt received much praise from the Archaeological Society (*JCAS* 1857, 337).

Penson can be credited with introducing this style to Chester; indeed it was a style which scarcely existed outside Chester[1]. His next Row project was at 36–38 Eastgate Street, a pair of half-timbered houses and shops erected in 1857 for William and Charles Brown (Figs 123, 142, 170)[2]. Although they are designed as a single building, the two frontages are each expressed in a different manner. This picturesque device became a standard technique of the Vernacular Revival and is one of the keys to its visual appeal. But in the early buildings, the styling is skin deep, for the timbering is insubstantial and the detailing unhistorical. A particular characteristic is the use of elaborately pierced bargeboards which are seen rarely in Cheshire's sixteenth- or seventeenth-century buildings, but are favourite features of Tudor Revival country houses and railway stations of the 1850s.

Another architect who pioneered the new style was James Harrison, the first architectural correspondent of

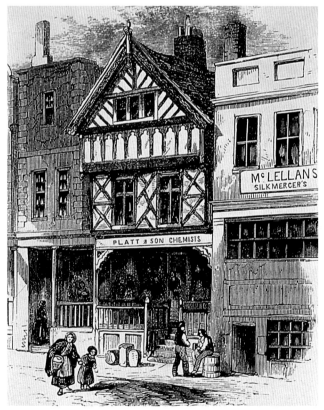

Fig 122   The house and chemist's shop for Mr Platt in Eastgate Street, Thomas Penson, 1852 (from The Builder, *30 August 1856)*

Fig 123   36–38 Eastgate Street, Thomas Penson for William and Charles Brown, 1857 (from The Builder, *30 August 1856)*

the Archaeological Society. Harrison was a scholarly architect, responsible for restoring many of the city's medieval churches. His speciality was Perpendicular Gothic, but for two buildings in the Rows he dabbled with vernacular sources. No 40 Bridge Street, built in 1858 for Welsby's, wine merchants, is the more straightforward; a Tudor Revival building in brick and stone with an oriel window[3]. Number 51–53 Bridge Street, situated opposite and erected in the same year, is half-timbered[4]; but apart from the timbering, which is planted on to a brick facade, there is little to differentiate the two.

Harrison was involved in the first recorded conservation case in Chester – the battle to save God's Providence House, 9 Watergate Street. The future of this seventeenth-century building was raised by Thomas Hughes (author of the 1856 edition of *The Stranger's Guide to Chester*) at a meeting of the Archaeological Society in November 1861[5]. It had recently changed hands and the new owner was reported to be intent on demolishing the building. Hughes urged that its existing character and the old carved timbers of the front facade be preserved. His plea bore fruit, for by the Society's next meeting, Harrison had been appointed as architect and his plans for the property were displayed (*JCAS* 1864, 405). In deference to public opinion, so the report went, the front was to be kept and as much of the ancient character as possible retained. The reality turned out somewhat differently, for in 1862 the house was completely rebuilt and the height greatly increased (Fig 124). Here the boundaries of contemporary opinion are not too clearly defined, for conservation and rebuilding in the same style seemed to meet with equal approval.

The new generation of buildings going up in the Rows enhanced the city's shopping status, which in turn demanded a more salubrious environment. With the introduction of the first Chester Improvement Act in 1845, serious attempts were made to improve the health and amenity of the city centre. Under the Act the Council was empowered to repair and drain the streets, and clear private responsibilities were established for maintaining the Rows and footpaths. Action was taken promptly to enforce repairs of dilapidated steps, and where owners defaulted, the Council authorised its surveyor to carry out the works and charge them[6]. Fines were levied for allowing livestock to stray in the highways, and traders petitioned the Council to remove cattle markets from the streets and prevent stallholders occupying the Rows on market days. With the opening of the Public Market building in 1863, the provision markets finally moved out of Eastgate Street. The change from an area of mixed uses and uncontrolled enterprise to a formalised shopping centre was well under way.

Browns' new premises of 1828 at 32–34 Eastgate Street had been the first shop to establish new standards of opulence (see Chapter 8). Contrasting it with its old-fashioned neighbours, Hemingway (1831, 410) visualised 'a brace of country clowns in tattered habiliments linked under each arm of a dashing exquisite of the nineteenth century, or... of a splendid family mansion flanked by a couple of mud wall cow houses' (Fig 168). The adjoining buildings did not last long, for Browns' success led to the expansion of their empire, and the 'country clowns' were swallowed up. Penson's proto-Vernacular Revival buildings of 1857 replaced the one, and his Crypt Building of 1858 replaced the other (Fig 125)[7]. The three buildings comprise a most extraordinary group, and illustrate the disregard that the mid-Victorians felt for stylistic harmony. The choice of sandstone and thirteenth-century Gothic for the Crypt Building was made to harmonise with the medieval undercroft over which it was built. Since High Victorian Gothic was Penson's strongest style, it is his most successful work in Chester. However, the building was not without its critics, for the Vernacular Revival lobby had become strong. The *Chester Chronicle*, taking sides in the battle of the styles, supported the design.

Fig 124 God's Providence House, 9 Watergate Street, before (left) and after (right) the 'restoration' of 1862

Fig 125 Browns' Crypt Building, Thomas Penson, 1857,
designed to complement the medieval undercroft over which
it stands (RCHME © Crown Copyright)

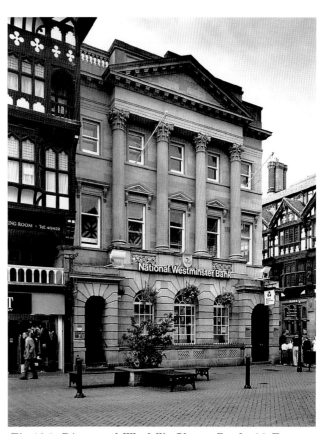

Fig 126 Dixon and Wardell's Chester Bank, 33 Eastgate
Street, George Williams, 1860 (RCHME © Crown
Copyright)

We cannot agree with those who withhold
commendation because the Crypt Buildings are
supposed to be out of character, simply because
they are not timber buildings. The remains of
ancient buildings in Chester are mostly so, but
they are of a later date: and the very Crypt from
which this edifice takes its name and which is
the only part of the original building still
remaining, indicates a style and date to which a
timber superstructure could not be appropriate,
but with which the present building strictly har-
monizes (Mass Observation 1947, 80).

There is no medieval source for the design, just as
Penson's half-timbered buildings lacked scholarship;
but if the architect was unaware of the contemporary
work of the Vernacular Revivalist, George Devey,
he was far from ignorant of the leading Gothic
Revivalists, for his design for Browns recalls the
University Museum, Oxford, of 1855–60 by Deane
and Woodward, and the abortive competition entry of
1857 by George Gilbert Scott for the Foreign Office
(Dixon and Muthesius 1978, 159, 161).

By the late 1850s the southern side of Eastgate
Street had become the best situation for retailers, and
commanded the highest rents. The north side of the
street remained, by comparison, relatively undeveloped.
On this side the Dark Row was notorious for prostitu-
tion and rowdiness, and when Messrs Dixon and

Wardell, the proprietors of the Chester Bank, decided
in 1857 to build their prestigious headquarters at the
junction with St Werburgh Street, they determined to
stop off the Row rather than run it through the new
building. In spite of public opposition to the proposed
enclosure, the bank was able to obtain approval from
the Improvement Committee by offering a strip of
adjoining land for widening St Werburgh Street,
together with land in Northgate Street[8]. The design of
the new building was also controversial. Ignoring the
disparaging remarks of the Archaeological Society, the
Bank attempted to introduce a metropolitan character
to Chester, and in 1860 erected a monumental classical
stone building, with a pediment and giant order of
Corinthian columns (Fig 126). It duly came in for
harsh criticism; Audsley (1891) describing it as
'distinctly out of place in such a street'. The architect
of the new bank, George Williams, was a competent
classical designer who put up large houses in both
Liverpool and the USA. The dominance of the
vernacular lobby is doubtless therefore responsible
for causing his subsequent buildings in Chester to be
half-timbered. These were 12 Eastgate Street, a tall
and fanciful building erected in 1861 for Messrs
Beckett and Co, drapers, and the adjacent and contemporary No 10 (Fig 127)[9]. For height, scale and
showiness, Williams' buildings outdid those of his
fellow architects, and they mark the culmination of
the early phase of the Vernacular Revival. The next

Fig 127   10 and 12 Eastgate Street, George Williams, 1861 (RCHME © Crown Copyright)

*Fig 128   20 Bridge Street, the first Row building by Thomas Lockwood, 1873 (*The Building News, *23 September 1872)*

generation of architects adopted a more scholarly and disciplined approach.

By the 1860s the Vernacular Revival was becoming a national style. George Devey shunned publicity, and his buildings were not widely known. They were however familiar to the young London architects W E Nesfield and R Norman Shaw, who introduced into their own projects elements derived from vernacular buildings of the home counties (Saint 1976). Their work was widely published, and it soon had an impact in Chester. Before this the Chester architects had been developing a truly local style; later it became one part of a wider movement.

Two local figures dominated the architectural scene in Chester during the latter part of the nineteenth century: John Douglas and Thomas Meakin Lockwood. They were principal architects to Chester's major landowners, the Grosvenors, Dukes of Westminster, who held substantial property in the city centre. Lockwood came to Chester as a pupil of Penson, setting up his own practice in the early 1860s. Following Penson's death in 1864, Lockwood became the Grosvenors' favoured architect for their Chester commissions. Like Penson he was brought up within the Gothic tradition, but in Chester he wholeheartedly adopted the burgeoning Vernacular Revival. His contribution to the Rows is more significant than that of any other single architect.

Lockwood's first Row project was at 20 Bridge Street, a pair of shops and houses erected for Mr Webb

in 1873 (Fig 128)[10]. It has a tall symmetrical front with a single gable and a rather stiff arrangement of timber-framing. Whilst the timbering has the insubstantial look of the early Vernacular Revival buildings, in other respects the building looks forward to the more mature style of the late nineteenth century. The most striking feature is the pargetted coving to the oriel window, a form of decoration which had been widely used by Shaw and Nesfield.

Lockwood's most famous Row building is 1 Bridge Street, erected for the City Council at The Cross in 1888[11]. At precisely the same time he designed the adjoining building, 2 Eastgate Street, for the Duke of Westminster (Harris 1979, 49). This building is bold and simple, a four-storey symmetrical facade surmounted by a broad gable, with jetties at each level. But the timbers are heavier and more closely spaced than in earlier buildings, and their surfaces are overlaid with a rich display of carved and moulded ornament. The decoration is derived from Renaissance rather than Gothic sources; at once more scholarly, but also more inventive than the work of Penson and James Harrison. At a glance it is hard to believe that 1 Bridge Street was designed and built at the same time, for the height and scale are quite different. But it is that contrast of scale, and the way the external elements are arranged that makes this corner so memorable (Fig 129). The essence of the composition is the treatment of the skyline. The lower building has at its centre a favourite Lockwood device, a domed turret rising

Fig 129   Thomas Lockwood's buildings at the corner of Bridge Street and Eastgate Street, 1888 (RCHME © Crown Copyright)

above the eaves; whilst behind it, the taller building is given greater height by the massive stone chimney with its vertical shafts and prominent capping.

Four years later the Duke gave Lockwood the opportunity to rebuild the opposite corner of Bridge Street[12]. The site was occupied by a number of separate plots, and as with the Eastgate Street corner, the new building was broken up to provide for a lively appearance. It was achieved not only by a varied silhouette, but also by mixing materials, for parts of the building are faced in brick and stone and others are half-timbered, the latter forming stops or book-ends to each side of the facade (Fig 130). The decoration here extends the vocabulary of Renaissance motifs, and introduces elements of English Baroque in the form of scrolls and broken pediments. But the eclectic composition is inspired principally by contemporary buildings, and Norman Shaw's New Zealand Chambers in Leadenhall Street, London are the source of the tripartite oriel windows.

Both these corner developments on Bridge Street replaced modest seventeenth- and eighteenth-century buildings. Whether they contained medieval undercrofts or other historic fabric is not recorded, but it is a feature of Lockwood's Row projects that all traces of earlier structures were removed. Conservation may have been one of the aims of the Archaeological Society, but Lockwood preferred the clean sweep. The contradiction is made all the more ironic by

Fig 130   2–8 Bridge Street, Thomas Lockwood for the Duke of Westminster, 1892 (RCHME © Crown Copyright)

Lockwood's apparent antiquarian interests. He was a bibliophile with an important book collection[13], and he produced a booklet on Bridge Street, with John Hewitt, for a meeting of the Royal Archaeological Institute, which records the interiors of many of the buildings (Lockwood and Hewitt 1886).

One restoration project in the Rows which Lockwood did undertake was at Bishop Lloyd's Palace, 41 Watergate Street (Fig 131). His client was Alderman Charles Brown, who, with his brother William, ran the expanding haberdashery store in Eastgate Street. In April 1899, a small party of local dignitaries and members of the Archaeological Society visited the building at Brown's invitation to inspect it prior to restoration[14]. Brown told the party that there was a danger of the building being sold to an American syndicate and he had therefore stepped in and purchased it himself for preservation. The value of the existing building was universally recognised, but Lockwood nonetheless contrived major alterations during the course of restoration. The left-hand gable was rebuilt and made to line up with the right, the eighteenth-century sashes were replaced by mullioned windows, and one of the stallboards was removed to make way for a new staircase from the street (Fig 131, right). Whilst the important carved panels on the front were retained, and the plaster ceilings and fireplaces sensitively restored, Lockwood could not resist adding his own decorative embellishments in the form of carved brackets with grotesque figures supporting the upper storeys at Row level (Fig 178).

Both Lockwood and Brown played a part in the most far-reaching redevelopment scheme to affect the Rows in the nineteenth century, the rebuilding of Shoemakers' Row. A picturesque group of mostly seventeenth-century properties on the west side of Northgate Street (Fig 132), the Row was notorious; it was the subject of regular complaints from local people for its tendency to attract low life and undesirable behaviour. At the same time the narrowness of Northgate Street at this point caused severe congestion, particularly on market days. In 1877 the City Council set up a special committee to consider ways of improving the area, and Alderman Brown was elected a member. At the first meeting on 25 May, the Town Clerk was ordered to investigate the possibility of acquiring St Peter's Church with a view to pulling it down[15]. Thomas Lockwood was engaged to advise the committee, and with the surveyor Robert Roberts, he submitted eleven possible proposals for widening Northgate Street[16]. Six involved demolishing the church and Harrison's News Room, as well as Shoemakers' Row, and three proposed a new wide thoroughfare running in a curve from Watergate Street to Northgate Street through what is now St Peter's Churchyard. Their clear recommendation was to demolish the church so as to improve traffic flow at The Cross, and to provide views of the Town Hall

Fig 131 Bishop Lloyd's Palace before (left), and after (right) 'restoration' in the 1890s (RCHME © Crown Copyright)

Fig 132 Early nineteenth-century view by G Pickering of Shoemakers' Row on the west side of Northgate Street (Photograph RCHME © Crown Copyright, from print in CAS Library, Chester Archives)

from Eastgate Street. What is revealing is Lockwood's ambivalent attitude to the Rows, for though he felt that reinstating a Row within the new frontage buildings would 'perpetuate a picturesque and interesting feature of the city', he actually favoured a conventional facade without Rows or even an arcade, on the grounds that introducing Rows 'may hamper resale of the property.'

The Committee took a less commercial view and asked that the 'features of the Row' be preserved[17]. Their preferred scheme was a compromise involving retention of the tower of St Peter's and building a new church to the west of the tower. The effect of this scheme would have been to widen the street from 15 feet (5m) to a minimum of 78 feet (26m), and Lockwood produced a perspective drawing showing the new frontage which he described as 'having the general Chester character, but not all of exactly the same style as it would naturally be built by several owners who would use their own style and notions'[18]. Whilst this proposal never came about, Shoemakers' Row was indeed ultimately rebuilt in 'the general Chester character' by several different owners, though Lockwood himself was to take no further part in it. Whilst his scheme was publicly exhibited in 1878, a resolution to proceed was never made, and in March 1881 the Northgate Street Committee itself was abolished[19].

From 1877, the Council had taken the opportunity to acquire properties in Shoemakers' Row whenever the occasion arose, and so had Charles Brown; and it was he who ultimately caused redevelopment to take place. Brown was a prominent member of the City Club which had taken over the premises of Thomas Harrison's Commercial News Room at 1 Northgate Street. Having acquired the adjacent plot, Brown submitted to the City Council in 1894 a scheme for rebuilding to provide an extension to the club[20]. His architect was the County Surveyor, H W Beswick, whose first design for the site included a Row. The Improvement Committee however, still seeking a coordinated scheme for Northgate Street, requested that the shop under the Row be abandoned and an arcade at street level be created. The new frontage was required to line up with the club. In 1897, after much negotiation, Brown accepted these changes[21], but only on condition that compensation was paid for the loss of a shop, and that the fronts of the three adjoining buildings which were in the ownership of the Council be demolished and set back to the same line. Thus the fate of the old buildings was sealed, and over the next 12 years the whole stretch of Shoemakers' Row was redeveloped.

The pattern of redevelopment corresponds closely to a proposal previously made by John Douglas in 1887 (Fig 133)[22]. Although the suggestion of running an arcade through St Peter's Church and the

Fig 133 *Proposals by John Douglas for the improvement of Shoemakers' Row, 1887*

Fig 134 *Shoemakers' Row, Northgate Street (photograph RCHME © Crown Copyright))*

Commercial News Room was not carried out, his half-timbered design for the new Shoemakers' Row was very much as executed (Figs 134 and 171)[23]. The first new building to be erected in Shoemakers' Row was 21–23 Northgate Street for Alderman Brown. Designed by Beswick, it is dated on the front elevation 1897 and inscribed with Brown's initials[24]. Only Brown's new building at 3 Northgate Street, erected in 1898–9, fails to follow the timber-framed tradition, being pebble-dashed within a broad timber framework. Behind the jettied upper storey of this building, and lit by coloured glass, was a new dining room for the members of the City Club, an interior which was inspired by the hall of the Leche House in Watergate Street. From his study of the Leche House, Beswick came to understand the medieval town house layout, and his facade to the tall City Club dining room is expressed as if it were chamber and attic, thus consciously reflecting the scale and rhythm of pre-classical Row buildings.

Douglas designed several of the new buildings in Shoemakers' Row. In 1899 he purchased 5, 7, and 9 Northgate Street from the Council and developed the site himself[25]. He designed Nos 11 and 13 for J F Densen and Sons, and he may also have been responsible for No 19[26]. When the Council acquired Nos 27–31, the corner property to the Market Square, Douglas was appointed as architect for the new building, which was erected in 1902[27].

Douglas' designs are recognisable by a strong sense of craftsmanship and a sensitivity to materials. This is

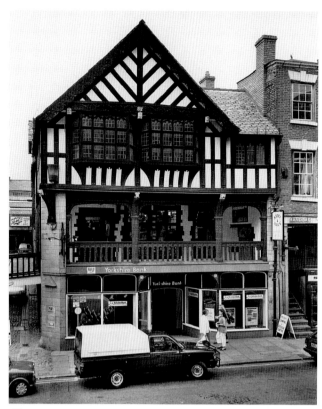

Fig 136 38 Bridge Street, John Douglas for the Duke of Westminster, 1897 (RCHME © Crown Copyright)

especially true of his woodwork which is always meticulously detailed (Fig 172). Unlike his colleagues in Cheshire, he had first hand experience of building crafts, having learned carpentry in the workshop of his father, a country builder, before he became the pupil of E G Paley, the Lancaster church architect. The frontages of 5–9 Northgate Street are a virtuoso display of the versatility of timber, their heavy bressumers and bargeboards carved with delicate Gothic cusping and trailing foliage (Fig 135). In his contemporary scheme for the east side of St Werburgh Street, Douglas broke up the long frontage into a series of separate units, each with its own identity. It was a technique that suited the narrowness of the street and the oblique viewpoints of the passer-by. But the irregular rhythm is contained by a unifying stylistic language, a common repertoire of materials and details, so that picturesque diversity is combined with visual order. This was not achieved so successfully in Northgate Street. Douglas set standards with the buildings that he designed, but he had no controlling interest, and the other architects lacked his sensitivity.

One of the other architects involved with Shoemakers' Row was Douglas' pupil James Strong, who designed Nos 15–17 built in 1909 to replace the Cross Keys Inn[28]. A comparison with the adjoining Douglas frontages reveals a lack of stylistic fluency and an over-fussy composition. The semicircular oriels with their elaborately carved cusping are repeated by Strong in his fire station building further up Northgate Street. Also seemingly by Strong is No 25 which was

Fig 135 Detail of 5–9 Northgate Street, designed and developed by John Douglas for the improvement of Shoemakers' Row, 1887 (RCHME © Crown Copyright)

Fig 137   55 Bridge Street, designed by Thomas Edwards, 1889 (RCHME © Crown Copyright)

refaced *c* 1914[29]. Photographs of *c* 1910 show an earlier Vernacular Revival frontage which had been built forward of the new street line; the replacement front was set back[30].

Although responsible for a huge number of buildings in the Chester area during his long career, Douglas contributed only one true Row building, 38 Bridge Street (Fig 136). This was erected for the first Duke of Westminster in 1897[31]. The design follows the medieval pattern of a stone undercroft (here at street level), with a timber-framed superstructure. The Row frontage is divided into three bays by octagonal posts supporting a jettied upper storey. The timbers are heavily ornamented with Gothic tracery patterns giving the surfaces a richness which was especially appealing to nineteenth-century taste.

A more shadowy figure is W M Boden (Hubbard 1991, 207, 229). A pupil of T M Penson, he was the designer of two buildings in Bridge Street: Nos 3–7, erected in 1889–90; and No 49, erected in 1891[32]. Both buildings are similar in appearance, each having a half-timbered upper storey with a brick facade below. The Row is protected by a shallow lean-to roof which is cut into by the canted bays of the storey above. R W Boden, presumably his son, designed 12–14 Northgate Street, erected *c* 1912, and probably also 16 Northgate Street[33]. Both these buildings are black and white from top to bottom, but are of little distinction.

Another architect who developed the black and white style with enthusiasm was Thomas Edwards. Together with his partner W H Kelly, Edwards took

over James Harrison's practice on his death in 1866. Edwards was responsible for 55 Bridge Street, built as an art gallery for David Sherratt in 1889 (Fig 137)[34]. It has an exuberant facade, incorporating jettying, carved timber panels in the manner of Bishop Lloyd's Palace, and a statue of Charles I. But the timbering of both Edwards' and Boden's buildings lacks the assured handling of a Douglas design, and has the look of applied pattern-making rather than an integrated element of the structure.

An assistant of John Douglas, belonging to an earlier generation, was Edward Hodkinson. He had a career with the Grosvenor Estate before joining the Douglas office, and designed extensions to Saighton Grange on the Eaton estate for the second Marquis of Westminster in 1861 (Hubbard 1991, 206, 228; de Figueiredo and Treuherz 1988, 159). He resided in a part of the remarkable seventeenth-century Mainwaring House (Fig 102) on Watergate Street until its demolition in 1851[35], and was responsible for the terrace of houses built for the timber merchants, Dixon and Myers, which replaced it (Hewitt 1887, 36–7). Hodkinson was no pioneer timber-frame revivalist, and his new houses were in a utilitarian Tudor Revival style, with brick gables and large plate-glass windows. He adopted a similar style for his other Row commissions before joining Douglas: 13 Bridge Street, erected in 1861 for Mr Ewen, hosier[36], and 37–41 Bridge Street, of 1864 for the second Marquis and first occupied by Beckett Brothers[37]. He was also responsible for a building erected in 1863 at 33–35 Bridge Street (Fig 138), which was later to be replaced by the controversial St Michael's Row building. This development received a good deal of attention, for when the site was cleared, substantial Roman remains were discovered (Brushfield 1871). Redevelopment gave the opportunity to excavate part of the impressive Roman bath house; and this was the first serious archaeological investigation carried out in Chester, although little was retained *in situ*.

As a rule, the reconstruction work of previous centuries had been far less destructive of older fabric. The eighteenth-century refacing and internal modernisation had often been carried out without affecting medieval undercrofts. By contrast, few nineteenth-century Row properties retain ancient stonework. One of the most serious losses was at 12 Eastgate Street, the premises of Messrs Becketts until its destruction in 1861. A proposal to demolish the vaulted undercroft came to the attention of the Archaeological Society early in 1861, whereupon they sent a plea to the company asking that it be retained (*JCAS* 1863, 405). At the subsequent meeting it was reported that Mr Beckett had instructed his architect, George Williams, to save the undercroft, but during the works it 'unavoidably' collapsed and all was destroyed (*JCAS* 1863, 410). Although a crude drawing was made of the undercroft, no accurate survey was ever carried out.

This event was criticised by John Hewitt, whose article in the *Journal* of the Archaeological Society of

Fig 138 Early photograph of the east side of Bridge Street; the prominent building with four gables was Nos 33–35 designed by Edward Hodkinson, 1863 (RCHME © Crown Copyright)

1887 was the first scholarly attempt to explain the origins of the Rows. He was also the first to condemn the reconstruction of God's Providence House, which he described as notable 'not so much for its well-known legend, nor its dated and inscribed beam, as for the unsatisfactory manner in which it has been restored'. This opinion was repeated in the 1890 volume of the *Journal*, where a photograph of the house 'before restoration' was included as a frontispiece (Fig 124). The same volume published the first criticism of the fashion for half-timbering, by Edward Hodkinson, whose long career allowed him a less prejudiced view of the architecture of the eighteenth century. 'It is much to be regretted', he wrote, 'that our fine old houses.... should not be restored in the spirit of their original design', remarking on the Old White Bear Inn in Lower Bridge Street where the Georgian front had been painted a black and white pattern in imitation of timberwork, and adding, 'it is almost incredible that such a piece of vandalism should take place in Chester' (*JCAS* 1890, 324).

Half-timbering in paint has never deceived, and thin planks applied to a brick or rendered wall in the fashion of present day speculative house builders are no better. The structural approach to nineteenth-century half-timbering in Chester took many different forms. Traditional methods of frame construction were not widely understood by Victorian architects, and

alterations to sixteenth- and seventeenth-century buildings were often carried out with disregard for historical accuracy. For the facades of their new buildings, the leading Vernacular Revival architects generally used load-bearing brickwork as backing to a timber frame, sometimes introducing steelwork to achieve wider spans and jettying. It was a pragmatic method which exploited new technology whilst giving the appearance of traditional construction. But the lofty scale, spindly proportions and structural daring of many of the buildings could not have been achieved by use of oak and plaster infill alone.

The architect who was finally to make a determined, though in the end unsuccessful, stand against the strait-jacket of the Vernacular Revival was W T Lockwood. With his brother, P H Lockwood, he had taken over the thriving practice established by their father, and, for a period, they continued to enjoy the patronage of the Grosvenor family. The building in question was 31–35 Bridge Street, which includes St Michael's Row (Fig 153), which is a typical Edwardian shopping arcade, not a true Chester Row. The design of this building was to be a *cause célèbre* which involved the second Duke of Westminster in considerable controversy and expense. Plans for the redevelopment of Hodkinson's building of 1863 came before the Improvement Committee in June 1909[38]. The scheme was approved, but, noting that the front elevation was

Fig 139 Extent of Row rebuilding during the nineteenth and twentieth centuries (basic mapping data © Crown Copyright)

to be of faience, the committee instructed the Town Clerk to write to the Duke urging that it be changed to half-timbering, 'in harmony with the characteristic architecture of the city'. Similar petitions were presented by the Archaeological Society and the Bishop of Chester. At first the Duke took no notice, replying that the matter was in the hands of Trustees in London and that they had decided not to erect a timber front as it would require repainting every three years at a cost of £150[39].

Construction started early in 1910, and by the middle of September the white and gold tiled facade, 'The White City' as it became popularly known, had reached its full height (Fig 140)[40]. It provoked a lively correspondence in the local newspaper. Central to the argument that developed was the merit of the new building and its suitability to Chester's Rows; all but James Williams, a member of the Archaeological Society, disliked it. Williams, by contrast, felt the style was unimportant, and chose rather to lambast the Corporation and the people of Chester for allowing the destruction of ancient buildings such as the old Shoemakers' Row, Lamb Row and the medieval city gates. In reply to the established view that only half-timbered buildings were suitable for Chester, he retorted

...when we see the truly cosmopolitan styles of architecture now so general, we may congratulate ourselves upon the varied styles used in the buildings in Chester. What sort of a place would

it look like if only one style of architecture was adopted? We should be appalled with the sameness. In our antiquarian researches let us not ourselves become antiquated. Whilst preserving the ancient–the old features–let us use the new styles also, and prosperity will bless us[41].

This was a very different message from that which the Archaeological Society had promoted 50 years before.

But the majority view gained support as the building progressed, and early in March 1911 a further petition was made to the Duke. He had already noted the correspondence in the *Chester Chronicle* and, sensitive to the public criticism his new building was receiving, made a visit of inspection. After consulting his mother, Countess Grosvenor, he summoned the architect, and also the contractor, John Mayers, and told them that whilst he admired the building, he had decided to have the tiled facade taken down and replaced in half-timber. The cost of reconstruction was estimated at £4,000 and was to be charged to his personal account[42].

The Duke's decision was greeted enthusiastically by the *Chronicle*, and the Improvement Committee instructed the Town Clerk to express their best thanks for the 'public spirit shown by His Grace in undertaking the alteration.'[43] It was reported that the new facade was that which Lockwood had originally proposed, but this is unlikely, for when completed the building had considerably increased in size. An extra bay was added to each side, involving the demolition of two further

Fig 140 The original white and gold facade of the St Michael's Row building, 31–35 Bridge Street, 1910–11 (photograph from private collection)

Fig 141 The half-timbered facade of the St Michael's Row building was the result of public pressure (RCHME © Crown Copyright)

Fig 142 Eastgate Street in the late nineteenth century; the Vernacular Revival buildings, all by Penson, are (from left to right) the Grosvenor Hotel, Mr Platt's shop and the Browns' department store extension. The stucco building on the extreme right is the Browns' original store. (The Howarth-Loomes Collection, courtesy of the Royal Commission on the Historical Monuments of England)

properties, and the height was also increased. Work started towards the end of March, and soon an advertisement appeared in the *Chronicle* drawing attention to a 'quantity of Doulton High-class CARRARA CERAMIC BLOCKS... just taken down from some new buildings, and suitable for re-erection as front elevation'[44]. It is not known where they ended up.

On completion in August 1911, the new design met with much approval. Yet, whilst the 'White City' facade was undoubtedly an incongruous insertion in the middle of Bridge Street, the same could be said about the new frontage too. Its height, its repetitious character, and its overall scale are quite alien to the irregular street facades of Bridge Street, and the E-plan layout expressed in the symmetrical elevation seems inappropriate to an urban setting (Fig 141). The bulkiness of the building is emphasised by the lack of a satisfactory relationship between the street level and the floors above, for the faience facing was retained at the base. The white tiled ground floor, together with the Row and the elegant arcade behind it (Fig 153), now stand as a reminder of the brief appearance of this notorious building.

This was the last major building to be erected in the Rows for more than 50 years. The Victorian redevel-

opment of Eastgate Street, Northgate Street and Bridge Street had transformed a nucleus of modest domestic brick and timber buildings into a shopping centre of metropolitan appeal (Fig 142). The new buildings, whatever the style, were bigger; they had extra storeys and, by combining plots, they were often wider too. In the 1850s and 1860s, the upper levels provided accommodation for the shopkeepers and sometimes for their staff; later they were designed as offices or additional retail space. No longer were Row buildings occupied as town houses by the families who erected them. In contrast to the enclosure of Rows which took place in the eighteenth century, the Row system largely survived its transformation to a modern shopping centre; indeed it was a major factor in Chester's appeal. Except for Shoemakers' Row, a replacement section of Row walkway was included in all the new buildings. Furthermore, opportunities were taken to make the Row more convenient and safer. According to T M Lockwood, when buildings were replaced, the walkway levels were evened out so that steps and slopes were eliminated (Brushfield 1895, 324), a process which had been going on at least since 1844 when the Assembly ordered 'That the owners and occupiers of property shall not alter the level of the

Fig 143   Early photograph of Bridge Street Row East (RCHME © Crown Copyright)

Rows without the consent of the Council'[45]. Ceiling heights in the Rows were increased to give a lighter and more salubrious character (Fig 143), and the levels of the stalls were often raised to allow more headroom for the entrances to undercrofts. Redevelopment also provided the opportunity for replacing staircases linking the Row with the street, and many petitions were made to form new sets of steps.

In contrast with these improvements to the fashionable public face of the Rows, the nineteenth century saw the continued build-up of the backland areas into a congested network of workshops and residential courtyards (Fig 144). These were often accessible only via narrow passageways leading from the Rows. Court building, begun in the eighteenth century and accelerated during the rapid population expansion after 1800, was largely halted by the 1845 Chester Improvement Act. But the congested courts thrown up behind Watergate Street and the west side of Northgate Street provided cheap lodgings for in-migrants and poor families. A report in the *Chester Chronicle* in 1879 described how once grand houses had

...become crowded tenements, and back gardens once flourishing with the rose and jessamine are covered with gloomy cottages and threaded with labyrinthine alleys upon which squalor, poverty, dirt and despair settle down like a thick November fog. Delapidation and decay are everywhere apparent, and the spectacle presented by these back courts is neither more nor less than a spectacle of Chester in ruins![46]

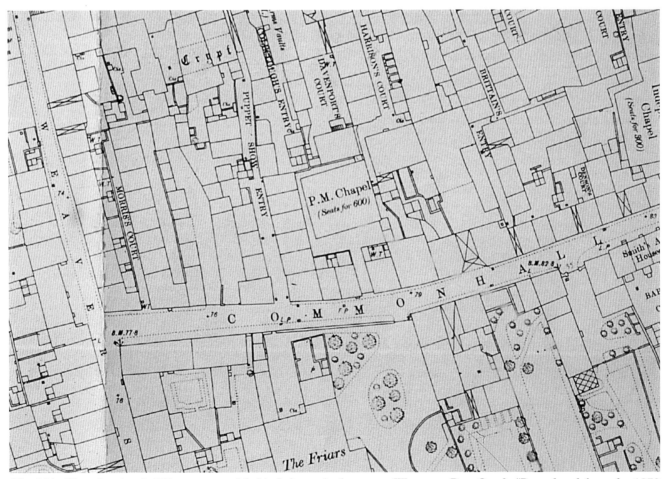

Fig 144   Plan showing buildings crammed behind the main frontages, Watergate Row South (Reproduced from the 1872 Ordnance Survey map)

This decay was symptomatic of changing patterns of use and occupation. In a few cases tenement buildings were erected at the same time as the Row building on to which they backed; more commonly they replaced outbuildings demolished when the families who owned the premises moved out[47]. The relationship between the showy frontage buildings and the labyrinth of insanitary courtyard development behind mirrored the inequalities in Victorian society.

As a result of commercial rebuilding there was also a growing contrast between the prosperous and the decaying areas of the Rows. Rateable values in Eastgate Street, Bridge Street, and Northgate Street increased, whilst those in Lower Bridge Street and Watergate Street declined. In the former streets the number of separate business premises decreased, squeezed out by larger, more successful shops; in the latter, property became increasingly divided, occupied by small, marginal businesses requiring cheap accommodation.

Although in the twentieth century the pace of change in Chester was initially slower, investment in prime Row buildings continued: retail areas were extended, shop windows enlarged, and display cases erected on the stallboards (Fig 143). As in the nineteenth century, Browns set the trend. In a series of improvements carried out from 1910, they converted their premises from a shop catering for wealthy and established customers into an emporium for the casual shopper, where, in the words of an advertisement of 1910, 'Ladies are assured of full freedom in visiting our showrooms, and are under no obligation to purchase.' (Mass Observation 1947, 182). The upper floors, where formerly the staff had lived – male assistants on one side, female on the other – were converted into additional retail space, and a new plate-glass frontage was installed at Row level to attract the passer-by. The aim was convenience, and the Rows, with their natural protection from the weather, made for a highly convenient mode of shopping.

Browns' rival, the department store of Richard Jones, was also expanding. Their premises at 9–13 Eastgate Street had been designed by T M Lockwood in 1900 in typical Vernacular Revival manner[48]. This was an unpromising site for a large store, since the shop was bisected by the Dark Row. The original premises only comprised the two central bays, but Lockwood's sons attempted to give it a more imposing look by adding the two flanking sections with their octagonal cupolas, the left side in 1915 and the right c 1930[49].

In national terms the use of half-timbering had by the 1920s become an anachronism. The style had been pirated and debased by the speculative house-builder, and most architects had long since turned back to the classical tradition for their sources. In Chester however the Vernacular Revival lived on. Although the style had mostly lost direction, one of the city's best timber-framed buildings, the former District Bank on the corner of Foregate Street and Frodsham Street, designed by Francis Jones, dates from 1921[50]. In the Rows, Penson's pioneering shop and house for Mr Platt at 40 Eastgate Street was demolished in 1912 to make way for W T Lockwood's three-gabled facade for Messrs Bollands[51]. At 8 Northgate Street a timbered front of the 1930s masks a flat-roofed steel-framed building, its gable propped up like a stage set. As late as the 1960s the facade of Woolworths former premises at 43 Eastgate Street was reconstructed in half-timber[52]. Modernism did not touch the Rows until very recently.

10 Postscript – renewal and conservation

The 1930s and 40s saw little change to the Row frontages, but growing concern for decent housing conditions led to dramatic restructuring of the backland areas. With the introduction of the 1936 Housing Act, the process of slum clearance began, and the dense network of nineteenth-century courtyard housing that existed behind the Watergate Rows was condemned[1]. In one order, confirmed in 1938, 286 people were dispossessed and offered new accommodation at the Lache Estate on the periphery of the city[2]. Following demolition of the back courts, roads were driven through the ancient plots, allowing access to the rear of the Watergate Street properties at Row level.

Chester's post-war 'Plan for Redevelopment', drawn up by Charles Greenwood, the City Engineer and Surveyor, in 1945, aimed at a balance between modernisation and preserving historic buildings. The priorities were seen as tackling poor housing and traffic congestion, but emphasis was also placed on safeguarding Chester's historic character. Greenwood drew attention to the poor condition of Row properties in Watergate Street, noting approvingly that the City Council had been purchasing problem buildings with a view to restoring them. But conservation was not then a popular issue, and Watergate Street was to decline a good deal further before the climate of opinion changed.

For Greenwood, the Rows had another dimension; they offered a model for the future, and in his plan for redeveloping Frodsham Street he suggested the creation of a new Row network (Greenwood 1945, 50–1). Twin-level streets were to become a fashionable concept for town planners in the 1960s. Whilst to some, Chester's Rows were seen as a prototype, the purpose of the twentieth-century elevated walkways was purely to segregate pedestrians from traffic. The systems briefly and misguidedly imposed on Liverpool and Manchester at that time envisaged a safe environment for shoppers at the upper level, with the streets below given over entirely to motor vehicles. In Chester it is quite different, for more than half of the trade is conducted at street level. This was a distinction acknowledged by George Grenfell Baines of Building Design Partnership, whose *Chester: a plan for the central area* was published in 1964. The possibility of throwing bridges across the streets to link the Rows together was explored in the plan, but then dismissed because the bridges would have needed to be considerably higher than the Row level to allow vehicles to pass beneath them. Nevertheless, Grenfell Baines did propose a bridge at the southern end of Bridge Street Row, and another close to the Cross in Watergate Street. The former was intended to be a lightweight glazed structure enclosing a restaurant which, it was argued, would form a new gateway to the inner city. A more realistic proposal was to bridge over Goss Street, Commonhall Street and Pierpoint Lane, three narrow side streets which broke the continuity of the Rows; and in time these bridges were constructed.

The early 1960s was a time of rapid change, and once again the Rows had to adapt to the pressures of commerce. The construction of the Grosvenor shopping precinct behind the Bridge Street and Eastgate Rows implanted 72 new shop units in the heart of the city, and reinforced the Cross as the retail focus. Its links with the Row system greatly extended the existing network of covered shopping areas. Meanwhile in Watergate Street a number of ambitious redevelopment schemes took shape.

The speed of demolition and rebuilding in the city centre at this time allowed scant opportunity for recording old structures, and major archaeological and architectural features were lost. During the erection of the Grosvenor shopping centre, important sections of the Roman baths were destroyed, whilst in Watergate Street a medieval undercroft was lost to make way for Refuge House. There were articles in the local press criticising the neglected state of the city centre and questioning the Council's development plans[3]. One of the most contentious issues was the proposal to demolish the Blue Bell, 63–65 Northgate Street, which the Council had allowed to fall into disrepair because it was in the way of a road improvement. It was in the fight to save this building that the Chester Civic Trust was founded.

Just as the Archaeological Society had influenced the course of Chester's Row architecture in the nineteenth century, so the Civic Trust was to play a similar role in the twentieth. During the early 1960s, Grenfell Baines was the city's architectural consultant and both he and the Civic Trust were involved in selecting a building to fill the notorious 'gap' site at 55–61 Watergate Street. The properties on this site were amongst those which the Council had purchased for renovation, but no works were done, and by the late 1950s they had fallen into such poor repair that they were demolished as dangerous structures (Fig 145). This left an unsightly and inconvenient gap in the Row. When redevelopment was proposed, the Civic Trust suggested an architectural competition be held, and called for a 'lively building completely in the style of our own time, to add to the existing jumble of styles'[4]. The Council agreed and a competition was staged with Grenfell Baines as assessor. The successful architects were Bradshaw, Rowse and Harker of Liverpool, and their completed building with its flat roofs, horizontal windows and finish of rough board-marked concrete was indeed a product of its time (Fig 146). It also revived the debate over how best to fit new buildings into Chester's historic streets.

Fig 145 55–61 Watergate Street before demolition in the late 1950s (this photograph RCHME © Crown Copyright: compare Pl 4)

Fig 146 55–61 Watergate Street, by Bradshaw, Rowes and Harker of Liverpool; the result of an architectural competition of the early 1960s (RCHME © Crown Copyright)

On this issue the Civic Trust and Grenfell Baines were in accord. The Trust praised the Council for appointing 'an architect known to have the courage to prefer the bold modern design to the safe compromise solution', and hailed the winning scheme as showing that 'providing new buildings are kept in scale with their older neighbours, style is no bar to a harmonious blending of old and new'[5]. But a later project at 42–48 Northgate Street divided them. This was a scheme by Harry S Fairhurst of Manchester to replace the picturesque half-timbered premises of Clemence's Restaurant. Surprisingly there was no dissension over the demolition, an indication that the Vernacular Revival had finally had its day, but Fairhurst's design for a new four-storey office building was less universally accepted. Grenfell Baines was a keen supporter, but the Trust criticised it for being considerably taller than the adjoining premises, and for its facing of smooth concrete and green glass panels. Some minor changes were made to the design, but on completion of the building in 1964, the Trust wrote critically to the *Chronicle* of its effect on the character of Northgate Street and questioned why the Council had not insisted on a Row being incorporated[6].

Another controversial scheme which was backed by the Council's architectural adviser was the redevelopment in 1970 of Messrs Astons' premises at 14–20 Watergate Street. At first the architects, W Campbell and Son of Hanley, proposed to take down all the existing Row frontage buildings including the eighteenth-century town house at the corner of Goss Street (Fig 147), and replace them by a concrete-framed structure with curtain-wall glazing. After much debate, it was agreed that the corner building should be rebuilt in replica, though using modern bricks, whilst the rest of the frontage was clad in concrete and slate[7].

A more positive approach to the conservation of historic buildings emerged after the publication in 1968 of Donald Insall's report, *Chester: a study in conservation*. Its survey of Row properties revealed serious physical decay and widespread disuse, with some 90 buildings needing repair. Insall warned that there were Row buildings '...where the mantle of prosperity is only skin deep. The mask could melt away with surprising speed if the underlying symptoms of decay are not soon remedied' (Insall 1968, 126). The remedies proposed were a phased programme of repairs; bringing upper floors into use; a series of environmental improvements; and a better system of everyday maintenance. Amongst the proposed improvement schemes were the pedestrianisation of Watergate Street, and, strangely, the redevelopment of Lockwood's corner building to the south west of the Cross to make way for a bridge over Watergate Street (Insall 1968, 129).

The programme of repairs began with the Dutch Houses, 22–26 Bridge Street. This was a complex scheme involving four separate ownerships, three of which the Council was obliged to purchase so as to ensure a comprehensive restoration. The whole facade

Fig 147 18–20 Watergate Street in 1969; this facade was rebuilt in replica the following year (RCHME © Crown Copyright)

was taken down and rebuilt, and much of the structural timberwork was replaced by steel. Another early project was the repair of Bishop Lloyd's Palace and its conversion to public meeting rooms and a flat (Figs 90 and 91). As Chester's Conservation Consultant, Donald Insall himself took on many projects. Most notable was his restoration of the Falcon, 6 Lower Bridge Street, which was on the verge of collapse (Pl 10 and 11a). The priority buildings tackled at the start of the programme were often in an advanced state of decay, and the scale of restoration was sometimes heavy, as at the Dutch Houses. In other cases buildings had deteriorated to such an extent that rebuilding a replica was the chosen solution, as at 34–42 Lower Bridge Street. But in the main, repairs have been, and still continue to be, carried out carefully and conservatively, using traditional materials and techniques (Chester City Council 1986,110–111).

Only one completely new Row building has been erected in the past 20 years, at 12 Watergate Street[8]. This replaced a two-storey flat-roofed structure of unprepossessing appearance, the demolition of which was uncontested because of an unfortunate failure to recognise that it contained archaeological material of considerable interest, including thirteenth-century timber-framing above an earlier undercroft (Ward 1988). The architect of the replacement building, Robin Clayton, adopted the prevailing spirit of contextualism and drew on elements of Chester's historic street architecture to produce an eclectic gabled facade with sash windows set in brickwork, and a central

pediment surmounted by a large ball finial. A more far-reaching scheme (1993–5), involved the block of buildings on the corner of Eastgate and Northgate Streets[9]. This project, by the Biggins Sargent Partnership, involved the total replacement of the corner properties, other than the facades, and was designed to increase trading at Row level. The dismal character of the Dark Row had long deterred public use of this area, and the scheme involved introducing new shopfronts at Row level and removing elements of the nineteenth-century frontages to create stalls between the Row and Eastgate Street. It was the first significant expansion of the Row system for many years.

The City Council continues to act as the guardian of the Rows. The principle of public access is strenuously maintained, licences have to be obtained for all obstructions to the Rows and stalls, and owners pay an annual rent for every showcase, sign or display of goods despite the fact that these are on their own private property[10].

It is a mark of their adaptability that the Rows have survived so long. Their evolution has reflected ever-changing patterns of habitation and trade, and over the past two centuries the pressures for change have never been greater. The medieval Row house evolved as a multi-use building, in which the family would live, work, trade and socialise. The strong local tradition of antiquarianism, which arose in the mid-nineteenth century and continued to influence architectural thought and practice in Chester well into the twentieth,

Fig 148 Restoration in progress at the Dutch Houses, 22–26 Bridge Street, during the 1970s (photograph © Chester City Council)

was essentially romantic. Victorian architects lavished attention on the facades of their buildings, incorporating the Row skilfully into their historicist designs. But behind the facade stood a modern commercial building, its plan unrelated to the form of the medieval town house, the spirit of which they sought to revive. Even when restoring ancient buildings, they showed scant regard for the nature of the interiors, apart from the celebrated stone undercrofts or 'crypts'. There were exceptions: Lockwood's restoration of Bishop Lloyd's Palace, and the survival of the remarkable interior of the Leche House are evidence of scholarly appreciation. The nineteenth-century galleried halls at 14 and 26 Eastgate Street and 11 Bridge Street also show an understanding of the original town house plan, but the gradual change in the use and occupation of Row buildings prevents accurate restoration of their domestic interiors. The nineteenth and twentieth centuries have seen the Rows adapted solely for trading, their upper storeys unused and often neglected. Now this complex system of ancient buildings provides retail space for a wide range of local shops, chain stores and multiples, but they remain largely unoccupied outside trading hours. The challenge for the future is not only to conserve the outward form of the Rows, but to give them back their medieval vitality.

Fig 149 'The heart of the Rows' (RCHME © Crown Copyright)

Appendix A: Notes on some of the property and building terms found in the medieval records of Chester

by A Thacker and J Laughton

For the early medieval period any study of property holding in Chester is inevitably based upon surviving deeds. The earliest date back to the twelfth century and they become more numerous in later centuries, although there are no long series of deeds referring to the same property. The records of the city's Portmote court provide additional information from the 1260s. For the fifteenth century these sources can be supplemented by material from the Mayors' Books and from the few surviving records of the murengers and the treasurers.

Burgagium

In a town such as Winchester, the term 'burgage' referred to the form of tenure rather than the property so held (Keene 1985, I, 137); to hold by burgage was to pay the *gablum* or gable-rent (Tait 1936, 99 n7). In Chester the word may generally have had similar force, since it occurs relatively rarely in the surviving deeds, despite the fact that from late Saxon times the city is known to have contained burgesses holding by burgage tenure (Thacker, forthcoming). In one case, however, the term clearly does denote a property in one of the four main streets. In a deed of 1313, Amicia, widow of Ranulph Peck, citizen of Chester, is said to have leased to Richard of Wheatley, a former sheriff, one third of a burgage, extending in length from Northgate Street to Crook Street. Amicia's property was clearly an important one. It stood on the west side of Northgate Street, and had been awarded to her after her husband's death[1]. In an earlier deed (1301) Ranulph Peck granted away all his tenements in Chester and its suburbs, and distinguished between his burgages, messuages, gardens, curtilages, rents, services, and liberties within the city[2]. Other early evidence confirms that the term could occasionally be applied to substantial properties held by important citizens or by local gentry, although in no other known instance is it applied to holdings within the area of the Rows[3]. By the mid-fourteenth century the term could be used interchangeably with 'messuage'; in 1349, for example, a property containing four shops is referred to in one deed as a 'burgage' and in another as a 'messuage'[4].

Camera

The term *camera* apparently denoted the room used for domestic accommodation, and typically contained beds and bedding, as well as chests in which clothing and valuables were stored. It was not uncommon for these rooms to be rented out to those in need of lodgings.

Domus

Domus appears to be the term most commonly used to describe the actual dwelling. However, there are several twelfth-century examples of *mansura*, a term which Keene (1985, I, 137) was surprised to discover absent from the Winchester records.

Messuagium

Towards the end of the thirteenth century, the term *messuagium* begins to appear in the sources (the earliest reference so far is in 1281–2). Thereafter, together with *tenementum*, it becomes the most commonly found term for structures in the main streets, although *terra* and *placea* continue in use. *Messuagium* is usually interpreted as indicating a plot of land supporting a dwelling and attached buildings, often a house and garden[5]. In the fourteenth century a messuage may be described as over an undercroft or as containing a solar[6].

Placea terre

See *terra*.

Seldae

In Chester the term seld appears to have been used in a number of senses from the early thirteenth century. It could mean simply a 'stall' or 'booth'. In the 1280s, for example, the monks of St Werburgh's alleged that during the midsummer fair goods could be sold only from the temporary *seldae* erected for that purpose outside the abbey gate, a claim which brought them into conflict with the citizens (Stewart-Brown, 1925, 122–3). In other instances, however, it clearly designated substantial structures resembling market halls (see p19). It is these later structures that are of particular relevance to the Rows.

A particularly interesting example is that provided by the seld of the Tailor (*cissor*) family. During the mayoralty of Richard the Clerk, possibly in 1260 or 1261, Wymarc, widow of John Tailor, granted to Hugh Tailor (presumably her son) half of the house, 27ft (8.23m) in length, lying behind the seld of John Grund, reserving to herself the other half. An especially curious feature of the arrangement was the provision that at fair times, Wymarc was to take down the wall which was to divide her property from Hugh's, to permit the extension of the latter's holding by a further 6½ft (1.98m)only[7]. The reason for this is apparent from a later deed; Hugh had converted his portion of the property into a seld, and the taking down of the wall was to increase the space available to him for trading during the period of the fair[8].

We can trace the later history of this property in further charters. In the 1270s, it was described as a seld and sold by Hugh Tailor's son to Robert Erneys. A deed of 1315–16 reveals that the Erneys family had a seld in Bridge Street, next to Commonhall Lane, behind which lay a substantial property which was let separately, and could well have been the half-house which Wymarc had granted to Hugh Tailor[9]. Behind that lay land, then held by John Bars, which presumably represents the remainder of the house retained by Wymarc herself. By then the Erneys family had acquired another seld on the street frontage, which in the 1260s had belonged to John Grund. In the early fourteenth century this still seems to have been a seld, whereas that which was formerly Wymarc's was merely described as a plot with buildings on it[10]. All this seems to suggest that a substantial house, in Bridge Street, near the Commonhall, was progressively given over to trade in the 1260s and 1270s, and at least in part retaining the same functions in 1315. The dimensions of Wymarc's house and the tenurial arrangements of 1315–16 suggest a long narrow plot, of sufficient size to be subdivided into at least three holdings. Such dimensions were probably characteristic of the selds as a whole. The evidence also indicates that existing buildings could be converted into selds, either permanently or temporarily at fair times. Selds were therefore defined by their usage rather than as a specific building type.

The deeds relating to the Shoemakers' selds suggest that the Chester selds resembled market halls (see p19). These premises are described as both *shopae* or *seldae*, possibly because the 11 units were all within, or attached to, a seld devoted to a single trade. This use of the selds is confirmed by other evidence. In 1288–9, for example, a suit came before the Portmote involving a seld in which a number of prominent citizens had an interest. It concluded when one of their number, Richard the Clerk, renounced his right of way through the seld in return for an annual rent of 3s 6d (three shillings and sixpence)[11]. This not only indicates that selds were halls with walkways between the stalls, but shows that they might belong to cooperatives of leading citizens. In this instance, an interest was held by Ranulph of Daresbury, Alexander Hurel, Ranulph Godweyt, and Richard the Clerk, all of whom belonged to families which had produced mayors or sheriffs. Clearly the selds were highly profitable concerns.

For a further illuminating discussion of *seldae* see Keene 1990.

Tabulae

In late medieval Chester the term *tabula*, like *selda*, had more than one meaning, but was perhaps most commonly used in the sense 'board and lodging'[12].

Occasionally it denoted a trestle or stall made of planks or boards[13]. There are, however, some indications that the term was sometimes applied to a more permanent structure. In 1355 the holdings of Henry Dunfoul included a tenement and two undercrofts (rent 16s), a quarter share in a *selda* (no rent because empty), a shop (2s 8d), and an undercroft and a *tabula* (4s)[14]. The inclusion of what would usually be considered a moveable object in the property holding of a leading citizen is surprising and suggests that something of a more fixed or substantial nature may have been involved.

That this was indeed the case is confirmed by entries in a mid-fifteenth-century rental of the city lands. From 1439 to 1442 Bartholomew Lyaldon paid an annual rent of 4d for a piece of land under the *tabula* of John Routon[15]. Lyaldon was a wealthy and influential citizen, who had served as sheriff in 1434–5 and treasurer in 1437–8; he was unlikely to have rented this land without good reason and it is difficult to envisage the use to which a piece of ground beneath the stall of another citizen could be put. If, however, the *tabula* referred to a Row stallboard (the sloping section that usually separates the Row walkway from the street frontage) then the entries in the rental begin to become clear (see Chapter 2). Lyaldon was paying rent for the parcel of ground which lay below it, at street level. In 1445 he is recorded as paying 4d a year to the city for a piece of waste ground in Bridge Street; it was described as lying between two undercrofts and extending from the house frontages towards the street for a distance of 4½ virgates[16]. It seems probable that this was the same piece of ground. The *tabula* above, which need not necessarily have extended so far streetwards, was held by a leading city tailor who had served as steward of his gild in 1432[17].

An entry in the Pentice Court rolls supports the idea that *tabula* sometimes describes the Row stallboard. In 1427, the city crier, John Conway, alleged that rent for his *tabula* was 1s a week and consequently the tenant who had taken it for a 12-week period commencing at the feast of the Purification owed him 12s[18]. This is a very high figure. In the mid-1430s the rents paid for shops under Pentice, generally acknowledged as a prime commercial site, ranged between 13s 4d and 16s 8d per annum while a shop at the Eastgate could be had for 6s 8d annually[19]. The implication is that some *tabulae* at least represented extremely attractive trading propositions.

Other references to *tabula* in the Chester records may also indicate stallboards rather than stalls or trestles, although certainty is impossible. The city's butchers, for example, were regularly presented for discarding their refuse into the street, but sometimes they were accused of throwing rubbish *subtus tabulis suis*[20]. In the fifteenth century butchers occupied tenements in Fleshmonger Row and perhaps used the stallboards as extra retailing space and the space below as an easy way of disposing of their rubbish.

Tenementum

In other towns, the term *tenementum* had been somewhat ambiguous in the thirteenth century, but after *c* 1300 it came to be used almost exclusively to denote a built-up site (Rosser 1989, 54 and n47; Keene 1985, I, 137–8). In Chester, the term seems to be used only occasionally in the thirteenth century[21], but more often in the fourteenth[22]. It seems almost invariably to imply buildings, both domestic and commercial, and is sometimes applied to property over an undercroft[23].

Terra

In the second half of the twelfth century and throughout the thirteenth century it was normal to describe properties in Chester as *terra* or *placea terre*. This was the term used in the fortified towns of Gascony funded by English kings in the thirteenth century, and Tout (1934, 78) proposed that it may indicate a burgage. Alternatively, it could denote a plot of land, which, unlike the burgage, was not of a uniform statutory size and for which the rent accordingly varied. This would accord well with archaeological findings in Chester where no standard plot width has been discovered. These terms could imply dwellings, as is shown by such usages as *terra quam mansi*, 'the land on which I live', and by numerous references to land or plots with buildings (*edificia*), houses (*domus*), and shops. *Terra* and *placea terre* may therefore denote 'real estate' and be used to define the property as a whole, irrespective of the buildings upon it.

Appendix B: Report on the dendrochronological sampling programme

by MK Hughes, PA Leggett, J Hillam and C Groves

This Appendix is a composite of a number of different dendrochronological sampling and analysis programmes. The majority of the sampling and analysis for this report was undertaken by Pat Leggett whilst at the University of Liverpool in 1988 and 1989. The sampling and analysis of timbers at 11 Bridge Street, the second series of cores from the Falcon, 6 Lower Bridge Street, and the analysis of the cores from 36 Bridge Street were undertaken in 1990 by Cathy Groves and Jennifer Hillam at Sheffield University. The first drafts of the Appendix were created by Rick Turner using separate reports of the work.

At a very late stage during the production of this volume, re-analysis became possible of some of the Liverpool data using more recently produced tree-ring chronologies. This work was completed by Ian Tyers of Sheffield University in 1999 and resulted in some new dating evidence for two of the buildings. Appropriate amendments to this Appendix have as far as possible followed the methods used in the original work. This Appendix is perhaps best seen as an interim statement of the dendrochronological results: in particular it should be noted that it has not been possible to rework all the original data using recently-produced tree-ring chronologies. It should also be noted that the methods and interpretations of the earlier work, although in accordance with the practice of the time, have now been refined and are rather different from those which would be used today (see English Heritage 1998).

Potentially, dendrochronology or tree-ring dating offers the most accurate method of dating the construction of a building, or its subsequent alteration or repair. The method relies upon the fact that as a tree grows, its size is increased annually by a growth ring, whose width is a reflection of the weather during that growing season. Over the life of the tree, these rings will record the varying climatic conditions of successive years. It has proved possible to build up a sequence of tree rings, starting with living trees, overlapping the beginning of their growth-ring pattern with those from timbers in historic buildings and, taking the sequence even further back, with those from timbers recovered from archaeological sites or peat bogs. In this way, sequences or chronologies have been extended over thousands of years.

The variations in growth rings are more marked in trees growing under stress – in poor soils or in dense woodland. Trees from hedgerows or parkland may not show sufficient variation in their growth-ring pattern for adequate matches to be established. Also, trees that are affected by disease or management practices such as pollarding or coppicing exhibit eccentric patterns of growth which make matching difficult.

Most tree-ring chronologies are based on oak, although in some parts of Europe chronologies based on beech and pine are being developed. As historically most structural timber in Britain has been oak, normally used green, the felling date established by dendrochronology can be assumed to be very close to the date when the timber was used for building. Structural timber, however, is normally dressed before use, the bark and the outer rings of sapwood being removed. The heartwood/sapwood boundary is very prominent in oak, and if it can be recognised a good estimate of the felling date can be made. If only heartwood is present, dendrochronology can offer only a general date after which the timber was used.

In a historic building, where a number of timbers survive, each can be sampled by drilling out a core as close as possible to the radius of the original timber or by measuring the rings visible on a cut end. Only timbers with at least 50 growth rings are normally considered. For each building or phase of building, internal cross-matching of the full range of samples is undertaken to build up the longest possible sequence. These internal sequences are then cross-matched with standard chronologies established elsewhere in the region or, if necessary, from further afield.

All cross-matching is based upon a statistical comparison between the sample or internal sequence and established tree-ring chronologies. Only when this comparison proves statistically significant can the date of the final ring be put forward. This means that only a percentage of samples will provide a date.

Also, only when the outermost ring of the growing tree is present can this be an exact felling date. Where the heartwood/sapwood boundary is present a reliable estimate can be given. Since the seasoning period for building timber was short and it was often used green (Salzman, 1952, 237–8), these timbers are likely to have been used soon after these dates.

During the Rows Research Project resources were limited, so dendrochronology was concentrated on those buildings which contained a range of early timber structures. The method was not used on buildings which could be dated from documentary sources or by distinctive stylistic characteristics. Dendrochronology proved vital in demonstrating the antiquity of the Rows and in suggesting a relatively narrow range of dates for the earliest Row buildings.

All the samples taken from the Row buildings were of oak, which was almost the only timber used for the construction of medieval buildings in Chester. Timbers were rejected for full dendrochronological analysis if the correct alignment of the core could not

Table 1 11 Bridge Street: details of timbers

Sample	Location	Timber	Total no of rings	No of sapwood rings	Period spanned	Estimated felling date
BSE11–1	undercroft	arcade post	115	–	–	–
BSE11–2	undercroft	beam	49	–	–	–
BSE11–3	undercroft	joist	<50	–	–	–
BSE11–4	undercroft	sole plate	<50	–	–	–
BSE11–5	undercroft	floorboard	56	–	–	–

be obtained or if they clearly contained less than 50 growth rings. Tree-ring samples with less than 50 rings have little value in cross-matching tests. However, information relating to cambial age, quality and preparation of a timber can be obtained from such samples. Details recorded in these cases included the number of growth rings, the presence of sapwood, pith, bark, and knots, and the general appearance of the timber.

Sapwood is the softer outer layer of wood which lies between the heartwood and the bark, and its presence (or traces of the heartwood/sapwood boundary) on a timber that has been absolutely dated allows the estimation of the felling date of the tree from which the timber was cut (Hughes *et al* 1981). Even when the felling date cannot be estimated, the presence of sapwood can provide information relating to cambial age. Oak has a predictable number of sapwood rings, so that if any have been removed, the number of missing rings can be calculated, the interpretations presented here use a sapwood range of 19–50, with a median value of 30 (see Hughes *et al* 1981). However, sapwood was often removed from oak timbers during their preparation since it was very susceptible to insect attack. Pith is the 'centre' of the tree. When both pith and sapwood are present on a dated or undated timber, it is possible to estimate the cambial age of a tree.

The timber cores were prepared and measured according to the methods described by Leggett *et al* (1978) and statistical cross-matching tests were carried out using the computer program CROS (Baillie and Pilcher, 1973). All the tree-ring samples not contained within a mean chronology were compared visually and statistically with each of the mean chronologies for evidence of cross-matching. Similarly, the mean chronologies were compared with each other. Each mean chronology was then compared visually and statistically with many established tree-ring chronologies dating from the tenth century to the present, from the British Isles and Germany. The chronologies included those from Chester (Hughes and Leggett 1985), Belfast (Baillie, 1977a), Dublin (Baillie 1977b), Lancashire, Cheshire and Merseyside (Leggett 1980), south-west Scotland (Baillie 1977c), and many more. Those analysed timbers that were not dated will be compared with other dated chronologies as they become available.

The undated timbers have provided information about growing conditions at the site at which the trees grew and about carpentry practices. The presence of sensitive growth patterns, with narrow rings (showing slow growth) and great variations in ring width, suggests that the trees had grown in close stands under stressed growing conditions. Trees growing in open woodland have a complacent growth pattern, with wide rings (showing fast growth) and exhibiting little variation in ring width.

11 Bridge Street

Cores were removed from five timbers in the undercroft of 11 Bridge Street. Table 1 gives details of the tree-ring samples, three of which were considered suitable for measurement. Comparison of the tree-ring graphs showed no similarities between them. Also, no consistent results were found when the sequences were tested against established chronologies and therefore the timbers remain undated.

Table 2 36 Bridge Street: details of timbers

Sample	Location	Timber	Total no of rings	No of sapwood rings	Period spanned	Estimated felling date
SWD1	undercroft	joist	18	7	–	–
SWD2	undercroft	joist	177	–	1073–1248	after 1267
SWD3	undercroft	joist	53	–	–	–
SWD4	undercroft	joist	159	–	1128–1286	after 1305
SWD5	undercroft	joist	97	–	–	–
SWD6	undercroft	joist	57	–	–	–
SWD7	undercroft	joist	42	15	–	–
SWD8	undercroft	joist	214	–	1104–1317	after 1336

36 Bridge Street

Eight timber joists in the undercroft of 36 Bridge Street were sampled, details of which are presented in Table 2. The seven measured sequences were compared and three were found to cross-match. These were combined to form a 245-year mean chronology, SWD–M1. This mean chronology and all the unmatched tree-ring patterns were tested against established chronologies. High 't' values and good visual matches were found for SWD–M1 (Table 2a) when it covered the period 1073–1317, but no consistent results were produced by any of the unmatched patterns.

None of the dated samples retained any sapwood. However, if they are contemporary they probably all have a *terminus post quem* for felling of 1336. This indicates that the joists were used in the construction of the undercroft ceiling after that date.

Table 2a 36 Bridge Street
Mean chronology SWD–M1
Period spanned AD 1073–1317
Crossdating of SWD–M1

Chronology	't' value	Years overlap
British Isles (Baillie and Pilcher pers comm)	7.24	245
The Falcon, Chester (see below)	6.71	162
Nantwich (Leggett 1980)	6.25	245

Table 3 Tudor House, 29–31 Lower Bridge Street: details of timbers

Sample	Location	Timber	Total no of rings	No of sapwood rings	Period spanned	Estimated felling date
T1	third floor, front bedroom, centre truss	tie beam	131	–	–	–
T2	third floor, front bedroom, centre truss	post	42	–	–	–
T3	third floor, front bedroom, centre truss	post	110	–	–	–
T4	third floor, front bedroom, front wall	post	c35	waney edge	–	–
T5	third floor, front bedroom, front wall	tie beam	131	18	1461–1591	1592–1623
T6	third floor, front bedroom, side wall	wallplate	c40	–	–	–
T7	third floor, front bedroom, side wall	purlin	127	–	1460–1586	after 1605
T8	third floor	beam	c35	6	–	–
T9	third floor	beam	75	–	–	–
T10	third floor, staircase partition	beam	80	14	–	–
T11	second floor, rear bedroom	purlin	70	H/S	1520–1588	1607–1638
T12	second floor, rear bedroom	purlin	77	8	–	–
T13	second floor, rear bedroom	tie beam	80	–	–	–
T14	second floor, rear bedroom	corner post	61	–	–	–
T15	second floor, rear bedroom	doorframe post (in two parts)	inner: 87 outer: 91	– 34	–	–

The Tudor House, 29–31 Lower Bridge Street

Fifteen timbers were sampled from the upper levels of the Tudor House (Table 3). There was highly significant cross-matching between samples T5, T7 and T11 and this made it possible to form a mean tree-ring chronology TUM 1 of 132 years (Table 3a). Samples T5 and T7 were located in the front bedroom of the Row + 2 level whilst T11 was from the rear bedroom of the Row + 1 level. Samples T3, from the front bedroom on the Row + 2 level, and T15 inner, from the doorframe of the rear Row + 1 level bedroom, also showed good cross-matching. These were averaged to form a mean chronology of 110 years called TUM 2. The remaining individual tree-ring samples did not cross-match with either of the two mean chronologies.

The mean chronology TUM 1 was dated to the period 1460–1591 (Table 3a). Consistent significant dates were not obtained in comparisons between the established chronologies and TUM 2. The only remaining

Table 3a Tudor House
Mean chronology TUM1
Period spanned AD 1460–1591
Crossdating of TUM1

Chronology	't' value	Years overlap
Belfast (Baillie 1977)	4.01	132
Bewsey Hall (Leggett and Hughes, unpub)	4.16	126
British Isles (Baillie and Pilcher, pers comm)	5.40	132
Lydiate Hall (Leggett, forthcoming)	3.74	69
Wales/West Midlands (Siebenlist-Kerner, 1978)	5.80	132
Yorkshire timbers (Hillam, pers comm)	4.59	132

Table 4 The Falcon, 6 Lower Bridge Street: details of timbers

Sample	Location	Timber	Total no of rings	No of sapwood rings	Period spanned	Estimated felling date
FAL1	undercroft	–	199	–	–	–
FAL2	undercroft	brace	80	–	–	–
FAL3	undercroft	reused tie beam	189	–	991–1181	after 1200
FAL4	undercroft	reused tie beam	126	–	1055–1180	after 1199
FAL5	undercroft	bridging joist	174	–	1060–1234	after 1253
FAL6	undercroft	joist	72	–	–	–
FAL7	row level	dragon beam	147	37	–	–
FAL8	Row level	joist	174	13	–	–
FAL9	Row level, N wall	cross beam	50	–	–	–
FAL10	Row level	joist	47	–	–	–
FAL11	Row level	joist	100	8	–	–
FAL13	Row level	joist	52	–	–	–
FAL14	Row level	joist	111	–	–	–
FAL15	undercroft	joist	81	12	–	–
FAL16	undercroft	joist	120	25	–	–
FAL17	undercroft	brace	78	H/S	–	–
FAL18	undercroft	joist	blackened	–	–	–
FAL19	first floor wall	post	41	–	–	–
FAL20	first floor, E wall	tie beam	61	H/S	–	–
FAL21	first floor, E wall	tie beam	72	9	–	–
FAL22	first floor, E wall	post	50	–	–	–
FAL23	first floor, E wall	post	35	–	–	–
FAL24	first floor, E wall	post	88	–	–	–
FAL25	first floor, E wall	beam	66	5	–	–
FALS1	undercroft	bridging post	61	–	–	–
FALS2	undercroft	post	<50	–	–	–
FALS3	undercroft	reused tie beam	79	–	–	–

tree-ring sample of reasonable length that had not been compared with the established chronologies was T1, but no significant results were obtained. This possibly results from the bands of very narrow rings in this sample that were scarcely measurable.

Only sample T5 retained sapwood and the last formed heartwood ring was absolutely dated to 1573; thus the felling date was estimated to be between 1592 and 1623. Whilst sapwood was absent from sample T11, sapwood in a crumbling state could be identified on the timber *in situ*. The poor condition of the sapwood probably explains its absence from the core sample. It is therefore likely that the outermost ring on T11, dated to 1588, lies very close to the last formed heartwood ring and hence the heart-wood/sapwood boundary. The felling date is therefore probably after 1607 but before *c* 1638. T7 included only heartwood and was probably felled after 1605.

The results of this dendrochronological analysis indicate that the trees used in the construction of the Tudor House are likely to have been felled in the early seventeenth century.

The Falcon, 6 Lower Bridge Street

Initial sampling was carried out at the Falcon during the latter half of 1988. The timbers under investigation were located in the undercroft, the front bar at Row level and the first-floor public room. A second sampling

investigated three further timbers in the undercroft. Table 4 gives details of the tree-ring samples of 27 timbers. There was highly significant cross-matching between samples FAL 7, FAL 8, and FAL 9 from Row level. These were averaged to form a mean tree-ring chronology (called FALM 1) of 191 years' length. A 244–year mean chronology (FALM 2) was formed from the timbers of the undercroft: FAL 3, FAL 4, and FAL 5. The 72–year mean chronology FALM 3 was constructed from timbers FAL 20 and FAL 21 which were taken from the first-floor public room. These two samples were so similar in appearance, span of years, relative position of the heartwood/sapwood boundary, and high level of cross-matching as to suggest that the two beams were derived from the same tree.

The mean chronology FALM 2 was absolutely dated against a number of established chronologies to 991–1234 (Table 4a). The chronologies FALM 1 and FALM 3 could not be consistently dated.

Four of the timbers retained sapwood: FAL 7 and FAL 8 in FALM 1, and FAL 20 and FAL 21 in FALM 3. In FALM 2, the mean chronology had been absolutely dated but sapwood was absent from the component timbers. However, by adding the figure 19 (for the minimum likely number of sapwood rings) to the date of the last heartwood ring on the sample, a date is obtained before which the tree is unlikely to have been felled (terminus date). Whilst this is an estimated

Table 4a The Falcon
Mean chronology FALM2
Period spanned AD 991–1234
Crossdating of FALM2

Chronology	't' value	Years overlap
Baguley (Leggett, unpub)	4.58	199
British Isles (Baillie and Pilcher, pers comm)	6.22	244
Dublin (Baillie, 1977)	5.53	244
Jaybank (Leggett, unpub)	4.39	178
Nantwich (Leggett, 1980)	4.02	244
28–30 Watergate Street (see below)	4.31	169
38–42 Watergate Street (see below)	9.16	170

date, that given for the most recently formed ring is absolute.

The three timbers from the Falcon that were absolutely dated span the eleventh, twelfth and thirteenth centuries, and are all located in the undercroft. The growth patterns of these, and of the other undercroft timbers, consist of long periods of very narrow growth rings. Such patterns are typical of those found in timbers dating from this period elsewhere in Cheshire (Leggett 1980, Hughes and Leggett 1983) and the north-west of England (Leggett and Hughes, forthcoming). In terms of the number of growth rings, the undercroft joists contained a greater number of rings than the undercroft braces. These two members also differed in their method of formation. The sampled joists all appeared

to be quartered timbers; the braces had been cleft radially. The joists in 28–30 and 38–42 Watergate Street which have been dated to the thirteenth century were also quartered timbers (Hughes and Leggett, 1985).

Timbers in other sections of the building were found to have a variety of types of growth patterns. Some contained sensitive growth patterns, some contained very even growth, whilst others exhibited bands of very narrow rings separated by very wide rings. Where the growth rings were exceptionally narrow they were often very distorted, indicating the presence of severe growth stresses in those trees.

In the Falcon, sapwood had been removed from some timbers and not from others, and in some cases was removed from only a portion of the timber length. The samples which retain sapwood are FAL 7*, FAL 8, FAL 10* (sapwood disintegrated on sampling), FAL 11, FAL 15, FAL 16, FAL 17 (heartwood/sapwood boundary), FAL 20* (heartwood/sapwood boundary), FAL 21*, and FAL 25. On those samples marked with an asterisk the waney edge was identified before sampling. (The waney edge is the roughened surface of the sapwood which lies immediately below the bark.) These samples are located throughout the building, and no relationship between sapwood removal and the location of a timber in the building can be identified. The identification of the waney edge on some timbers before sampling indicates that the only form of timber preparation that took place in these cases was the removal of the bark. This minimal treatment left the sapwood intact.

Several of the ceiling timbers at Row level had numerous knots along their lengths: FAL 7, FAL 10, and FAL 11. FAL 7 and FAL 10 were two of the timbers which exhibited the waney edge (ie minimal timber preparation). The presence of many knots suggests that these trees had grown in a very open stand or hedge which allowed an extensive network of branches to develop. In close stands, the proximity of other trees prevents such a network from developing. In terms of quality of finish, the obvious presence of knots indicates that there had been little attempt to remove or hide them. The quality of timber preparation does not appear

Table 5 The Old King's Head, 48–50 Lower Bridge Street: details of timbers

Sample	Location	Timber	Total no of rings	No of sapwood rings	Period spanned	Estimated felling date
OKH1	ground floor	post	28	–	–	–
OKH2	ground floor	post P1	not measured	–	–	–
OKH3	ground floor	brace	>20	–	–	–
OKH4	ground floor, B6	arcade plate	32	–	–	–
OKH5	ground floor, B3	arcade plate	49	H/S	–	–
OKH6	ground floor	joist	17	–	–	–
OKH7	first floor	brace, truss VI	c23	–	–	–
OKH8	first floor	post, truss VI	88	–	–	–
OKH9	first floor	brace, truss VI	51	–	–	–
OKH10	first floor	post, truss VII	124	–	–	–
OKH11	first floor	rafter, truss VII	29	–	–	–
OKH12	first floor	tie beam, truss VII	83	5	–	–

to have been a high priority at the Falcon, particularly at Row level. Some of the trees used in the construction of the Falcon were approximately 90–150 years old, but the timbers from the undercroft were probably 200 or more years old. The small number of trees for which both pith and sapwood was present prevents a detailed statement on the age of trees felled for the construction.

Using tree-ring analysis, two timbers at the Falcon were dated to the late twelfth century and one timber to the mid thirteenth century. After allowance for missing sapwood it appears that these two groups were unlikely to have been felled before the early thirteenth century and the latter half of the thirteenth century respectively.

Two of the three cores taken during the second sampling were suitable for dating purposes (FALS1 FALS3, Table 4). Their ring sequences were compared with the mean tree-ring chronologies previously established from the Falcon, FALM 1 and FALM 2, but no similarities were found either visually or by computer comparison. The two new individual sequences were then compared with established chronologies but no consistent results were produced.

The Old King's Head, 48–50 Lower Bridge Street

Twelve timbers were sampled from the ground and first floor of the Old King's Head (Table 5). Significant cross-matching was obtained between samples OKH10 and OKH12 only and these were averaged to form a mean chronology, 124 years long (called OKHM). The relative positions of these series are given below.

OKH10 Year 1 to year 124
OKH12 Year 1 to year 83

Consistent significant datings were not obtained from these comparisons. OKHM was also tested for cross-matching with undated chronologies from the north-west of England (Leggett 1980) but again no significant dates were found. Sapwood was identified on two

samples, OKH5 and OKH12. For OKH5 and OKH12 the cambial ages are approximately 79 years and 108 years respectively.

Only those samples containing 80 or more rings had sensitive growth patterns, and all the sampled timbers were located on the first floor of the building. The remaining nine samples all exhibited wide rings and complacent growth patterns. One of the samples with sensitive growth, OKH8, was taken from a timber showing many knots. This indicates that the tree from which this timber was taken grew in an open stand, since such conditions encouraged the growth of many side branches.

The dendrochronological analysis indicates that the construction of the Old King's Head included the use of fairly young trees with a fast growth habit. Slower grown trees were used for some of the timber at first floor level.

The Three Kings, 90–92 Lower Bridge Street

Samples were removed from oak timbers in various parts of the Three Kings, of which eight were measured (Table 6). There was significant cross-matching between samples K3 and K7 only ('t'=5.19 at 65 years overlap). These were averaged to form a mean chronology of 121 years (called TK1M). The relative positions of K3 and K7 in TK1M are shown below.

Sample K7 spans the period year 1 to year 86.
Sample K3 spans the period year 22 to year 121.

No consistent significant dating was identified for TK1M. Comparisons were also made with undated chronologies but the presence of relative dating was not evident.

Four timbers were not measured because they did not contain a sufficient number of tree rings. These timbers all contained wide rings showing a complacent growth sequence, in contrast to the measured timbers, which exhibited sensitive growth patterns. Timbers in

Table 6 The Three Kings, 90–92 Lower Bridge Street: details of timbers

Sample	Location	Timber	Total no of rings	No of sapwood rings	Period spanned	Estimated felling date
K1	staircase, 2nd landing	beam	121	–	–	–
K2	second floor	tie beam	30	3	–	–
K3	second floor	purlin	100	17	–	–
K4	second floor	purlin	21	5	–	–
K5	second floor	principal rafter	70	H/S	–	–
K6	staircase, 3rd landing	beam	62	–	–	–
K7	first floor	central post	86	–	–	–
K8	first floor	beam	43	10	–	–
K9	first floor	brace	<30	–	–	–
K10	first floor	beam	69	4	–	–
K11	first floor	post	99	25	–	–
K12	staircase, 1st landing	post	42	–	–	–

Table 7 The Blue Bell, 63–65 Northgate Street: details of timbers

Sample	Location	Timber	Total no of rings	No of sapwood rings	Period spanned	Estimated felling date
BB1	street level	post (BP2)	18	–	–	–
BB2	street level	rail (R1)	46	–	–	–
BB3	street level	joist (JP2)	31	–	–	–
BB4	first floor	tie beam (TB1)	51	–	–	–
BB5	first floor	brace (TB1)	33	–	–	–
BB6	first floor	tie beam (TB2)	30	10	–	–
BB7	first floor	wallplate (PL28)	32	–	–	–
BB8	first floor	post (PL6)	70	–	–	–
BB9	first floor	tie beam (TB3)	45	–	–	–
BB10	first floor	brace (CP2B2)	17	4	–	–
BB11	first floor	wallplate (PL3)	161	9	–	–
BB12	first floor	tie beam (TB4)	150	–	–	–
BB13	cellar	post (BP3)	25	–	–	–
BB14	first floor	tie beam (TB6)	125	–	1118-1242	after 1261

Table 7a: The Blue Bell
Timber BB14: period spanned AD 1118–1242
Crossdating of BB14

Chronology	't' value	Years overlap
Dublin (Baillie, 1977b)	4.17	125
Baguley Hall 2 (Leggett, 1980)	4.33	125
British Isles (Baillie and Pilcher, pers comm)	5.74	125
Scotland (Baillie, 1977c)	4.62	125
Falcon, Chester (see above)	7.36	117
36 Bridge Street, Chester (see above)	5.19	125
Nantwich (Leggett, 1980)	4.69	125

both categories and from different locations still showed the presence of sapwood. An estimate of cambial age could be made for samples K4 (46 years) and K8 (63 years). None of the timbers examined had a particularly knotty form.

The Blue Bell, 63–65 Northgate Street

Timbers were sampled from various locations in the Blue Bell Inn. The tree-ring samples from five timbers were tested and there was highly significant cross-matching between two: BB8 and BB12 (61 years overlap; 't'=6.75). These were averaged to form a mean chronology of 159 years (called BBM). BB8 is a post

located on the first floor and BB12 is a tie beam located in the first floor box room, both part of the northern structure (No 65). The relative position of the two series are shown below.

BB8 spans the period year 1 to year 70.
BB12 spans the period year 10 to year 159.

There was no consistent cross-matching with established chronologies for this sequence. In addition, no cross-matching was found between BBM chronology and undated chronologies from the north-west of England. Sample BB14 did exhibit consistent significant cross-matching with established chronologies (Table 7a) and is dated 1118–1242 inclusive. Since this sample has no sapwood a date of after 1261 is indicated for the felling of this first floor timber.

Sapwood was identified on three of the prepared samples, two of which were not measured: BB6 and BB10. Pith could also be identified on these samples.

The four samples with 70 rings or more exhibited sensitive growth patterns with narrow growth rings. On the innermost end of those samples with over 100 tree rings, the rays were running parallel. This suggests that this end of the sample is not near the pith since the rays converge as they reach the centre of the tree. At the outermost end of the samples, missing sapwood also needs to be accounted for. Consideration of these two factors indicates cambial ages in excess of 100 years for BB8 (pith present), 180 years for BB11, 180 years for BB12 and 160 years for BB14. For those samples lacking sapwood the figure is likely to be a gross underestimate since it is unlikely that the last formed heartwood ring on the sample is close to the heartwood/sapwood boundary.

The remaining samples show great contrast to those above, in that the ring patterns (fairly wide) are generally complacent. Apart from samples BB1 and BB9, these show pith located part way along the sequence so that a portion of the longer tree-ring sample is repeated on the other side of the pith. This

Table 8 The Leche House, 17–19 Watergate Street: details of timbers

Sample	Location	Timber	Total no of rings	No of sapwood rings	Period spanned	Estimated felling date
LEC1	undercroft, truss 1	brace	16	–	–	–
LEC2	undercroft, truss 1	tie beam	not sampled	–	–	–
LEC3	above street entrance	door lintel	39	–	–	–
LEC4	undercroft	joist	39	–	–	–
LEC5	undercroft	joist	47	–	–	–
LEC6	undercroft	joist	50	15	–	–
LEC7	undercroft	joist	72	–	–	–
LEC8	undercroft	joist	c40	–	–	–
LEC9	undercroft	joist	36	–	–	–
LEC10	undercroft	joist	67	–	–	–
LEC11	undercroft	joist	47	–	–	–
LEC12	Row passage	post	40	–	–	–
LEC13	Row passage	tie beam	56 and 58	12	–	–
LEC14	Row passage	post	26	–	–	–
LEC15	Row passage	post	62	–	–	–
LEC16	Row passage	tie beam	98	23	–	–
LEC17	Row passage	post	31	1	–	–
LEC18	Row passage	post	76	–	–	–
LEC19	Row passage	floorboard	38	–	–	–
LEC20	Row passage	threshold	23	–	–	–
LEC21	Row +1	post LEC12	76	12	–	–

indicates that relatively young trees were used to form those timbers and that their preparation simply required the removal of the surplus outer wood. The results suggest that two different populations of trees are represented in the timbers sampled at the Blue Bell.

The Leche House, 17 Watergate Street

Twenty samples were taken from nineteen timbers in the Leche House; ten from the undercroft and ten samples from nine timbers at Row level and above. Table 8 gives details of the timbers sampled in each part of the building.

Five of the timbers sampled from the undercroft had insufficient rings for analysis to be undertaken. One of these contained sapwood (LEC6). There was no cross-matching whatsoever between any of the samples, and therefore a mean site chronology could not be constructed. Equally it was not possible to match these samples with any established chronologies.

One of the principal posts in the passage was sampled at Row level (LEC12) and again at Row + 1 level (LEC 21). On LEC12 the ring series extended almost to the centre of the tree (to pith) and contained no sapwood; LEC21 showed no evidence of pith but contained 12 sapwood rings. By cross-matching these samples, it should have been possible to calculate the cambial age of the tree. However, the presence of distorted areas in LEC12 prevented the calculation being made.

LEC21 and four other samples had sufficient growth rings for analyses to be made, but no cross-matching was found. Each sample was then compared with established chronologies, but no significant cross-matching was present.

The timbers showed great variation in their growth ring patterns. Samples LEC13, LEC16 and LEC18 contained the largest number of rings, most of which were fairly narrow (0.5–2.0mm). Sample LEC14 exhibited the widest growth rings (many 12.0mm). The marked variation in the widths and patterns of the tree rings suggests that the timbers used in the building of the Leche House derived from different timber stands.

37 Watergate Street

Six samples were obtained from the beams over the undercroft: the details are given in Table 9. Duplicate cores were taken from two timbers because, in each case, the first core broke during extraction. Sample STU3A was the only core containing less than 50 rings. This would normally be rejected for analysis but it was included since there was a possibility that it might extend the series of the second core, STU3B. In fact, this was the case. STU3B contained 82 rings plus approximately 25 rings that were too narrow to be measured accurately. Cross-matching was found between STU1A and STU1B and between STU3A and STU3B. These two series were averaged to form two mean chronologies: STU1M and STU3M. The tree-ring series of STU2 also cross-matched with those from STU1M and STU3M; these were combined to form a 100 year mean chronology for the undercroft, STURM. It was tested against established chronologies and dated to 1320-1419 inclusive (Table 9a). No sapwood

Table 9 37 Watergate Street: details of timbers

Sample	Location	Timber	Total no of rings	No of sapwood rings	Period spanned	Estimated felling date
STU1A	undercroft	tie beam D	69	–	1346–1414	after 1433
STU1B	undercroft	tie beam D	59	–	1348–1406	after 1425
STU2	undercroft	tie beam E	80	–	1340–1419	after 1438
STU3A	undercroft	tie beam C	44	–	1320–1363	after 1382
STU3B	undercroft	tie beam C	82	–	1328–1409	after 1428
STU4	undercroft	tie beam B	83	–	–	–

Table 9a: 37 Watergate Street
Chronology STURM
Period spanned AD 1320–1419
Crossdating of STURM

Chronology	't' value	Years overlap
East Midlands (Laxton and Litton, 1988)	4.67	100
British Isles (Baillie and Pilcher, pers comm)	4.65	100
Upwich 2, Droitwich (Groves and Hillam, 1997)	7.24	96
High Town, Hereford (Boswijk and Tyers, 1997)	4.87	100
Sinai Park, Burton on Trent (Tyers, 1997)	4.80	100
Nostell Priory, Wakefield (Tyers, 1998)	5.59	100
Commandery, Worcester (Pilcher, pers comm)	5.01	100

was present on the cores and thus a felling date after 1438 is indicated. This suggests that this building was partially reconstructed, most probably in the mid-fifteenth century.

The Deva, 10 Watergate Street

Samples were obtained from 11 structural timbers in the Deva (Table 10). Timbers which obviously had less than 50 rings were not sampled. Five samples that had an insufficient number of rings were not measured. The 32 rings shown for DE11 is only part of the sample that could have been extracted: the remaining wood could not be removed because of tarring of the sample which prevented extraction. Whilst DE1 contained only 42 rings, these did form a sensitive growth pattern. This may have been contemporary with other series in the building and therefore DE1 was measured and subsequently tested.

Six samples were tested but no consistent significant cross-matching was found. The series for DE4 (132 years), DE6 (73 years) and DE10 (86 years) were subsequently tested with established chronologies. DE6 was absolutely dated by a number of these chronologies to span the period 1437–1509 (Table 10a). There were no significant dates for DE4 and DE10.

Sample DE6 retained sapwood and the date of the last formed heartwood ring is 1505. The felling date can be estimated as 1524–55. The sample DE6 also contained pith, and this allows an estimate of cambial age of 99 years, with a range of 88–119 years. This calculation may also be made for the undated series DE4 for which the figure is 147 years, with a range of 136–167 years.

Dendrochronological analysis of timbers from the Deva show that trees with both sensitive and complacent patterns of growth were used in its construction. This suggests different growing conditions for these trees.

Table 10 The Deva, 10 Watergate Street: details of timbers

Sample	Location	Timber	Total no of rings	No of sapwood rings	Period spanned	Estimated felling date
DE1	street level	beam	42	–	–	–
DE2	street level	beam	37	–	–	–
DE3	street level	beam	45	–	–	–
DE4	street level	post	132	15	–	–
DE5	street level	post	48	–	–	–
DE6	street level	post	73	4	1437–1509	1524–1555
DE7	street level	brace	22	3	–	–
DE8	street level	brace	<30	–	–	–
DE9	street level	tie beam	56	–	–	–
DE10	Row level	corner post	86	–	–	–
DE11	Row level	corner post	32	–	–	–

Table 10a: The Deva
Timber DE6: period spanned AD 1437–1509
Crossdating of DE6

Chronology	't' value	Years overlap
Belfast (Baillie, 1977a)	4.25	73
Bishops House (Morgan, 1977)	4.37	73
British Isles (Baillie and Pilcher, pers comm)	3.85	73
Farington Hall Farm 2 (Leggett, unpub)	6.06	65
Lydiate Hall (Leggett, forthcoming)	5.13	73
Stayley Hall (Leggett, 1980)	6.19	73
Wales/West Midlands (Siebenlist-Kerner)	4.69	73
Yorkshire timbers (Hillam, pers comm)	3.78	73

22 Watergate Street

Table 11 gives details of the six samples taken from timbers at 22 Watergate Street. Two samples were not measured; sample GR3 contained less than 30 growth rings and sample GR5 contained approximately 50 rings but was broken in a number of places. Subsequent cores removed from GR5 continued to break during sampling.

Sample GR1 contained 123 growth rings including 26 rings of sapwood. Therefore this individual series was analysed further, but as no consistent significant date was obtained, GR1 could not be given an absolute date. It is possible that this may result from the bands of very narrow, scarcely measurable, rings in the sample. In addition, this series differed from the others by containing many more rings and by having a growth sequence that was extremely sensitive (with great variations in ring width). It is possible that this timber was from a different tree population.

Sample GR6 contained pith and sapwood, allowing an estimate of cambial age of 87 years, with a range of 76–107 years. None of the other samples from this building contained both pith and sapwood.

Booth Mansion, 28–34 Watergate Street

Fourteen cores were taken from the joists over the eastern undercroft in Booth Mansion. There was sufficient cross-matching of five of the samples to permit the formation of a mean site chronology and this was compared with established chronologies to provide absolute dating for the last rings (Tables 12 and 12a). This suggests that these joists were taken from trees felled during the second half of the thirteenth century.

Five cores were taken from the arcade in the western undercroft and three of these provided sufficient cross-matching to establish a mean chronology. When compared with established chronologies this provided dates from 1201 to 1231 for the last rings. One of the dated timbers (LP1325) possessed bark, but it was not possible to take a sample of the sapwood suitable for measurement. Even so, it would be reasonable to assume that the last dated ring predates felling by little more than 30 years, suggesting a date of *c* 1260 for this arcade.

38–42 Watergate Street

Nine timbers were sampled from the floor over the eastern undercroft at 38–42 Watergate Street (Table 13). It proved possible to date only the three samples which had the greatest number of rings and these all came from the joists. LP1360 and LP1362 matched one another strongly ('t'=7.27, 114 years of overlap) and so were merged to form a mean chronology, IND4. This and LP1361 were then compared with established chronologies to give firm dates for the last rings present in each sample (Tables 13a and 13b). The sapwood was absent and it is therefore not possible to estimate the felling dates. It is, however, likely that the trees from which these timbers were taken were felled within 50 years of the last dated ring, suggesting that the floor over this undercroft dates from the first half of the

Table 11 22 Watergate Street: details of timbers

Sample	Location	Timber	Total no of rings	No of sapwood rings	Period spanned	Estimated felling date
GR1	street level front	tie beam	123	26	–	–
GR2	street level rear	post	34	–	–	–
GR3	street level rear	joist	<30	–	–	–
GR4	street level front	tie beam	39	–	–	–
GR5	street level front	post	<50	–	–	–
GR6	street level front	beam	59	2	–	–

Table 12 Booth Mansion: details of timbers

Sample	Location	Timber	Total no of rings	No of sapwood rings	Period spanned	Estimated felling date
28–30 Watergate Street						
LP1329	undercroft	joist	148	–	1165–1213	after 1232
LP1332	undercroft	joist	180	–	–	–
LP1336	undercroft	joist	189	–	–	–
LP1337	undercroft	joist	87	–	–	–
LP1340	undercroft	joist	168	–	1175–1243	after 1262
LP1341	undercroft	joist	213	–	–	–
LP1342	undercroft	joist	110	–	–	–
LP1343	undercroft	joist	70	–	–	–
LP1346	undercroft	joist	166	–	1169–1235	after 1254
LP1347	undercroft	joist	122	–	1117–1239	after 1258
LP1348	undercroft	joist	125	–	–	–
LP1351	undercroft	joist	67	–	1181–1248	after 1267
LP1353	undercroft	joist	146	–	–	–
LP1354	rear undercroft	joist	77	–	–	–
32–34 Watergate Street						
LP1324	undercroft	bolster	73	–	–	–
LP1325	undercroft	post	77	–	1154–1231	after 1250
LP1326	undercroft	bridging joist	125	–	–	–
LP1327	undercroft	bolster	124	–	1076–1201	after 1220
LP1328	undercroft	post	68	–	1145–1213	after 1232

Table 12a Booth Mansion: *Crossdating*
Mean chronology: period spanned AD 1165–1248

Chronology	't' value	Years overlap
British Isles (Baillie and Pilcher, pers comm)	13.15	183
Farington Hall (Leggett, unpub)	4.48	155
Jaybank (Leggett, unpub)	8.09	174
Nantwich (Hughes and Leggett, 1983)	11.03	183

fourteenth century. Three samples were also taken from the arcade in front of the Row walkway of 40 Watergate Street; unfortunately none produced any date.

Conclusion

Despite its relatively low success rate (only 27 dated samples from the 171 cores taken – 15.8%) dendrochronology provided an important and cost-effective contribution to the Rows Research Project. As the sampling programme was limited by resources, it was largely targeted at the earliest buildings so as to establish more precise dating. This meant that the programme was also limited by the relative rarity of medieval timber structures compared with the common occurrence of

Table 13 38–42 Watergate Street: details of timbers

Sample	Location	Timber	Total no of rings	No of sapwood rings	Period spanned	Estimated felling date
LP1355	undercroft, no 38, frame 1	archbrace	19	–	–	–
LP1356	undercroft, no 38, frame 1	archbrace	23	–	–	–
LP1357	undercroft, no 38, frame 1	tie beam	40	–	–	–
LP1358	undercroft, no 38, frame 2	tie beam	37	–	–	–
LP1360	undercroft, no 38	joist	187	–	1106–1293	1312–1343
LP1361	undercroft, no 38	joist	288	–	998–1286	–
LP1362	undercroft, no 38	joist	114	–	1115–1229	–
LP1364	undercroft, no 38	joist	28	–	–	–
INRL1	row walkway, no 40	post	43	–	–	–
INRL2	row walkway, no 40	post	27	–	–	–
INRL3	row walkway, no 40	bressumer	66	–	–	–

Table 13a 38–42 Watergate Street
Mean chronology IND4 (LP1360 & LP1362)
Period spanned AD 1116–1293
Crossdating of IND4

Chronology	't' value	Years overlap
Baguley Hall (Leggett, 1980)	4.07	184
British Isles (Baillie and Pilcher, pers comm)	5.16	187
Farington Hall (Leggett, unpub)	4.46	187

Table 13b 38–42 Watergate Street
Timber LP1361
Period spanned AD 998–1286
Crossdating of LP1361

Chronology	't' value	Years overlap
Baguley Hall (Leggett, 1980)	5.40	250
British Isles (Baillie and Pilcher, pers comm)	7.33	288
Nantwich (Leggett, 1980)	4.50	288

medieval masonry (Chapters 3 and 4). In addition, opportunities for sampling the few medieval timbers above Row level were limited, as such structures were either in public areas or inaccessible.

Nevertheless, dendrochronology has provided independent evidence that there are a number of buildings in the Rows dating from the second half of the thirteenth century and the first half of the fourteenth century. Unfortunately, the general absence of sapwood means that only general dating estimates can be given.

The absence of sapwood is a testimony to the quality of the carpentry, and the size and slow-growing nature of the trees from which the timbers were selected is shown by the length of the ring counts. Many of the joists, for example, were quartered timbers and proved to have ring counts exceeding 150 years.

Frustratingly, most of those buildings believed to have a late medieval date, such as the Leche House, 17 Watergate Street, did not produce any dated samples. The exceptions were a single timber from the Deva, 10 Watergate Street, and three dated tie beams from 37 Watergate Street. Except for 37 Watergate Street the medieval buildings failed to produce cross-matching internal chronologies. The samples from these buildings generally had ring counts of less than 100 and sapwood was commonly present. This implies that the carpenters working on these buildings had to use poorer timber from a variety of sources, such as hedgerows, parkland and managed woods, rather than the better quality timber available during the earlier period.

Appendix C: Documentary references for the enclosure of the Rows

by J Laughton and R Turner

As the Rows were considered part of the 'common soil' of the city any projected development had to be submitted to the Assembly for approval. This inevitably generated considerable bureaucratic activity, the written records of which survive in Chester Archives. All known documentary sources relating to the enclosure of the Rows are listed in this Appendix by address (where it has been identified), and therefore individual references have been omitted from the main text. Petitions to the Assembly appear in the Assembly Files (AF), occasionally accompanied by counter-petitions from indignant neighbours stressing the loss of light, access, custom, or other amenity which would ensue if permission were granted. The Assembly Books record the deliberations, together with orders to view the premises, the resulting decision, and the fine and rent imposed. The references are presented either, for example, as A/B/3/71V which refers to the folio number, or A/B/3/27.7.1715 which is the date of the meeting. The Treasurer's Accounts complement these sources, by recording payments (or occasionally the failure to pay), and the Quarter Session Files record disputes. Corporation deeds and collections of family papers have helped with the precise identification of properties and have also provided the more personal element.

Sometimes the evidence has been gathered from secondary sources, including collections of deeds deposited or transcribed by Lawson, Simpson, or Faulkner and stored under their names in the City Record Office. Occasional items have also been published in the *Cheshire Sheaf* or the *Journal of the Chester Archaeological Society*.

The information is presented street by street, under modern addresses. The location of historic properties has been made possible from topographical information given in the documents or by building up blocks of adjacent owners and fixing them into the street pattern. However, the picture is not complete and several petitions cannot be placed with certainty (these are indicated by a question mark [?] after the address). Other petitions can only be placed generally and these are listed separately. The problem is compounded by the fact that successful petitions did not necessarily lead to the taking in of the Row and later owners needed to reapply.

Bridge Street – West side

52 Bridge Street

1697	Francis Skellern Alderman	3s rent	A/B/3/2.10.1697

According to Simpson (unpublished manuscript, Chester Archives CR 112/3) this caused strong resentment and the obstruction was removed. The Row walkway was blocked again in c 1810 by the present building erected by Mr Swannick and an alternative passage from The Row to Bolland Court provided.

Unlocated petitions in the vicinity of Pierpoint Lane

1733	Laurence Corless Wetglover	rejected	AF/52/234
1733	George Taylor	oversail granted, enclosure rejected	AF/52/234
1733	Joseph Soreton Innkeeper	rejected	AF/52/236
1733	Robert Jones Watchmaker	rejected	AF/52/235

Lower Bridge Street – East side

1–3 Lower Bridge Street

1703	Richard Penketh Ironmonger	6s 8d rent	AF/47f/62

TAP/3 August 1703, shows house 'in the holding of Mary Throppe, widow, and Mr Low has a shop to the north'

5 Lower Bridge Street

1703	William Bennett Alderman	6s 8d rent	AF/47f/61

House 'in the holding of Robert Comberbach, Recorder of Chester'

7 Lower Bridge Street (formerly the Red Lyon Inn)

1703	William Bennett Alderman	6s 8d rent	AF/47f/30

CMD/2/41 and TAP/3 19 August 1703 grants land $11^{1}/_{2}$ x 4yd to Bennett and later views of this building show it set back with imperial stairs to first floor entrance.

9 Lower Bridge Street

| 1728 | John Dicas Barber | 30s fine | AF/51 |
| 1759 | William Dicas Peruke maker | reapplication 30s fine | |

For earlier encroachment into row see AF/50e/48 and a series of deeds relating to this property D/L 110–150.

11 Lower Bridge Street

| 1728 | Roger Barnston | £5 fine | AF/51 |

In 1711, Barnston granted leave to build on stallboard, A/B/3/18.4.1711, but this property remains unenclosed.

13 Lower Bridge Street

| 1728 | Lawrence Gother Alderman | 30s fine | AF/51 |
| 1741 | Thomas Gother City Treasurer | reapplication 30s fine | AF/53 |

In 1709, Lawrence Gother was granted a Row chamber, AF/49a/38. This was built but the Row remained unenclosed until 1876 (Lawson and Smith 1958, 9).

15 Lower Bridge Street

| 1741 | Samuel Hinton Druggist | | AF/53 |

17–19 Lower Bridge Street

The Row walkway is concealed behind chambers but is unenclosed and is called Unity Passage.

21 Lower Bridge Street

Shown as unenclosed in early nineteenth-century print, perhaps remaining so until present house built in 1895

23 Lower Bridge Street

Date of enclosure not known

25 Lower Bridge Street

1725	John Dewsbury Assembly Member	counter petition to Bulkeley (see below)	AF/51
1727	John Dewsbury	enclosure petition no report	AF/51
1728	John Dewsbury	provision of steps	A/B/4/8.3.1728

27 Lower Bridge Street

1725	William Bulkeley Ironmonger	petition	AF/51
1726	William Bulkeley	rejected	A/B/4/4.3.1726
1728	William Bulkeley	£5 fine and provision of steps	A/B/4/8.3.1728

29–31 Lower Bridge Street (Tudor House)

1725	Roger Ormes	petition	AF/51
1726	Roger Ormes	rejected	A/B/4/4.3.1726
1728	Roger Ormes	£5 fine and provision of steps	A/B/4/8.3.1728

33 Lower Bridge Street

1725	Mary Whitfield Widow	petition for two messuages	AF/51
1726	Mary Whitfield	20s fine for part only	A/B/4/4.3.1726
1728	Mary Whitfield	£7 fine for remainder	A/B/4/8.3.1728

35 Lower Bridge Street

| 1720 | John Warrington Carpenter | 40s fine | AF/50c/28 |

37–41 Lower Bridge Street (Park House)

| 1703 | Madam Elizabeth Booth | rejected | AF/48a/13 |
| 1717 | Elizabeth Booth | £8 fine | AF/50c/18 |

43–47 Lower Bridge Street

Date of enclosure not known but this site was formerly occupied by a large eighteenth-century house with no Row

49 Lower Bridge Street

| 1716 | Peter Bristow | £3 fine | AF/50a/15 |

51 Lower Bridge Street

| 1699 | John Mather Gentleman | petition | AF/47c/8 and 38 |
| 1700 | John Mather | £10 fine | A/B/3/12.1.1700 |

53 Lower Bridge Street (formerly the Crown and Angel Inn)

1708	Richard Lawrence	complaint against Mather	AF/48c/39

No enclosure details known for this plot

St Olave's Church

No petitions have been traced for the enclosure of the Row in the properties below St Olave's Church.

Lower Bridge Street–West side

2 Lower Bridge Street

1698	Randle Holme III	5s rent	A/B/3/18.2.1698

This seems to have been a major encroachment rather than an enclosure. This property disappeared when Grosvenor Street was built.

4 Lower Bridge Street (Lamb Row)

1715	John Thomas Tailor	rejected	AF/40g/51–2
1715	Mary Griffith		A/B/3/27.7.1715

Only the Row at the south end appeared to have been enclosed before this building was demolished in 1821 for the construction of Grosvenor Street.

6 (The Falcon) and 8–10 Lower Bridge Street

1643	Sir Richard Grosvenor	26s 8d fine 2s 6d rent	AF/26/7

12 Lower Bridge Street (formerly the Upper White Bear)

1675	Thomas Gibbons Feltmaker	5s fine	A/B/2/18c

14 Lower Bridge Street

1681	Thomas Wright	3s 6d rent	TAP/3 Faulkner 19
1699	Thomas Wright, jnr Sheriff		A/B/3/71v

16 Lower Bridge Street

1686	Laurence Gualter Joiner	5s rent	AF/42b/32

Bridge House, 18–24 Lower Bridge Street

1676	Lady Mary Calveley	40s fine 5s rent	AF/41a/16
1678	Lady Mary Calveley	added stairs	AF/41d/30

24–26 Lower Bridge Street[?]

1668	Thomas Weston Clerk	2s 6d rent	AF/39e/25

26 Lower Bridge Street[?]

	Edward Cooke	mentioned in Alban Grey's petition (see below)

28 Lower Bridge Street

1691	Alban Grey	£2 fine 12s rent	AF/46a/26

30 Lower Bridge Street (formerly the Sign of the Angel)

1676	Ralph Leighe	10s fine 3s 6d rent	A/B/2/183v
1703	Thomas Leigh Innholder	petition	AF/47f/69
1704	Thomas Leigh	rejected	AF/48a/15
1717	Thomas Leigh	10s fine	AF/50c/9 and 15

32 Lower Bridge Street

1717	William Hunt (formerly M Croughton)	included in 38–42	AF/50c/3

34–36 Lower Bridge Street

1717	Ambrose Wheawell (encroachment only)	40s fine	AF/50c/4,47,54

38–42 Lower Bridge Street

1717	Thomas Hunt	20s fine	AF/50c/3

Collection of deeds (CR 165) show the subsequent stormy history of Nos 32–42

44–46 Lower Bridge Street[?]

1734	John Dutton Baker	report delayed	A/B/4/15.8.1734
1741	John Dutton	30s fine	A/B/4/17.4.1741
1740	Deborah Clegg Widow	£5 fine	A/B/4/8.10.1740

The locations here are not certain and A/B/4/2.12.1748 and A/B/4/24.8.1749 are also relevant.

48–50 Lower Bridge Street (The Old King's Head)

| 1741 | William Ball | no report traced | A/B/4/20.8.1741 |

52–60 Lower Bridge Street (Gamul House)

Fronted by a raised walkway: not a true Row. G Batenham's view of 1816 shows No 60 as a stair tower/solar block projecting forward, blocking the walkway. (See also Pl 8.)

62–68 Lower Bridge Street

Fronted by a raised walkway, as Gamul House. Batenham's view implies a series of properties in which the Row was enclosed.

70–78 Lower Bridge Street

No petitions have been traced for the enclosure of the Row in these properties.

80 Lower Bridge Street

| 1704 | Thomas Williams Innholder | 2s 6d rent | AF/48a/60 |

82 Lower Bridge Street

| 1723 | John Brerewood | 30s fine | AF/51 |

84 Lower Bridge Street (Shipgate House)

| c 1705 | Sir John Werden | no petition traced house dated stylistically | |

Unlocated petitions in Lower Bridge Street

| 1734 | Isaac Powell Barber | no report traced | A/B/4/15.8.1734 |

Eastgate Street – North side

All the petitions listed below relate to properties east of St Werburgh Street, where the buildings appear to have oversailed a street-level pavement and therefore did not contain true Row walkways.

35 Eastgate Street

| 1742 | Nathanial Hall | no report traced | A/B/4/4.3.1742 |

37 Eastgate Street

| 1742 | John Moulson | no report traced | A/B/4/4.3.1742 |

39–41 Eastgate Street

1742	David Williams (No 39)	no report traced	A/B/4/4.3.1742
1742	Richard Moulson (No 41)	no report traced	A/B/4/4.3.1742
1749	Richard Moulson Grocer	petition	A/B/4/24.8.1749
1750	Richard Moulson	shop only 5s 4d rent	A/B/4/10.10.1750
1772	Thomas Moulson	petition with plan	AF/55
1773	Thomas Moulson	5s fine	A/B/4/13.5.1773

43 Eastgate Street

1742	Thomas Hincks	no report traced	A/B/4/4.3.1742
1749	Thomas Hincks	petition	A/B/4/24.8.1749
1750	Thomas Hincks	shop only 5s rent	A/B/4/10.10.1750

45 Eastgate Street

1742	Ralph Probert Hatter	no report traced	A/B/4/4.3.1742
1748	Ralph Probert	petition	A/B/4/2.12.1748
1750	Ralph Probert Alderman	shop only	A/B/4/24.8.1750

Eastgate Street – South side

58 Eastgate Street

| 1714 | Charles, Duke of Shrewsbury | £10 fine | AF/49g/35 |
| 1716 | Charles, Duke of Shrewsbury | rejected | AF/50b/9 and 15 |

This property now forms the eastern end of the Grosvenor Hotel, where the street-level arcade does not continue across the full width of the hotel frontage.

Northgate Street – West side

1 Northgate Street (part only?)

| 1699 | William Wilson Alderman | 1s rent | A/B/3/31.3.1699 |

3 Northgate Street

| 1699 | Abigail Burroughs | 40s fine | A/B/3/31.3.1699 A/B/3/19.5.1699 |

5 Northgate Street

| 1699 | John Dob Cordwainer | no report traced | A/B/3/31.10.1699 |
| 1699 | Abigail Burroughs | counter petition | A/B/3/31.10.1699 |

Unlocated petitions in Northgate Street

In 1613–14 William Mercer, tallow chandler, and Richard Stockton, blacksmith, 'enclosed and stopped uppe the Rowe' illegally (QSF/62/48 – 20 October).

| 1670 | Elizabeth Throppe Widow | rejected | AF/40b/24 |
| 1681 | Thomas Dod | rejected | A/B/2/16.12.1681 |

Watergate Street – South side

69 Watergate Street

| 1711 | Eleanor Massie Widow of Dublin | 50s fine | AF/49d/14 |
| 1714 | Bernard Fielding Innholder | 50s fine | A/B/3/1.6.1714 |

71–73 Watergate Street

| 1703 | Henry Pemberton | rejected | A/B/3/20.9.1703 A/B/3/25.2.1704 |
| 1711 | John Pemberton | 50s fine/ messuage | AF/49d/11 |

75 Watergate Street

| 1711 | Thomas Alcott Smith | 50s fine | AF/49d/12 |

77 Watergate Street[?] (Yacht Inn)

| 1711 | Thomas Biggins Innholder | 50s fine | AF/40d/13 |

The building on this site was demolished to allow the widening of Nicholas Street.

Watergate Street – North side

44–46 Watergate Street

| 1713 | Robert Bavand Doctor of Physick | £2 10s fine | AF/49f/6 |

CR/45/24 includes the conveyance of the Row.
CR/45/25–31 has later transactions including the sale of the property to Dame Philadelphia Cotton.

48–50 Watergate Street

| 1701/2 | Robert Denteth Merchant | rejected | AF/47e/34 |

This was a counter petition to that submitted by James Doe (see below).

| 1713 | Sir Thomas Cotton | £2 10s fine | AF/49f/5 |

CR/45/1–13 gives the earlier history of the house.
CR/45/14–19 has transactions between Denteth and Cotton.
CR/45/20 includes the conveyance of the Row.
CR/45/21–3 records a later sale.

52 Watergate Street

| 1713 | John Martin Yeoman of Eastham | £1 10s fine | AF/49f/7 |

54–56 Watergate Street

| 1701 | James Doe Gent | £5 fine £5 rent | AF/47e/13 |

60–66 Watergate Street

| 1675 | Sir Peter Pindar Collector of customs | 3s rent | AF/40g/32 |

For earlier references to encroachment and enclosure of this property see

> *TAR 3/51 (1643–6)*
> *TAR 3/52 (1655–6)*
> *QSF/78/6*
> *Trevor Mss (Flintshire Record Office, Mold)*

68 Watergate Street

| 1686 | Michael Johnson | | A/B/3/6v |
| 1703 | John Williams | rent not recorded | AF/47f/13 |

Related documents are

> *TAP/3 (34.4.1703)*
> *CHD/8/11*

Gazetteer

(This gazetteer was finalised during the summer of 1993.)

Bridge Street – East side

1 Bridge Street, 1 Bridge Street Row, and 2 Eastgate Street

A Vernacular Revival building designed by T M Lockwood for Chester City Council and dated 1888. It replaced a timber-framed building which incorporated the sixteenth-century cistern. For this prominent corner site, Lockwood produced an enjoyable design in half-timbering which has served as a popular symbol of Chester's nineteenth-century Row architecture. (See pp 118–9, Figs 129 and 150.)

3–7 Bridge Street, 3–7 Bridge Street Row

A Vernacular Revival building designed by W M Boden and erected 1889–90. The structure is of cast iron columns and beams, with internal partitions of Ruabon pressed brick. The facade is half-timbered above a tiled lean-to canopy to the Row level. (See p 124.)

9 Bridge Street, 9 Bridge Street Row

A rendered facade of *c* 1840 conceals a seventeenth-century building. Medieval masonry survives at the rear of the undercroft, with a modern lavatory and a cloakroom to the north having sandstone walls; while on the south, a chamber, 4.33m in length, is also of stone construction. At Row + 1 level there are lamb's tongue stopped beams and fleur-de-lys plasterwork, and there are clear indications that a jetty has been removed. The rooms above have classical fireplaces. Part of a timber frame may survive, but the south wall is of twentieth-century brick. (See p 91.)

11 Bridge Street, 11 Bridge Street Row

A partially surviving seventeenth-century timber-framed building with a medieval undercroft (Fig 151). The upper part of the facade was rebuilt as a replica in the twentieth century. The undercroft measures 12.15 x 5.50m and contains part of a medieval timber arcade supporting large square joists for which dendrochronological analysis has yet to produce a dating. This level is divided into two by an eighteenth-century crosswall, access to the rear being via the Row-level shop. The rear section has sandstone walls and a corbel in the east wall that originally supported the end of the arcade beam. In the north wall a timber sole plate, joist, and section of floorboard are preserved. At Row level, there is a good Edwardian shop interior with an arcaded gallery, which probably reflects a seventeenth-century arrangement. At Row + 2 level the seventeenth-century trenched-purlin roof truss is exposed. (See pp 45–6 and 83.)

Fig 150 Bridge Street looking south; Nos 1 and 3–7 first and second left (RCHME © Crown Copyright)

Fig 151 Timber arcade post in undercroft of 11 Bridge Street (RCHME © Crown Copyright)

Fig 152 Ceiling at Row + 1 level in 15 Bridge Street, 1942 (RCHME © Crown Copyright)

13 Bridge Street, 13–15 Bridge Street Row

A tall brick building of 1861 designed by Edward Hodkinson for Mr Ewen, hosier, containing no evidence of earlier fabric. The undercroft is L-shaped with the return projecting south behind 15 Bridge Street. At Row level a narrow rear wing leads to a former courtyard dwelling, which was probably independently occupied.

15 Bridge Street, 17–19 Bridge Street Row

The eighteenth-century brick facade conceals a seventeenth-century timber-framed structure above a short stone-walled undercroft, 10.5m long. The undercroft is spanned by a pair of two-ordered chamfered pointed arches dating from the mid-fourteenth century (p 49 and *cf* 36 Bridge Street, pp 38, 163). These carry large medieval flat oak joists. The walls are covered with a modern lining, but Lawson and Smith (1958, 11) recorded evidence for the lowering of the undercroft floor and a recess in the south wall (*cf* 28 Eastgate Street). Seventeenth-century plasterwork (Fig 152) survives on the upper floors, and the way this has been truncated shows that the building was jettied. The southern boundary of the property encroached southwards to include the steps up to Row level; the resultant distortion is shown on the 1875 OS map. (See p 91.)

17–19 Bridge Street, 21–23 Bridge Street Row

A late eighteenth-century building with sandstone flanking walls to the rear undercroft, which are probably medieval. The facade has been altered since its construction; the Row + 1 level windows have lost their heavy cornices and brackets, and the projecting pediment, shown on nineteenth-century photographs, has been replaced by a less substantial version.

21 Bridge Street, 25 Bridge Street Row

An early nineteenth-century brick facade fronts a building containing elements from previous centuries. The narrow undercroft has large square joists with evidence of a sandstone corbel table on the south side. Below the back of the stallboard is a chamfered oak beam, stopped at the south end. Late seventeenth- or early eighteenth-century brickwork and timber framing are visible on the south wall at Row + 1 level.

23 Bridge Street, 27 Bridge Street Row

An early nineteenth-century brick building with cast-iron Doric columns at Row level and a medieval undercroft. The walls of the undercroft are lined, but are reported to be of sandstone. Cross beams and chamfered flat oak joists with stops at the rear end are partly visible.

25–27 Bridge Street, 29–31 Bridge Street Row

The brick facade is of *c* 1800, but inside, only the undercroft is of this date. At Row level and above, the interiors were altered in the twentieth century to accommodate newspaper presses.

Fig 153 St Michael's Arcade (RCHME © Crown Copyright)

29 Bridge Street, 35 Bridge Street Row

An early nineteenth-century brick building with cast iron Doric columns at Row level. The site of any medieval undercroft is largely obliterated by a vast subterranean printing press room. A storeroom towards the front has early nineteenth-century joists, bridging joists and cast iron columns. Several of the joists have unused mortices and are manifestly reused.

31–35 Bridge Street, 37–39 Bridge Street Row

A large Vernacular Revival steel framed building of 1910–1911 with half-timbered facade designed by W T Lockwood for the first Duke of Westminster. It replaced a similar scaled building of the mid-nineteenth century by Edward Hodkinson (p 124, Fig 138), and incorporates the Row-level entrance to St Michael's Arcade. At first built with a facing of white faience tiles, the front was taken down and rebuilt on the Duke's instruction, following local protest at its appearance. Little interior detail from 1910–11 survives, although deeply embossed Art Nouveau wallpaper below dado level on the Row to Row + 1 level staircase at 39 Bridge Street Row gives an indication of the lost interior, as does the undercroft of No 31 with its egg-and-dart moulded bridging joists. (See pp125–8, Figs 140,141 and 153.)

37–41 Bridge Street, 43–47 Bridge Street Row

A neo-Jacobean style brick building erected in 1864 for the second Marquis of Westminster and designed by Edward Hodkinson (p 124). It incorporates a medieval undercroft (14.5m in length), now subdivided and reduced in height by the insertion of a street level floor. Originally 4.2m high, the undercroft was perhaps used as a seld (see Appendix A). In the west cellar wall are sections of Roman bath house masonry, and the medieval rear wall contains a rebated doorway opening into an exposed Roman hypocaust, and is footed on to Roman concrete. Also in the east wall are compound corbels, probably *c* 1300, with that over the doorway comprising four stones (p 40, Fig 43). The Row and above levels have entirely modern clad interiors. Across a rear court is a group of brick tenements (45, 45a and 45b Bridge Street Row) contemporary with the frontage building of 1864. They are rare surviving examples of nineteenth-century courtyard housing.

St Michael's Rectory, 43 Bridge Street, 49 Bridge Street Row

A mid-seventeenth-century timber-framed building which was bequeathed in 1659 by Lettice Whitley to St Michael's Parish and used until 1907 as the Rectory.

Fig 154 St Michael's Rectory, 43 Bridge Street (RCHME © Crown Copyright)

The undercroft is lined, but there are post-medieval oak joists partly visible at the rear. The Row-level interior has a fine seventeenth-century plastered ceiling and an eighteenth–century twist baluster staircase up to Row + 1 level. At this level a galleried room is open to the roof, with a chamber over the Row. The rear wall of the seventeenth-century structure, incorporating a 6-light mullion window, is now an interior wall, with the rearward extension apparently a twentieth-century rebuild of an eighteenth-century precursor. Below the window are three plaster panels of scenes of the Crucifixion and Deposition, probably installed when the building was restored by Mr Crawford, an antique dealer, shortly after he purchased it in 1907. The purlin roof is seventeenth-century, but has been severely altered; the rear truss of the rear chamber is the most intact. A warehouse at the rear, which was recently demolished, contained seventeenth- and nineteenth-century features (See p 91, Figs 66 and 154).

45–47 Bridge Street, 51–55 Bridge Street Row

A brick building of the early to mid-nineteenth century, with no evidence of earlier fabric. The undercroft to No 45 has a fine early twentieth-century butcher's shop interior with a cast iron column and cashier's office.

49 Bridge Street, 57 Bridge Street Row

A Vernacular Revival building by W M Boden, dated 1891 on the gable, and in a similar style to his later work at 3–7 Bridge Street. The 1891 interior has been largely removed, with only a single late nineteenth-century cornice surviving at undercroft level. (See p 124.)

51–53 Bridge Street, 59 Bridge Street Row

A proto-Vernacular Revival facade of 1858 by James Harrison encases a much altered seventeenth-century timber-framed building above a pair of modern clad undercrofts. Evidence for this structure is fragmentary and is best seen in the passageway at the south. The Row level is open to the roof and there is a gallery; this is of nineteenth-century construction, but probably perpetuates the seventeenth-century form. The over-Row chamber has remains of timber studwork in the south wall. The eastern truss of this room is a twentieth-century non-structural creation from reused timbers planted on to the wall face. (See pp 83, 115.)

55 Bridge Street, 61 Bridge Street Row

A Vernacular Revival building by Thomas Edwards, built as a commercial art gallery for David Sherratt in 1889. The half-timbered facade has inscriptions, statuary and carved panels of biblical scenes in the manner of Bishop Lloyd's Palace. The elaborate wrought iron hanging sign is contemporary with the building. The brick and stone undercroft is probably eighteenth-century, and retains large-scantling bridging joists that support the Row storey. The interiors at Row level and above are little altered and contain tall top-lit galleries for the display of paintings and other works of art. (See p 124 and Fig 137.)

57 Bridge Street, 63 Bridge Street Row

A brick-built structure of the early nineteenth century incorporating fragmentary evidence of a seventeenth-century timber frame, which is most apparent in the stop-chamfered timber in the Row level passage, and a medieval undercroft. This undercroft is lined with modern cladding, though sandstone flank walls were revealed in recent refitting. At the rear is an intact medieval chamber (3.7 x 3.47m), entered via passages at east and west. It is of one phase of sandstone construction with a small cupboard, 0.40m deep, in the west wall (p 43). The rear wall of the main undercroft is visible, extending 1.05m south of the chamber, and the interconnecting passage is 1.67m long. The upper floors contain simple classical interiors of the early nineteenth century.

59 Bridge Street, 67–69 Bridge Street Row

A late seventeenth-century building, altered in the eighteenth century and refronted in the 1950s. The new

Fig 155 South end of Bridge Street Row East (RCHME © Crown Copyright)

Fig 156 Nineteenth-century drawing of Bridge Street Row East from porch of St Michael's Church (reproduced by courtesy of Chester Archives)

front crudely replicates the elevation recorded by G Batenham in 1816. Internally there is a good staircase, panelled doors and plasterwork; all date from the late seventeenth century. The south wall is reported to be timber-framed.

61 Bridge Street, 71–73 Bridge Street Row

A brick building of *c* 1760, employing heavily reused timbers with seventeenth-century detailing as bridging joists and ceiling beams at Row level. The rear wall of a medieval undercroft survives (now lined) with a doorway towards the north leading through to a second chamber or undercroft. An eighteenth-century twist baluster staircase runs from Row level to Row + 2, and there is an impressive over-Row parlour.

63 Bridge Street, 75 Bridge Street Row

This predominantly late eighteenth-century brick building reveals no earlier fabric and the interior is entirely modern clad. However, the occupier recalls the exposure of a sandstone wall at undercroft level, adjacent to St Michael's Church, and presumably medieval.

St Michael's Church

The south end of the Row passes through the west tower of the church and serves as the porch. The church is fifteenth-century in origin, but was largely rebuilt by James Harrison in 1849–50. The chancel roof of 1496 is narrower than the present chancel, which was widened in 1678. Also surviving from the

fifteenth century is the north arcade with octagonal piers. The building has been used as a Heritage Centre since 1975. (Fig 156)

Bridge Street – West side

2–8 Bridge Street, 2–6 Bridge Street Row, and 1–3 Watergate Street, 1–3 Watergate Street Row

A Vernacular Revival building by T M Lockwood, erected for the first Duke of Westminster in 1892. The brick, stone and half-timbered facade shows Lockwood's eclectic and inventive use of Renaissance and Baroque ornament. No earlier fabric survives, despite this being the site of the medieval 'Staven Selds' (see p 69). Photographic and map evidence reveals that before 1892 an earlier nineteenth-century brick building occupied the site, extending further north into Watergate Street. (See pp 119–20, Figs 130 and 157.)

10 Bridge Street, 8 Bridge Street Row

This is a largely intact seventeenth-century timber-framed building on an undercroft which is lined and thus undatable. The deep stallboard (3.58m) is mainly of seventeenth-century fabric with only a minor nineteenth-century encroachment. The facade above Row level has a distinctive band of 5 quatrefoils, over which is painted mock timber framing. Internally, a gallery at Row + 1 level survives, with chambers at front and rear. A modern suspended ceiling breaks up the former galleried hall. The rear Row + 1 level chambers reveal

Fig 157 Early photograph of Bridge Street, west side. The brick buildings on the right and the two timber-framed buildings alongside were replaced by Nos 2–8 Bridge Street by Lockwood in 1892; his 1873 rebuilding of No 20 can be seen just before the Dutch Houses. See also Fig 158. (RCHME © Crown Copyright)

the timber frame most clearly, particularly the braced trenched purlin roof structure. A nineteenth-century warehouse at the rear contains the remains of a belt drive power take-off system. (See p 65.)

12 Bridge Street, 10 Bridge Street Row

One of the more impressive buildings in the Rows, this comprises a medieval vaulted undercroft with a seventeenth-century timber-framed building above. The undercroft is of two parts; the front section is lined, but 16.8m from the street is a 6-bay pointed quadripartite rib-vault (12.95 x 4.6m) of the mid- to later thirteenth century. The east wall is of 1839, when the undercroft was rediscovered, but is on medieval foundations. At the west end is a light well. The three round-headed windows are higher than their still detectable thirteenth-century trefoil-headed precursors. The south wall has a trefoil-headed doorway to a 0.75m wide mural staircase up to Row level. The vault has chamfered diagonal and cross-ribs springing from plain sub-conical corbels. The seventeenth-century timber-framed building at Row level and above has a reasonably intact elaborate facade, with strapwork and the inscription *TC 1664* ('T C' referring to Thomas Cowper, Mayor of Chester 1641–2, and a Royalist). The timber frame behind the facade is more fragmentary, although a trenched purlin roof is partly preserved. At Row + 1 level a sandstone fireplace is dated 1661. (pp 17, 35, 42, 69, 90–1, and Figs 17 and 46)

14 Bridge Street, 12 Bridge Street Row

Some medieval stonework is visible at the rear of an otherwise lined undercroft. The south wall has been breached to create an extension to the south behind No 16. There is no visible evidence of the staircase arrangement in the north wall, which can be seen in No 12. At Row level and above, the building is a shallow timber-framed structure. Despite the absence of any interior detail earlier than the nineteenth century, and a rendered facade, the building can be dated to the seventeenth century on the basis of the over-Row carved bressumer and the trenched purlin roof construction. Behind this structure is a modern flat roof over the rear part of the undercroft, with a freestanding three-storey nineteenth-century brick building beyond. There is no evidence for the rearward extent of the medieval or seventeenth-century buildings.

16–18 Bridge Street, 14 Bridge Street Row

Two contemporary properties of the early nineteenth century (a rainwater head is inscribed 1804) that form a symmetrical frontage. No fabric earlier than this is visible.

20 Bridge Street, 16–18 Bridge Street Row

A tall Vernacular Revival building dating from 1873, with a half-timbered facade infilled with brick. It was designed by T M Lockwood and is his earliest work in the Rows. No earlier fabric survives. The oriel window with pargetted panel is derived from Shaw and Nesfield. An Art Deco lavatory at undercroft level, classical panelling at street level, and large bread ovens at Row level are interesting early twentieth-century additions when the property was in use as the Plane Tree Café. (See p 118, and Fig 128.)

The Dutch Houses, 22–26 Bridge Street, 20–24 Bridge Street Row

This structure, with its distinctive facade and twisted columns, appears to have been built as a single impressive property. It had, however, been subdivided into a complex of different ownerships, before the need for

urgent repairs led the City Council to purchase all the individual sections in the 1970s. Following a heavy and extensive restoration by the City Council, which involved the insertion of much steelwork, only the four stone piers, some plasterwork, a series of sandstone fireplaces, and some timber framing survive from the late seventeenth-century town house. The undercrofts are largely lined, although No 24 reveals seventeenth-century joists. The Row level and above are notable chiefly for the sandstone columns, which rise through the full four storeys. Lamb's tongue stops to the chamfers, the smaller dimensions of the column second from the south, and the seeming lack of compatibility with the seventeenth-century interior detail led J T Smith (unpublished articles) to propose a thirteenth-

Fig 158 Pre-1873 photograph of the Dutch Houses, 22–26 Bridge Street. Lockwood's No 20 is not yet built. (The Howarth-Loomes Collection, courtesy of the Royal Commission on the Historical Monuments of England)

Fig 159 Ceiling at Row + 1 level in the Dutch Houses, 22–26 Bridge Street, 1972 (RCHME © Crown Copyright)

century date. Their condition, detail and an absence of medieval fabric elsewhere make this improbable. Furthermore, the photographic evidence of the fabric removed in the 1970s rebuild indicates eighteenth- or nineteenth-century alterations which could account for plasterwork overlapping seventeenth-century detail on the columns. At the rear of the Row + 2 and Row + 3 front parlours, a major timber-framed wall has been preserved, with three trenched purlin trusses and blocked windows to a central light well. A heavy seventeenth-century plaster ceiling survives at Row + 1 level in No 24. (See pp 91, 132–3, and Figs 158 and 159.)

28 Bridge Street, 26 Bridge Street Row

A late eighteenth-century corner property of brick, with a rainwater head dated 1789. Early twentieth-century alterations replaced the facades and interiors at undercroft and Row levels. Heavy cornices have been added in keeping with those on the Dutch Houses. A concrete footbridge built over Commonhall Street in the 1970s connects the Row with that of No 30.

30 Bridge Street, 28 Bridge Street Row

A brick and timber-framed building, formerly a public house. A design by John Douglas exists for rebuilding, dated 1873, but this was not executed. More modest proposals, perhaps by Douglas and Minshull, were carried out in 1900. The previous structure was recorded by Douglas, and is most notable for having a large chamber on the stallboard next to Commonhall Street.

32 Bridge Street, 30 Bridge Street Row

An early nineteenth-century building (a rainwater head is dated 1811) standing on a medieval undercroft. This extends back 40.85m and is the longest in the Rows.

Fig 160 34 and 36 Bridge Street (RCHME © Crown Copyright)

Its extreme length combined with its narrowness (between 3.5m and 4.75m) and its location near the Commonhall mean that it may well be a surviving seld (see Chapter 2 and Appendix A). The back side of the rear medieval wall has been exposed by a nineteenth-century extension, but was built against solid earth. The heavy timbers spanning the undercroft are not medieval and probably date from the early nineteenth-century rebuilding. A cottage at the rear contains an early eighteenth-century staircase and panelled room.

34 Bridge Street, 32 Bridge Street Row

A late eighteenth-century brick building with no earlier fabric visible. A good open well staircase with panelled dado leads up from Row level, and several rooms retain eighteenth-century features. (Fig 160)

36 Bridge Street, 34 Bridge Street Row

A wide and impressive medieval sandstone undercroft spanned by two mid-fourteenth century two-centred chamfered pointed arches. These carry quarter-sawn joists, three of which provided dendrochronological dates for felling after 1327 (see Appendix B). At the rear these joists can be seen to be carrying rubble fill. In the south-west corner furniture blocks the medieval rear access. The present floor, three steps below street level, is inserted, with the lower part of the undercroft

*Fig 161   Undercroft in 36 Bridge Street (RCHME ©
Crown Copyright)*

concealed beneath. At Row level and above, a late eighteenth-century brick facade conceals a largely intact
late sixteenth-century timber-framed building. Some
wainscot and studwork survive, but it is mainly the
major structural members that have been preserved.
Lawson and Smith (1958, 3) noted a joist in the cellar
inscribed 1593, but this has been removed. This was
most probably the bressumer from the frontage, reused
in the eighteenth–century rebuilding. An impressive
studded door at Row level previously opened to a passage
(see 1875 OS map) and probably dates from the sixteenth century. (See pp 49, 51, and Figs 160 and 161.)

38 Bridge Street, 36–38 Bridge Street Row

A Vernacular Revival building of stone, brick and timber
framing by Douglas and Fordham, erected in 1897 for
the first Duke of Westminster. An asymmetrical design,
with heavy timbering ornamented by delicate Gothic
carving, this shows Douglas's sensitivity to craftsmanship. No earlier fabric survives. (See p 124, Fig 136.)

40 Bridge Street, 40 Bridge Street Row

A Tudor style building of 1858 designed by James
Harrison and built for Welsby's wine merchants. The
front is of brick and stone with a canted oriel window.
The side elevation to Pierpoint Lane is of slightly
earlier construction, but no internal features of interest
survive.

42 Bridge Street, 42 Bridge Street Row

An early eighteenth-century town house, refaced in
brick and stone *c* 1860. No early fabric exists at undercroft or Row level, but the upper storeys retain a staircase, panelling and plasterwork of early eighteenth-
century character.

44 Bridge Street, 44 Bridge Street Row

A late nineteenth-century building with a plain brick
facade, erected as part of a department store. A three-
aisled arrangement of cast iron columns supports the
building at undercroft, Row, and Row + 1 levels.

46 Bridge Street, 46 Bridge Street Row

The rebuilt facade of the 1890s, in Ruabon brick, is
a facsimile of the previous late eighteenth-century
building on the site. Behind the facade, the department store has removed evidence of this or any earlier
interior.

48–52 Bridge Street, 48–50 Bridge Street Row, and 2 Whitefriars

These properties formed the largest known Row
building, and Nos 48 and 50 still retain extensive medieval
fabric. No 52, and 2 Whitefriars are almost entirely of
the late eighteenth century, but previously formed the
service bay of the medieval mansion. The earliest fabric
is the 'Three Old Arches' facade of No 48. This is a
stone frontage at undercroft and Row levels, with an
arcaded Row and no stallboard. The thinned spandrels
of the three round-headed arches indicate timber-
framed over-Row chambers. Stylistically assignable to
the thirteenth century, this was probably the frontage of
a right-angled hall building. During the early or mid-
fourteenth century this appears to have been combined
with the properties to the south to allow the construction
of a major medieval town house with a hall parallel to
the street. The hall (12.40 x 8.88m) is the largest
surviving in the Rows and has an impressive east wall.
This extends to Row + 1 level and contains four
medieval doorways at Row level. A 1970s restoration
of the east wall has not disguised the location of the
screen partition. Of the fourteenth-century undercrofts
only No 50 has kept its spanning chamfered arch,
No 48 having lost its double arch and central octagonal
column arrangement *c* 1900. Nos 50 and 52 are the
only examples of Row enclosure in Bridge Street. (See
pp 24–6, 38–9, 43, 51, 99; Figs 25, 26, 30 and 40.)

Lower Bridge Street – East side

Windsor House

An office block of 1974–5 by John Taylor of Edmund
Kirby and Partners built on the corner of Pepper
Street, formerly the site of the Red Lion Inn.

9 Lower Bridge Street

The facade of this building dates from the early nineteenth century, but it masks a section of Windsor
House (see above) and so contains no early internal
features. There are steps up to former Row level to the
right, the Row having been absorbed into the house.

11 Lower Bridge Street, 11a Lower Bridge Street

This house preserves the last section of Row left open in Lower Bridge Street, which is three bays in length with Tuscan piers supporting the brick facade above. Inside, the building is unusual in that it has a deep basement cut out of the natural rock and faced with late eighteenth- or early nineteenth-century bricks. Also unusual is the fact that the floor at street level is slightly higher than the street, rather than lower, as is the norm in Chester. A barrel-vaulted extension to the rear of the plot is eighteenth-century. The Row has a very wide stall at *c* 3.30m. The paired shopfronts have tall risers embellished with quatrefoils, and the windows above have Gothick glazing bars. (See p 99.)

15 Lower Bridge Street

The facade of this building, which occupies a narrow medieval plot, is early to mid-eighteenth century. It is a single bay building with a twentieth-century shopfront at street level. Medieval fabric survives to the rear of the undercroft where two recessed cupboards with reveals for doors are let into the south wall. Good eighteenth-century panelling survives in the front room at Row + 1 level.

15a Lower Bridge Street

A three-storey, two-bay nineteenth-century stucco facade. Steps to the former Row level to the right. At parapet level there is a central round-headed panel bearing a shield. No internal features of note.

17–19 Lower Bridge Street, 1–2 Unity Passage

This four-storey, two-bay stucco frontage of the early nineteenth century conceals a vestigial Row, now manifesting itself as a spinal corridor within the building. Until recently this was a passage that gave access to further properties to the south, and it was separated from the street by a narrow chamber constructed on the former stallboard (p 110). The street level is divided into two undercroft-like spaces, their ceilings carried on heavy timber cross-beams of probable medieval date. The windows to the upper storeys have Gothick glazing bars.

21–23 Lower Bridge Street

A Vernacular Revival building of 1895, probably designed by W M Boden for J R Crawford. There is no evidence of earlier fabric.

25–27 Lower Bridge Street

A late 1960s office building with shops at street level designed by the Biggins Sargent Partnership.

The Tudor House, 29–31 Lower Bridge Street

An early seventeenth-century building characterised by flamboyant decorative framing (Fig 77) and fine internal features. The roof and other elements have been dated by dendrochronology to *c* 1618 (see Appendix B). A cellar has been dug out of the bedrock. At street level, the building is divided into two undercrofts, each containing well-preserved ceiling frames of massive crossbeams with joists housed and morticed into them. The Row above was enclosed by Roger Ormes in 1728; its disposition is clearly indicated in the framing of the inner wall of the southern room on the former Row frontage. The former Row + 1 level is notable for the plaster ceiling of the great chamber which closely echoes that of the western room of Bishop Lloyd's Palace in Watergate Street and is doubtless by the same craftsmen or workshop. (See pp 83–4, 93, and Figs 85, 86, 90 and 91.)

33 Lower Bridge Street

A nineteenth-century frontage, although the building appears to occupy a narrow medieval plot. The brick front is rendered at street level. The interior contains a barrel-vaulted undercroft to the rear but no other features of note.

35 Lower Bridge Street

A rendered brick building of four storeys and two bays, built for John Warrington in 1720. Timbers in the dividing wall to No 37 exposed during recent refurbishment provide evidence of an enclosed Row.

Park House, 37–41 Lower Bridge Street

Built in 1715, the building later became the Albion Hotel, and then the Talbot Hotel. It briefly housed the city's Assembly Rooms in the mid-eighteenth century. A three-storey, five-bay rendered brick facade with an undercroft well below street level. The former Row level is dominated by a Doric porch sheltering a six-panelled door. The interior contains early eighteenth-century panelling and a fine central staircase lit by a glazed oculus. A ballroom with a barrel-vaulted ceiling was added to the rear in the early nineteenth century. (See p 102 and Fig 162.)

43–47 Lower Bridge Street

A brick faced office building in neo-Georgian style designed by Peter Catherall and erected 1990–91.(Fig 162)

49 Lower Bridge Street

A single-bay, three-storey brick building of the mid-eighteenth century with stone quoins and a pedimented doorcase. No internal features of note.(Fig 162)

Fig 162 Lower Bridge Street looking north showing No 51 on right, and Park House with projecting porch (RCHME ©️ Crown Copyright)

51 Lower Bridge Street

A three-storey, three-bay house with an undercroft, built in 1700 for John Mather, a lawyer. The brick facade has a rendered stone plinth to the former Row level. A staircase parallel with the front leads to an entrance with substantial stone doorcase. The two projecting bays at the rear probably contained closets. The interior retains features of the early eighteenth century, including a rebuilt staircase with barley-sugar balusters. (See pp 98, 102, and Figs 101 and 162.)

53 Lower Bridge Street

A pedestrian nineteenth-century brick facade fronts an interesting timber-framed structure, possibly dating from the early sixteenth century. This is visible from St Olave's Lane. The framing is not of particularly high quality; its interest lies in the evidence it provides for an original Row and in the details of its construction. (See pp 67–8, 98, and Fig 101.)

St Olave's Church

The church was founded in the eleventh century, though the present building dates from the mid-fifteenth century. It was restored by James Harrison in 1859, and converted to an exhibition gallery in the early 1980s. A set of stone steps lead up to a forecourt at former Row level; this formerly supported a building in front of the Row walkway.

57–71 Lower Bridge Street

The present large concrete and brick motor garage erected in the 1960s replaced a block of seventeenth-, eighteenth- and nineteenth-century houses, some of which contained traces of a Row. This was the site of Pareas Hall, the house of Richard the Engineer (see p 15). Nineteenth-century prints show a Row walkway running in front of the buildings and supported on a stone retaining wall.

Lower Bridge Street – West side

The Falcon, 6 Lower Bridge Street

The present building is the surviving half of a still more impressive thirteenth-century town house which extended further down Lower Bridge Street. In 1643 Sir Richard Grosvenor successfully petitioned to enclose the Row, and set a trend which was to transform Lower Bridge Street. The thirteenth-century stone piers forming the front of the former Row are still visible, as is the late medieval shop front at the rear of the Row (this spans the middle of the present front bar [Fig 98]). The well preserved undercroft has a doorway to the street with flanking windows and clear evidence for an earlier structure in the reused timbers that now support the Row level floor. The sixteenth- and early seventeenth-century timber framing represents another rebuilding, when the open hall was probably removed. This timber frame was repaired by John Douglas *c* 1879, who also removed eighteenth-century sash windows and installed the mullions. The whole building was restored for the Falcon Trust by Donald Insall during the 1970s. (See pp 16, 40, 41, 46, 68, and Figs 27, 45, 51, 79, 99, and Pls 10 and 11a.)

8–10 Lower Bridge Street

A Vernacular Revival building of 1886 by E A Ould. The stone archway of the Row is visible in the north wall on the upper floor. (See p 96.)

12 Lower Bridge Street

A modern brick building with a gable facing on to the street.

14 Lower Bridge Street

A four-storey, early eighteenth-century building on a narrow plot that presumably replaced a medieval building of the same basic outline. It has no surviving Row. The floor of the undercroft is 0.6m below street level, and at the rear the medieval side walls still exist.

Bridge House, 16–24 Lower Bridge Street

Built by Lady Mary Calveley in 1676 as a 5-bay town house, a further wide bay has been added at the north end. The house was set back from the street frontage and an Edwardian extension now breaks forward at street level in the position of a pair of curved steps shown on G Batenham's etching of 1816. The original symmetrical frontage is articulated by Ionic pilasters. A central 12-pane sash with a floating dentilled cornice replaces the original first floor entrance and is flanked by sashes in eared surrounds; the second floor has very tall 24-pane sashes in plain architraves. The interior contains some very fine features including good late seventeenth- or early eighteenth-century panelling and a round-arched door architrave leading from the entrance hall into the body of the house. The lower saloon, panelled at its south end, is dominated by a profusely carved wooden chimney breast. The staircase, with its bulbous turned balusters, is late seventeenth-century, but the Venetian window above it dates from the late eighteenth. Remodelling during this later period is indicated by the lighter panelling and Doric friezes of the second floor. (See pp 95, 101–2, and Figs 98, 105 and 106.)

26–42 Lower Bridge Street

A group of buildings dating from 1982–3 with some of the facades being facsimiles of the eighteenth-century houses which stood on the site. (Fig 163)

Fig 163 26–42 Lower Bridge Street before redevelopment in 1982–3 (RCHME © Crown Copyright)

44 Lower Bridge Street

A four-storey brick building, probably the result of a successful petition by Thomas Hunt for the enclosure of the Row in 1717. Ceiling beams at the former Row level contain mortices for partitions, representing the line of the Row and of the shop unit behind. In the centre of the building is a good early eighteenth-century closed-string staircase with twisted balusters.

46, 46a and 46b Lower Bridge Street

An early nineteenth-century brick building with a staircase leading to the former Row level. No evidence of earlier fabric.

The Old Kings Head, 48–50 Lower Bridge Street

The earliest written reference to this site dates to 1208 and refers to the stone-built house belonging to Peter the Clerk. It is likely that the thick stone walls of the cellar belong to this building. Above this stone-built section in Castle Street is a timber-framed wing with a second-floor jetty on bull-nosed joists, possibly of fifteenth-century date. The main part of the building, consisting of a long range parallel to Lower Bridge Street with the three bays in front at right angles to the street, probably dates from the later sixteenth century. The undercroft is a timber-arcade construction, similar to that at 10 Watergate Street. The line of the former Row can clearly be seen running through the building. A curiosity is the treatment of the timber post at the north-east corner of the building, which was rounded off in the eighteenth century to resemble a Tuscan pier. Mortice evidence shows that the floors are all original to the building and not later insertions. The roof trusses are of V-strut construction and the principal rafters have wind-braced purlins trenched into their backs. The original internal arrangement of this building is not clear. The unpartitioned space at street level was probably used for storage. The Row above was fronted by narrow shops with a large undivided room beyond. The internal subdivision of the Row + 1 level is uncertain. (See pp 65, 67, 68, 87, 105, and Figs 70, 72, 80 and 111.)

1 Castle Street

A three-storey Georgian building on a narrow medieval plot at the corner with Castle Street. The brick barrel-vaulted undercroft is reached by a set of external steps parallel to Lower Bridge Street. No evidence exists for a former Row.

Gamul House, 52–58 Lower Bridge Street

This building contains a medieval stone-built open hall. There is enough evidence to reconstruct the position of

Fig 164   Gamul House, 52–58 Lower Bridge Street (RCHME © Crown Copyright)

Fig 165   The interior of the hall of Gamul House, 52–58 Lower Bridge Street, in 1968 before restoration (RCHME © Crown Copyright)

the screens passage. One doorway to the service end is still in use, and the position of another is visible. The door to the solar survives, although the solar itself has long been demolished. Windows looking into the hall from the solar and rear range have led to suggestions that the hall itself was formerly a courtyard, but this seems unlikely. The roof is not visible, but several trusses from a collar purlin roof were recorded during restoration of the building in the 1970s. Important interior features include an impressive early seventeenth-century fireplace in red sandstone, curious pendants in the centre of the barrel-vaulted ceiling and a three-plank medieval door at the rear of the screens passage.

Fig 166 Shipgate House, 68 Lower Bridge Street (RCHME © Crown Copyright)

The building was refronted in brick in the late seventeenth or early eighteenth century, and has a fine pedimented doorway of that date. The hall is at Row level, reached by a set of external steps leading to an open gallery. In G Batenham's view of 1816 a brick stair tower is shown on part of the gallery. The undercrofts at street level have brick barrel vaults of eighteenth-century type. (See pp 53, 69, 70, 91, and Figs 94, 164, 165 and Pl 8.)

60–68 Lower Bridge Street and 2–6 Gamul Terrace

Five lock-up shops and five cottages built in 1872 by T Fluitt on the site of Boarding School Yard. The shops are below an open access gallery leading to the cottages at Row level above. A stepped access passage between the shops leads up to Gamul Place, a courtyard development of eleven cottages built at the same time. Restored by Chester City Council in the mid 1970s, Gamul Place is the only surviving example of occupied courtyard housing in the city centre.

70–74 Lower Bridge Street

Two late eighteenth-century, four-storey, brick town houses. The position of the external staircases leading up to recessed doorways suggests that there was formerly a Row through these properties which was enclosed in the eighteenth century.

76 Lower Bridge Street

A three-storey, two-bay brick building of *c* 1800 with no features of special interest.

78–82 Lower Bridge Street

A facsimile facade of the previous buildings, concealing a modern steel-framed building of 1983. The warehouse and town houses formerly on this site were erected in the mid- to late eighteenth century; their four-storey front had a full-height loading bay at the north end and an external stone staircase to the south.

Shipgate House, 84 Lower Bridge Street

A late seventeenth-century house, re-fronted in the mid-eighteenth century in brick with finely carved stone dressings and external staircase. The interior retains walls, floor beams and other features of the late seventeenth century, including an open-well oak staircase. (Fig 166)

The Old Edgar, 86–88 Lower Bridge Street

This is a building of fifteenth- or sixteenth-century date, occupying an important site on the corner with Shipgate Street. The ceilings are original and the house is jettied on both main facades, with a dragon beam carried on a braced post. The jetty is supported on bull-nosed joists. The roof has king posts set on cambered tie beams and some trusses have raking struts. It is likely that the building has always formed two or more tenements. (See p 68.)

90–92 Lower Bridge Street

A brick facade of the early nineteenth century conceals a timber frame of unusual form and probably very early date. At street level the internal plan has been obliterated by later alterations. Above, the framing has jowled posts with very long straight braces. The front section of the house was reordered in the early seventeenth–century to form a panelled parlour with plastered beams carrying relief friezes with fruit motifs. Evidence for a former Row is flimsy, resting as it does on a hollow sound when the north wall is tapped. The framing of the upper storey is quite different in construction, with timber of slight scantling and principal trusses with raking struts.

The Bear and Billet, 94 Lower Bridge Street

A timber-framed building, formerly the town house of the Earls of Shrewsbury, Serjeants of the Bridge Gate, and dated 1664 on a jettied beam. There is a cellar but no undercroft, then three storeys, plus an attic, each jettied up to a single symmetrical gable. Mullioned and transomed windows occupy the full width of the facade at first and second floor levels, whilst the attic storey has a central loading door and remains of a hoist, with paired casement windows to each side. A seventeenth-century carved door at street level leads to a former side passage. The building became a public house in the late eighteenth century. (Pl 11b)

Eastgate Street – North side

1 Eastgate Street

A predominantly twentieth-century building with some eighteenth-century brickwork in the rear wall at Row and Row + 1 levels. The Row walkway at the rear of the building, known as Dark Row, is on solid ground and is not oversailed. This is a medieval arrangement probably dating back to at least 1270, when the Buttershops were already in existence on this site. A late eighteenth-century brick building, with a similar curved facade, preceded the present timber-framed design. The rock-cut cellar is probably eighteenth-century. The Dark Row project (1993–95) has involved extensive rebuilding of the internal structure and fabric of Nos 1, 3, and 9–15 Eastgate Street. (See pp 15 and 18 and Fig 116.)

3 Eastgate Street

Apart from some early nineteenth-century brickwork facing the Dark Row at the rear, this rendered brick building is entirely of the 1860s and later. The cellar is rock-cut and does not extend northwards under the Row walkway. Print evidence shows that a medieval jettied timber-framed building preceded the present structure.

5–7 Eastgate Street

A Vernacular Revival building of 1874 designed by T M Lockwood for Mr Spence as a shop and tailors' premises. It has a timber-framed facade with herring-bone brickwork, pargetting and an oriel window. There is no earlier fabric visible, although the medieval Dark Row arrangement is perpetuated at the rear. The two former undercrofts, which are the most westerly on the north side of Eastgate Street, have been combined to form a single shop, the walls of which are concealed by modern cladding.

9–15 Eastgate Street, 7 Eastgate Street Row

A Vernacular Revival iron-framed building of 1900 designed by T M Lockwood as a department store for Richard Jones, and extended to each side by Lockwood's sons in 1915 (left) and c 1930 (right). The facade is timber-framed, with broad oriel windows at Row + 1 level. Dark Row survives at the rear, and is oversailed by a nineteenth-century structure that connects the narrow frontage buildings to the bulk of the department store behind. Print evidence shows that this section was oversailed from the late medieval period, if not earlier. (See p 130.)

The Boot, 17 Eastgate Street, 9 Eastgate Street Row

This is the first building east of the Dark Row and the Buttershops area with a stallboard, and consists of a medieval undercroft with a mid-seventeenth century timber-framed building above, known from at least 1750 as the Boot Inn (Cheshire RO ? 63/2/133/17). The front section of the undercroft is mostly lined, but some visible painted sandstone blocks reveal its medieval origins. Behind is a separate sandstone undercroft, used as the cellar of the Row level building. Divided into two chambers in the medieval period, this most probably opened off the front section (cf 57 Bridge Street). At Row level and above a relatively intact seventeenth-century timber-framed building survives (dated 1643), albeit with a rebuilt facade largely of the late nineteenth century. Extending back 21.1m, this two-storey structure had no open hall or gallery. Over the modern stairwell there is a complete trenched-purlin truss with overlapping wind braces. In front of this, the over-Row parlour is clad almost entirely with seventeenth-century wainscot. (See pp 38, 84, and Fig 167.)

Fig 167 The Boot, 17 Eastgate Street (RCHME © Crown Copyright)

17a Eastgate Street, 11–13a Eastgate Street Row

A mid-twentieth century neo-Georgian facade conceals a late eighteenth- or early nineteenth-century brick building. At the rear is a separate early nineteenth-century building, connected to the front at Row level only. The party wall between the rear yard and the adjoining yard of the Boot Inn is partly built of medieval sandstone, marking the boundary of the burgage plot. Interior detail is mainly twentieth-century, but an over-restored trenched-purlin roof truss, with lengths of purlin intact, survives at the rear of the front building.

19–21 Eastgate Street, 15–17 Eastgate Street Row

Formerly two properties, this was rebuilt as a single broad-fronted brick town house in the early nineteenth century. No earlier fabric is discernible, but the western section retains a relatively unaltered late Georgian interior.

25 Eastgate Street, 19 Eastgate Street Row

An early Vernacular Revival building of 1861, designed by T A Richardson for Dutton and Miller, grocers. The half-timbered front elevation is almost symmetrical. At street and Row levels the interior has no visible features of interest, but above this the mid-nineteenth-century character is preserved to a degree unusual in Row properties.

27 Eastgate Street, 21 Eastgate Street Row

An eighteenth-century building, extended at the rear in the early nineteenth century. The Georgian brick facade, with cast iron columns at Row level, is embellished with later Jacobean-style ornamentation. Some eighteenth-century features survive on the upper floors.

29 Eastgate Street, 23 Eastgate Street Row

An eighteenth-century building of one bay width, altered in the mid-nineteenth century. The facade is of painted brickwork with stone quoins and windows with heavy architraves and cornices. The nineteenth-century staircase from Row to Row + 1 level is intact, but little other interior detail of that date has been retained.

31 Eastgate Street, 25 Eastgate Street Row

A Vernacular Revival building of 1889 designed by T M Lockwood. It replaced a building which was destroyed by fire. The tall timber-framed facade has pronounced jetties. The interior detail, where surviving, is of this date.

33 Eastgate Street

An impressive stone faced Neo-classical bank by George Williams built in 1859–60 for Dixon and Wardell's Chester Bank. It entirely replaced the previous building, the Mitre Inn, and enclosed the Row which formerly ran into St Werburgh Street. The northern-most bay fronting St Werburgh Street was probably designed by John Douglas as an extension of 1867–8. The large mid-nineteenth-century colonnaded banking hall is preserved. (See p 117 and Fig 126.)

Eastgate Street – South side

4 Eastgate Street, 2 Eastgate Street Row

A richly detailed Vernacular Revival building by T M Lockwood, built for the first Duke of Westminster in 1888. It is contemporary with 1 Bridge Street by the same architect. The black and white facade uses broad timbers intricately carved with Renaissance ornament, and windows fitted with patterned leaded glazing. (See p 119 and Fig 129.)

6 Eastgate Street, 4 Eastgate Street Row

A mid-nineteenth-century brick building, with a pair of Edwardian oriel windows at Row + 1 level. No interior features of interest are visible.

8 Eastgate Street, 6 Eastgate Street Row

An early nineteenth-century building with a yellow sandstone facade. The interior is almost totally lined, but masonry within a cupboard at undercroft level may indicate a medieval party wall.

10 Eastgate Street, 8–10 Eastgate Street Row

With 12 Eastgate Street, this is one of a pair of tall Vernacular Revival buildings designed by George Williams and built in 1861. Stylistically it belongs to the early phase of revived half-timbering, where the timbers are applied for purely decorative effect. The interior is mostly stripped-out and lined. (See p 117, and Fig 127.)

12 Eastgate Street, 12 Eastgate Street Row

A Vernacular Revival building of 1861 by George Williams built for Messrs Beckett and Co. A thirteenth- or fourteenth-century two-bay vaulted undercroft on the site collapsed during the construction of the new building. The side walls of the medieval undercroft may in part survive, though they are now coated in textured plaster. (See pp 33, 124.)

14 Eastgate Street, 14 Eastgate Street Row

A late nineteenth-century Vernacular Revival building of four storeys and an attic. The Row and upper level adopt the form of an open-galleried hall. No earlier fabric survives.

16 Eastgate Street, 16 Eastgate Street Row

A late eighteenth-century brick building with no evidence of earlier fabric.

18 Eastgate Street, 18–20 Eastgate Street Row

An early nineteenth-century brick building with no evidence of earlier fabric.

20 Eastgate Street, 22 Eastgate Street Row

This narrow property has an early nineteenth-century brick facade concealing two partially surviving seventeenth-century buildings, one behind the other. Most walls are lined, but exposed sections reveal the frame with wattle and daub infill panels of the seventeenth century. The west walls of both sections are of nineteenth-century brick.

22 Eastgate Street, 24–28 Eastgate Street Row

A modest three-storey building with the initials and date *16:CB:10* on a jettied gable. It was altered in the eighteenth century and comprehensively refurbished by T M Penson for the second Marquis of Westminster in the 1850s. However, much of the structure behind the facade is of 1610. At Row + 1 level a disused space over the Row-level suspended ceiling exposes the bay posts and roof trusses of the seventeenth-century structure. The Row stallboard is completely occupied by a nineteenth-century cabin. (See p 110.)

24 Eastgate Street, 30 Eastgate Street Row

A late nineteenth-century Vernacular Revival building with a cabin occupying the Row stallboard. The interior has a twentieth-century cellar below a modern clad undercroft (now open to No 22).

26 Eastgate Street, 32 Eastgate Street Row

A seventeenth-century building with eighteenth-century alterations, restored by T M Penson for Butts, Jewellers, in 1858 in Vernacular Revival style. There is no sign of medieval fabric in the modern clad undercroft. At Row level a twentieth-century shop adopts the form of a previous galleried hall. An eighteenth-century staircase leads to the upper floors. At Row + 1 level there is a good over-Row parlour with visible timber framing and seventeenth-century wainscot.

28–30 Eastgate Street, 34 Eastgate Street Row

A Gothic Revival stone facade by T M Penson built in 1858 as an extension to Browns' drapers shop. It fronts two medieval plots. That to the west has one of the most impressive vaulted sandstone undercrofts in the Rows (see pp 16, 35, 42, and Figs 15, 16, 31 and 36). Measuring 12.95 x 4.2m internally, it has a four-bay quadripartite vault with chamfered cross, diagonal and ridge ribs. Of the same construction phase is the restored former street frontage with a doorway and flanking lancets (p 39). The distinctive sunk chamfers on the jambs place the undercroft between the late 1290s and *c* 1320. To the east of the undercroft is a medieval passage 875mm wide, which must have led to a separate rear structure, either at undercroft or, less probably, at Row level. The eastern plot is all modern cladding at undercroft level. Usage as a department store has removed most of Penson's interior detail, although at the front of the Row + 1 level there is an intact mid-nineteenth-century office. (See p 116, and Fig 125.)

32–34 Eastgate Street, 36 Eastgate Street Row

A Greek Revival building erected in 1828 as the first part of what was to become Browns' celebrated department store. The symmetrical facade has stone Doric columns at street and Row levels, and heavy architraves around the Row + 1 level windows. A balustrade

Fig 168 Frontage of Brown's original store, 32–34 Eastgate Street (RCHME © Crown Copyright)

Fig 169 Nineteenth-century view of Eastgate Street Row South, by W Tasker (RCHME © Crown Copyright)

Fig 170 36–38 Eastgate Street (RCHME © Crown Copyright)

obscures a later penthouse at Row + 3 level. The interior is mostly modern cladding, although the segmental vaults of the two undercrofts are probably early nineteenth-century and small sections of sandstone walling at the extreme east and west survive from the medieval undercrofts. (See p 110 and Figs 168 and 169.)

36–38 Eastgate Street, 38–40 Eastgate Street Row

A pair of half-timbered buildings of 1857 designed by T M Penson, his first substantial work in the Vernacular Revival. They were built for Charles and William Brown, but did not become part of the department store until 1912. Before this, No 38 was leased to Bollands, wedding cake makers by appointment to Queen Victoria and King Edward VII. The timber framing, which is applied to a brick structure, is unscholarly and idiosyncratic, with richly carved bargeboards, finials and colonnettes. At Row + 1 level within No 36 there is a two-storey high barrel-vaulted space with ironwork skylights. The steps up to Row level shown on the 1875 OS map have been removed, and an elaborately carved mid-Victorian shopfront was lost when the Grosvenor Precinct was built. (See p 114 and Figs 123, 142 and 170.)

40–44 Eastgate Street, 42–48 Eastgate Street Row

A symmetrical three-gabled facade in close-studded timber framing unites these properties. The building was erected in 1912 for Bollands confectioners and designed by W T Lockwood. There is no visible fabric earlier than this and the interiors are all modern clad. (Fig 122 shows Penson's 1852 building at No 40.)

50 Eastgate Street Row

The brick facade to this building of 1963–5 is a replica of the early eighteenth-century town house on this site, which was demolished for the construction of the Grosvenor Precinct. The Row walkway is too low to permit an undercroft.

Grosvenor Hotel, 52–58 Eastgate Street

A bulky Vernacular Revival building of 1863–6 designed by T M Penson and completed by his son R K Penson and Ritchie for the second Marquis of Westminster. It does not contain a Row walkway but a ground level colonnade. There is no earlier fabric visible. (Fig 142)

60 Eastgate Street

A building of *c* 1770, erected at the same time as the present Eastgate to the plan of either Joseph Turner of Hawarden or Mr Heyden, Surveyor of Buildings for Lord Grosvenor. At street level there is a Tuscan colonnade and there is no Row walkway. Three parallel cellars survive with eighteenth-century segmental vaults on post-medieval sandstone walls. At the east end, adjacent to the city wall and the Eastgate, there is fragmentary Roman stonework.

Northgate Street – West side

1 Northgate Street

An impressive Neo-classical stone building of 1807, designed by Thomas Harrison as the Commercial News Room, and now the City Club. The wide facade (11.70m) has a rusticated arcade of three bays behind which a walkway was crudely inserted in the 1960s. On the first floor, the former News Room retains its fine Neo-classical interior. The building replaced the Sun Inn, and the News Room Committee erected the Commercial Tavern behind in St. Peter's Churchyard to take its place. The mid-thirteenth century Ironmongers' Row was located here. (See pp 15, 108 and Fig 115.)

3 Northgate Street

This Vernacular Revival building of 1898–9 was erected for Charles Brown and designed by H W Beswick. It is of roughcast faced brick and timber framing. The upper floors were designed as an extension to the City Club, and take the form of an open hall with a false hammer-beam roof, modelled on the hall of Leche House, 17 Watergate Street. Between 1897 and 1909,

Fig 171 West side of Northgate Street showing, from right, Shoemakers' Row, the City Club, and the east end of St Peter's Church (RCHME © Crown Copyright)

Fig 172   Detail of Shoemakers' Row, Northgate Street (RCHME © Crown Copyright)

3–31 Northgate Street were rebuilt as part of a municipal road widening project (see pp 121–3). They replaced the so-called Shoemakers' Row and all now have a colonnaded walkway slightly above the street level. This walkway is the result of a lowering of the former Row and, as a result, any former undercrofts are now cellars. (See Figs 132–5 and 171.)

5–9 Northgate Street

A good Vernacular Revival range of 1900 by John Douglas, acting as both architect and developer. The timber-framed facade unites three medieval plots. An arcade of six bays supports an upper storey with oriel windows. Each pair of windows is separated by a niche containing a carved figure. Within No 9 there is the remains of a medieval undercroft. (See p 123 and Figs 135 and 172.)

11–13 Northgate Street

A Vernacular Revival building by John Douglas erected in 1900 for J F Densen and Sons. The two-bay timber-framed facade has wide oriel windows and jettied gables. The Row walkway has been lowered, but the medieval sandstone undercrofts have been preserved. No 11 is distinguished by a rear passage and central pier. (See p 123.)

15–17 Northgate Street

A three-bay Vernacular Revival building of 1909 designed by James Strong, a pupil of Douglas. It replaced

the Cross Keys Inn. Two short sandstone undercrofts survive, probably originally a pair belonging to one medieval house. A passage, with no certain medieval fabric, provides access to the rear of No 17. The party wall has been demolished, although the sandstone footings are preserved. The front wall and a chamber in No 17 are of brick. In the north-west corner a pre-medieval pit has been cut by the construction of No 17; this is probably from the first phase of the Roman *principia*. (See p 123.)

19 Northgate Street

A Vernacular Revival building of *c* 1900, possibly designed by John Douglas, with a three-bay arcade to the lowered Row walkway. The undercroft was inaccessible, but a medieval sandstone wall survives at Row level at the rear of the south side, and stands to a height of 1.75m.

21–23 Northgate Street

A Vernacular Revival building of 1897 designed by H Beswick for Charles Brown, whose initials are inscribed in a pargetted panel on the facade. The interior is largely modern clad, but in the former undercroft of No 23 Roman columns and bases survive from the north arcade of the basilica in the *principia*. These haphazardly collapsed remains were excavated in the late nineteenth century and indicate that there cannot have been a medieval undercroft on this site.

25 Northgate Street

A Vernacular Revival building with a facade of *c* 1914 by James Strong (p 123–4). Formerly the site of the Woolpack Inn, the plot was first redeveloped *c* 1903, but with a front which projected further into the street. The long narrow stone cellar is largely medieval, although the stones immediately above the bedrock at the east end of the north wall may be Roman, possibly reused.

27–31 Northgate Street

This terminal building of the redeveloped Shoemakers' Row was designed by John Douglas and erected for the Corporation in 1902. With its lively half-timbered facades, it makes an effective corner to the Town Hall Square. The present cellar preserves medieval sandstone walls that indicate a cellar, rather than an undercroft with street access. The south wall has the springing course of a stone barrel vault. Above, the interior is all modern clad. (See pp 38, 123.)

The Blue Bell, 63–65 Northgate Street

A relatively intact pair of medieval buildings incorporating a ground level arcaded walkway and stallboard arrangement similar to the *bona fide* Row buildings.

Fig 173 The Blue Bell, 63–65 Northgate Street (RCHME © Crown Copyright)

Fig 174   Crown-post roof in the Blue Bell, 63–65 Northgate Street (RCHME © Crown Copyright)

The buildings were extended and made into a single property in the eighteenth century. The northern building (No 65) is largely clad but has a well-preserved trenched purlin roof, and is mid-fifteenth to mid-sixteenth century. The southern building, No 63, has a fine crown-post roof and close studded walls of the mid-fifteenth century (but see pp 53, 69). There is a solar surviving over the walkway and street-level cabin, but the open hall at the rear has suffered the insertion of a first floor. The narrow space between the two buildings is now occupied by stairs and interconnecting lobbies. Beneath the two buildings is a single medieval sandstone cellar. (See pp 29, 69–71, and Figs 73, 76, 173 and 174.)

Northgate Street – East side

4 Northgate Street,
4 Northgate Street Row

The brick facade of the late eighteenth century conceals an earlier eighteenth-century structure. The south facade, overlooking Dark Row, a panelled over-Row chamber, and the twisted baluster staircase date from *c* 1700. The stallboard is virtually non-existent, no doubt due to the narrowness of Northgate Street at this point. No earlier fabric is discernible. The Dark Row project (1993–5) involved extensive rebuilding of the internal structure and fabric of Nos 4, 6, and 8 Northgate Street (see p 106).

6 Northgate Street,
6 Northgate Street Row

Replacing a wide (7.75m) timber-framed building recorded by G Batenham *c* 1816 (print in Chester Archives), this brick building is of the 1820–30s. Above the modern clad shop levels, the interior is largely nineteenth-century, with no earlier fabric visible. There is no stallboard.

8 Northgate Street,
8 Northgate Street Row

A mediocre early twentieth-century Vernacular Revival building. The Row + 1 and Row + 2 levels have little depth, with the gable being a facade only. G Batenham recorded a seventeenth-century timber-framed building of similar proportions on this site in *c* 1816. There is no stallboard.

10 Northgate Street,
10 Northgate Street Row

An early nineteenth-century brick building which preserves elements of the previous timber-framed structure. The undercroft is all clad and has a modern cellar beneath. Above, the interior is nineteenth- and twentieth-century. There is a steeply-sloping narrow stallboard *c* 1.3m deep.

12–14 Northgate Street,
12–14 Northgate Street Row

A Vernacular Revival brick building, with a half-timbered facade, erected in 1912–13 by R W Boden for Walker and Knight. A major rebuild was carried out at the rear in the 1930s to convert the premises into a restaurant and ballroom, complete with motor garage, and with the stallboard turned into a rock garden.

14–16 Northgate Street,
14–16 Northgate Street Row

As with Nos 12–14, with which this now forms a single building, No 16 has a Vernacular Revival frontage.

Although not erected until 1913, it is of similar appearance and is therefore probably also by R W Boden. The 1950s work revealed a now largely lost parallel pair of undercrofts with chamfered segmental stone arches, corbels and an interconnecting doorway. The earlier rebuild of the rear part brought to light a Roman hypocaust, which is still visible, and demolished another undercroft parallel to the street with a timber-framed crown-post building above, with halls at Row and Row + 1 levels. Recorded evidence for a wing connecting this to the front double-plot building, and the survival of Leen Lane to the north, show that this was a medieval courtyard property, probably of the fourteenth century. (See pp 27, 42, 50, 54.)

18–20 Northgate Street

This was built for the Chester United Gas Company in 1936 and is steel-framed, faced with a timber frame and vertical studwork. There is no evidence of fabric from the previous two-storey timber-framed building on the site. This is the most southerly building of a group that once had some form of Row, since all enclosed.

22 Northgate Street

This wide (9.94m) late eighteenth-century building, with a modern shop frontage at street and first floor levels, is built over a pair of medieval sandstone undercrofts. The low walls of these support segmental brick barrel vaults, and the front wall of the north undercroft survives intact with a medieval doorway (pp 16, 41). This has plain jambs and opens into a stone built chamber, presumably equating with the encroachment of the stallboard. The southern undercroft has a similar arrangement, but the jambs are modern brick. Above, the modern interior at street and first floor levels has removed all evidence of the former Row walkway and the central passage visible on G Batenham's drawing of *c* 1816 in Chester Archives. The building was converted to electricity showrooms in 1924 by P H Lawson for Chester City Council.

26 Northgate Street

A brick building of the 1820s. This has removed all evidence of the minute timber-framed building (3.45m wide), with Row walkway, that preceded it. The interior is entirely modern and, at street level, forms a single shop with No 28.

28 Northgate Street

A narrow brick building (3.44m) of the 1830s, with no earlier fabric surviving and no interior detail of this period. As with No 26, it replaced a narrow timber-framed Row building.

Watergate Street – South side

5–7 Watergate Street,
5–7 Watergate Street Row

A symmetrical brick building with stone dressings, dated 1803. The undercroft of No 5 has rubble sandstone walling, into which is inserted a brick barrel vault. The stone steps to the rear formerly rose to Row level. The structure of the undercroft of No 7 is hidden.

God's Providence House, 9 Watergate Street, 11–11a Watergate Street Row

A four-storey timber-framed building reconstructed in 1862 by James Harrison and loosely based on the preceding building of 1652. The facade is enriched with mechanical plaster detailing. The west wall of the undercroft is shared with the late thirteenth-century undercroft of No 11, but is extended forward to enclose the steps and encroach on to the street. The east wall is of rubble stone and has two corbels, 1.3m apart. The timber ceiling beams are seventeenth-century or later. The Row level and above is all of 1862 or later, but retains a passage overlooked by a blocked window. Drawings of the earlier building show a rather lower, small-framed, understated facade, slightly sagging and carried on plain timber posts. (See pp 41, 115–6, and Fig 123.)

11 Watergate Street,
15–15a Watergate Street Row

A good symmetrical four-storey, three-bay brick building with stone dressings, dated 1744 in deeds. The undercroft has the best stone vault in Chester, with four bays of quadripartite vaulting divided by an arcade of three octagonal piers. It measures 13.5 x 6.2m internally with walls 1.2m thick. The east and south walls contain rebated cupboards. Parts of the original front wall survive, showing remains of blind

Fig 175 Undercroft in 11 Watergate Street (RCHME © Crown Copyright)

arcading on the inside, behind an encroachment of
2.4m on to the street. An original doorway in the rear
wall leads into an extension of the undercroft with rubble
stone walls and brick barrel vault. The upper levels of
the building were rebuilt in the mid eighteenth century.
At Row + 1 and Row + 2 levels there is good panelling
and plasterwork, some being features which were
rearranged when the building was converted in the early
1980s. At the back, an inglenook with oak bressumer
at Row level suggests that the rear wing may have been
built as a separate dwelling in the seventeenth century.
(See pp 33–35, 42, 69, 104, and Figs 32, 34, 35, 36,
108 and 175.)

13 Watergate Street,
17 Watergate Street Row

A single tenement occupied by a house dated 1771,
with a two-storey two-bay brick facade. The undercroft
seems to utilise the stone walls of Nos 11 and 15, and
has an inserted brick barrel vault. During alterations in
1986 a blocked stone staircase was found against the
western wall, leading up to Row level.

15 Watergate Street,
19 Watergate Street Row

The mid-twentieth-century brick facade, which
replaced a similar three-storey facade of the early
nineteenth century, conceals an earlier structure. The
undercroft has coursed sandstone rubble walls and on
the eastern side, towards the rear, the wall steps in and
has four stone corbels at 1.0m centres. This suggests a
medieval date but the ceiling is now spanned by
massive, chamfered seventeenth-century beams. At
Row level the building is one continuous shop. At Row
+ 1 level there is a line of post-medieval collar and tie
beam trusses. These suggest a hall range behind a small
shop fronting the Row. The chamber over the Row was
raised in height in the seventeenth century to give a
room of similar dimensions to that in the Leche House.

The Leche House, 17 Watergate Street,
21 Watergate Street Row

This is a very important timber-framed building with a
complex history. The original undercroft is of good
quality ashlar sandstone and measured 14.6 x 5.8m
internally. It is divided into five equal bays with braced
ceiling beams carried on stone corbels, the two to the
rear being partly hidden by a later brick barrel vault
over a rear extension. The east wall steps in towards
the rear to carry the fireplace above. A moulded timber
bressumer from the original street frontage survives,
with mortice holes that indicate close-studding and a
central doorway. The encroachment of 1.4m into the
street includes posts carrying the early seventeenth-
century chamber above the Row. The upper storeys
consist of a late fifteenth-century timber-framed box of

Fig 176 The Leche House, 17 Watergate Street (RCHME © Crown Copyright)

Fig 177 Fireplace in rear parlour at Row level in the Leche House, 17 Watergate Street (RCHME © Crown Copyright)

posts carrying the roof trusses, tied by beams at their feet and resting on a sill beam placed on the undercroft walls. The bay spacing is different from the undercroft beneath. The plan at Row level retains a two-bay open hall at its centre with a false hammer-beam central truss and king-post trusses at either end (Figs 67 and 75). The hall is top-lit through dormer windows and contains a gallery over a passage along the western side. The stone jambs of the hall fireplace are contemporary with the undercroft, but a stupendous overmantel of the early seventeenth century has been added. A squint window overlooks the hall from an upper rear room. In front of the hall was a small shop and to the rear was a screens passage with staircase, entered from the side passage. Beyond the screens passage was a parlour with chamber above. In the early seventeenth century the chamber above the Row was raised in height and carried forward on posts. At the same time two closets and the 'Lady Bower', a gallery carried on wooden Renaissance columns, were added around a small courtyard at the rear. The early eighteenth-century Lion House (23 Watergate Street Row) to the south may occupy the site of the former kitchen and dining room. Later alterations include encroachment on to the street, the addition of sash windows to the facade, (graffiti on the glass are dated 1736) and the insertion of a floor in the over-Row chamber. Extensive dendrochronological sampling failed to provide any dates, but on stylistic grounds the development of the building can be summarised as

> *late fourteenth century*
>> original undercroft
>> stone jambs of the fireplace above

> *late fifteenth century*
>> extension of undercroft
>> framework of timber-framed house

> *early seventeenth century*
>> new street facade
>> rebuilding of the Row chamber
>> additions to rear
>> internal decoration

The probate inventory of Alderman John Leche of Mollington (died 1639) can be fitted to the present plan of the house. (See pp 16, 49, 51, 64–5, 69–71, 83, 91, 105, and Figs 74, 75, 89, 96, and Pl 7)

21 Watergate Street, 27 Watergate Street Row

The four-storey, early eighteenth-century brick facade conceals an earlier building. The core of the undercroft is late fifteenth-century, with a quadripartite stone vault of three bays, each 4.2m square. The ribs are chamfered and have the same profile as those in No 11, but spring from moulded capitals. The undercroft is well below street level and has walls 0.5m thick. It has been extended to the rear in stone with a brick barrel vault, probably contemporary with the seventeenth-century work above. The front of the undercroft has been brutally cut away by the creation of a rock-cut cellar and a shop extending 1.6m into the street. The Row-level plan has an enclosed passage on the eastern side of the building, alongside a continuous shop. A nineteenth-century door from the passage gives access to the stairwell. A lower range at the rear is mid-seventeenth-century and has been truncated at both ends. (See p 105.)

25 Watergate Street, 29 Watergate Street Row

A mid-nineteenth-century four-storey brick building occupying a single tenement plot. The undercroft is 4.4m wide and extends for 27.1m. The walls are in poor quality masonry and the rear portion contains an inserted brick barrel vault. Print evidence shows that the earlier building was timber-framed and jettied forward on posts in the street. The undercroft is shown with a stone front wall containing a central pointed arched doorway of late medieval date with a window at either side (see p 16).

Refuge House, 27–33 Watergate Street, 31–41 Watergate Street Row

The erection of this over-scaled mid-twentieth-century concrete and brick block led to the total demolition of three Rows buildings known from print evidence, two of whose undercrofts are recorded (Lawson and Smith, 1958, 21). No 27–29 Watergate Street was a substantial twin-gabled, timber-framed house of the late sixteenth century. No details of the undercroft are known, but access to the Row was up an L-shaped flight of steps with a carved newel post. The Row + 1 chambers were carried forward on posts rising from the street and braced to the bressumers. 31 Watergate Street had a four-storey, two-bay brick facade of the late eighteenth century. The stone undercroft was 4.42m wide, with a corbel table on either side for a distance of 7.62m from the front of the Row walkway. 33 Watergate Street was a four-storey, three-bay brick house of the late seventeenth or early eighteenth centuries. The undercroft was 6.25m wide and 13.40m deep from the front of the Row walkway, and had walls of large, well-coursed masonry. There was a later stone extension forward to the street frontage.

35 Watergate Street, 43 Watergate Street Row

A Vernacular Revival building of 1890 with a half-timbered facade. There is no evidence of earlier fabric. The base and lower shaft of a Roman column stand *in situ* in a sunken yard behind the undercroft.

37 Watergate Street,
45 Watergate Street Row

A four-storey building with a nineteenth-century facade, stone to street level and timber-framed above. The undercroft is five and a half bays in length. The two bays to the rear are roofed with quadripartite stone vaults of the late thirteenth century. This vaulting sits somewhat clumsily in an irregular space and is built across a round-arched doorway in the rear wall. This suggests that it was an insertion into an earlier, stone-walled structure, probably of the twelfth century, which is therefore the earliest surviving structure in the Rows system (see pp 33–5 and Fig 33). The front bays of the undercroft are spanned by timber beams and the front half-bay represents encroachment into the street. From Row level upwards the building is substantially a rebuild of the nineteenth century with radical twentieth-century alterations, but one section of sixteenth- or seventeenth-century timber framing survives in the west wall.

39 Watergate Street,
47–49 Watergate Street Row

An early eighteenth-century building with painted ashlar at street level and brick with rusticated quoins above. The walls of the undercroft are of coursed red sandstone rubble to a height of 1.40m, and carry an eighteenth-century brick barrel vault. The chamber above the Row is subdivided but contains some fine early eighteenth-century bolection-moulded panelling, with dado rail and dentilled cornice. The door to the landing with a radial fanlight, and the open-string staircase with slender column-on-vase balustrade are late eighteenth-century. (See p 104.)

Bishop Lloyd's Palace, 41 Watergate Street, 51–53 Watergate Street Row

These two tenements, although clearly of different construction, are now one property and are considered together. The building was extensively restored in the 1890s by T M Lockwood and again in the 1970s by Chester City Council. Lockwood's alterations replaced the eastern street entrance with a staircase, and entry is now gained through the western tenement only. At Row level the eastern stallboard has been replaced by the staircase and the positions of the posts holding the chamber above the Row have been altered. The western unit has a wide stallboard with nineteenth-century posts and balustrade next to the street and seventeenth-century posts approximately 1.0m back, with carved brackets depicting bearded giants on the street side and animals and an owl to the Row. At Row level and above, both buildings have timber-framed frontages, that to the east being a complete nineteenth-century rebuild, while the other retains many elaborate carved panels depicting biblical and heraldic subjects.

Fig 178 Detail of brackets over the Row stallboard at Bishop Lloyd's Palace, 41 Watergate Street (RCHME © Crown Copyright)

One panel gives the date 1615 and another shows the arms of Bishop George Lloyd. The undercrofts have brick barrel vaults on medieval coursed sandstone rubble walls. At Row + 1 level there is a series of remarkable seventeenth-century plaster ceilings and fireplaces in two large chambers. The decorative scheme in the eastern unit seems to be inserted and the oversized fireplace and ceiling may have been imported from the Bishop's Palace, partially destroyed in the Civil War. The western unit contains a more restrained ceiling, probably original to the building and a fine fireplace with plaster overmantel depicting Cupid mounted on a lion. (See pp 84, 88, 90–3, 120, and Figs 88, 90, 91, 93, 131, 178 and Pl 6.)

51 Watergate Street,
55–57 Watergate Street Row

This building was rebuilt from Row level upwards in the early 1970s, to a design which approximately reflects the seventeenth-century timber frame which had previously been rendered. The only original feature is the carved frieze above the Row which matches that on Bishop Lloyd's Palace. Fragments of the medieval coursed sandstone rubble wall are visible inside, and the western section of walling carries two double corbels, 1.15m apart, with clear signs of burning between (see p 41).

Fig 179 The Old Custom House, 69–71 Watergate Street (RCHME © Crown Copyright)

53 Watergate Street, 59 Watergate Street Row

A mid-eighteenth-century four-storey brick building with a late Georgian shopfront at Row level. The interior at street level is completely clad, but its proportions (4.55m x 9.55m) suggest a typical medieval undercroft with an eighteenth-century brick barrel vault. Access to the upper floors is by a very tight staircase with Chinese Chippendale balustrade. Early maps show a passageway on the west side of the building, but this no longer exists.

55–61 Watergate Street, 61–67 Watergate Street Row

A block of four reinforced concrete shop units with flats above, erected in the 1960s to the design of Bradshaw, Rowse and Harker, winners of an architectural competition held by the City Council. The front is of board–marked concrete with horizontal bands of windows. In the 1950s and 60s the undeveloped site formed a notorious gap in the Rows. (See pp 131–2, Figs 145, 146 and Pl 4.)

63–67 Watergate Street, 71–77 Watergate Street Row

Only the early eighteenth-century stone and stucco facade and other isolated fragments survived when this property was entirely rebuilt during the early 1970s. A large external stack to the south-west is of sixteenth- or seventeenth-century origin, and one section of rubble-stone walling is visible in the undercroft, suggesting a medieval structure. Pre-alteration plans show two wide, short undercrofts, that to the east containing some form of stone arcade (see p 50). The plans at Row level appear to show two main rooms at either end of the building at right angles to the Row, with a number of passages and smaller rooms in between. (See pp 68–69.)

The Old Custom House, 69–71 Watergate Street

This public house occupies two buildings both of which have recently refaced stonework at street level. No 69 has a much restored timber-framed gable, dated 1637 and bearing the initials *T & AW*. The undercroft of No 69 has coursed rubble walls and measures approximately 4.90 x 10.80m. A staircase leading up from the rear appears to be original. The Row was enclosed in 1711 and the plan at that level suggests its position. Also two walls at right angles to the street suggest a passage, now incorporated into the building. (Fig 179)

73 Watergate Street

An early nineteenth-century brick building with no evidence of earlier fabric. The rear wing formerly comprised a pair of courtyard dwellings which have survived twentieth-century slum clearance.

75 Watergate Street

A poor quality half-timbered building of the early twentieth century. No evidence of earlier fabric survives.

Watergate Street – North Side

St Peter's Church

The church stands on the site of the former Roman *principia*, and is said to have been founded by Queen Ethelfleda in 907. The present building dates from the fourteenth, fifteenth and sixteenth centuries. It is roughly square in plan, with a continuous nave and chancel of four aisles. The tower, now capped with a low pyramidal roof, formerly supported a spire, which was rebuilt in the sixteenth century, taken down in the seventeenth, then rebuilt and finally removed in the eighteenth. The south face of the church was refaced by Thomas Harrison in 1803 when the pentice which adjoined it was taken down. The south door of the church is reached from a set of steps leading to Watergate Street Row. Below the floor of the Perpendicular north aisle is the undercroft of a medieval town house which was filled and paved over.

2–4 Watergate Street,
2–4 Watergate Street Row

A seventeenth-century timber-framed building, concealed by an early nineteenth-century brick facade. The structure of both undercrofts is hidden, but a short stretch of rubble wall is visible to the rear of No 4, and the proportions (4.01 x 12.84m and 4.28 x 12.62m) suggest a medieval origin. At Row level and above elements of the timber frame are visible in the two stairwells and two seventeenth-century doors survive. The building was originally divided into two at Row level. (Figs 18 and 180.)

6–8 Watergate Street,
6 Watergate Street Row

This building was substantially rebuilt during the 1970s. It has a nineteenth-century brick facade, similar to Nos 2 and 4, but there is no indication that this ever concealed a timber frame. None of the internal layout survives, but pre-alteration plans show two undercrofts, 3.35m and 3.20m in width, and two sections of stone rubble wall are visible. The rear facade on to St Peter's churchyard, although much rebuilt, is early eighteenth-century. (Figs 18 and 180.)

10 Watergate Street,
8 Watergate Street Row

A major timber-framed building behind an early nine-teenth-century brick facade, with a Row-level passage to the west. The undercroft with rubble stone walls is approximately 8.8m in width and divided by a massive timber arcade carrying beams with four-way bracing from posts (see pp 68–9), which has been dated by dendrochronology as early to mid-sixteenth-century (see Appendix B). The timber-framed construction above is probably seventeenth-century. At Row level there is a wide fireplace with moulded mantelpiece and a closed-string staircase with pierced splat balusters, both of the early seventeenth century. On the floor above is a massive fireplace with a painted plaster chimney breast depicting the Royal Arms and the arms of the Corbett family, and with a frieze of sea monsters. (See pp 91 and 93, and Figs 71 and 95.)

12 Watergate Street,
10 Watergate Street Row

A brick and reinforced concrete building of 1985, designed by Robin Clayton and Partners in a neo-Vernacular style. The redevelopment involved the destruction of an early medieval undercroft and timber framing at Row level. The undercroft had stone walls with corbel tabling and a central timber arcade with braced post. Dendrochronology provided a single date of 1207 from a timber without sapwood at Row level (Ward 1985). (See pp 45–6, 50, 51, and Figs 48 and 57.)

14–20 Watergate Street,
12–20 Watergate Street Row

A redevelopment of the early 1970s in textured concrete and glass designed by W Campbell and Son. The front elevation was substantially amended by the City Council's architectural consultant, Harry Tasker of Building Design Partnership. The facade of Nos 18–20 was rebuilt in replica using modern bricks (Fig 147), though a rare surviving eighteenth-century cabin in the Row was not replaced because of the construction of the pedestrian bridge over Goss Street. (See pp 110, 132.)

22 Watergate Street,
22 Watergate Street Row

Enclosed within this mid-eighteenth-century brick building is an earlier house. The undercroft has some masonry in the eastern and rear walls. The front post and beam of a later, jettied, timber-framed facade remains. This was cut away when the brick facade was built, leaving a half-sawn, carved bracket typical of the early seventeenth century. The western wall contains a medieval timber arcade which may have been a partition within a larger building or may provide the only evidence for a non-masonry party wall between undercrofts (see p 47). At Row level there is a similar line of posts of smaller scantling and narrower spacing, probably contemporary with the jettied facade.

Fig 180 View from Watergate Street Row South (RCHME © Crown Copyright). Note steep slope of stallboard.

Fig 181 Timber arcade in west wall of undercroft in 22 Watergate Street (RCHME © Crown Copyright)

A substantial brick fireplace survives, whose seventeenth-century plaster overmantel has been moved into No 24. (See p 105 and Figs 52, 181.)

24 Watergate Street, 24 Watergate Street Row

A timber-framed building behind an early nineteenth-century brick facade with stone dressings. A large bay window projects above the Row. The undercroft is the same width internally (5.6m) as No 22, with which it must share the timber arcade at undercroft level. At Row level there is evidence of a passage to the west with a late medieval open hall, behind a shop fronting the Row. In the seventeenth century a staircase was inserted into the shop space. The roof was raised at least once in the sixteenth or seventeenth century and again in the nineteenth century. (See Fig 113.)

26 Watergate Street, 26 Watergate Street Row

A good four-storey building of *c* 1720, with an added bay window above the Row, as at No 24. The undercroft is wider (7.6m) than the usual tenement width,

and contains a pair of eighteenth-century brick barrel vaults. The plan at Row level is double-pile with no through passage and the rooms fronting the Row were domestic, not commercial. There is a good early eighteenth-century staircase and other contemporary fittings. At Row + 1 level the thirteenth-century stone wall of the eastern house within Booth Mansion is exposed with its moulded eaves cornice. This cornice implies that the adjacent house was free-standing, or stood above its neighbours when built. (See p 104, and Fig 113.)

Booth Mansion, 28–34 Watergate Street, 28–30 Watergate Street Row

The largest house in Watergate Street with a fine brick facade and ornate baroque cornice. It was created in 1700 for George Booth of Dunham Massey by remodelling two medieval houses to provide the impressive elevation and the large panelled reception rooms above the Row. These rooms were later combined, probably *c* 1740 when the building became Assembly Rooms. The remains of the two earlier buildings are described separately. (See p 104 and Fig 107.)

Eastern House – The present undercroft measures 13.0 x 7.0m and is walled in coursed sandstone. It is divided longitudinally by an arcade of pointed arches (originally 5) with octagonal piers. A series of closely spaced massive joists, halved above the arcade, are carried on the outer wall, by a corbel table. In the rear wall are two stone cupboards and a blocked doorway. This doorway probably gave access into a further undercroft beyond. The Row walkway is spanned by two chamfered, pointed arches, similar in profile to those in the undercroft and set within the side walls of the house which continue up to the original moulded eaves cornice (see 26 Watergate Street). A late thirteenth-century wooden doorway at Row level was originally part of a partition wall dividing the front of the building from the hall. At the centre of the west wall of the former hall is a corbel carved like a squatting man, which may have carried the central open truss over the hall. Old plans imply further stone-walled rooms beyond the hall, now demolished. There is evidence of substantial seventeenth-century alterations to the building. A Jacobean stair was inserted into the hall and the remains of a good plaster frieze were found in the room above the Row. Dendrochronology gives estimated dates of 1260–80 for the undercroft timbers. (See pp 23, 33, 39–43, 45, 48, 50, 93, and Figs 23, 42, 44, 50, 58, 97, and Pl 12.)

Western House – This is much less intact than the eastern house with which it shares a masonry wall. The undercroft was originally 8.0m x 10.7m and isolated within it is a timber arcade using timbers with felling dates estimated at 1260–80. At the rear of the undercroft there are two spaces covered with pointed barrel vaults in sandstone masonry. No similar vaulting is

Fig 182   Row level in 38–42 Watergate Street showing fourteenth-century doorway and displaced balustrade of Jacobean stair (RCHME © Crown Copyright)

Fig 183   End of arch-braced beam in undercroft of 38–42 Watergate Street (RCHME © Crown Copyright)

known to survive in Chester. Old plans of the Row level and above show walls of sufficient thickness to be of masonry. (See pp 38, 45–8, and Fig 49.)

36 Watergate Street, 32 Watergate Street Row

A twentieth-century brick building in Georgian style, said to have been rebuilt following a fire. The only early evidence is the west stone wall of the undercroft shared with No 38.

38–42 Watergate Street, 34–38 Watergate Street Row

The washed brick and weakly composed timber-framed facades of this building hide an exceptionally important and well-preserved stone medieval town house, spanning three tenement plots. The property width (17.5m in total) allowed the stone-walled hall to be placed parallel to the street. The three service doorways between the screens passage and the hall survive, as does a similar door in the front wall of the hall. The braced ceiling beams and massive joists of the easternmost undercroft have produced estimated felling dates of the early fourteenth century. In the late sixteenth century back-to-back fireplaces and a cross-beam floor were inserted into the hall to create four heated rooms. One of these rooms has a good plaster overmantel with Renaissance columns and there are the remains of two Jacobean staircases. The medieval screens passage is still shown as an access through the building on maps pre-dating 1875. This building may have been the 'Mansion place' at the corner of Gerrard's Lane, now Crook Street, mentioned at the time of Edward III. (See pp 24, 29, 38, 40, 42, 49, 83, 91, and Figs 24, 47, 54, 55, 84, 182, 183, and Pl 1 and 3.)

Fig 184   44–46 and 48–50 Watergate Street (RCHME © Crown Copyright)

44–46 Watergate Street

A four-storey corner property with an eighteenth-century facade, gable end to Watergate Street. On the west side a flight of steps leads to the former Row level. The undercroft has stone walls and is 6.7m in width. It contains a number of cross-beams and joists but

Fig 185 Frontage of 68 Watergate Street in 1942 before the alterations which removed the Ionic pilasters at first floor level (RCHME © Crown Copyright)

these are all re-used. The seventeenth century closed-string twisted baluster staircase descends to street level. No early features survive *in situ* at the former Row level, except for a deep moulded cornice, probably early eighteenth-century in date, and some re-used seventeenth-century panelling. At Row + 1 level the main chamber has bolection-moulded panelling of the early eighteenth century. (See Fig 184.)

48–50 Watergate Street

A four-storey building with an early nineteenth century brick frontage concealing at least three earlier phases. The undercroft has coursed rubble stone walls and measures 5.3m x 14.95m. The medieval building line is only 46cm behind the present street front. The Row is enclosed, but the Tuscan column which formerly supported the chamber above is visible behind a window shutter at Row level. The room above has mid-eighteenth-century wall panelling and a fireplace flanked by full-height fluted pilasters. The closed-string staircase with bulbous balusters is early eighteenth-century. (See p 100 and Figs 103 and 184.)

52 Watergate Street

A late nineteenth- or early twentieth-century gabled brick building containing no early features.

54–56 Watergate Street

A building of *c* 1840 with steps leading up to the entrance at former Row level. Below this is a short undercroft, possibly truncated, with wide unchamfered ceiling beams. The east wall of the undercroft is of coursed sandstone of *c* 1300. Remains of corbelled stone steps formerly leading to Row level are visible within a cupboard. A passageway existed on the east side of this building up to the early nineteenth century and is shown on maps of 1789, 1816 and 1833.

58–66 Watergate Street

A terrace of five brick gabled buildings of 1852 by Edward Hodkinson for Messrs Dixon and Myers (p 124). They replaced a seventeenth-century timber-framed mansion belonging at one time to the Mainwaring family, for which there is good evidence from the 1816 print by G Batenham. This shows a warehouse on the site of No 58 and to the left a four-bay gabled house above a number of undercrofts. Access was by a central flight of steps beneath a gabled chamber to a vestigial Row. The first, second and fourth bays of the Row are enclosed. This building was very similar to contemporary Cheshire manor houses, such as Moss Hall, Audlem, dated 1616. (See pp 88, 100 and Fig 102.)

68 Watergate Street

An early eighteenth-century brick house with rusticated stone ground floor. The front elevation was partially rebuilt and considerably altered in the mid twentieth century. Steps on the east side lead to the entrance at former Row level. The facade to Trinity Street shows evidence of window alterations, including the insertion of a large Venetian window, presumably contemporary with the fine late eighteenth-century open-string staircase which it lights, and the Adamesque decorative scheme to the saloon. The house was built by Alderman Henry Bennett and remained in the family of his descendants, the Heskeths, until the second half of the nineteenth century. (See p 104 and Fig 185.)

Church of the Holy Trinity

A prominent building with a tall steeple, built on the site of the medieval church in 1865–9 to the design of James Harrison, but completed after his death by Edwards and Kelly. The interior, stripped of most of its fittings, is now used as the Guildhall.

Glossary

Terms italicised in the definitions given are themselves defined separately in the Glossary.

Abacus	The flat slab on top of a capital
Acre	See *Measurement, area*
Arcade	A range of arches on columns, or timber beams on posts
—— plate	The longitudinal timber beam placed directly on top of *arcade posts*, or with a *bolster* between, and supporting the *bridging beams*
—— post	The vertical timber post of an arcade
Arch-braced beam	See *Beam*
Ashlar	Masonry cut to an even square finish, with straight courses, exact joints, and smooth surfaces
Assembly	The medieval and early modern corporation of the city of Chester
Baroque	A style of architecture originating in late sixteenth-century Italy. In Britain it is manifested in the early eighteenth-century work of Vanburgh and Hawksmoor.
Barrel vault	A continuous vault of semicircular, segmental or two-centred section
Bay	The external division of a building by windows, between columns or, in timber-framed buildings, the internal units formed between principal structural frames or trusses
—— post	A substantial vertical timber forming part of a main framework and marking bay divisions
Beam, arch-braced	A transverse timber beam with its span reduced by curved braces. In Chester these braces usually spring from masonry side walls.
——, bridging	A longitudinal or transverse timber beam directly supporting common joists. It rests either directly on top of the *arcade posts* or on the *arcade plate*.
——, dragon	A diagonal beam carrying a projecting corner post or hip rafter
——, false hammer	Resembles a *hammer beam* but has no hammer post; instead it is braced to a *principal* or *collar*.
——, hammer	A horizontal roof timber, supported on a brace and bearing a hammer post
——, sill	Horizontal timber at the bottom of a timber-framed wall

Beam, tie	Main transverse timber in a roof truss, sitting on the wall plates and connecting the feet of the principal rafters
Bolection-moulded panelling	Rebated panelling with a moulding which stands above the face of the framing
Bolster	A short horizontal timber placed above an arcade post and below the *arcade plate*
Boulting	Sifting (of flour, meal, etc) through wide mesh textile to remove coarse particles
Bressumer	Horizontal beam over a fireplace opening or set forward to support a jettied wall
Burgage plot	Land or tenement held by a burgess or in a borough. Such property, which was heritable and alienable, was subject to special customs, most notably to money rent or land-gavel.
Canted oriel window	A window, with splayed sides, projecting from the face of a wall and supported by corbels or brackets
Capital	The topmost section of a column or pier
Chain	See *Measurement, linear*
Closed string	See *Staircase*
Cogged joist	See *Joist*
Collar	Horizontal roof timber connecting a pair of rafters, between foot and apex levels
Colonnade	A range of columns
Corbel	A stone block projecting from a wall and usually supporting a beam
—— plate	A horizontal timber resting on a corbel table
—— table	A closely spaced series of *corbels* and the longitudinal timber, or corbel plate, which the corbel table supports
Cornice	A projecting moulding at the top of a wall or arch
Cross passage	The passage across one end of an open hall, normally with a wall or partition towards the hall and often with doorways at either end
Crown plate	The plate in a crown post roof, carried by the crown posts and supporting the collars
—— post	A vertical timber in a roof, carried by the tie beam, supporting the crown plate, and not rising beyond the collar
Cruck	A pair of timbers, straight or curved, serving as the principals of a roof and reaching from a point at, or near, the apex to a point well down the side wall

Currency	Pounds, shillings and pence (pennies) are abbreviated as £, s, and d. There were 12 pence to 1 shilling and 20 shillings to 1 pound.
Dais	The raised platform at the upper end of a hall
Dendrochronology	The science of dating annual growth layers of wood (tree rings) to their year of formation
Double-pile plan	A building plan two rooms deep through-out
Dragon beam	See *Beam*
Ell	An obsolete measurement of 45in (1.14m). A 'royal ell' is equivalent to one yard (0.91m) and a 'woollen ell' might be the longer Flemish ell (ie 45in).
Entasis	The outward curvature of a column shaft to counteract the optical illusion of concavity given by a straight-sided shaft
False hammer beam	See *Beam*
Fee farm	1 A form of tenure by which land is held in fee simple (in absolute possession) subject to a fixed rent 2 The rent paid for land so held
Fine	Before the nineteenth century the mean-ing is generally closer to 'tax' or 'fee' than the current usage of the word.
Flemish ell	See *Ell*
Foot (ft)	See *Measurement, linear*
Fresco	Wall painting on wet plaster
Gunstock	See *Jowl*
Hammer beam	See *Beam*
Impost	A bracket from which an arch springs
Inch (in)	See *Measurement, linear*
Jack rafter	A rafter set obliquely where two roofs converge, on which are set the progres-sively shorter common rafters
Jamb	The vertical side of a window, doorway or archway
Jetty	A projecting or overhanging part of a building
Joist, cogged	The end of the joist is placed in a recess in the supporting beam
——, lodged	A joist resting on top of its supporting beam
Jowl (or Gunstock)	Enlargement at the top of a post to accom-modate housings for plates or beams
King post	A vertical roof timber supported by a tie beam or collar and rising to the apex of the roof to support a ridge piece
Lamb's tongue stop	A flat ogee moulding at the end of a chamfer
Lancet	A narrow two-centred arched window
Lodged joist	See *Joist*
Measurement, area	Units of area measurement cited in this volume are *acre* and *virgate*. An acre is an imperial measurement equalling 4840 sq yd (square yards): 2.471 acres equals 1 hectare. The virgate (as an area measure) was a variable unit, but aver-aged 30 acres.
Measurement, linear	Units of imperial linear measurement cited in this volume are *chain*, *yard* (yd), *foot* (ft) and *inch* (in). There are 12 inches to 1 foot, and 3 feet to 1 yard. One chain = 22 feet (ft). One yard = 0.9144 metre (m). One *virgate* (as a linear measure) was equal to 0.915m.
Measurement, weight	There are 16 ounces (oz) to 1 pound (lb); 2.2lb = 1 kilogram (kg)
Mortice	A socket cut in a timber to receive a tenon, forming the commonest joint between two timbers
Murenger	An official responsible for keeping the walls of a city in good repair
Neo-classical	Late eighteenth- and early nineteenth-century architecture based on classical models
Open hall	The principal room of a medieval house, open to the roof
Open string	See *Staircase*
Ounce	See *Measurement, weight*
Overlapping wind braces	Pairs of diagonal roof timbers in adjacent bays overlapping above the principal truss and designed to prevent distortion of the structure
Pargetting	Ornamental plasterwork
Passing brace	A long straight timber halved across other roof timbers, commonly running from wall post or aisle post to the opposing rafter
Penny	(pl: pennies or pence) See *Currency*
Pier	A column-like support, often square, octagonal or compound in section
Pilaster	A shallow rectangular pier attached to a wall
Plate	A horizontal timber, commonly on top of a wall, arcade or crown post
——, sole	A short timber set across a wall to take the foot of a rafter
Podium	A ground or basement storey, usually rusticated, treated as a plinth for the building above

Portmote	The court of a borough (a term used especially within the County Palatine of Chester)	Staircase, open string	In an open or cut string staircase, the inclined support at the side is shaped to the outline of the steps.
Pound	See *Currency*, also *Measurement, weight*	String course	Projecting horizontal band in a wall, sometimes moulded
Principal	The most important member in a timber frame	Stud	A subsidiary timber, usually vertical, in a framed wall or partition
Raking strut	A strut at an angle to the tie beam and framed into the principal rafter	Tenon	A rectangular projection on the end of a timber which fits a mortice to make the commonest joint between two timbers
Rebate	A continuous recess cut on an edge, and having a rectangular section	Tie beam	See *Beam*
Respond	Half-pier bonded into a wall, from which an arch springs	Truss, principal	A rigid (transverse) framework consisting of a pair of principal rafters with *tie beam* and/or *collar* constructed across a roof, defining bay intervals. It carries purlins, supports the roof structure, and prevents spreading.
Rib vault	See *Vault*		
Ridge-rib	A rib along the longitudinal or transverse ridge of a vault	——, spere	A truss dividing the cross entry or cross passage from the hall proper
Roodee	A large expanse of marshland or water meadow, south west of Chester, between the city walls and the River Dee	Tuscan	One of the classical orders, its columns being an unfluted variant of Doric with a base added
Royal ell	See *Ell*	Two-centred arch	A pointed arch struck from two centres
Ruabon (pressed) brick	A hard, smooth facing brick from Ruabon, North Wales	Undercroft	part of a building, wholly or partially below ground
Rustication	Style of ashlar where the surfaces of large blocks are left rough, smooth with V-joints, or vermiculated	Vault, quadripartite	A vault divided into four parts
Scantling	The cross-sectional size of a timber	——, rib	A vault with diagonal ribs along the groins
Scarf joint	The joint between two timbers meeting end to end	Venetian window	A three-light window with a central semi-circular-headed light, flanked by narrow square-headed lights
Scribing	The shaping of one timber to fit around the moulding or *waney edge* of another	Virgate	See *Measurement, area* and *Measurement, linear*
Service bay	Service accommodation usually divided into a buttery and pantry	Voussoir	A wedge-shaped component of an arch
Shilling	See *Currency*	Wainscot	Wooden panelling, or fine quality oak used for that purpose
Sill beam	See *Beam*		
Soffit	The underside of an arch, lintel or beam	Waney edge	The irregular surface on converted timber, being originally the roughened surface of the sapwood lying immediately below the bark on the tree
Solar	Upper floor living room or bedchamber of a medieval house		
Spandrel	The near-triangular surface between the outside of an arch, a horizontal drawn from its apex and a vertical drawn from its springing	Wattle and daub	An interwoven arrangement of wicker-work (wattle) covered with plaster-like material (daub)
Springer	The lowest stone of an arch	Weights	See *Measurement, weight*
Staircase, closed string	In a staircase of this kind a closed string is an inclined support at the side, with the treads and risers housed into it.	Woollen ell	See *Ell*
		Yard (yd)	See *Measurement, linear*

Bibliography

The following abbreviations have been used throughout the book

BAR	British Archaeological Reports
BL	British Library
BL Add Ch	British Library Additional Charters
BL Harl Ms	British Library Harleian Manuscripts
BPR	Register of Edward the Black Prince, HMSO
Cheshire RO	Cheshire Record Office
Cheshire Sheaf	This is a collection of unattributed notes published in three series.
Chester CRO	Chester City Record Office (now *Chester Archives*)
JCAS	*Journal of the Chester Archaeological Society*; the same abbreviation denotes the *Journal* of this Society by various earlier forms of its name (The Chester and North Wales Archaeological and Historical Society, The Architectural, Archaeological and Historical Society for the county and the city of Chester and North Wales, The Chester and North Wales Architectural, Archaeological and Historical Society). Where only the date is given the reference is to unattributed notes or reports of meetings.
JRUL	*Journal of the John Rylands University Library*, Manchester
PRO	Public Record Office
RSLC	Record Society of Lancashire and Cheshire
RCHME	The Royal Commission on the Historical Monuments of England
THSLC	*Transactions of the Historic Society of Lancashire and Cheshire*
TLCAS	*Transactions of the Lancashire and Cheshire Antiquarian Society*
TRHS	*Transactions of the Royal Historical Society*
VCH	*Victoria County History*

Addy, J (ed), 1987 The diary of Henry Prescott, LLB, Deputy Registrar of Chester Diocese, *RSLC*, **127**

Aldsworth, F G, and Harris, R, 1988 The tower and 'Rhenish helm' spire of St Mary's Church, Sompting, *Sussex Archaeol Collect*, **126**, 105–44

Alldridge, N J, 1981 Aspects of the topography of early medieval Chester, *JCAS*, **64**, 5–31

Allott, S, 1974 *Alcuin of York, c 732 to 804 AD; his life and letters*, York

Audsley, G A, 1891 *The stranger's handbook to Chester*, Chester

Babbington, C (ed), 1869 *Polychronicon Ranulphi Higden Monachi Cestrensis*, Rolls ser, **2**

Baillie, M G L, 1977a The Belfast oak chronology to AD 1001, *Tree-Ring Bull*, **37**, 1–12

——, 1977b Dublin medieval dendrochronology, *Tree-Ring Bull*, **37**, 13–20

——, 1977c An oak chronology for south central Scotland, *Tree-Ring Bull*, **37**, 33–44

——, and Pilcher, J R, 1973 A simple crossdating programme for tree-ring research, *Tree-Ring Bull*, **33**, 7–14

Baker, A, 1895 The Rows of Chester, *JCAS*, **5**, 400–1, 433–4

Baker, N J, Lawson, J B, Maxwell, R, and Smith, J T, 1993 Further work on Pride Hill, Shrewsbury, *Trans Shropshire Hist Archaeol Soc*, **68**, 1–64

Barker, E E, 1953 Talbot deeds 1200–1682, *RSLC*, **103**

Barraclough, G, 1957 *Facsimiles of early Cheshire charters*, Gloucester

Barraclough, G (ed), 1988 The charters of the Anglo-Norman Earls of Chester *c* 1071–1237, *RSLC*, **126**, 279–82

Beresford, M, and St Joseph, J K S, 1979 *Medieval England: an aerial survey*, 2 edn, *Cambridge air surveys*, **2**, Cambridge

Blair, J, and Ramsey, N (eds), 1991 *English medieval industries*, London

Boydell, J, 1749 *South prospect of the city of Chester*, Woodbridge

Brown, A N, 1984 The Rows debate: where next?, *JCAS*, **67**, 77–83

——, Grenville, J C, and Turner, R C, 1986 Watergate Street: an interim report of the Chester Rows Research Project, *JCAS*, **69**, 115–45

——, Howes, B, and Turner, R C, 1985 A medieval stone town house in Chester, *JCAS*, **68**, 143–53

Brown, R A, Colvin, H M, and Taylor, A J, 1963 *The history of the king's works*, **1**, *The Middle Ages*, London

Brownbill, J (ed), 1913 Calendar of Moore manuscripts, *RSLC*, **67**

——(ed), 1914 Ledger book of Vale Royal Abbey, *RSLC*, **68**

Brushfield, T N, 1871 The Roman remains of Chester, *JCAS*, **3**, 1–106

——, 1895 The Rows of Chester, *JCAS*, **5**, 207–338

Carver, M O H (ed), 1983 Two town houses in medieval Shrewsbury: the excavation and analysis of two medieval and later houses built on the town wall at Shrewsbury, *Trans Shropshire Archaeol Soc*, **61** (for 1977–8)

Chester City Council, 1986 *Conservation in Chester*, Chester

Chibnall, M (ed), 1969–80 *The Ecclesiastical History of Orderic Vitalis*, Oxford

Christie, R C (ed), 1887 *Annales Cestrienses*: or Chronicle of the Abbey of St Werburgh at Chester, *RSLC*, **14**

CliftonTaylor, A, 1978 *Six English towns*, London

Compton, E H, 1916 *Chester water-colours*, London

Coppack, G, 1990 *The archaeological recording and analysis of timber-framed buildings*, in ICOMOS UK 1990 Understanding timber-framed buildings: archaeology, recording and repair, Papers given at a conference organised by ICOMOS October 1990, privately circulated

Cowan, W (ed), 1903 *A Journey to Edinburgh in Scotland by Joseph Taylor, Late of the Inner Temple, Esq*, London

Cox, E W, 1895 The origin and date of Chester Rows, *JCAS*, **5**, 299–303

Davey, P (ed), 1973 *Northgate Street brewery*, Grosvenor Museum, Chester

Dean, R, 1983 *Chirk Castle*, National Trust guide, London

de Figueiredo, P, and Treuherz, J, 1988 *Cheshire country houses*, Chichester

Defoe, D, 1726 *A tour through the whole island of Britain*, Everyman edn 1976, London

Dixon, R, and Muthesius, S, 1978 *Victorian architecture*, London

Dobson, R B, 1977 Urban decline in late medieval England, *TRHS*, 5 ser, **27**, 1–22

Dodgson, J McN, 1981 Place-names of the city of Chester, *The place-names of Cheshire*, **V (I:i)**, English Place-Names Soc, **XLVIII**

Dyke, A F E, 1946 A Cestrian looks at Watergate Street, *JCAS*, **26**, 21–30

English Heritage, 1998 *Dendrochronology: guidelines on producing and interpreting dendrochronological data*, London

Evans, J W, 1991 *St David's Bishop's Palace*, Cadw – Welsh Historic Monuments, Cardiff

Evans, and Gresty, 1857 *Stranger's guide book to Chester*, Chester

Faulkner, P A, 1966 Medieval undercrofts and town houses, *Archaeol J*, **123**, 120–35

Forestry Commission, 1984 *Census of woodlands and trees, Cheshire 1979–82*

Fuller, T, 1662 *The history of the worthies of England*, (ed P A Nuttall, 1840) London

Giles, C, and Goodall, I M, 1992 *Yorkshire textile mills 1770–1930*, London

Girouard, M, 1985 *Cities and people*, London

——, 1992 *Town and country*, London

Grant, L (ed), 1990 *Medieval art, architecture and archaeology in London*, Trans British Archaeol Assoc Conference 1984

Greenhalgh, M, 1989 *The survival of Roman antiquities in the Middle Ages*, London

Greenwood, C, 1945 *Chester: a plan for redevelopment*, Chester

Grenfell Baines, G, 1964 *Chester: a plan for the central area*, Chester

Grenville, J C, 1990 The Rows of Chester: Some thoughts on the results of recent research, *World Archaeol*, **21** (3), 446–60

——, and Turner, R C, 1986 Two timber-framed houses in Chester, *JCAS*, **69**, 97–114

Hamilton, N E S A (ed), 1870 *Willelmi Malmesbiriensis Monachi: de Gestis Pontificum Anglorum*, Rolls ser, Chronicles and memorials, **52**

Harris, B E, 1979 *Chester*, Edinburgh

——, 1984 The debate on the Rows, *JCAS*, **67**, 7–16

—— (ed), 1987 *The Victoria County History of Cheshire*, **I**, Oxford

Harris, J, and Lever, J, 1966 *Illustrated glossary of architecture, 850–1830*, London

Harris, R, 1989 The grammar of carpentry, *Vernacular Architect*, **20**, 1–8

——, forthcoming *The English medieval town house*, Oxford

Harrison, J, 1864 Report of meeting on December 2nd 1861, *JCAS*, **2** (pt 7, 1864), 405

Harrod, H D, 1902 The Rows of Chester, *JCAS*, **8**, 48–66

Harvey, J H, 1971 *The master builders: architecture in the Middle Ages*, London

Hemingway, J, 1831 *A guide to the city of Chester*, Chester

Hewett, C A, 1980 *English historic carpentry*, Chichester

Hewitt, H J, 1967 *Cheshire under the three Edwards*, Cheshire Community Council, **38**

Hewitt, J, 1887 Notes on the medieval architecture of Chester, *JCAS*, **1**, 30–52

——, 1895 The Rows of Chester, *JCAS*, **5**, 277–98

Hopkins, A (ed), 1950 Selected rolls of the Chester city courts, *Chetham Soc*, 3 ser, **11**

Hubbard, E, 1991 *The work of John Douglas*, London

Hughes, M K H, and Leggett, P A, 1983 Tree-ring dating of the timbers, in McNeil, R, Two twelfth century houses in Nantwich, Cheshire, *Medieval Archaeol*, **27**, 69–71

Hughes, M K H, and Leggett, P A, 1985 Dendrochronology, in Brown, A N, *et al* 1985, 132–4

——, and ——, 1986 Dendrochronology, in Brown, A N, *et al* 1986, 149–51

Hughes, M K H, Milsom, S J, and Leggett, P A, 1981 Sapwood estimates in the interpretation of tree-ring dates, *J Archaeol Sci*, **8**, 381–90

Hughes, T, 1856 *The stranger's handbook to Chester and its environs*, Chester

Hulton, W A (ed), 1847 Coucher book of Whalley Abbey II, *Chetham Soc*, 2 ser, **11**

Hunter, J, 1789 *Survey of the ancient and loyal city of Chester*, Chester

Hyde, J K, 1966 Medieval descriptions of cities, *Bull John Rylands Library*, **48** (2), 308–40

Insall, D, 1968 *Chester: a study in conservation*, London

Irvine, W F, 1904 Chester in the twelfth and thirteenth centuries, *JCAS*, 1–29

Jones, B C, 1986 House building in Carlisle in the Middle Ages, *Cumberland Westmorland Archaeol Antiq Soc*, **86**, 101–8

Jones, D, 1957 The church in Chester, 1300–1540, *Chetham Soc*, 3 ser, **7**

Jones, R H, 1986 *Excavations in Redcliffe, 1983–5: survey and excavation at 95–97 Redcliffe Street, Bristol: an interim report*, Bristol

Keene, D, 1985 Survey of medieval Winchester (i and ii), *Winchester studies*, **2**, Oxford

——, 1990 Shops and shopping in medieval London, in Grant 1990, 29–46

Kennett, A M, 1984 The Rows in the city records, *JCAS*, **67**, 47–54

——, (ed), 1987 *Georgian Chester*, Chester

King, D (ed), 1656 *The vale-royall of England*, London

Krautheimer, R, 1982 *Three Christian capitals*, Univ California, San Francisco

Laughton, J W, 1988 'The house that John built': a study of the building of a seventeenth century house in Chester, *JCAS*, **70**, 99–132

——, 1993 Aspects of the social and economic history of late medieval Chester, 1350– *c* 1500, unpubl PhD thesis, Univ Cambridge

Lawson, P H, and Smith, J T, 1958 The Rows of Chester: two interpretations, *JCAS*, **45**, 1–42

Leggett, P A, 1980 The use of tree-ring analyses in the absolute dating of historic sites and their use in the interpretation of past climatic trends, unpubl PhD thesis, Liverpool Polytechnic

——, Hughes, M K, and Hibbert, F A, 1978 A modern oak chronology from North Wales and its interpretation, in Fletcher, J M (ed), *Dendrochronology in Europe*, BAR International ser, **51**, 157–161

Lockwood, T M, and Hewitt, J, 1886 *Notes on Bridge Street*, Chester

Maddison, J M, 1983 The choir of Chester Cathedral, *JCAS*, **66**, 31–46

——, 1988 Master masons of the diocese of Lichfield: a study in fourteenth-century architecture at the time of the Black Death, *TLCAS*, **85**, 107–72

Mason, D, 1976 Chester: the evolution and adaptation of its landscape, *JCAS*, **59**, 14–23

Mason, D, 1985 *Excavations at Chester: 26–42 Lower Bridge Street 1974–6: Dark Age and Saxon occupation*, Grosvenor Museum archaeological excavation and survey report, **3**, Chester

Mass Observation 1947, *Browns and Chester – Portrait of a shop 1780–1946*, London

Matthews, K, 1995, Excavations at Chester – the evolution of the heart of the city: investigations at 3–15 Eastgate Street 1990–1, *Chester City Council: Archaeology Service excavation and survey report*, **7**, Chester

McNeil, R, and Turner, R C, 1987–8 An architectural and topographical survey of Vale Royal Abbey, *JCAS*, **70**, 51–74

Mercer, E, 1976 *English vernacular houses; a study of traditional farmhouses and cottages*, London

Minns, G W, 1913 Relics of old Southampton, *Proc Hampshire Fld Club Archaeol Soc*, **6**, supp, 1–2

Mitchell, S I, 1980 Retailing in eighteenth and early nineteenth century Cheshire, *THSLC*, **130**, 33–60

Montgomery, R M, 1918 Some early deeds relating to land on the north side of Eastgate Street, Chester, *JCAS*, **22**, 117–41

Moran, M, 1994 Shropshire dendrochronology project – phase two, *Vernacular Architect*, **25**, 31–6

Morris, C, 1982 *The illuminated journeys of Celia Fiennes, 1685–1712*, London

Morris, R H, 1894 *Chester in the Plantagenet and Tudor reigns*, privately printed, Chester

——, 1899 Bishop Lloyd's Palace, *JCAS*, **6**, 245–8

Ockrim, M, 1988 Life and work of Thomas Harrison of Chester 1744–1829, unpubl PhD thesis, Univ London

Ormerod, G, 1882 *The history of the county Palatine and city of Chester*, 2 edn (revised and enlarged by T Helsby), London

Oswald, A, 1965 The Old Palace, Croydon, Surrey, pt 1, *Country Life*, April 8 1965, 806–10

Packham, A B, 1924 The Marlipins, New Shoreham, *Sussex Archaeol Collect*, **65**, 158–95

Palliser, D M, 1980 *Chester: contemporary descriptions by residents and visitors*, Chester

Pantin, W A, 1947 The development of domestic architecture in Oxford, *Antiq J*, **27**, 120–50

——, 1963a Medieval English town-house plans, *Medieval Archaeol*, 7, 202–39

——, 1963b Some English medieval town houses: a study in adaptation, in Foster I Ll, and Alcock L (eds) *Culture and environment: essays in honour of Sir Cyril Fox*, 445–78

Parker, J H, 1856 Unsigned review in *Gentleman's Magazine*, **126**, II, 291–297

Parker, V, 1971 *The making of King's Lynn*, Chichester

Parkin, E W, 1973 The ancient buildings of New Romney, *Archaeol Cantiana*, **38**, 1–14

Pennant, T, 1883 *Tours in Wales* (ed J Rhys), **I**

Pevsner, N, 1958 *The buildings of England: Shropshire*, Harmondsworth, Middlesex

——, and Hubbard, E, 1971 *The buildings of England: Cheshire*, Harmondsworth, Middlesex

Platt, C, and Coleman-Smith, R, 1975 *Excavations in medieval Southampton, 1953–1969*, **1**, *The excavation reports*, Leicester

——, 1976 *The English medieval town*, London

Prestwich, M, 1988 *Edward I*, London

PRO, 1875 *36th report of the Deputy Keeper of the Public Records*, Public Record Office, London

Rackham, O, Blair, W J, and Munby J T, 1978 The thirteenth-century roofs and floor of the Blackfriars Priory at Gloucester, *Medieval Archaeol*, **22**, 111–2

RCHME, 1916 *Inventory of the county of Essex*, Royal Commission on the Historical Monuments of England, London

——, 1977 *Inventory of the town of Stamford*, Royal Commission on the Historical Monuments of England, London

——, 1981 *Inventory of the city of York*, **5**, *The central area*, Royal Commission on the Historical Monuments of England, London

Reynolds, S, 1977 *An introduction to the history of English medieval towns*, Oxford

Rosser, G, 1989 *Medieval Westminster: 1200–1540*, Oxford

Rutter, J A, 1984 Lifestyle in the Rows, with particular reference to a collection of pottery from 11 Watergate Street, Chester, found in 1884, *JCAS*, **67**, 55–76

Saalman, H, 1968 *Medieval cities*, London

Saint, A, 1976 *Richard Norman Shaw*, London

Salzman, L F, 1952 *Building in England down to 1540*, Oxford

Sawyer, P H, and Thacker, A T, The Cheshire Domesday, in Harris 1987, 293–341

Schofield, J, 1984 *The building of London from the Conquest to the Great Fire*, London

Selfridge, H G, 1918 *The romance of commerce*, London

Simpson, F, 1915 The Leche House, Chester, *JCAS*, **21**, 5–22

Smith, L T (ed), 1908 *The itinerary of John Leland in or about the years 1535–1543*, **III**, London

Smith, P, 1975 *Houses of the Welsh countryside*, London

Smith, R, and Carter, A, 1983 Function and site: aspects of Norwich buildings before 1700, *Vernacular Architect*, **14**, 5–18

Stewart-Brown, R, 1925 *Calendar of Chester county court rolls*, Chetham Society, 3 ser, **84**

Strickland, T J, 1984 The Roman heritage of Chester: the survival of the buildings of *Deva* after the Roman period, *JCAS*, **67**, 17–36

Stukeley, W, 1776 *Itinerarium curiosum*, **I**

Tait, J (ed), 1920–3 Chartulary of the Abbey of St Werburgh, Chester, *Chetham Soc*, 3 ser, **79, 82**

——, 1936 *The medieval English borough*, Manchester

Taylor, A J, 1989 *Caernarfon Castle*, Cadw – Welsh Historic Monuments, Cardiff

——, 1982 Scorched earth at Flint in 1294, *J Flintshire Hist Soc*, **30**, 89–105

——, 1985 Castle-building in thirteenth century Wales and Savoy, *Studies in castles and castle-building*, 1–28, London

Taylor, H, 1888 Notes upon some early deeds relating to Chester and Flint, *JCAS*, **2**, 149–85

——, 1897 Six early deeds relating to property in Northgate Street, Chester, *JCAS*, **6**, 49–59

Taylor, J, 1878–9 The Dominican Priory, Bristol, *Trans Bristol Gloucestershire Archaeol Soc*, **3**, 234–7

Taylor, M V (ed), 1912 Obits of St Werburgh's Abbey, *RSLC*, **64**, 91

Thacker, A T, 1987 The Anglo-Saxon period, in Harris 1987, 240–92

——, forthcoming, VCH Cheshire, **5**, Chester

Thompson, P, 1981 *Ince Manor*, Cheshire County Council Archaeol Monograph, Chester

Trappes-Lomax, R, 1930 The diary and letter-book of the Rev Thomas Brockbank 1671–1709, *Chetham Soc*, new ser, **89**

Turner, L A, 1927 *Decorative plasterwork in Great Britain*

Turner, R C, 1988 Early carpentry in the Rows of Chester, *Vernacular Architect*, **19**, 34–41

——, 1991 *Lamphey Bishop's Palace*, Cadw – Welsh Historic Monuments, Cardiff

Ward, S, 1984 The Rows: the evidence from archaeology, *JCAS*, **67**, 37–46

——, 1988 *Excavations at Chester: 12 Watergate Street 1985*, Grosvenor Museum archaeological excavation and survey report, **5**, Chester

——, 1990 *The lesser medieval religious houses: sites investigated 1964–83*, Grosvenor Museum archaeological excavation and survey report, **6**, Chester

Webster, G, 1951 A Roman inscription found in Watergate Street, *JCAS*, **38**, 176

Wilson, K P, 1965 The port of Chester in the later Middle Ages, unpubl PhD thesis, Univ Liverpool

Wood, M E, 1965 *The English medieval house*, London

Woodward, D M, 1970 The trade of Elizabethan Chester, *Univ Hull Occasional Paper*, **4**, Hull

Endnotes

Abbreviations

BL	British Library
BPR	The Black Prince's Register
Cheshire RO	Cheshire Record Office
Chester CRO	Chester City Record Office
	(NB At the time of going to press, *Chester CRO* had recently been renamed *Chester Archives.*)
JRUL	John Rylands University Library, Manchester
PRO	Public Record Office

Chapter 1

1 Chester will be referred to as a 'city' throughout, although in the medieval period the terms 'city' and 'town' appear to have been interchangeable.

2 The first evidence for buildings oversailing the pavement at Totnes is in a document of 1584 (Clifton-Taylor 1978, 136).

3 The location of a number of Roman military establishments all imply sea-borne links centred on the legionary fortress at Chester. These include: the industrial complexes at Wilderspool, Cheshire, and Walton-le-Dale, Lancashire, which are at the tidal limit of their respective rivers; Carlisle, the service centre for the western part of Hadrian's Wall; the trading base at Caer Gybi, Holyhead; and the tile kilns and pottery works at Holt, Clwyd.

4 The massive nature of these remains seems to have inhibited subsequent building work, or at least to have established boundaries. On the north side of Watergate Street between St Peter's Church and Goss Street the rear walls of the medieval undercrofts abut against one of the main walls of the *principia*; a relationship demonstrated during excavations at No 12 (Ward 1988). The same is true for Nos 51–67 on the opposite side of Watergate Street where the undercrofts are built in front of the walls of the Roman granaries. In some cases the lower levels of the Roman structures were reused, as at 37–41 Bridge Street where the front of the nineteenth-century building is supported by the walls of the legionary bath house. Some idea of the problems faced by the medieval builders can be gauged from the fallen columns of the *principia* which survive in the undercroft of 23 Northgate Street and from the fact that the remains of the legionary bath house were found to be still standing to a height of 4m in the 1960s.

5 All four Roman gateways straddle the later main streets and considerable stretches of the Roman wall survive in the northern and eastern sections of the present city walls (Strickland 1984).

6 This was certainly the case in other cities. In Lincoln 166 houses were lost as a result of the construction of the castle, and in Norwich 98 (Reynolds 1977, 43).

7 Alldridge (1981) argues that the southern extension came first, but this must have been completed by 1150 when work began on the western extension. St Martin's parish, laid out *c* 1190–5, uses the line of the new walls as its western boundary.

8 The Franciscan (or Greyfriars) precinct occupied 7 acres on the north side of the lower section of Watergate Street, while the Dominicans (or Blackfriars) had approximately 5 acres on the south side. However, when the Carmelites (or Whitefriars) were established in Chester in 1277 they were unable to find a site until they purchased seven houses on what is now Whitefriars in 1290. This would suggest that the availability of land was much reduced by the end of the thirteenth century (Ward 1990).

9 The earliest description of an English town being an eighth-century poem by Alcuin about York (Allott 1974, 157).

Chapter 2

1 The main collections of deeds that have been consulted are the Aston Charters (BL Add Ch 49,968–50,217); the Shrewsbury (Talbot) Deeds (BL Add Ch 72,203–72,296; 75,107–75,237); the Cartulary of St Anne (BL Harl Ms 2061, printed *Cheshire Sheaf*, 3 ser, xxxvi); the Cartulary of St Werburgh (Tait, 1920–3); the Cartulary of Whalley Abbey (Hulton 1847, 339–61); the Arley Family Deeds (John Rylands University Library); the Barnston Family Deeds (Cheshire RO DBA/35, calendared in *Cheshire Sheaf*, 3 ser, xliii); the Eaton Charters (Eaton Hall, Chester); the Vernon Family Deeds (Cheshire RO DVE); the Henry Taylor Collection (Chester CRO D/HT); the Moore Manuscripts (Liverpool Library, calendared Brownbill, 1913); deeds relating to Chester property which passed to the Crown in the sixteenth century (PRO Cat Anct D; Wale 29); deeds enrolled in the Chester Portmote Rolls (Chester CRO MR).

2 For the comparable terminology of the Winchester deeds see Keene 1985, 137–9.

3 Measurements are recorded only rarely and at random. For example: in Northgate Street in the 1270s there was a plot 18ft (5.49m) wide (BL Add Ch 50,005) and in Bridge Street in 1358 there was a messuage with appurtenances, which at its longest point stretched back 52yd (48.24m) from the highway and was some 10yd wide (9.83m) (Chester CRO DVE 1/CI/41). Outside the Rows, in Pepper Street, a property was recorded in 1324/5 as being 9 'royal' ells (8.23m) long and 7 'royal' ells (6.86m) wide (BL Add Ch 72,270). Other deeds refer to a 'woollen' ell, perhaps the longer Flemish ell of 45in (1.15m) (pers comm Dr D Keene). In 1311, for example, a plot of land in Bridge Street with buildings upon it was described as 9 'woollen' ells wide and 30 'woollen' ells long (BL Add Ch 50,090/99). None of this suggests uniformity.

4 An attempt to identify if there had been some early uniformity of wide plots that had been concealed by later irregular subdivision was made by J Grenville during the course of fieldwork, but no clear pattern emerged.

5 BL Add CH 50,032

6 Cheshire RO DBA 35; BL Add Ch 49,982

7 PRO E 315/47

8 PRO CHES 15/1 and Thacker in Matthews 1995, 33

9 Barraclough 1957, 34–6; Barraclough 1988, 281–2; BL Add Ch 40,177

10 BL Add Ch 72,224. Compare the *camera* of Richard del Holt with its *palisadium* (1328) (BL Add Ch 72,273).

11 Chester CRO D/HT/6

12 *Cheshire Sheaf*, 3 ser, xix, 72–3; Brown *et al* 1963, 468; Hopkins 1950, 114–15

13 BL Add Ch 75,178

14 JRUL Arley Charters, Box 25, nos 13–14

15 For the Daresburys' property in Pepper Street see Tait 1920–3, 339. According to the Aldersey manuscript 'old evidences' showed that there was a house called Daresbury's Hall on the south side of Pepper Street: Chester CRO, CR 469/542.

16 JRUL Arley Charters, Box 25/16

17 The premises in the Buttershops, which changed hands in 1361 and comprised a shop with two *solaria* above and one adjoining, perhaps provide an example of an arrangement of this kind (BL Add Ch 75, 161).

18 Chester CRO D/HT/13. Here 'seld' probably means simply 'shop'.

19 For example Chester CRO D/HT/18; BL Add Ch 50,021/2, 50,082, 75,154; *Cheshire Sheaf*, 3 ser, xxxvi, 47, 49, 51

20 For example BL Add Ch 50,082; Irvine 1904, 42

21 There is evidence from 12 Watergate Street that the rear ground level was still rising during the medieval period and that the Row level was originally above the contemporary rear ground surface (Ward 1988).

22 BL Add Ch 50,081–2

23 Chester CRO D/HT/44

24 *Cheshire Sheaf*, 3 ser, xxxi, 6804; xxxvi, 7921. There are examples of cellars used as taverns bearing this name in Winchester and London (Keene 1985, **ii**, 563–4).

25 The phrase used is '*contra ecclesiam sancti Petri, versus ecclesiam sancti Werburgae*' (BL Add Ch 49,975; Irvine 1904, 17).

26 Cheshire RO DBA 35 (no 4); BL Add Ch 49,982; Chester CRO D/HT/20

27 PRO CHES 25/1

28 PRO CHES 25/1

29 Chester CRO D/HT/13; D/HT/43; BL Add Ch, 50,051/2

30 Flesher's Row was certainly in existence by 1355 when it included, significantly, a tenement with two shops and two undercrofts (Morris 1894, 294). For the Doncaster holdings in Watergate Street see PRO CHES 15/1; Chester CRO MR/3, mem. 12; MR/8, rot, 6d; D/HT/20, 40–4; Cheshire RO DBA 35. For a fuller analysis see Thacker (forthcoming).

31 Chester CRO D/HT/20, 42–3

32 Chester CRO MR/64

33 Barker 1953, 30; cf BL Add Ch 50,196, 75,161; Cheshire RO DVE CII/8 1412

34 PRO CHES 25/1; Chester CRO D/HT/18, 20, 24; MR/30; BL Add Ch 50,151; Taylor 1988, 166–8, Brownbill 1913, 144

35 Chester CRO MR/48

36 *36th Report of the Deputy Keeper of the Public Records*, 374 (PRO, 1875); *cf* the reference to the need for a new hall for the holding of eyres and courts at Macclesfield, in which the Black Prince might have *shoppae* rented out at 40 shillings per annum (BPR, III, 273).

37 PRO SC 6/783/15, mem 3; 783/16, mem 2v; 783/17, mem 2; 784/5, mem 2

38 For example BL Add Ch 50,058; 50,152; Chester CRO D/HT/46; MR/5, mem 5; MR/30; MR/35

39 Cheshire RO DVE 1/CII/21

40 Chester CRO CR 469/542. See also Chester CRO MR/30, mem 3; BL Add Ch 50,152.

41 Chester CRO CHD/2/1

42 We can be certain of the location since the fishboards are known from other sources to have lain at the east end of Watergate Street at the junction with Bridge Street (Morris 1894, 295). It should be noted, however, that by the mid-seventeenth century Corviser Row was apparently on Eastgate Street or the east side of Bridge Street (Dodgson 1981, 21).

43 PRO E 315/47/139

44 PRO E 326/3474

45 Compare the seld of Hugh Tailor, 27ft (8.1m) long, which comprised half a house and lay behind another seld (BL Add CH 49,997).

46 At 32 Bridge Street, for example, there is an undercroft 40.85m long and about 3.65m wide.

47 Cheshire RO DVE 1/CII/21

48 PRO CHES 25/1

49 Chester CRO CHD/2/7

50 Chester CRO CHD/2/1

51 Chester CRO MR 1, mem 1; MR 3, mem 2v

52 Two shops at the west end of Foregate Street in 1303/4 are recorded as being 8 x 28ft (2.4 x 8.5m) and 7 x 20ft (2.1 x 6.1m) respectively (BL Add Ch 50,053). Also a shop 15 x 7ft (4.57 x 2.13m) was the subject of a dispute in the Portmote in 1297 (Chester CRO MR/3 mem 12v).

53 At 12 Watergate Street the superstructure extended beyond the rear wall of the undercroft, although this may be the result of the break in building operations that has been postulated (Ward 1988). At 32 Bridge Street it is unlikely that the 40.85m long undercroft carried purely domestic buildings for its full length, but this may also be an exception as it is in the area of the selds.

54 The plot of 36 Watergate Street is wedge-shaped, does not extend back to Hamilton Place, and contains no medieval fabric.

55 Chester CRO D/HT/6; Taylor 1897, 55

56 BL Add Ch 50,032; Dodgson 1981, 41

57 PRO E 315/47/139; PRO WALE/29/272

58 BL Add Ch 75,179. For a further and more detailed description see BL Add CH 75,202; *cf* BL Add Ch 75,154, possibly the same messuage and if so taking the Row at this point back at least to 1349.

59 A full history of the Dark Row and the modern developments which have significantly altered the historic arrangement of this part of the Row system are described in Matthews 1995.

Chapter 3

1 BL Add Ch 72,224

2 Peter the Clerk was the earl's chancellor, and Ranulph of Oxford was a chamberlain of Chester (Thacker, forthcoming).

3 Bye-laws of this nature are a feature of many other towns and cities. In London the earliest surviving building and fire regulations were probably issued between 1192 and 1212, with additional regulations added in 1212 following a serious fire (Schofield 1984, 75–6). Regulations can be inferred from the frequency of stone construction in Southampton during the thirteenth and fourteenth centuries (Platt 1973, 39–41).

4 This vault is mentioned in Hughes (1856, 50) and an illustration was reproduced in a critical review (unsigned, by J H Parker) in the *Gentleman's Magazine*, 1856, 126. This illustration is described in Lawson and Smith 1958.

5 Description by Randle Holme III in BL Harl Ms 7568, fol 154

6 It appears, particularly in outer window arches, throughout many of the Southampton undercrofts.

Chapter 4

1 For example Scolland's Hall, Richmond Castle, *c* 1080 (Turner 1988, 39), Hall of Great Tower, Chepstow Castle, *c* 1090 (Wood 1965, pl III), St Etheldreda's Church, Ely Place, London, probably 1290s (Hewett 1980, 123–4)

2 Analysis and dimensions supplied by R B Harris, 1990

3 For illustration see Oswald, 1965

4 Information generously supplied by John McCann

5 This is contrary to an Anglo-Saxon origin for the joint, favoured by Hewett (1980, 14–29) based solely on his misdating of the Sompting Tower Rhenish helm. This has been dated by comprehensive dendrochronological sampling to the early fourteenth century (Aldsworth and Harris 1988). A further example, of exactly the same period, is on the southern arcade post at the Marlipins, Shoreham-by-Sea (Packham 1924).

6 First known under the choir stalls at Winchester Cathedral by 1309, and at Baythorne Hall, Essex, in the late thirteenth/early fourteenth century, and surviving as late as 1398 at the Abbot's Court House, Battle Abbey, Sussex (Hewett 1980, 136, 140–1, 279)

7 For example the Great Hall, Caernarfon Castle, *c* 1300 (Taylor 1989)

8 It is possible that this was a king-strut or king-post roof, but the remaining post appears to be largely intact and is only long enough to be suitable for a crown post.

9 16–17 St Paul's Street, Stamford (RCHME 1977, fig 193, 148)

10 Various grants are recorded in the *BPR*, 3, (Cheshire)

Chapter 5

1 In an earlier publication (Grenville 1990, 453) it was stated that recent work at 58 French Street, Southampton had revealed the former existence of a gallery in front of the shop. This comment was based on a personal communication from Glyn Coppack, the recorder of that building, but it is an interpretation that is no longer tenable. In the light of Coppack's subsequent explanation (1990, 8) that the 'final critical analysis sprang not from the building itself but from the paper record', changes in interpretation are not surprising.

2 References to town houses are very scattered, with the only summary of evidence for undercrofts being in Wood 1965, 95–7, and Faulkner 1966. For Southampton, see

Platt 1973; for Winchelsea, Beresford and St Joseph 1979, 234–42; for Shrewsbury, Carver 1983 and Baker *et al* 1993; for Norwich, Smith and Carter 1983; for Oxford, Pantin 1947; for York, Salisbury, and Stamford, the relevant inventories produced by the RCHME.

3　Observation by R C Turner

4　Cumbria Record Office (Carlisle) D/LONS/L.9.

5　Cumbria Record Office (Carlisle) D/LONS/L 5/2/11/273.

6　For example, the Herefordshire school of Romanesque masons and sculptors seem to have drawn on ideas brought back from pilgrimage to Santiago de Compostela, Spain. The 12 round-nave churches of England, constructed by the Knights Templar, are based on the church of the Holy Sepulchre in Jerusalem. Advances made in the design of the crusader castles were adopted in England and features of the Edwardian castles of Wales were used in Savoy.

7　Observation by A N Brown

8　Perhaps the most interesting man linking Edward's new town policies in both France and England was Henry le Waleys, who was mayor of both London and Bordeaux. He had a hand in the planning of New Winchelsea and Berwick-upon-Tweed, and in 1284 was appointed to farm the revenues of six of the bastide towns.

9　The tensions between private and public spaces in towns and cities are explored in detail in Saalman 1968, 28–35.

Chapter 6

1　The main documentary sources used for this chapter are the accounts that were rendered annually by the city's sheriffs for the fee farm (PRO SC6/789/6 – SC6/800/4); the administrative records of the majors (Chester CRO MB1–5) and sheriffs (Chester CRO SB1–4); the Portmote Rolls (Chester CRO MR); the Pentice Rolls (Chester CRO SR); the Treasurers' accounts which no longer survive (BL Harl Ms 2158); collections of deeds cited in note 1 of Chapter 2. Records of the city's council do not survive from the medieval period and this important source of the evidence is therefore unavailable. Also, Chester's palatinate status resulted in the city's exclusion from national taxation assessments, although the palatinate records in the PRO do provide valuable information.

2　BPR iii, 275, 292, 298; PRO SC 6/783/16, m1d.

3　BPR iii, 154; PRO SC 6/783/16, m1d.

4　PRO SC 6/784/9, mm1, 2d, 3.

5　Chester CRO CH/28; CH/30; CH/31.

6　Analysis of the claims made by the citizens of Winchester in 1440 has shown that they did not greatly exaggerate the impoverished state of their city and that their petition contained very precise information. They claimed that pestilence and loss of trade during the previous 50 years

had left 17 parish churches, 11 streets and 987 messuages in ruins. A 12 per cent loss of property and a 30 per cent drop in population has been traced from *c* 1300 to 1417, with a further 68 per cent drop in population to *c* 1550 (Keene 1985, i, 96–8, 143–5).

7　PRO SC 6/789/6–SC 6/800/4 and Laughton 1993, Appendix 2

8　PRO SC 6/784/5, m5d; SC 6/784/9, m3

9　PRO SC 11/890, m1

10　Chester CRO CHD/2/4

11　BL Harl Ms 2158, fols 213–4

12　For example BL Harl Ms 2158, fols 212, 212d, 213, 213d

13　BL Harl Ms 2158 fols 197d, 200

14　Chester CRO CHD/2/5; BL Harl Ms 2158, fol 199. The rent due was 16d, which may indicate four posts.

15　Chester CRO SB2, fols 85d, 86

16　PRO SC 6/800/1, m1d; SC 6/800/6, m1d

17　Chester CRO SB3, fol 67

18　PRO SC 6/799/9, m4d; SC 6/800/7, m4; SC 6/801/1, m4d

19　BL Harl Ms 2158, fol 224d

20　See Simpson 1915 for a discussion of the name of this building, its history, and its appearance in the early twentieth century.

21　Chester CRO MR52, m1

22　PRO CHES 25/11, m18

23　PRO CHES 25/11, m18; Chester CRO MR77, M1

24　PRO WALE 29/126; BL Harl Ms 2020, fol 403

25　For example Chester CRO MB2, fols 6d, 89; MB3, fols 12d, 60d; MR65, m1; MR78, m1; BL Harl Ms 1994, fols 288, 289.

26　Photographs of the building, before its restoration in the late 1970s, illustrate this element and indicate that it continues to occupy the same position. No mention is made of the present central section of the screen, suggesting that this may have been introduced from elsewhere (Cheshire RO 942.2 INS).

27　Cheshire RO DVE 1/C11/21; Morris, 1894, 250–1; Chester CRO CHD/2/7

28　Report held by National Monuments Record, Swindon.

29　There are a number of Cheshire churches with similar seventeenth-century false hammer-beam roofs, eg Handley, Harthill, Hargrave, and Lower Whitley (Pevsner and Hubbard 1971).

30 In Cheshire, these examples of crown-post roofs were largely discovered during the listed building resurvey of the early 1980s and include three associated with base crucks: Tabley Old Hall *c* 1380 (now collapsed but see Mercer 1976, 32) and two from the fifteenth century, Willott Hall, Prestbury, and Lower Garden Hall, Tilston. Gawsworth Old Hall and Puddington Old Hall, both dating from the fifteenth century, provide examples of crown-post roofs in box-framed buildings. Two examples are known in box-framed buildings from north-east Wales; Llay Hall, Denbighshire and Basingwerk Abbey (Smith 1975, 408–9). Two examples are known north of Cheshire, of which one, in the north aisle of Ribchester church, Lancashire (observation by R C Turner), is comparable in scantling to the reused trusses in the Falcon, 6 Lower Bridge Street. The most northerly example is from another town house, the Guildhall, Carlisle, dating to *c* 1400 (observation by R C Turner).

31 Examples such as Edge Hall, Gawsworth Old Hall, Haslington Hall, Little Moreton Hall, and Vale Royal House, (de Figueiredo and Treuherz 1988).

32 PRO CHES 25/12, m6d

33 For example Chester CRO MR 80/1; BL Harl Ms 2037, fol 309d.

34 BL Harl Ms 2158, fol 211

35 Chester CRO MB4, fol 53d

36 Chester CRO MUR 2, m3

37 Chester CRO MUB 1, fols 10–11d

38 Chester CRO MR44, m1d; SR118, m1d

39 *Cheshire Sheaf*, 3 ser, xxxvi, 8004

40 Chester CRO SR230, m1d; SR235, m1; SR321, m1d, SR432, m1d

41 For example Chester CRO SB1, fols 41d, 102; SB3, fol 41

42 For example Chester CRO SB1, fol 65; SB3, fols 39d, 92; MB6, fols 167d, 170

43 Chester CRO SR 239/3; SR 287/1d; SR 290/1

44 For example Chester CRO SR175/1d; SR180/1

45 Chester CRO MB5, fols 4d, 184

46 Chester CRO MB7, fol 123

47 Chester CRO MB5, fol 87d; MB6, fols 3, 4d; MB7, fol 81.

48 The monks later included his name among the obits of the abbey (Taylor, M V [ed] 1912)

49 *Cheshire Sheaf*, 3 ser, xxxvi, 8004

50 Chester CRO SB3, fols 19d, 20d, 70; MB4, fol 8.

51 BL Harl Ms 2158, fol 195d; Taylor 1888, 163; Chester CRO MB2, fols 59, 92

52 Chester CRO SB3, fol 85; SR196, ml; SR377, m1d; SR460, m1d. A late sixteenth-century, timber-framed, wattle and daub smoke hood survives in Castle Street, indicating that the use of combustible materials in vulnerable locations continued for a considerable period (Grenville and Turner 1986, 113).

53 Chester CRO AB1, fol 170d; Kennett 1987, 42

54 BL Harl Ms 2037, fol 309d

55 Chester CRO SR337, m1d; SR351, m1d; SR399, mld; SR418, m1d

56 Chester CRO QCR11, ml; MB3, fol 8

57 Chester CRO MB1, fol 61

58 Chester CRO SR457, mlv

59 PRO SC11/890, ml

60 For example Chester CRO SR239, m2; SR316, m1d; SR432, m1d

61 PRO SC11/890, m1

62 Cheshire RO WS 1666 Farrington

63 Chester CRO SB4, fol 53

64 Chester CRO SR362, m1d; SR363, m1.

65 Chester CRO SC6/784/5, m5d; SR366, m1

66 BL Harl Ms 2158, fol 209d

67 Chester CRO SR445, m1d

68 Chester CRO SR391, m1d

69 Chester CRO SR169, m1d

70 Chester CRO SR389, m1d

71 JRUL Arley Charters Box 25, 13–14

72 Chester CRO SB358, m1d

73 For example Chester CRO MB1, fol 2; MB2, fol 95d; MB5, fols 1, 41d; MR 78/1

74 Chester CRO MR 81/1d

75 For example PRO SC 6/784/5, mm5, 5d; SC 6/797/1, m1d; Chester CRO MR 59/1; MR 60/1d; MR 69/1, 1d; MR 75/1; MR 81/1; MR 104/1

76 For example Chester CRO MR 45/1; MR 69/1; BL Harl Ms 2158 fols 193, 195d, 198d

77 For example Chester CRO MR 44/1; MR 54/1; MR 65/1; MR 71/1d; MR 78/1; MR 104/1

78 For example Chester CRO MB1, fols 15d, 27; MB2, fol 4; MB3, fols 60d, 71d

79 For example Chester CRO SR 223/1; SR 272/1; SR 319/1. In 1425 a leading vintner leased two cellars in Bridge Street under the 'Stonesels', *Cheshire Sheaf*, **66** (1961), 10832.

80 For example Chester CRO MR 78/1; SR 311/1

81 For example BL Harl Ms 2158, fols 209d, 210, 212d, 216

82 For example BL Harl Ms 2158, fols 192d, 195

83 PRO WALE 29/291

Chapter 7

1   The main documentary sources used for this chapter are the Assembly Minute Books and Assembly Files (Chester CRO AB and AF); the Mayors' Books (Chester CRO MB); family records (Chester CRO CR); Coroners' Inquisitions (Chester CRO QCI); Quarter Sessions Files and Quarter Sessions Examinations and Depositions (Chester CRO QSF and QSE); Treasurers' Account Rolls and Rentals (Chester CRO TAR); probate records (Cheshire RO WS); seventeenth-century transcripts of deeds in the Harleian Collection (BR Harl Ms).

2   Chester CRO QSF/48, 79; QSF/49, 43, 46; QSF/53, 3; QSF/54, 3; MB/28, fols 72, 76, 306d

3   BL Harl Ms 2082, fol 111. Thomas Whitby also had to rebuild a house in Parsons Lane (the present Princess Street) because it had been 'insufficientlie erected' (Laughton 1988, 116).

4   Chester CRO AB/1, 327

5   Chester CRO QSF/53, 6; Cheshire RO WS 1608 Aldersey; *Cheshire Sheaf*, 3 ser, xxxii, 7168.

6   Cheshire RO AB/1, fol 340; TAR 2/38; TAR 2/40; TAR 3/51

7   Cheshire RO WS 1639 Whitby

8   Cheshire RO WS 1688 Fletcher

9   Chester CRO QSF/53, 6, 77. The inventory of Rivington's goods (Cheshire RO WS 1616 Rivington) refers only to a new parlour so perhaps he was prevented from carrying out a major building project on his own home by the effect of Aldersey's rebuilding.

10 Chester CRO AB/1, fol 327

11 Chester CRO MB/30, fol 28d

12 BL Harl Ms 2037, fol 310

13 It has been possible only to sample the available documentation, but every effort has been made to select records most likely to refer to the Rows.

14 Chester CRO QSF/54, 39

15 Chester CRO QCI/11; QCI/18, 6

16 For example Cheshire CRO CR 69/3/25

17 BL Harl Ms 2099, fol 454

18 Chester CRO AF/36, 26

19 Cheshire CRO TAR 2/23

20 Chester CRO AF/13, 34

21 These fines, paid by traders from outside the city, were an important source of revenue.

22 Chester CRO AB/3, 61, 1697; AB/3, 70d, 1699

23 Chester CRO AF/13, 30; AB/3, 201

24 Chester CRO AF/33, 25

25 Chester CRO AF/33, 18

26 Chester CRO AF/36, 27

28 Chester CRO AF/39a, 9

29 Chester CRO AB/2, 151d; AB/2, 162

30 Chester CRO AB/2, 185; AB/2, 185d

31 This 'common soil' was granted to the mayor and citizens of Chester by Edward I in his charter of 1300, and they as 'Lords of the soil' were empowered to grant it out for building or otherwise improve it.

32 It is possible that this process of encroachment was encouraged when work on a new conduit led to the gutters, hitherto located on either side of the street, being moved to the centre. These channels may have delineated the boundary between the common soil and king's highway and thus have hindered substantial encroachment. This reorganisation was authorised for Eastgate Street in 1584 and for Bridge Street in 1586–7 (Chester CRO AB/1, 197d; AB/1, 207).

33 Chester CRO TAR 1/8

34 Chester CRO AB/1, 269; TAR 2/23

35 Chester CRO AB/1, 337d, 338d

36 Chester CRO AF/10, 70

37 Chester CRO TAR 2/23, m3d

38 Chester CRO TAR 2/23, m3d

39 Chester CRO TAR 1/20

40 Chester CRO TAR 2/23, mm.1d, 3

41 Chester CRO AB/1, 345

42 Chester CRO AF/13, 34

43 Chester CRO AF/14, 22

44 Chester CRO AB/2, 92d

45 BL Harl Ms 2022, fols 140–1

46 For example Cheshire RO WS 1604 Maddock; WS 1607 Lingley; WS 1617 Leycester; WS 1619 Thropp.

47 Cheshire RO WS 1604 Lawton (60yd); WS 1617 Leycester (58yd plain and 9yd of cutwork); WS 1614 Wall (88yd). Robert Brerewood had over 100 yards of wainscot in his new hall (Cheshire RO WS 1602 Brerewood), but this room was not typical as his house was exceptionally large.

48 Cheshire RO WS 1607 Lingley

49 Cheshire RO WS 1617 Leycester

50 Cheshire RO WS 1662 Butler

51 Cheshire RO WS 1661 Thropp

52 Cheshire RO WS 1602 Amery; WS 1613 Amery

53 Cheshire RO WS 1617 Leycester; WS 1621 Thropp

54 Cheshire RO WS 1609 Fletcher; WS 1612 Hunt

55 Cheshire RO WS 1617 Leycester; WS 1621 Thropp

56 See especially Cheshire RO WS 1609 Fletcher. He had served as mayor 1595–8.

57 Cheshire CRO QSF/27, 131

58 Cheshire CRO QSF/51, 63; QSF/61, 6

59 See Schofield 1984, 159 for similar arrangements in London. Of the inventories studied only those of Robert Brerewood (Cheshire RO WS 1602 Brerewood) and of Robert Fletcher (Cheshire RO WS 1688 Fletcher) specifically refer to a shop in the Row.

60 Cheshire RO WS 1609 1612 Hunt

61 Cheshire RO WS 1666 Farrington

62 Cheshire RO WS 1604 Lawton; Chester CRO QSF/48, 25

63 Cheshire RO WS 1638 Roberts

64 Chester CRO QSF/50, 56

65 Chester CRO QSF/13, 17

66 Cheshire RO WS 1619 Allerton; WS 1621 Thropp

67 Chester CRO QSF/44, 56

68 See maps of Braun (c 1560) and Speed (1610). For references to gardens and orchards in deeds see *Cheshire Sheaf*, 3 ser, xliv, 9138 (Eastgate Street, 1584); xvii, 4106 (Watergate Street, 1610–11); xxxv, 7769 (Northgate Street, 1614–15).

69 BL Harl Ms 2022, fols 140–1

70 Cheshire RO WS 1689 Rock

71 PRO CHESTER 38/48, 10

72 Cheshire RO WS 1609 Fletcher; WS 1625 Aldersey

73 Cheshire RO WS 1632 Poole; WS 1673 Hulton

74 Cheshire RO WS 1602 Brerewood; WS 1605 Aldersey with Chester CRO CR 63/1/47; WS 1641 Leche

75 Chester CRO QSF/36, 57

76 Cheshire RO WS 1615 Wall; Chester CRO AF/30, 20. In 1595 smoke from a cellar in Northgate Street led the neighbours to complain, because no chimney had been provided (Chester CRO QSF/44, 14).

77 Chester CRO AB/1, fol 313

78 Cheshire RO WS 1621 Thropp

79 Chester CRO AB/1, fol 289d

80 Chester CRO AB/2, fol 172

81 Cheshire RO WS 1609 Fletcher

82 PRO CHESTER 38/48

83 Cheshire RO WS 1625 Aldersey

84 BL Harl Ms 2022, fols 136, 136d, 137

85 Chester CRO AB/2, fol 170d

86 Chester CRO AB/2, fol 102d; Laughton 1988, 104, 117–8

87 The removal and resiting of plaster ceilings, whilst not common, was certainly not beyond the skills of contemporary plasterers; the drawing-room ceiling and chimneypiece at New Place, Shedfield, Hampshire, were moved from Bristol in c 1640 (Turner 1927, 93).

88 One parallel, dated c 1628, is from Moray House, Canongate, Edinburgh (Turner 1927, 114).

89 Cheshire RO WS 1617 Leycester

Chapter 8

1 This is supported by the Cotton family papers (Cheshire RO 45/1/31)

2 Chester CRO CR 69/3/95

3 PRO CHESTER 16/133, quoted in Mitchell 1980, 49

4 Calveley Hall, the country house Lady Mary built at Handley, 7 miles from Chester, has an elaborate staircase with double-twisted balusters. This fits rather awkwardly into the house and it is possible that it is the original

staircase from Bridge House, moved during alterations by the Williams family of Bodelwydden (Harris 1979, 140).

5 Chester CRO AF/47c/19; AF/47c/65; AB/3/13/4.1700.

6 Chester CRO 70/30/10

7 Chester CRO AB/3/2.3.1744

8 Chester CRO AB/4/252

9 Chester CRO AB/4/211V

10 Chester CRO 63/2/133

11 Chester CRO AB/4/85v

12 Chester CRO AF/55/67

13 Chester CRO AB/4/257

14 Chester CRO AB/4/336

15 Chester CRO AB/3/29.3.1701–2

16 Chester CRO AB/3/12.1.1700

Chapter 9

1 Only George Devey, an architect working in Kent, can be said to have developed a coherent revival of timber-framing earlier than Penson.

2 *The Builder*, 30 August 1856, 471. Also Hughes 1856, 399.

3 *The Builder*, 17 April 1858, 269.

4 *The Builder*, 17 April 1858, 269.

5 *JCAS* 1864, 399; *The Building News*, 29 November 1861, 952.

6 Chester CRO Imp Cttee, February 1847, 689.

7 *The Building News*, 18 May 1860, 400–401; *The Builder*, 26 February 1859, 160; *Chester Record*, 11 June 1864.

8 Simpson, F, unpublished manuscript, The Rows of Chester, v 2, Chester CRO CR 119/18.

9 Hughes 1882, 65; Chester CRO Imp Cttee, 20 June 1860.

10 Chester CRO Imp Cttee, 15 September 1875; *The Building News*, 23 September 1872.

11 Simpson, F, *Chester past and present*, unpublished photographic albums, v 3, ill 93, Chester Library, 23; Harris 1979, 49.

12 Chester CRO Imp Cttee, 24 December 1890; Eaton Estate Office drawings; *Academy Architecture* 1891, 21

13 In 1897 Lockwood mounted an exhibition of illustrated books at the Grosvenor Museum. Most were from his own collection. Lockwood, T M, 1898, *Notes on illustrated books*, Chester Library.

14 *The Builder*, 29 April 1899, 422

15 Chester CRO Northgate Street Imp Cttee, 25 May 1877

16 Chester CRO Northgate Street Imp Cttee, 17 August 1877

17 Chester CRO Northgate Street Imp Cttee, 13 December 1877

18 Chester CRO Northgate Street Imp Cttee, 28 January 1878

19 Chester CRO Northgate Street Imp Cttee, March 1881

20 Chester CRO Imp Cttee, 9 May 1894

21 Chester CRO Imp Cttee, 11 November 1897; 11 August 1897

22 Published in *The Cheshire Observer*, 8 January 1887

23 The present arcade below the Commercial Newsroom, now the City Club, dates from *c* 1970 (Fig 115)

24 Chester CRO Imp Cttee, 11 August 1897

25 Chester CRO Imp Cttee, 14 June 1899; *The Architect*, **64**, 1900, 200; **79**, 1908, 288; Hubbard 1991, 272

26 Hubbard 1991, 272; (James Strong may also have been involved, see Chester CRO Imp Cttee, 6 July 1898).

27 Chester CRO Imp Cttee, 26 September 1899; *The Architect*, **79**, 1908, 288; Hubbard 1991, 273

28 Chester CRO Imp Cttee, 13 July 1910

29 Chester CRO Imp Cttee, 16 January 1907; 29 May 1907

30 Photograph at Chester Library, 69/251

31 Eaton Estate Office drawings 01539, Eaton Hall, Chester; Building News, 73, 1897, 471; Hubbard 1991, 268

32 Chester CRO Imp Cttee, 18 September 1889; 26 October 1889

33 Chester CRO Imp Cttee, 16 October 1912

34 Chester CRO Imp Cttee, 18 September 1889

35 Census Enumerators' Returns, Holy Trinity Parish, 1841–1842, Chester CRO.

36 Chester CRO Imp Cttee, 11 June 1861

37 Chester CRO Imp Cttee, 4 February 1863; 11 February 1863

38 Chester CRO Imp Cttee, 2 June 1909

39 Simpson, F, 1910 *New Bridge Street Row Premises*, unpublished notebook in the possession of Peter de Figueiredo

40 *Chester Chronicle*, 17 September 1910

41 *Chester Chronicle*, 28 October 1910

42 Simpson, F, 1910 *New Bridge Street Row Premises*, unpublished notebook in the possession of Peter de Figueiredo

43 Chester CRO Imp Cttee, 15 March 1911

44 *Chester Chronicle*, 31 March 1911

45 Chester CRO City Assembly, 20 December 1844

46 *Chester Chronicle*, 27 December 1879

47 Numbers 45a, 45b, and 47a Bridge Street Row are a rare surviving group of courtyard dwellings behind Bridge Street. They were erected *c* 1864 in conjunction with 43, 45 and 47 Bridge Street, and were therefore presumably designed by Edward Hodkinson.

48 Chester CRO Imp Cttee, 12 July 1899

49 Advertisements in *Chester Directory*, 1912–13 and 1928–29, Chester CRO; Kelly's Directory, 1938, Chester CRO.

50 Chester CRO Imp Cttee, 3 October 1921

51 Chester CRO Imp Cttee, 3 April 1912; 3 July 1912

52 Information from Peter Howell

Chapter 10

1   Chester CRO Clearance Area application, CBI 130C/A.

2   Chester CRO Clearance Area application, 6B2 6/B.

3   Chester CRO Civic Trust correspondence file, CR 251/13.

4   Letter from the Secretary of the Chester Civic Trust to the Town Clerk, 19 June 1960, Chester CRO 251/13.

5   *Chester Chronicle*, 8 November 1963

6   *Chester Chronicle*, 15 July 1964

7   Chester CRO Planning application file p21.6.

8   Chester City Council Planning application file, 6/13230.

9   Chester City Council Planning application file, 6/22988.

10 Under the Cheshire County Council Act 1980 the City Council has the right to ensure public access to the Row walkways and stalls at all times.

Appendix A

1   BL Add Ch 50,089

2   BL Add CH 50,064

3   Tait 1920–3, 468; Cal Inq iii, nos 409–9; v, nos 33,62; 26 D.K.R. 54; BL Add Ch 49,984

4   *Cheshire Sheaf*, 3 ser, xxxvi, 35. These deeds, from the cartulary of the fraternity of St Anne, survive in a seventeenth-century copy only.

5   For examples relating to Chester see BL Add Ch 50,120; 75,137; 75,139; 75,142;75,153; 75,158; Chester CRO D/HT/5, 10

6   BL Add Ch 50,147: 50,163; Chester CRO D/HT/18; Cheshire RO DBA 35; *Cheshire Sheaf* deed no 9

7   BL Add Ch 49,997

8   BL Add Ch 50,004

9   BL Add Ch 50,089; 50,099

10 BL Add Ch 50,117/18; *Cheshire Sheaf*, 3 ser, xxviii, 6282

11 PRO CHES 31/File 1A

12 For example Chester CRO SR 177/1d; SR 237/1d; SR 272/1d; SR 280/1d

13 For example Chester CRO SR 119/1d; SR 254/d

14 PRO SC 6/784/5, m5. Dunfoul's residence appears to have adjoined the Bridgegate, but this tenement possibly stood near to St Bridget's Church (SC 6/784/9,m1).

15 BL Harl Ms 2158, fols 194v, 195, 195v

16 Chester CRO CHD/2/3

17 Chester CRO SR 191/1

18 Chester CRO SR 166m.1v

19 BL Harl Ms 2158

20 For example Chester CRO SB 4, fol32v

21 For example Eaton Charters 34, Eaton Hall, Chester

22 For example Chester CRO D/HT/8; MR/30, mem.3

23 For example BL Add Ch 50, 81–2, 75, 154

24 For example BL Add Ch 49,976; 49,983; 50,020; 50,028; 50,054; 72,232; 72,242; 75,136; 75,143; 75,146; PRO WALE 29/387, 395; Chester CROD/HT/3–4; Cheshire RO DBA 35; JRUL Arley Ch, Box 1/40; Box 25/24; Box 27/53

25 BL Add Ch 50,032

26 BL Add Ch 49,982; 72,203; 72,253; 75,148; PRO WALE 29/272; Chester CROD/HT/40; Cheshire RO DBA 35; Eaton Charters 84, Eaton Hall, Chester; JRUL Arley Ch, Box 25/5

Index

by Indexing Specialists

Note: Page numbers in *italics* refer to illustrations and tables.